Elvis

Icons of Pop Music

Series Editor: Sarah Raine, Research Fellow, School of Arts and Creative Industries, Edinburgh Napier University.

Books in this series, designed for undergraduates and the general reader, offer a critical profile of a key figure or group in twentieth-century pop music. These short paperback volumes will focus on the work rather than on biography, and emphasize critical interpretation.

Published

Björk
Nicola Dibben

Bob Dylan
Keith Negus

Brian Wilson
Kirk Curnutt

Buddy Holly
Dave Laing

Elvis Costello
Dai Griffiths

James Brown
John Scannell

Nina Simone
Richard Elliott

The Beatles
Ian Inglis

The Velvet Underground
Richard Witts

Elvis

Roots, Image, Comeback, Phenomenon

Mark Duffett

SHEFFIELD UK   BRISTOL CT

Published by Equinox Publishing Ltd

UK: Office 415, The Workstation, 15 Paternoster Row, Sheffield, South Yorkshire, S1 2BX
USA: ISD, 70 Enterprise Drive, Bristol, CT 06010

www.equinoxpub.com

First published 2020

© Mark Duffett 2020

All rights reserved. No part of this publication may be reproduced or transmitted in any form or by any means, electronic or mechanical, including photocopying, recording or any information storage or retrieval system, without prior permission in writing from the publishers.

British Library Cataloguing-in-Publication Data

A catalogue record for this book is available from the British Library.

ISBN-13 978 1 84553 830 9 (paperback)
         978 1 78179 992 5 (ePDF)

Library of Congress Cataloging-in-Publication Data

Names: Duffett, Mark, author.
Title: Elvis : roots, image, comeback, phenomenon / Mark Duffett.
Description: Bristol : Equinox Publishing Ltd, 2020. | Series: Icons of pop music | Includes bibliographical references and index. | Summary: "Elvis interprets the image and music of Elvis Presley to reveal how they have evolved to construct a particularly appealing and powerful myth. Following broad contours of Presley's rollercoaster career, the book uses a range of analytical frames to challenge established perspectives on an icon. Its shows that the controversy around Elvis has effectively tested how far a concern for social equality could be articulated through the marketplace, and ultimately challenged how popular music itself should be assessed"-- Provided by publisher.
Identifiers: LCCN 2019050681 (print) | LCCN 2019050682 (ebook) | ISBN 9781845538309 (paperback) | ISBN 9781781799925 (ebook)
Subjects: LCSH: Presley, Elvis, 1935-1977. | Rock musicians--United States--Biography.
Classification: LCC ML420.P96 D73 2020 (print) | LCC ML420.P96 (ebook) | DDC 782.42166092--dc23
LC record available at https://lccn.loc.gov/2019050681
LC ebook record available at https://lccn.loc.gov/2019050682

Typeset by S.J.I. Services, New Delhi, India

Contents

	Acknowledgements	vii
	Introduction	1
1	Roots	14
2	Image	70
3	Comeback	106
4	Phenomenon	136
	Appendices	168
	Notes	197
	Bibliography	224
	Index	233

Acknowledgements

Creating any artist profile is an act of impersonation. That places me alongside all of Elvis's many other stylists as a kind of academic tribute artist. Elvis himself therefore deserves thanks. His music is an inspiration. It is my hope that anyone who seeks to profoundly understand Elvis will read this work alongside my other writing on the subject, notably *Counting Down Elvis: His 100 Finest Songs* (Rowman & Littlefield, 2018).

I first studied the Elvis phenomenon back in 1995, when I embarked upon a PhD for what was then the University of Wales, Aberystwyth. In relation to that grounding, I would like to thank Professors Richard Phillips and Mark Goodwin, as well as various people in the Elvis world, including Julie Mundy, Nigel Patterson, Paul Richardson, and other fans such as Eileen Weston.

For subsequent conversations, I am indebted to many music lovers, including the late and much missed David Sanjek, Ben Halligan, Jon Hackett, Tim Wall, Ian Inglis, Tom Attah, and my partner Julie. I would also like to thank Amanda Nell Edgar, Michael Bertrand, Robbie Fry, and everyone else who contributed to the 2017 Memphis conference we held on the subject.

I wish to express gratitude to colleagues at the University of Chester for organizing my timetable to help me pursue my research interests. I am grateful to Professor Darren Sproston and CCRAM at Chester for providing a travel grant to return to Memphis late in 2011. In relation to that visit I would also like to thank the following interviewees, who gave me their time, information and attention: Jane Ellen White at Sun Studio, Jonathan Lyons (then of the Memphis Convention and Visitor's Bureau), Mike Freeman, Hal and Julie Lansky.

Equinox deserve many thanks for giving me the opportunity to dedicate this book to debates on the Memphis Flash, and for waiting patiently for the manuscript.

The history of popular music is not just one of changing sounds. Considered as a cultural field, it proceeds from dialogues between living cultures, from diverse scenes and musicians, and from a parade of stellar characters who left their mark on the art. Academic disciplines are like that too, more so than we often acknowledge. I would like to dedicate this book to the memory of Dave Laing, a pillar of popular music studies as it emerged in the UK, whose work was an inspiration to many, including myself. Without Dave, what you have in your hands would not exist... So thanks, Dave, for your support.

Introduction

> It was a Saturday afternoon, a busy, busy afternoon, and for some reason I happened to be alone in the office. The office was full of people wanting to make personal records. It was a stand-and-wait-your-turn sort of thing. He came in, said he wanted to make a record. I told him he'd have to wait and he said okay. He sat down. Of course he had his guitar... I said, "Who do you sound like in hillbilly?" He said, "I don't sound like nobody". When we went back to make the record, a ten-inch acetate, he got about half way through the first side and I thought, I want to tape this. Now this was something we never did, but I wanted [label owner] Sam to hear this.
>
> Sun Records secretary Marion Keisker[1]

In a recent book discussing meanings of the term "event", the political philosopher Slavoj Žižek described his subject as "something shocking, out of joint, that happens all of a sudden and interrupts the usual flow of things; something that emerges seemingly out of nowhere, without discernable causes".[2] Žižek's definition of an event as *the effect that seems to exceed its causes* applies precisely to Elvis Presley.[3] In the context of mid-1950s America, Elvis appeared both shocking and unprecedented—a break or rupture in the order of things. He was one amongst several rock'n'roll pioneers: not the first, but so spectacularly successful that in the minds of many he came to represent the genre. His contribution demonstrated the political power of the youth market. It placed rock'n'roll firmly in the mainstream. With his sensual gyrations and racial associations, Elvis caused national controversy, put rockabilly on record, transformed country music, and sent out international shockwaves. Nicknames such as the "Memphis Flash" and "Atomic Powered Singer" appeared immediately in the local press, but the idea that Elvis was the *source* of the sea change came later when the era was historicized. After Elvis's own *NBC Comeback Special*, Nik Cohn's rock history *Awopbopaloobop Alopbamboom* described an originating talent: "Elvis is where pop begins and ends. He's the great original and, even now, he's the image that makes all others seem shoddy, the boss".[4] In 1977, the same year that Elvis died, director Tony Palmer's British television documentary series *All You Need is Love* firmly located the singer as the centre of the rock'n'roll explosion. That explosion is, arguably, still having its extended aftermath. As a legacy artist, Elvis Presley is inescapable. Without a doubt, he remains the single most important artist in twentieth-century popular music. He is the alpha and omega figure of the rock and pop era.

The goal of this book is to paint an analytical portrait that introduces the major debates around Elvis Presley. It interprets his music and image to reveal how they have united to construct a particularly powerful and appealing myth, a myth that still has important functions in wider society. One of the main problems with studying Elvis is the overload of available information. The facts of his life, music, and career, are broadly known to historians. With Elvis, we already have the answers. What we do not always have are the questions to apprehend his phenomenon in a way that will make it speak from a more enlightened perspective. Since academic theories remain underdeveloped, immediate stories about his life have often led the conversation. As the decades have gone by, historical detail has frequently been ignored in favour of legend. We might never quite have a full picture of the Memphis singer as an individual, but by closely examining certain facets of his image, we can develop a better understanding of what he has meant as a public phenomenon.

Elvis's career has often been interpreted as a rollercoaster ride which ascended when he found popularity by leading social change, but declined when his embrace of commodification lost its social value and degenerated into safe and predictable entertainment. The rollercoaster supposedly ascended again when Elvis rediscovered his passion for music at the end of the 1960s, but descended once more after the start of the next decade as personal problems and the demands of touring gradually overtook him. What follows in this book is not a strict chronology. Readers who want that can find a timeline in the first and second appendix. Instead, the book uses that broad "rollercoaster" shape of Elvis's career to consider different issues at different points. Before examining his early career and the things which made him popular, the rest of this introduction will offer four perspectives on Elvis to introduce debates about his place in society.

A Tale of Four Elvises

It has been said that we get the Elvis we deserve. Instead, if we do not make independent investigations, we might get the Elvis who reflects someone else's agenda. Presley is, after all, associated with a certain baggage. Elvis has always been, to some extent, linked to the mainstream at its most commercial. As the late sociologist Pierre Bourdieu pointed out, the way that we live and share meaning, creates hierarchies of taste.[5] In their displays of carefully cultivated knowledge, individuals position themselves on these social hierarchies as higher in status than those nearby.[6] Bourdieu called this knowledge *cultural capital*, and suggests that those who appropriately display it are judged as superior by others because they demonstrate that they are more cultivated. Some researchers have suggested that the display of cultural capital does not just mean endorsing high cultural forms, such as ballet; it also happens when individuals display "cool" tastes within popular music fandom.[7] Since Elvis was always a mainstream performer, one, furthermore, often associated with working-class fans, expressing a taste for his music has rarely, if ever, won followers status in wider society. To many non-fans, he has appeared too popular, not creative enough, too emotional, or not "political" enough, to consider. Declaring oneself an Elvis fan, they believe, gains one little or nothing in displays of taste, and may, if unqualified—partly because of the way that his fans have been portrayed in the past—might be seen as a detrimental *display of tastelessness*. This is the reason that Elvis even has closet fans. Perhaps because popular music studies often tends to be middle-class people talking about artists they like, the icon represents a neglected concern: a founding figure in postwar music, a rebellious and iconoclastic artist who became an icon, yet someone that the field of study, with a few exceptions, has barely acknowledged.

To talk about the singer, his creative contribution and his career, is to tread on a complex territory, a territory where realities are overshadowed by bigger arguments and associated simplifications that they create. There is what the singer actually did, how it was taken at the time, and how it has been recycled later, both in nostalgic celebration, and a wider range of debate. Debates about Elvis are complex in part because his image is multifaceted and open to interpretation. They will, however, be briefly rehearsed here. America is a racially diverse capitalist nation with a share of problems that, depending on one's viewpoint, Elvis has either come to embody or challenge. For some opening questions, we might therefore consider: What good can be done through the mechanism of the marketplace? Is it nothing but an obstacle to revolution? How much can it register and inspire useful social change? To begin addressing those issues, what follows in this section will explore a series of different takes on Elvis.

Perhaps the most rudimentary stereotype of Elvis Presley has been portrayed in the comedy of Andrew Dice Clay, who regularly evokes Presley as a hunk o' love parody figure: a big, dumb, macho guy who has enough social awareness to recognize that his innate charisma can take him far. Chuck Berry's 1958 Chess Records hit 'Johnny B. Goode' describes an illiterate country boy who has a golden talent for musicianship. Dice Clay's loose impersonation locates Elvis as a kind of *Johnny B. Goode* figure: someone with great instinct and good fortune who lacks conventional intelligence, and becomes popular in spite of himself. To some extent, this image does connect with iconic moments portrayed in some of Elvis's own screen roles. However, the dumb Southerner stereotype can also reduce Elvis to an opportunist or narcissist: a song salesman who got lucky. It neglects the "real" Elvis's depth of learning and interest in high and low culture, something we might call his *cultural literacy*.[8] It also ignores his shrewd studio craft, vital collaborations, and, more importantly, his complex relation to race and American identity. Finally, it completely glosses over the complexity of Elvis's own personality and beliefs. A dumb Southerner, for example, would have had no special motivation to meditate, or immerse himself in New Age spiritual literature in the 1960s. Andrew Dice Clay's formulation misses Elvis Presley's cultural contribution, the places where he personally made a difference both to society and to popular music. Even Elvis's early Hollywood roles, which drew on perceptions of rock'n'roll to shape his image, portrayed a much more complicated persona. Yet, some people wish to see Elvis only on the basis of his supposedly untutored gut instincts, his opportunism, his acquiescence to fortune, or personal entrapment. For those who do not know much about him, the Dice Clay stereotype seems attractive.

As a young upstart, Elvis angered racists, moralists, defenders of high art, and their politicized brethren, the mass culture critics. In various King Canute-style attempts to reduce the pace of social change, those detractors highlighted what they saw as Presley's crass commercialism. The radical scholar Theodor Adorno, for example, argued that Elvis's commercial success meant that conformist music critics would inevitably defend the singer's "screeching retinue".[9] Of course, Elvis never screeched. Adorno's deafness to Presley demonstrated his own willingness to use artistic judgements in service of political ones. His research could not concede that political change might *first* be registered in the marketplace.

Original criticism was associated with perceptions of Presley's teasing *performance of gender*. From their perspective "Elvis the Pelvis"—to quote his 1950s nickname—used vulgar seduction to court controversy and make money. That his performance was perceived as an appropriation of race made it even more incendiary. So was Elvis nothing but a tacky prop for women's sexual fantasies? In December 1977, *Playboy* men's magazine ran a spoof feature on Elvis-related memorabilia. At that point there was a general obsession in the press with the idea that hawkers were exploiting gullible fans by selling tacky merchandise outside Graceland, Elvis's Memphis home. Lambasting this vulgar mass merchandising, one item featured in the *Playboy* cartoon was a vibrator: "ten full inches of lifelike flesh-tone latex, erotically sculpted in the shape of Elvis… [so you can] feel those legendary hips gyrate in places you never realized were there". The "El-Dŏ" sex toy, it said, also came in an advanced "Treat Me Mean & Cruel" model "for serious fans". Given that the cartoon was released less than six months after Elvis's death, it seemed rather disrespectful. Coverage of Elvis was rarely concerned with respect. Ironically, however, if Elvis and *Playboy* both used sex to sell themselves, neither could quite be reduced to that. The "El-Dō" spoof revealed *Playboy*'s position of Presley: one that, somewhat hypocritically, claimed the kudos of caviar over cornbread, sex and sophistication over a crass, direct, Southern hillbilly approach. *Playboy*'s joke about Elvis merchandise therefore based itself on a certain displacement: posthumous smut peddlers, only existed, they implied, because Elvis himself had made his career *being* tacky merchandise. Commodification is the process of treating a thing as if it is merely an object to be exchanged in the marketplace. As nothing but a sex object, the argument went, Presley vulgarly raised expressions of female desire in the public sphere. To understand this position, it is important to consider its roots.

On the broadest scale is the mass culture critique, a mode of thinking that says commercial cultural products offered to the mainstream fail to fully serve humanity, replacing full satisfaction with illusions and gimmicks which can only serve to subvert social opposition to inequality. In the 1950s, mass culture thinking held sway in certain circles of the upper classes and academia, but was contested by the increasingly popular pleasures of youth culture. Hence the "Elvis the Pelvis" argument, that the King was hoodwinking his audience by gyrating his hips, helping to pass off rock'n'roll as "good" music when there was nothing positive about it. The genre was considered noise, not music. Instead of offering sincere sentiments, it seemed to be nothing more than marketing based on inciting lust. Instead of instilling compassionate values, rock'n'roll prompted riots, caused media controversy, and divided generations. Associated with all this was a racial question. By being so openly sensual, was young Elvis not just crossing the colour line between White and Black musical traditions? For his detractors, this made him a thief. When added to the repetitive movie schedule and touring of later years, such views help cement the idea that Elvis was a dumb country boy who opportunistically embraced his own commodification *until it exploited him*. We might call this the "crass commercialism" argument.

A second, more complex version of Elvis is to be found in the musical preferences of the quirky, masterful Hollywood film director, Quentin Tarantino. Like Dice Clay, Tarantino loves Elvis, and like Dice Clay he also uses that love in his professional life, in this case someone who has made it their business to curate "cool" references to pop culture. Tarantino's fannish interests are a good barometer, not so much of his personal identity, but of how literate American popular music lovers generally think about Elvis as multifaceted: someone who was *both* the "coolest" and "uncoolest" performer. On one list of his favourite albums, he included *The Sun Sessions*, a compilation LP of Elvis's early music, and justified it by saying, "If you grew up loving Elvis, this is it. Forget the Vegas period: if you really love Elvis, you're ashamed of that man in Vegas. You feel like he let you down. The hillbilly cat never let you down".[10] The beauty of art is called its *aesthetic* dimension. Tarantino's judgement might be purely aesthetic—after all, later on, Elvis had, at least on occasions, arguably sang less interesting songs, offered less inspired performances, and even sang a few bum notes—but that would be to ignore the value of Presley's 1970s achievements *and* to locate rock'n'roll itself purely as an aesthetic activity.

To many people, a bit like, say, folk music before or punk afterwards, the genre had a political dimension that could not be disentangled from its form. In other words, it marked a shift in which a new generation of record buyers embraced previously segregated and sometimes marginal forms of music, creating a socially monstrous hybrid which took over the mainstream. To be more specific, rock'n'roll, exciting as it was, spoke for youth by peddling sexual liberation—allowing young women to feel aroused and express that in public—and also became a precursor to civil rights because it offered mainstream recognition to Black musicians, and by extension attacked racism. Elvis was the genre's chief representative. So when he reported to the army and to the Hollywood studios, the argument goes, he resigned his designated role as a champion of social change. That he was discovered in a provincial city or on a small, independent label helps to prove the point. This approach compartmentalizes Elvis Presley, arguing that his youthful dynamism and social relevance coincided with a brief period in which he ascended and changed the world.

A comparison with Dice Clay's Elvis might be instructive, by way of another character. In 1994, Robert Zemeckis directed *Forrest Gump*, a film in which a charming, but physically and mentally challenged man accidentally, but positively, changes the course of several key moments in American life. In the film, Gump unintentionally inspires a young Elvis Presley. In Dice Clay's formulation, Elvis himself can at best only be a kind of *Forrest Gump* figure, accidentally making positive social changes because his instinctual approach contains some folk wisdom. Dice Clay's Elvis cannot let us down by "selling out" to commerce, he can only *roll* with it. Instead of "selling out", he is constantly *buying in*. The logical point, by contrast, that Tarantino's Elvis can let us down and therefore "sell out" any faith that audiences place in him, means he has a stake in the game. If, because of his youthful rebellion, at first he represented the will of the people to make social progress—away from racism, sexual repression, and pointless individual conformity—then the threat of mainstream rejection or repetitive demands of commerce eventually beat that spirit out of him, and he played it safe. Again, as this book will show, that version of Elvis is somewhat inaccurate and drastically simplified, making him a kind of stooge of the genre of music that made him famous, and ignoring the complexity of both his earlier and later career.

Nevertheless, some would have Elvis play the role of a kind of rock'n'roll messiah, someone come to save the world. This reading suggests that in the 1950s he was challenging sexual repression, uniting races through music, and helping his own generation speak its truth. This perspective makes Elvis Presley stand up against the unmarked traditions of racism and sexual hypocrisy that have dogged the USA, and enthrones him to reign triumphant as a democratic emblem of the renewed will of the people. It also positions him as a smooth ambassador for America as melting pot, a place where different races and ethnicities can, at least theoretically, live in harmony. Elvis came into the music scene as an inadvertent destroyer of the very distinctions that allowed others to maintain their cosy lives and ideas. A lot of the theories about Elvis, however, make him a figment of the change he led, and ask what consequences it had *for him*. In the commentaries written by music critics, this shift represents a "loss of nerve" in which the singer was afraid his stardom would disappear so he tied himself to a lucrative treadmill and became stifled creatively. In this model, his success as a rock'n'roll rebel ended when he went in the army and served Hollywood.

The historical figure we see today is trapped like a fly in amber behind a series of fixed conversations that have continued to the point where we can no longer quite see him. Elvis is often located as an ordinary labourer with a genius gift—a poor boy who achieved the American dream and eventually faced its fatal consequences—but his impact on popular music and society was more like the revolutionary change wrought by business or *capital* in its purest form. So how did it happen? To set the ball rolling, it might be worth thinking about authenticity. Directly or indirectly, both fans and critics often talk about the music they like being authentic, but what does that mean? Academic studies of musical authenticity have taken the concept apart, showing that rather than something *inside the music*, an *essence*, it is instead a way of speaking, a *discourse*, that, when attributed, helps people to discriminate and make judgements about genres, artists and songs.[11] Those judgements are necessarily based on adopting particular distinctions. *Authentic* music, it is often argued, comes from "genuine" communal or representative individual expression, something outside of commerce, outside of the mainstream, from ordinary folk.

At one point during a scene that was deleted from Tarantino's 1994 film *Pulp Fiction*, a central character explained: "There's only two kinds of people in the world: 'Beatles people' and 'Elvis people' ... nobody likes them equally. Somewhere you have to make a choice, and that choice tells you who you are".[12] The claim sounds absurd, but in one way it has some grounding. By the mid-1960s, the Beatles symbolized a significant change which located popular music as something based on each individual's or group's songwriting creativity; something that could be art, speak for a generation, give marginalized people a voice, express political protest, and bring about social change. On this score, we might say, the Beatles won. As one commentator wrote in 1972, "Elvis Presley must appear low-brow as against the Beatles, but that is only because he 'peaked' at the wrong time".[13]

Both early Elvis and the Beatles represented modern life in their own eras and ways. We might say that the 1950s Elvis, historically, made the Beatles possible, but equally, the world *they* then helped to create made the priorities of that era obsolete. Elvis both helped to lay the foundations for popular music's gradual response to such critiques and was caught out by them. The Elvis we know is refracted as a missing link between two musical epochs: more edgy and vernacular than his predecessors, but more obviously yoked to commerce than those who came later. He was a performer whose signature style was popular, commercially successful, but ironically, neglected by those who came to believe that song writing was the deepest form of personal expression in popular music. The updated equation framed Elvis, who had no significant credentials as a songwriter, as unworthy of critical scrutiny compared to myriad other artists, whether Robert Johnson or Bob Marley, John Coltrane or Miles Davis, Bob Dylan or the Beatles, Kraftwerk or Pussy Riot. It positions the Tin Pan Alley tradition of music making, where songwriters often work in teams and sell their compositions to publishers who then broker them to recording artists, as comparatively inauthentic. It also ignores the significant value of song interpretation and performance. If nobody could deliver a song quite like Elvis, and that was part of why he ascended to such phenomenal heights as an iconic artist, how do we evaluate the *work* involved? What, culturally and financially, is its worth? One answer might be to say that it is whatever can be extracted from the audience and their brokers in the music industry, such as record labels and concert promoters. This question, then, signifies a potential class issue, perhaps even a Marxist one: a case of labour against capital. As a cultural worker, someone who sells his highly skilled labour as a singer, we want Elvis to get his due, his critical and financial worth. When we talk about him, we also want to explore the dimensions of that struggle, reflected in the drama of his working life. This approach, however, also locates Elvis as someone who is not entrepreneurial or in full control of his own destiny.

Concerns about Elvis as a cultural worker set the stage for a third way to discuss him. What Dice Clay's and Tarantino's versions of Elvis have in common is that they suggest, first, that Presley is rarely seen as a *primarily* creative or socially conscious figure. Instead, his ability to steer his own career (autonomy) and make a difference to history (agency) is presumed to have limitations. These are reflected in perceptions of both his manager, post-rock'n'roll career, working collaborations, and personal decline. A third version of Elvis, however, begins to transcend these assumptions. Music critic Greil Marcus specializes in the study of American roots music, and Elvis's relationship to it. For him, the Elvis Presley that emerges is more mature insofar that he is a figure who has the ability to inflect and respond to his own story.[14] Not only is Marcus's Elvis more socially and historically situated, and more active in his art and career, but he is also quintessentially American: an individual *and icon of individualism*, a figure of unity and majesty, someone for who the line between art and commerce is blurred, and new things arise in the blurring. Marcus sees younger Elvis as a hero who has the nerve to bring races together, and older Elvis as both worshipped and made a victim, someone trapped within, and responsive to, the vast size of his own legend. This, at least, captures some of the ways in which Elvis was able to make reference to his own story by using it to perform comedy or tragedy in his act. Signs consist of signifiers, such as words or images, which stand in for the shared meanings they represent. Overall, Marcus locates Elvis as someone who embodies America's democratic ideals, a *sign* for something that does not die in 1977, but gets used as a resource by those who come after.[15] Malleability is a term used to suggest that things can easily be put to different uses. The notion of Elvis as a malleable signifier was popular in the 1980s and 1990s, when, in his absence, the King appeared to be everywhere because he had become used as a way to talk about the commercial imperatives of popular culture.

Marcus's Elvis transcends questions of commercial pressure or social relevance, not by sidestepping them, but by encompassing them. It would be useful to find more refined ways to locate the singer in his musical and social context, in order to note where his story fits and departs from the more stereotypical portrayals. At this point, it is worth briefly considering the thoughts of Herbert Marcuse. This cultural Marxist thinker has some unusual parallels to Elvis. He lived at the same time and in the mid-1950s he carefully synthesized Marxist and Freudian ideas. In his 1969 article "An Essay on Liberation", Marcuse talked of "Black music, invading the White culture".[16] He located it as something that paralleled classical music in its revolutionary possibilities:

> In the subversive, dissonant, crying and shouting rhythm, born in the "dark continent" and in the "deep South" of slavery and deprivation, the oppressed revoke the Ninth Symphony and give art a desublimated, sensuous form of frightening immediacy, moving, electrifying the body, and the soul materialized in the body... The affinity between Black music (and its *avant-gardistic* White development) and the political rebellion against the "affluent society" bears witness to the increasing desublimation of culture.[17]

What is crucial here is that although Elvis, of course, performed rock'n'roll, the statement takes in effect the focus off him and begins to places it back on the music's form and audience. It also suggests that the struggle was not simply to express sexual excitement; that was only *one* aspect of *challenging social conformity*. From that perspective, couched in the language of self-expression, it was Elvis's generation that demanded social change. He was simply one of them.

Marcuse realized that working-class consciousness no longer fostered radical social change. Instead, he believed, there was a *cultural revolution* in which the arts could challenge conformity by expressing authentic human demands neglected by capitalism. This would, Marcuse believed, help people rediscover their *commitment* to living a genuine life rather than being shaped by forces imposed on them from outside by a capitalist social system which ultimately prioritized the ethics of big business over basic human compassion. Marcuse was rediscovered by the next generation. He became required reading for 1960s radicals working for the counterculture, civil rights movement, and women's liberation. What is interesting about his work, in this context, however, is that over the years it recognized the complexity of art. It was not only a case of civilization imposing conformity on individuals and art then liberating them, but rather that the aesthetic elements of *some* forms of artistic production from *within* the capitalist system—such as rock music and fringe theatre—lent themselves to a push for liberation. Marxists traditionally described ruling classes who own business assets as the *bourgeoisie*. For Marcuse, although their capital system was stifling society, bourgeois art could nevertheless be used to help the seeds of change grow from within. More importantly, he believed that prior, less obviously radical, artistic work could be plundered for aesthetic forms that would help in this process.[18] In other words, perhaps the binary distinctions between "revolutionary" and "non-revolutionary", or "progressive" and "regressive", are too simplistic a way to talk about culture, the individuals who remake it, or the times they live in.

In light of Marcuse's ideas, the problem of limiting Elvis to a messianic role becomes obvious. Rock'n'roll, and the cultural revolution that it helped to start, contributed to significant changes in society, but the initial major legal challenge to school segregation in 1954 proves that the music was not *solely* responsible.[19] Genres are also bigger than artists. Although it is worth acknowledging that artists who take fresh paths within the mainstream may, inadvertently or deliberately, play a valuable role in *accelerating* the pace of social change, another concern should be to avoid restrictive simplifications. This, of course, is reminiscent of Karl Marx's classic line, "Men make their own history, but they do not make it as they please; they do not make it under self-selected circumstances, but under circumstances existing already, given and transmitted from the past".[20] At certain times, Elvis, and artists who have played similar roles, have *represented* the changing course of the music mainstream, but not one of them has single-handedly determined its fate. It is worth adding that the next line from Marx's famous essay was, "The tradition of all dead generations weighs like a nightmare on the brains of the living".[21] This recalls a recent lecture by the African American public scholar Cornel West, who discussed the continuing pervasiveness of racism:

> I've got a lot of vanilla brothers and sisters that walk with me and say, Brother West, Brother West, you know I'm not a racist any longer. Grandma's got work to do, but I've transcended that. And I say to them, I'm a Jesus-loving, free, black man, and I've tried to be so for 55 years, and I'm 62 now, and when I look in the depths of my soul I see White supremacy because I grew up in America.

And if there's White supremacy in me, my hunch is you've got some work to do too.[22]

For West, in the USA at least, White supremacy has been part of the social environment for a long time, so it has some degree of hold over *all* our thinking, even in the twenty-first century. If we are all influenced by it to different degrees, an approach that points at others and makes absolute distinctions has its limitations. This does not mean, however, that the aim of working towards a society without racism is invalid. Instead of making judgements that ignore the complexity of real balances of power, we might be better off assessing whether, *in light of all the contradictions*, the *summation* of what any one person did was positive. We might also ask what lessons might be learned from them about how to improve the world despite all of us being imperfect people in a limited environment.

Speaking of accommodating contradiction makes it worth considering Elvis's linking or bridging function. Modernity refers to the period of social experience that occurred between the early and late twentieth century. For anybody who delves into Elvis's universe, his attitudes can appear contradictory. It is hard to fathom whether such contradictions stem from a lack of knowledge about him, or from the man himself. This book suggests that such contradictions characterize our construction of Elvis's celebrity persona in part because we already see him as a bridge figure between the quaint communality of the early twentieth century and a later period of high modernity. When his life and career ended in the 1970s, he was at home in a comparatively alienated, technologically orientated world. Elvis's music, and what we know of his life, reflected the changes. In this formulation, Elvis is consistently contradictory, hybridized, or compromised, yet he also appears to ride these things out without much effort because they signify the strength and source of his appeal. Somewhat inadvertently, that also makes him a figure of nostalgia now too. This book has the task of bringing all these different aspects into and out of focus, where appropriate, and unpacking them as it discusses his changing career.

A fourth portrayal of Elvis takes this approach even further. Music critic and biographer Peter Guralnick presents Presley in a much more historical light, quietly noting the singer's responses to his situation, and celebrating moments when he visibly adopts higher ethical ideas. As one review of Guralnick's first Elvis biography *Last Train to Memphis* explained, the singer handles both his success and the older generation's critical reactions to it "with impressive grace".[23] Guralnick's version of Elvis is not a stooge used to talk about the limitations of personal freedom within commodity capitalism; he takes the singer more on his own terms. Taking its cue from the word "pathology", meaning the study of disease, "pathography" is defined as *biography that focuses on failure or misfortunes*. Of Elvis, the biographer explained: "The last few years of his life amounted to little more than a sad diminution; this is what has become the basis for the caricature that we so often see repeated in our pathographic times".[24] It is not that Guralnick's Elvis is a totally free individual, however. Sometimes the singer has to compromise or otherwise suffer, but, equally, he can *redeem* himself, as it were, moment by moment.

Perhaps the "real" Elvis is out there somewhere, but will we ever find him? One aim of this book is to take readers beyond simplifications which locate Elvis *only* as a struggling worker in order to better consider what he did and how he did it. Nevertheless, when we attempt to avoid the simplifications, and just see Elvis as a historical figure, in some form they almost inevitably come back. Elements such as Elvis's commodification tend to guide our thinking because they connect to the concerns of our own age. Aspects of all four Elvises—Dice Clay's, Tarantino's, Marcus's and Guralnick's—and the debates they raise will come up frequently in the sections that follow, not because this book necessarily agrees with them. Rather, the debates that these portrayals connect with are the ones that shape how Elvis has been seen. This is no accident either, as Elvis's screen and celebrity image has periodically played upon them. Think, for example, of the "real" Elvis, performing during his NBC TV *Comeback Special* in 1968. After members of the live audience express their disappointment that 'One Night' will be his last song, he quips, "Man, I only work here". Muddying these proverbial waters is therefore a question of how we, as audiences, tend to piece together diverse aspects of Elvis's musical persona, screen image and private life by making them interrogate each other. Music critic Greil Marcus has talked of "another Elvis Presley, a [public] figure made of echoes not facts".[25] Although Marcus was speaking about the things communicated by those who knew Elvis *only* as a myth, what follows suggests that even for diligent researchers the "echoes" never quite disappear as they continually guide and shape what he means. Advanced biographic study might help us unearth a "real Elvis" privileged by details found out about his private life, but this too is our own construct. Different readings have been made by different groups of people at different times, variously coming to the forefront of debates about Elvis. They arguably shape discussions about the degree of control he had over his career (commerce), the role of his following as a kind of support structure (totemism), family and its impact on his working life (in Freudian terms, Oedipal issues), the drama of his mental struggle and its portrayal in music (existentialism). Though not all of these frames are common in popular music studies, together they arguably offer a high level of insight into the singer's public profile.

By discussing Elvis's roots, image, comeback and posthumous phenomenon, the rest of this book examines ongoing debates about a popular music icon. The first chapter considers a series of moments from the singer's early career. It focuses on Elvis's early recordings, his complex relation to issues of race, grounding on the tour circuit, and controversial performances on national television. It also discusses perceptions of his amateurism as a musician, his embrace of gospel music, and audience support. What unites these things is the way that they negotiate the common idea that Elvis was authentic because his roots were in the world outside of show business. In the next chapter, the issue of Elvis's social conformity is considered by looking at his army and Hollywood years. While his close relationship with parents Gladys and Vernon Presley was part of his identity, it also fed into his screen image, and had interesting connections to an era where courtship, youth and sexual relations were changing their meanings. The chapter traces these meanings through the film roles that framed Elvis as a country cousin, juvenile delinquent, innocent hedonist, and potential husband. Notions of conformity move the discussion back to consider how ideas about exploitation shaped Elvis's image off-screen, and the roles assigned to his father and manager in his story. The third chapter of this book continues the theme of Elvis's struggle for autonomy by looking at how he bought commercial success and compassion together in a series of more "adult" career achievements, including his 1968 television *Comeback Special*, American Sound recording sessions, Las Vegas years, and *Aloha from Hawaii* concert. Along the way it discusses Elvis's fan support, political persuasion, relation to nostalgia, and personal decline. The final chapter considers how Presley's posthumous reputation has fared with changing times, first by considering the argument that Elvis's ultimate downfall was supposedly caused by his careless embrace of commodification, then by discussing how his fans have actively curated his music.

1 Roots

In 1990 Richard Peterson wrote an article called "Why 1955?" in which he explained the advent of rock'n'roll. Peterson argued that some of the cultural explanations for the emergence of the genre were relatively poor. Members of the famous 1960s "baby boomer" generation were still children in the 1950s. Star musicians could not create a social shift *by themselves*. Peterson suggested that a series of enabling socio-economic factors were responsible for the environment that gave birth to the music. These included the invention of vinyl singles, a doubling in the number of licensed radio stations, the rise of BMI (a performance royalty collection agency that supported vernacular artists), the success of independent distribution networks, and the rise of television. By shifting focus away from the performers to their environment, Peterson offered an argument that questioned the importance of individual behaviour. Inevitably, however, there was an interaction between context and participants. Elvis and others took full advantage of the new opportunities available. Building on Peterson's work, we might therefore consider the cultural and political landscape that facilitated the momentous shifts of the mid-1950s era. What follows in this chapter discusses how Elvis started out as an artist on the Sun label and examines some of the bases for his appeal as a popular musician. It covers not only the existential drama of his 1950s music, but also issues such as Elvis's relation to race, his performance of gender, the appeal of his amateurism and abiding love of gospel, and the audience support which guaranteed his stardom.

In the Beginning: The 1950s, Memphis and Sun Records

Vernacular music consists of genres such as blues and gospel that emerge from everyday creativity rather than show-business professionalism or high art. Elvis's story has often been painted as a tale about an unusual music enthusiast who was steeped in the rich vernacular musical heritage of his geographic region, and who gave it back to the world as his own creation. While that story is true, it deserves more framing through cultural changes that were taking place in 1940s and 1950s America. After World War II, a new generation of Americans lived in the shadow of the Cold War, the Korean conflict and compulsory conscription. In a social transformation epitomized by Alfred Kinsey et al.'s book *Sexual Behaviour in the Human Female* (1953), women had started to assume greater freedom and independence. By adding scientific weight to the reluctantly acknowledged actuality of female desire, Kinsey's claim that one in four wives had experienced extra-marital sex by their forties began to generate public discussion and dispel taboos around female sexuality. Young people were also starting to find a voice as part of the new consumer society. The introduction of the seven-inch single in 1949 and the switch in profit emphasis from sheet music to record sales within the next two years brought with it an era in which music consumption could conveniently be used to express both individual and shared identity. Although Elvis was located in a city where he was able to seek out live music of different sorts, he also enjoyed recorded sounds from Hollywood and the mainstream music industry. The mid-1950s were a joyous time when new technology, materialist aspiration and social progress combined; young people began to define themselves around a quest for style. Once famous, Elvis became the poster boy for a new generation less interested in the protestant work ethic than in collecting cars, clothes and music.

Sam Phillips was the person who produced Elvis's first professional recordings and guided the development of his early career. Phillips visited Memphis in 1939 and later moved there to work as a disc jockey on WREC. In January 1950 he started a mobile recording unit called The Memphis Recording Service. It made audio recordings of weddings and other occasions. Sam's calling card read, "We record anything—anywhere—any time".[1] To create a home for his operation, he opened a small studio at 706 Union Avenue, a street best known for its used car lots. The modest operation consisted of a small front office plus studio room and console. Bands played more quietly than they do today and the place had little sound separation. The whole facility used only five microphones per session. Sun was a site of possibility and experiment, more like an ongoing talent contest than other labels. Where his competitors usually went with what was already proven popular, Phillips's approach was more akin to the field recordist, John Lomax, who scoured the South in the 1930s for Black performers he considered unspoiled by modern society. Sam created a funnel system that was rather like an *inverted* version of John Lomax's field recording venture: Black artists *came to him* and, if they created something commercial together, he paid them.[2]

In the summer of 1950 Sam met local disc jockey Dewey Phillips and created the short-lived Phillips label. Before it sunk into debt, the Phillips label managed to press 300 copies of a Joe Hill Louis blues single, the riotous, semi-spoken word 'Gotta Let You Go'.³ Promotional material called Louis the hottest thing in the country. When he lost his label, Sam organized recording sessions, paid the musicians a flat fee, then licensed the results to companies such as Chess Records. His studio's most significant early recording was 'Rocket 88' by Jackie Brenston and his Delta Cats, a number dedicated to flirtation and driving General Motors' top selling automobile line, the Oldsmobile 88. The song is often acclaimed as the first significant rock'n'roll single. Ike Turner played piano on the record and soon became a scout for Sam, seeking out undiscovered local blues musicians.

In March 1952, Phillips started a new independent label called Sun Records as a way to bring local talent direct to the marketplace. Twenty years later he told an interviewer from the *Radio Times*:

> I'd grown up to a large degree with both poor Black people and poor Whites ... they had come to think of themselves as something different [and inferior] over the years, so that the only things they could do privately were their music and their religion.⁴

He recalled that Black artists were trying to be like professional balladeers, but he wanted them to do their own thing. In his search for raw emotion, Phillips encouraged his artists toward "perfect imperfect" recordings. As Sam saw it:

> The most difficult thing I had to do was to impress upon them that they were welcome to come and try to do what they did best, but that I didn't want anyone trying to sound like Nat King Cole or something they weren't.⁵

Sun started as a White-owned singles label, promoting the talent of local Black artists. Its spate of hits began in the wake of a legal wrangle with two R&B songwriters who were later central to Elvis's RCA story: Jerry Leiber and Mike Stoller. The pair of up-town New York Jews crafted a song called 'Hound Dog', which became a national hit in 1952 on Peacock Records for Big Mama Thornton. A year later, Sun artist Rufus Thomas, who got his start in the Rabbit's Foot Minstrels, recorded a lively but unoriginal answer record called 'Bear Cat'. Leiber and Stoller issued a lawsuit and Sun lost the case. Thomas—who was a pivotal figure for decades in the Memphis music scene—recorded no other releases for Sun.⁶ Then, in June 1953, the Prisonaires—who formed as part of a Tennessee Penitentiary rehabilitation programme—recorded 'Just Walkin' in the Rain'. It sold 250,000 copies as a regional doo-wop hit single, and was picked up nationally in 1956 by the pop balladeer Johnnie Ray, who sold eight times as many records.⁷ With his achingly sentimental trademark delivery, Ray became a youth idol at the start of the 1950s with a chart-topping double A-side for Columbia's Okeh subsidiary featuring the heart-breaking 1951 ballads 'Cry' and 'The Little White Cloud That Cried'. Creating hits throughout the decade, Ray formed a link—at least in terms of audience phenomena—between Sinatra's bobby soxers and Elvis's mighty following. Johnnie Ray's popularity was eventually somewhat diminished by his rather static style of performance and limited television exposure. Nevertheless, his popularity was immense at the time. He was so well known that when Elvis first appeared in the US and UK national media, he was compared to Johnnie Ray.

Sam was cognizant of stars like Ray and the rising demand for R&B amongst young White radio listeners:

> It seemed to me that the young people couldn't identify with the music the adults liked, and the only music they could identify with was race music. It had a certain abandon, and it was something that parents didn't particularly dig.[8]

So how did Elvis find his way to Sun? He told host Wink Martindale on a Memphis TV show in 1956, "I never even thought of singing as a career. In fact I was ashamed to sing in front of anybody except my mother and daddy".[9] From an early age, though, Elvis had taken an interest in recorded and broadcast music. By the early 1950s he would listen to both Memphis's Black station WDIA and the *Grand Ole Opry*.[10] Elvis also collected records, browsing and buying discs at Charlie's record store and Poplar Tunes. His interest in playing music had developed from an early age in Tupelo, where both his pastor Frank Smith, and uncles Johnny and Vester, encouraged him on guitar. Following that, Elvis essentially taught himself. There were several moments when he sang in public before he found fame.[11]

After using a Presto mixing board for years, Sam Phillips obtained an RCA 76-D radio console with hand-built transformers and a playback speaker. For a few dollars, he would make a personal acetate for anyone who wanted to record.[12] Starting in 1953, Elvis cut two acetates over a year-long period, perhaps as a shy way of auditioning for the label.[13] Sam claimed that Elvis's first visit to Sun had been inspired by knowing that the label had created hits for Black artists.[14] Elvis experts Peter Guralnick and Ernst Jørgensen speculate that the young singer may have been prompted to enter following a story in the *Memphis Press-Scimitar* on July 15, 1953 that celebrated the success of the Prisonaires.[15] It is quite surprising that a *White* teenager would audition for a label that predominantly released Black artists. Other local White musicians had never considered such an idea, though *after* 1953 some began to participate in Sun sessions.[16] Elvis's story not only portrayed a boy from Tupelo who was colour-blind and desperately hungry for stardom; it combined those two aspects in interesting ways.

When Elvis entered Sun in the summer of 1953, Sam Phillips was talking to his associates in the back room and went next door with them to Taylor's restaurant. Since Sam was too busy to deal with casual custom, Marion Keisker helped Elvis cut his first recording. According to Guralnick she recalled seeing a "shy, a little woebegone" 18-year-old "cradling his battered, beat-up child's guitar".[17] Elvis chose to record 'My Happiness' by a Black doo-wop group from Indianapolis called The Ink Spots. Cover versions in different styles were commonplace back then. According to music researcher John Potter, it was "a time when there was a great deal of fluidity between listening publics that had previously been considered separate".[18] The song had already been a country hit before Elvis sang his tender, lilting, bittersweet rendition around July 18.[19] At the same session he also recorded the syrupy 'That's When Your Heartaches Begin', another hit for the Ink Spots. Although Sam Phillips had missed the first session, Keisker told him about the young singer. He gave Elvis's first recording a listen. On January 4, 1954, Elvis dropped by Sun again and recorded Italian-American singer Joni James's tender pop ballad 'I'll Never Stand in Your Way' plus country star Jimmy Wakely's 'It Wouldn't Be The Same Without You'.[20] Sam Phillips recalled:

> I remember one day I was in the studio and I noticed this young boy walking up and down outside ... he came in, hung his guitar round his neck, and we talked a little bit, and I gathered that he was called Elvis Presley, was 18 and lived in a very poor area. I saw in his eyes that same look of fear that was in the Black man's eyes, that he might be somewhere off bounds for the likes of him. I tried to put him at ease, and I let him sing a little to practice before I cut the record, and we used a piece of scrap record I had lying around, just so that he could get the confidence. I'll never forget the look of amazement when he heard himself on record—amazement not at the way he sounded when he sang, but also that someone should be treating him with such respect.[21]

While Elvis *said* that he made his first records to see how he sounded and as a present for his mother, he may have had other motives. Sun was a place where anyone with enough money and confidence could go and make a record; though he or she would not be paid any money so far as royalty advances were concerned. Elvis could not have walked into any other record company; none would have been quite so willing to experiment.

Elvis's entry into Sun Studio has become the stuff of legend. Sun Records secretary Marion Keisker's description of the youngster's vanity recording of doo-wop group The Ink Spots' 'My Happiness' and 'That's When Your Heartaches Begin' has become akin to the book of Genesis in terms of its status as a founding myth of rock'n'roll. Elvis biographies inevitably include this brief story as a matter of seeming innocence, but in doing so they continue to promote the interpretation it makes, not least in the way it marks Elvis as a commodity. Interpretations of music are influenced by what we know about its popularity, something measured through the marketplace. In that sense "hype" is not about *artificially swindling* the public: it is instead an *integral part* of music consumption, even if that is as simple as the audience's knowledge of a single's chart position. While some have argued that fandom is an independent phenomenon, it is still inspired by commercial products. Marketing helps audiences to discover and understand artists in ways that make fandom possible. The story of Elvis's entry into Sun Studio, like many others, has grown hazy over the years.[22] It is now remembered, arguably, in relation to the commercial marketplace. Elvis's lucky break story paints his entry into commerce as a matter of total innocence—he was just singing for his mother—yet it also acts as a vouchsafe for his music as different and independently selected by a female admirer. Reading the accounts again, it is hard not to be struck by the way that they construct Elvis as a *commodity*: authentic (singing to hear himself, not for money), original ("I don't sound like nobody"), universal ("I sing all sorts"), and female friendly (singing for his mother, selected by Marion Keisker). Part of this is to do with how we process historical information by looking in retrospect for congruity in the lineaments of a popular artist's celebrity myth. In that sense, it is interesting that one of Elvis's first biographers, Favius Friedman, mistakenly recorded the surname of the singer's discoverer, Marion Keisker, as "Risker".[23] Ms Keisker took a chance by recommending the boy's singing.

A while after those early, self-funded studio visits, Sam decided to see if Elvis had the potential to succeed in a commercial context. At this point he had been dabbling for around six months with the idea of making Elvis a Sun artist.[24] What started to galvanize him was that he had received an acetate demo from the song publisher Red Wortham called 'Without You'. It was a sentimental song and needed a tender vocal. On Saturday June 26, 1954, Sam told Marion to call Elvis.[25] He invited him to the studio that afternoon to try out, but, unfortunately, did not hear anything inspiring. This first professional session was a gamble on Sam's part. Quickly, he called upon two local musicians to see if they would accompany the young singer.

Scotty Moore and Bill Black were both older than their young charge; both had more life experience and were settled down. Both had also served in the Korean conflict.[26] Black's family had lived in Lauderdale Courts at the same time as the Presleys. Mrs Black knew Mrs Presley. Bill's brothers Johnny and Ken also went to school with Elvis, but Bill was grown up and had moved out. Scotty was a competent guitar player with a gentle, quirky, angular style. Bill, on the other hand, came from the Opry tradition in which a "country bumpkin" player would leap around on stage with a "bull fiddle" (standing double bass) and banter with the band leader.[27] Scotty and Bill had regularly played live together when they backed the local sensation Dorsey Burnette. Their association continued in an ensemble dance outfit called the Starlite Wranglers. In the Memphis country scene of the 1950s, "barn storming" was the accepted form of wisdom. Conventional thinking said that bands should make records not to generate sales income, but instead to use them as advertisements: calling cards distributed to radio to secure airplay and thus create live bookings. Scotty earned a great local reputation for the way he had developed the Starlite Wranglers. Moore had marshalled the band to the point where it had a distinctive lead vocalist in the shape of Doug Poindexter, a repeat radio spot on KWEM, and a regular booking at the Bon Air club. Near the end of May 1954, the Starlite Wranglers recorded a first single for Sun in a kind of Hank Williams inspired, hillbilly style. Scotty was characteristically modest about his musical skills: "I just stole from every guitar player that I could over the years".[28]

Sam had been talking to Scotty about Elvis as early as mid-May. A week after he first tried to record the youngster, the Sun producer told Scotty Moore to call Elvis and work with him directly. During a phone call to the Presleys on Alabama Avenue, Scotty invited Elvis to his house on Belz Street, which was near to where Bill lived. That Sunday, July 4, all three musicians started jamming together and trying to find common ground in ballads like Hank Snow's 'I Don't Hurt Anymore', Jo Stafford's 'You Belong to Me' and the Ink Spots' 'If I Didn't Care'. Scotty concluded that Elvis could sing, but was not exceptional. Nevertheless, Sam set up a studio session for the trio, aiming to start at about 7pm the next day.[29]

Elvis's professional Sun Studio sessions are listed in the third appendix of this book. His first accompanied Sun session is one of the most discussed moments in popular music. Sam Phillips did not necessarily know he was making history, but he realized he had to be patient.[30] He described himself as a facilitator: able to discern others' gifts and to remove any constraints that prevented their free expression.[31] As he explained, "I ran the show, but it was run in such a way that they were part of it". He added:

> The studio had to be a place where we knew that nothing is perfection, and the worst thing we could hunt for is perfection ... We had to have enough belief in each other to say, hey, we're going to make mistakes, and that just might be the thing that's going to be different about it.[32]

On July 5, 1954, the first number that the trio recorded was Leon Payne's 'I Love You Because', but the song was no better than its original release. The musicians kept looking for inspiration.[33] It was then that they stumbled on a different kind of sound. During a break in the session, a song popped into Elvis's head and he just started singing it and jumping around. Scotty and Bill joined in, but the tape was not rolling, so Sam asked them to back up and do it again. Elvis may have practised his own unique version of 'That's All Right' for a while, as Johnny Black claimed that he heard him sing it when the Presleys lived at Lauderdale Courts.[34] The song was not a new composition, even at that point, but Elvis performed it in a completely new style. In August 1956 he explained to a fan magazine:

> When I was called to make my first record, I went to the studio and they told me what they wanted to sing and how they wanted me to sing it. Well, I tried it their way, but it didn't work out so good. So while most of 'em were sitting around resting, a couple of us just started playing around with 'That's All Right', a great beat number ... It came off pretty good, and Mr [Sam] Phillips, the man who owned the record company, said I should go ahead and sing all the songs my own way, the way I knew best.[35]

From his perspective, Sam Phillips explained:

> Well here is this Cat, 18 years old, and I said, "Elvis: what in the hell have you been holding out on me all this time?" You know. The next thing you knew, I had Scotty and Bill pick up their instruments. I nipped back in the control room and it was just a matter of two or three takes. Man, that was delivered on a silver platter to me.[36]

The other tune definitely recorded on the trio's first Sun session was the melancholic ballad 'Harbor Lights'.[37] It was 'That's All Right', however, that had something special. The song's most obvious undercurrent was a racial one, as the trio had mixed country and blues, genres that were relatively segregated in terms of marketing and recording, if not live music. Discussing Elvis, Sam also explained:

> I knew then there was something distinctive about him. He liked the same music that I did, good gut-bucket blues, and he really was a student of Arthur Crudup and Leadbelly and people like that, which was amazing in a boy so young.[38]

The idea of Elvis as a "student of ... Leadbelly" is interesting; he recorded one Leadbelly song ('Cottonfields'), which he may have played live as early as 1954.[39] I mention this because Sun is often portrayed as a *starting point* for the emergence of rootsy and raw blues, while in reality to some extent it was a more ethical *continuation* of previous field recording practices. Sam added: "I knew we had something that wasn't fish and wasn't fowl, but that had tremendous excitement and abandon".[40] To elaborate on the metaphor, 'That's All Right' was, of course, neither fish (White country), nor fowl (Black blues). According to George Klein in a *Radio Times* interview: "Sam was the guy who kicked it all off. He took Black music and he made White guys sing it".[41] Elvis pushed the tune away from Crudup's casual, showy blues style, instead creating a breezy country pop number with its vocal careering over some bopping, percussive bass work.⁴² John Potter observed, "What is unusual about it is the direct engagement that Elvis makes with the listener, a kind of creamy urgency that is unsettling to listen to".⁴³ When the lyrics, too, are considered, the song explores how a young man might cope with warnings from parents telling him to avoid a bad girl—a theme that links sexual mischief to parental disapproval.

'That's All Right' appealed to Sam precisely because it represented the moment when Elvis's musical tastes connected with his longstanding interest in the blues. Although Sam had known Arthur Crudup's version for at least five years, neither Scotty nor Bill had ever heard the song before. What they created over Elvis's vocal was, in effect, totally improvised.⁴⁴ The song's engaging, up-tempo style was enhanced by the qualities that Sun bought to the expression of Elvis's voice: the little room on Union Street had an especially warm, live sound. Explaining the musical backing of the first session, Elvis said:

> Well, actually there's only two [musicians]. See, I'm just singin', I'm not ... I play the guitar but they didn't record it ... We just more or less landed upon it accidentally. Nobody knew what they were doin' until we had already done it.⁴⁵

His last line emphasized the improvisational and perhaps instinctual nature of the session. Bill Black provided such enthusiastic percussive bass on the early Sun material that the trio did not need drums. The percussive effect he created became known as *slapback*, a combination of Bill "alternately plucking and slapping the string back down against the neck" and Sam creating delay by flipping the magnetic tape back over the recording head.⁴⁶ It gave the trio a "big" sound. Indeed, RCA tried to duplicate the innovative slapback echo for their first Elvis single 'Heartbreak Hotel' by recording it in a hallway. As Scotty also recalled, there were no sophisticated banks of studio equalizers back then. Microphone placement was what changed the sound.

Elvis's vocal style stood out on his gently rollicking rock'n'roll rendition. Sam mixed Elvis's voice as part of the music. According to Scotty, "He treated Elvis's voice like an instrument".⁴⁷ Guralnick explained, in more detail:

> Elvis brings a melodic sense, a kind of swinging country sense to a blues song whose blues roots he never betrays and I think stands as a kind of homage, in a way, to a singer he enormously admired: Arthur Crudup. But it's an entirely different song ... The classic sound of these Sun sides that Elvis made really relies upon the feeling you get, no matter how many times that you listen to them, that they're unrehearsed, they're spontaneous, they're springing right from the soul.⁴⁸

It was this urgent performative style that, in part, characterized Elvis's up-tempo delivery. Against the traditional timing of the beat, he could sing like a horse bolting for freedom.[49]

At this point it is relevant to consider the racial politics of Memphis in the 1950s. After the Great Depression, the increasingly urbanized national Black population pursued an ethic of material aspiration.[50] Though African Americans were only around 10% of the nation, by 1950 they were 37% of the city's population.[51] Memphis had been defined by the separation of different races, a long period of segregation still maintained by its notorious mayor, Edward Hall "Boss" Crump. After 44 years presiding over the city, in 1954 Crump stood down for health reasons. The racial environment was just beginning to change and that movement was reflected nowhere more clearly than on the airwaves. Southern Blacks generally remained poor, but were slowly beginning to make a difference as a consumer group. WHBQ had shows pitched at the Black audience as early as the 1930s. Two White men—John Pepper and Bert Ferguson—tried Black programming in 1947 after their station's all-White format failed to make money. The result was WDIA, a station that was successful because African Americans made up 47% of the audience in its catchment area.[52] When the charismatic Black disc jockey Nat D. Williams started at the station, "Most callers made it clear that they felt Black people should not be on the radio at all".[53] In such an intolerant environment, almost all of the station's music programming was relatively tranquil. Initially WDIA did not play the blues or any other form of folk music. WHBQ then entered the same marketplace as WDIA, but it had a policy of not hiring Black announcers and instead started looking for a White disc jockey with an interest in R&B.[54]

Dewey Phillip's first music job was selling records from a booth in Grant's department store. His enthusiastic and untrained style attracted a wide range of customers. Phillips was hired by Gordon Lawhead to play tunes on WHBQ. Ironically, such disc jockeys played fresher sounds than their Black counterparts and helped to popularize Black vernacular genres.[55] The Chisca Hotel had some tiny radio rooms on its mezzanine level. Dewey was given his own room there because he bought in the most advertising revenue. He broke radio equipment, was untidy, and constantly championed music that station programmers did not follow. Dewey introduced his listeners to a range of Black artists including the Coasters, the Drifters, Ivory Joe Hunter, Ruth Brown, LaVern Baker, Muddy Waters, Howlin' Wolf, Little Richard, Lightnin' Hopkins and Fats Domino. His on-air style was highly unorthodox. He did not read ad copy or pronounce things straight. Instead he enthusiastically talked over records and spouted catchphrases like, "Tell 'em Phillips sent ya!" Audiences loved his show. Initially Dewey had no competition from WDIA, since it was purely a daytime station. Listeners who liked Black performance styles would tune to WDIA by day and Dewey at night. His *Red, Hot, and Blue* show began as a 45-minute slot starting at 10.15pm, but was soon expanded to begin at 9pm and fill three hours. Its core audience, unlike WDIA, was predominantly young and White. Any casual visitor tuning his or her radio dial, however, may have been unsure of Dewey's racial identity. According to Louis Cantor:

> In essence, by making Black music acceptable to White teenagers, Phillips also helped crack the taboo on open sexual expression in music. White teenagers might secretly listen to WDIA in the early days and identify with the more open sexuality in Black music while in the privacy of their rooms, but not until Phillips could they do so openly.[56]

While Dewey began on only a pittance, he was eventually paid $250 a week. At its peak, *Red Hot, and Blue* had a broadcast audience of 100,000— 20% of the Memphis population.[57]

Sam Phillips knew that Dewey had a great ear for potential hits and was interested in quirky, up-tempo R&B songs. The disc jockey was, in effect, his test marketer. As soon as Sam had an acetate, he took 'That's All Right' along WHBQ in downtown Memphis to see how Dewey would respond. Sam later said:

> Until rock'n'roll music came along the grossest of all racial discrimination in America was in music. You had pop music—which was for a certain type of people; you had country and western music, which was supposedly for another class, and you had what we called in those days "race" music. So if you're talking about segregation there was no better example of it than in music, and I just hope that I played some part in breaking that down in some way.[58]

As the first take of 'That's All Right' was played back, Scotty—with his background in country music—reportedly said to his band mates, "My God, when they hear that they'll run us out of town!"[59] He knew that even Black mainstream artists like Nat King Cole pursued sedate music; a White singer doing an up-tempo country blues hybrid would have been seen as positively incendiary. When Dewey first heard 'That's All Right' he exclaimed, "That'll flat git it!"[60] The initial public playing of the song caused a strong reaction. Young listeners immediately tried to contact the station. Dewey's phone started ringing off the hook and he immediately received a flood of telegrams requesting it again. In response, Dewey decided to interview the singer—who was just 19 years old at that point—so he found a telephone number and called the Presley residence on Alabama Avenue. Elvis had been a regular WHBQ listener, but was shy and had never been interviewed before. He had slipped out the door to watch a Western at the Suzore No. 2 movie theatre on North Main. Finally, the message got through to him and he rushed over to the Chisca Hotel to speak to Dewey in the studio. In order to calm the youngster's nerves, Dewey craftily conducted the interview before he told Elvis that the microphone was live. He also asked Elvis on air which high school he had attended. When the singer said he went to Humes High, the audience would have understood the profound racial implications of his answer. In an age of segregation, it meant that while 'That's All Right' sounded "Black", its singer was actually White. WHBQ's airing of 'That's All Right' indicated a shift in attitudes towards the tradition of musical segregation and therefore initiated a sea change in popular culture. Dewey played the song around 15 times just on that first evening in response to audience demand. Explaining the impact of Elvis's rock'n'roll sound, the Rolling Stones' guitarist Keith Richards said, "He hit like a bomb shell. It was like the world went from black and white to technicolour".[61]

In response to exceptional public interest in the new song, Dewey immediately passed the acetate demo along to Elvis's friend George Klein who had his own show at WHBQ. The next afternoon, Klein became the second disc jockey to play the demo. Given the indications of public demand, Sam immediately planned a single but needed a B-side. At the next session, bassist Bill Black began to improvise a version of bluegrass player Bill Monroe's 'Blue Moon of Kentucky'. Elvis took up the vocal.[62] The singer knew Monroe's music from a childhood listening to the *Grand Ole Opry*—a show that had already been established for a decade before he was born.[63] In the studio, Sam was amazed. He said, "Fine, man. That's different. That's a pop song now, near about".[64] In some ways, 'Blue Moon of Kentucky' was even more interesting than 'That's All Right' because it *reversed* the band's previous approach to genre, bringing the up-tempo energy of R&B to a country number. That new version of the song was so daring that Elvis apologized when he met Monroe at the *Grand Ole Opry*. The bluegrass mandolin player took it in good humour.[65]

When Elvis's first recording aired in Memphis, he had not yet signed a contract with Sun Records. With the help of radio airplay and other local interest, his first single (catalogue number Sun 209), 'That's All Right' / 'Blue Moon of Kentucky', took 5,000 in advanced orders before going on sale, but promoting it was no easy matter. As Sam Phillips recalled, "I went on the road with that one record, and although I couldn't actually find anyone who was prepared to play it, I kept getting favourable reactions from both the Black disc jockeys and the White ones".[66] On July 29, 1954, about ten days after the single's initial release, Sam wrote to the record pressing plant:

> It is the BIGGEST record—bar none—that has ever hit the Memphis territory. *Both* sides are hitting, and in every category: pop, R&B and Hillbilly. Our Memphis distributor has sold more than four thousand on it, and I am sure that, although tastes may

be a lot different on the West Coast, this record has the potential to sell in any territory in the country.⁶⁷

Whilst Elvis's hybridized music appealed to teenagers, its commercial success was limited by radio formatting. Some country programmers thought 'That's All Right' disrespected their genre by mixing it with blues.⁶⁸ For instance, the Miami representative of Sun's distributor, Pan American, said that responses to the record were mixed. In Gladewater, Texas, the KSIJ country disc jockey Tom Perryman recalled that his station did not want him to play it.⁶⁹ Some places would not take the Sun single as they considered it too Black (like an R&B or "Race" record):

> Your record 209 is giving me a little problem in that certain locales throughout the State have operators which have them on every [jukebox] machine and in other locales they won't even touch it. That is one of the strange things about the record business. I think it is a great record, my immediate reaction in Miami was good but in the northern part of Florida, they won't touch it as they consider it too racy.⁷⁰

The mixed pattern was characteristic of a nation still negotiating its heritage of racial segregation. That pattern of reception was not true of *all* of Elvis's Sun singles, however: 'That's All Right' had been surprisingly successful, but Sam Phillips also realized he could not single-handedly demolish radio formats overnight. He knew that country radio would help him secure national status, but to crack country formats he needed a recording in the appropriate style.⁷¹ Despite Sam's general lack of experience selling country, and despite the format's difficulties, 'That's All Right' was a hit with young audiences, achieving 20,000 in local and regional sales by the end of the year.⁷² It reached number three on the *Billboard* chart for Memphis.⁷³ Although 'That's All Right' is often seen as the Rosetta Stone of rock'n'roll for teenagers, its flip side 'Blue Moon of Kentucky' was highly popular, perhaps due to its closer fit with country formatting. Elvis's band was therefore billed as the Blue Moon Boys.

Remapping Vernacular Genres

It is important to understand that Elvis was not the first "colour blind" public figure in his geographic region. Several people around him were pursuing a path of racial integration well in advance of changing social norms. The list included producer Sam Phillips, radio DJ Dewey Phillips, clothier Bernard Lansky, plus the Black artist and radio DJ Rufus Thomas. What made Elvis different was that he developed a high profile as a *mainstream music artist*.

During his youth, Elvis Presley was clearly interested in Black cultural forms. He was a fan at a time when taking an interest in culture on the other side of the colour line in some ways appeared as a daring if not dangerous thing to do—though it was a much more commonplace activity for marginalized, Southern, working-class, and young people. During his childhood, Elvis would visit the Shake Rag ghetto area in East Tupelo and sing along as local Blacks played in public.[74] In his teens, he often went with White friends to East Trigg, the Black missionary Baptist church run by Dr W. Herbert Brewster.[75] WHBQ did outside broadcasts from the church. Word got round that East Trigg had a proper band and showcased great Black singers. In one of Elvis's first verified radio interviews outside of Memphis, presenter Frank Page described his style as "rhythm and blues" and "something new in the folk music field". Elvis, in turn, explained that, "We just stumbled upon it".[76] Of course, at that point, "folk" was widely used to reference vernacular music as opposed to the mainstream. Elvis Presley was marketed as folk blues, a category associated with Black performers. Indeed, Elvis was also an accomplished blues performer.[77] On January 29, 1955, *Billboard* said of 'Milkcow Blues Boogie', "Item here is based on some of the best folk blues. The guy sells all the way".[78]

So what was Elvis's relation to Black culture, and, more importantly, how *should* his music be understood? This complex question is essentially a matter of perspective. At a most basic level, there are two positions. The first suggests that Elvis was a *culture thief* who *appropriated* Black music. The second is that Elvis was practising a pioneering form of racial integration.

It is crucial to put these arguments in a much broader historic context. In the period before the mid-twentieth century, Western countries controlled other ones called colonies by building trade and administrative empires. Many of the colonized countries were in Africa. Black folk were sent from the colonies to work as slaves in America. When the slaves were freed in 1863, society continued to be shaped by the class divisions formerly associated with slavery. Popular culture exploited racist attitudes. Blackface, for example, was a type of stage performance in which White performers "blacked up" and parodied Black identity. It continued well after Abraham Lincoln's Emancipation Proclamation. Primitivism was an artistic movement which later emerged from racial biases, but was slightly more empathetic. It was racist insofar that it positioned non-White races as backwards and more savage in relation to modern society, but it also celebrated other cultures as representing something lost from the modern world.

The appropriation argument is often premised on Sam Phillips's supposed claim, "If I could find a White man with the Negro sound and the Negro feel, I could make a billion dollars".[79] Elvis's "Negro sound and Negro feel" performativity might have put him closer, from one perspective, to unmarked Blackface. After all, just before they recorded 'I'll Never Let You Go (Little Darlin')', Elvis, Scotty and Bill bantered in a Black style or idiom. From the sound of Elvis's voice and music, a number of his early listeners guessed that he was Black.[80] The blackface historian Eric Lott has adopted this position, arguing:

> Underwritten by various kinds of public cultural interaction, minstrel men appropriated styles of racialized masculinity as much as any other particular cultural product, a gendered obsession easily converted into profitable minstrel show counterfeits. It's [sic] modern resonance is articulated in White guitarist Scotty Moore's remark to Elvis Presley at one of the recording sessions in which Elvis first found his voice: "Damn, nigger!"[81]

We have to remember Scotty's comment was made in a recording studio where a White producer worked with musicians of both races. Sun, at the time, was therefore an exceptional, *desegregated* space. Moore knew that the people around him in the studio that day were living in a city dominated by Whites who supported the tradition of racial segregation. His exclamation almost certainly indicated that he knew Elvis's style would upset a lot of White people.

Music writer Michael Ochs once claimed, "Elvis Presley had a Black soul with a White face".[82] Ochs's position is a starting point for discussions associated with the view that Elvis articulated Blackness in order to rethink Whiteness. However, Och's position falsely locates expressive "soul" as an *essence*: a quality that is characteristic *only* of African Americans. It therefore makes an argument that both specify cultural property (if a White man has expressive "soul" then he necessarily has "Black soul" because expressive "soul" is *essentially* Black) and can, in turn, support primitivist and/or liberal humanist perspectives. The primitivist interpretation is that unrestrained sensual abandon is more available to Blacks because they have less baggage of civilization to restrain them. Unless it is explicitly recognized as a *White* projection, this connects to some old and entrenched racist assumptions. It supports the idea that Elvis—as a privileged "Black souled" interpreter—gave the White public an emancipatory choice to accept or reject Black music and raw sexuality.[83] The term *liberal humanism* broadly reflects the idea that individuals are free and have certain rights. The liberal humanist view of Ochs's statement on Presley is, conversely, that Black folk, as possessors of expressive "soul", have had their last remaining property unfairly appropriated by Whites (an argument in which music *stands for* labour). Here Elvis is portrayed as the *necessarily* White face of a rapacious culture industry that puts Black musicians in a parallel predicament to their enslaved and exploited forebears.

The primivist and liberal humanist arguments roughly pre- and post-date Elvis's arrival. Neither is mutually exclusive. Furthermore—and this is the key issue—both are much bigger than Elvis. Their historical roots go back further and their consequences are much broader than even his myth. Because he brought different genres together, for many people he *personified* those issues.

America is a nation originally predicated on racial trauma—the dispossession of both First Nations land and Black slave labour—and its vast repercussions.[84] In popular music those issues played out in relation to the ethics and reception of folk blues as a genre. At different times, various arguments have dominated, depending not primarily on the music, but on the social and political climate. Because of Elvis's great success, he effectively began to symbolize the nation, so discussing his association with Black cultural forms has become a means to formulate wider social questions as *issues of personal ethics*. For example, Chet Atkins recalled that in 1955, Elvis had been billed below country act the Louvin Brothers on live tours, but by the next year they were opening for him:

> "Elvis does his show and comes back afterwards", says Louvin. "He sits down at a piano, hits a few chords, says 'Here's what I like', and sings a gospel song, an old hymn". Ira says, "You fuckin' White nigger. If that's the kind of music you like, why don't you do that out there instead of that shit you do?" Elvis just looked at him—that was before his karate—and he said, "When I'm out there I do what they want to hear. When I'm back here, I do what I want to do".[85]

It is hard to say whether the story is true or not. Atkins produced both artists, but his relationship with Elvis was never overly positive. The story references two things that are now known about Elvis: his desire to serve his public even while performing material that he cared little about—a pattern repeated during his movie era—and his deep love of gospel. It uses these premises to say that if Elvis did smooth the way to racial integration, it was only because he was a conduit for market forces; he had no moral code of his own. My point in recounting this story is not that it is true, but rather that it demonstrates how discussions about Elvis are really evaluations of the melting pot project reduced to a personal scale.

Did Elvis simply pantomime or burlesque Black music for profit? The appropriation argument has problems. The first is that it rests on primitivist baggage or liberal humanist property assertions. The notion of *reparations* suggests that African Americans should be financially rewarded for the unpaid work their slave forebears were forced to do. Arguably, the liberal humanist argument leads to a kind of "musical reparations" perspective which tends to exaggerate (to "*over Blacken*") Elvis's style. For example, Gael Sweeney has claimed:

> The Black body in American culture is forever linked with labor and the savage discipline of slavery: power, fear, and sexuality are joined to make a combination that was, to middle-class White teenagers, as alluring as it was illicit. When Elvis adapted Black music, dress, and style, he also appropriated some of the sexuality and

scandalizing power of Black bodies. Elvis, the White boy who sang Black, was doubly dangerous because he could appear so innocent and polite: reporters always commented on how Elvis always said "Yes, Ma'am" and "No, Sir" (in much the way of "good Negroes") and was so soft-spoken—right up until he began to sing and cause the daughters of Suburban America to have public orgasms.[86]

Such arguments draw racial lines rather too heavily and bluntly. Sweeney is correct, for the reasons that she suggests, to say that Black bodies were already understood as expressive of sensual abandon in a way that White bodies were not. The perceived racial shock of Elvis was a direct result of his willingness to seize the moment with an equal level of abandon. His reasons for doing so may have been justified as musical, but the act of genre-blending was inevitably *interpreted* as social in a context where society and music had been segregated. However, although some of Sweeney's ideas reflect ways that national commentators have perceived Elvis, it is a step further in interpretation to claim, for example, that Elvis "sang Black" or *appropriated* Black dance. Such oversimplifications obscure the facts of history at hand. Musical traditions in the South were *already* subject to race mixing, much more than music publishing catalogues would have us believe. Elvis got his deferential manners from his *class* background. Just because Blacks shared a deferential approach it did not mean that Elvis was appropriating *their* style. The problem with appropriation arguments is that they are really *authenticity* arguments, liable to proliferate at particular times because they continually reinforce the idea that any White performer who mixes music genres has no significant prior identity of their own.

Elvis constantly expressed a willingness to embrace Black culture in various ways, from clothing to music. That willing embrace made him a unique kind of leader, articulating a process of *integration*—bringing races together through action and the marketplace, not policy or preaching. There is much evidence to support the integration argument, the idea that Elvis was an *assimilator*, a remarkably "colour blind" and "transracial" musician whose style heralded an era of racial integration by refusing to accept the segregation of popular music genres. Vernon Chadwick summarized this position in 1997 by saying, "Elvis names musical integration and, by extension, racial and cultural integration".[87] Against a backdrop of traditional segregation and then civil unrest, Elvis's music rarely offered a direct *verbal* challenge to the racial turmoil of the era. That does not mean, however, that Presley was not an archetypal assimilationist in his field.

First, Elvis entered the public sphere just after the passing of anti-segregation legislation. He consistently brought mixed-race pop to the mainstream. According to Sam Phillips:

95% of the people I'd been working with had been Black. Most of them, of course, "no name" people. So Elvis fit right in: he was born and raised in poverty. He was around Black folks an awful lot. He was around people that had very little in the way of worldly goods ... So Elvis was the perfect one for the "transition" that I wanted to make to have the Black person get a broader reception, and to help the White person feel that, "Hey, we got a kinship", especially in the South.[88]

Second, Elvis angered White supremacists who wanted America's racial cultures kept apart. Two months after the release of 'Heartbreak Hotel', *Billboard* magazine reported that the executive secretary of the North Alabama Citizen's Council urged a jukebox ban on rock'n'roll for subversively encouraging racial integration.[89] Its editor Paul Ackerman received telephone calls from two Nashville music executives in one day demanding that the magazine stop listing Elvis's records on the country chart. *In their view*, Elvis played Black music.[90] As Guralnick said in 2007: "He was simply seen as too low class, or perhaps just too no-class, in his refusal to deny recognition to a segment of society that had been rendered invisible by the cultural mainstream".[91] Music scholar George Plasketes also claimed, "Elvis blurred distinctions not only between musical forms, but races and classes as well".[92] To some extent, Presley ignored the social road map and *ripped it up*. Dave Marsh observed, "The crime of Elvis's rock'n'roll was that he proved that Black and White tendencies could co-exist and that the product of their co-existence was not just palatable but thrilling".[93]

Third, Elvis was also initially accepted and favoured by Black audiences; some of his early singles topped R&B charts. Using George Klein as an intermediary, in 1956 Louis Cantor asked Elvis to come to the WDIA Goodwill Revue.[94] The event attracted a crowd of 9,000, packing both of Ellis Auditorium's two theatres. Backstage, Elvis talked to Rufus Thomas and B.B. King. Don Kern wanted to put Elvis on stage right away, but, anticipating the audience would explode, Rufus asked him to save his public appearance until the end. Elvis was announced and only shook a leg (without any music), which was enough to generate immense excitement. After the Revue, Thomas was able to play Elvis's records on WDIA without any opposition.[95] It is also fascinating that in February 1957, fresh off his last *Ed Sullivan* television show appearance, Elvis may have briefly dated outside his race with the Latin starlet Rita Moreno. Moreno was the most prominent female Puerto Rican in Hollywood back then and had graced the cover of *Life* magazine three years earlier. At the end of that year Elvis also returned to the WDIA revue and was photographed backstage by the local press with Little Junior Parker and Bobby "Blue" Bland.[96] His commitment to racial progress was in no doubt.

Crucially, the argument that Elvis was a White agent of cultural appropriation, somebody taking what was not his—driven by self-interest or not—forgets what he did for *both* White audiences *and* Black artists. Guitarist Keith Richards of the Rolling Stones has discussed the off-meter quality of Elvis's early music:

> I guess they were the first White band that anybody heard of with a good lead singer, that was sellable, that could actually play Black, sound like that. They had the rhythm. They had that fluidity which White music, especially then, didn't have. It was very "meter, meter, meter", you know. One, two, three, four. The beautiful thing about Elvis is that he's just sort of turned everybody into everybody. It doesn't matter: "Is the guy Black or White?" anymore. And maybe even you can do it. It at least sparked a dream.[97]

This suggests that it is worth exploring how Elvis's unusually integrated sound began to rip up genre boundaries. His aural cross-fertilizations raised questions of racial import about how such music should be marketed and received. What is interesting about Richards's claim is how it connects spontaneity with issues of race. In other words, in his view, Elvis is not *racialized* by genre conventions—*countrified* as White or *bluesified* as Black—but rather, Elvis's particular approach to musical feel *deracinates* popular music by giving it a universal quality: anyone *who has soul, who feels the music and can express it* now has the right to make music. What is more, they may have the capacity to shake off the audience's racial prejudices as part of that process.[98] Elvis therefore "broke down the door" for a lot of musicians who played vernacular music, to help them gain mainstream recognition for their styles and therefore find them a place on the airwaves and music charts. By familiarizing White audiences with Black sounds he paved the way for Black artists to enter the mainstream. The *commercial mainstreaming* of Black music changed the fortunes of a range of previously marginalized artists. James Brown met Elvis after being introduced by George Klein. He thanked the Memphis singer for helping Black artists get airplay on White stations.[99]

Elvis did not, however, immediately or single-handedly change race politics. Keith Richards's interpretation makes more sense in relation to recent years and the mainstream outside the South. Memphis was still characterized in the 1950s by *significant* racial segregation in life, recorded music, and its airplay, though there was *some* race mixing in live music. Audiences *did* notice the race of performers, and music genres and conventions still had racial connotations. It was not until 1957, after a Black rights organization organized a boycott, that local papers the *Memphis Commercial Appeal* and *Memphis Press-Scimitar* even capitalized the word "Negro", and accorded Black men and women the titles of Mr or Mrs.[100] African Americans were not allowed into the Peabody Hotel until the 1960s. In fact, during the next decade Memphis saw some of the most tragic incidents in the struggle for civil rights: the Sanitation Strike of February 1968, and the shooting of Martin

Luther King two months later. The city struggled with a painfully slow process of racial integration long after Elvis started recording. All through that time, Elvis's reputational currency fluctuated significantly. In March 1957, he told one interviewer a false rumour had blown up in Memphis that he did not like African Americans.[101] During the 1960s, meanwhile, Hollywood represented Elvis as a *creolized* figure of racial integration. He toured with an extended, multicultural band in his final years. However, the "appropriation" reading or interpretation was commonplace during the 1980s and 1990s, when a new generation of artists questioned his representative status as a national hero. Discussing commentaries in song from that period, Plasketes noted:

> Like the various accounts which present another side of Elvis, many songs are part of the demystification process as they portray Elvis as a racist, junkie, fraud, and failure, among other things, and emphasize the commercial sprawl surrounding his name. Such critiques commonly originate from the younger generation of musicians, the underground, and the African American community. In contrast, the older generation of artists, even in their cursing and criticism of the King's demise, display a sense of reverence and debt to Elvis.[102]

A key point here is that the appropriation/integration discourse has become a vehicle to address issues stemming from the changing racial politics of America, a cultural field larger than Elvis himself. Many of the facts of his story are actually neutral and cannot decide the issue by themselves. These neutral facts include that race mixing was already a tradition in live music; that Elvis was interested in Black forms; and that he stumbled upon a new sound. He inaugurated a reorientation of traditions—with all their racial baggage—partly in the service of his own individual stardom. He was marketed as both country and folk blues, and topped all charts. Equally, he expressed a sense of abandon that had traditionally been coded as Black. None of these malleable premises is sufficient to decide the argument in one direction or the other. For example, the fact that his music effortlessly *blended* genres of diverse origins is conceivable either as a *repression* of racial issues (ignoring what was already there) or as a form of integration (changing what was unacceptable).

In an era of digital sampling, the idea that anyone can contribute to the social conversation that is music is increasingly accepted. Back in the 1950s, Elvis Presley was controversial amongst unreconstructed traditionalists *not* for cultural appropriation, but precisely for promising *racial integration*. The process of bringing races together is often called assimilation. Elvis's music suggested a forward-thinking, assimilationist politics that, to traditionalists, seemed naïvely colour blind and disrespectful of segregated genre traditions. White segregationists angrily criticized Elvis for breaking racial taboos. It was only after decades of racial progress that the opposite notion gained ground and suggested that he was a culture thief. He was therefore criticized as an *integrator* (by White separatists in the 1950s) *and* as an *appropriator* (by Black separatists in the 1980s) *for the same musical activity*. Both critiques positioned him as an unworthy national hero. Specifying a single "colour" for Elvis's music has always been a way to stall the fraught possibility of racial integration.

Presley was radical because he actively sought to expand and popularize crossover in *both* directions.[103] By the 1950s, the country genre was changing and diversifying, developing into a professional, glamorous, modern business. Elvis tended to be billed as "Western" rather than country—"Western" signifying theatrical, aware, "cowboy"-themed music. One advertisement for a Fair Park Coliseum show in Lubbock, Texas billed him as "The Be-Bop Western Star of the LA. Hayride".[104] The "bop" element suggested a new beat, the aspirational call of new times as the country circuit catered to a different market. Elvis was understood as the sound of modern times coming to the genre, offering youth-orientated, up-tempo sounds that included drums. His success had multiple *musical* influences on country. It broke the taboo that excluded percussion from the genre: initially, the percussive element in Elvis's music was supplied by rhythm guitar and slap bass, later by the burlesque-inspired drumming patterns of Shreveport's house player, D.J. Fontana. Elvis's runaway success at Sun inspired Sam to seek out other White Southern singers who could reference lively R&B within a matrix of country styles. The resulting subgenre was known as rockabilly.[105] According to Guralnick, discussing Elvis's early country blues number, 'Baby Let's Play House', "that kind of burbling hiccup [vocal] is probably one of the most influential songs—in terms of that early rockabilly sound—of any song that was ever recorded".[106] Then, particularly after Elvis moved labels and starting working with the country guitarist and RCA producer Chet Atkins, he adopted a new, ensemble-based approach—which by that point included gospel singing group, the Jordanaires. It refined country into a more balanced, commercial form. John Potter writes:

> The "Nashville sound" associated with Atkins' RCA artists dropped the traditional fiddle and steel guitar (increasingly an anachronism for all but the oldest players) in favour of two acoustic guitars and background vocal harmonizing. It was this sound which Elvis appropriated when he signed up for RCA and took on the Jordanaires (a resident Nashville group) as his backing musicians.[107]

The approach modernized country to create a smoother, swinging up-tempo fusion style that could include vocal backing ensembles, piano and electric bass.[108] Elvis's emergent success changed practices in both the recording studio and radio station, with a new sound that began to revolutionize and dominate country radio station formats. As Nicholas Dawidoff explained, "Presley devastated traditional country music. Once they heard The King, people wanted their popular music to grind and bounce."[109]

Touring the Country Circuit

Elvis biographer Peter Guralnick has said, "The thing that is most remarkable about Elvis's early career is that there was never a moment of faltering; it just kept opening up."[110] Guralnick is broadly correct: while Elvis faced many difficult moments during his early days, they were never significant enough to finish his expanding career as a professional singer. To begin with, his trio the Blue Moon Boys were guided, in effect, by Scotty Moore's talents. Moore never had the voice to be a singer, but he had both musical ability and knowledge of the business. He had experience and a track record. During Elvis's first year as a recording artist, to shield him from predatory business interests, Sam Phillips installed Scotty as the youngster's manager. The Blue Moon Boys had an uncanny ability to transform musical source material. At first they had very few songs to perform. Scotty was impressed with Elvis's knowledge of music from various genres. Upon forming the band he gave Elvis his record collection in order to open up an even broader choice of inspiration. As they jammed above Scotty's workplace, the trio began to develop a 15-minute live show.[111] Most local and regional country bands in 1950s Memphis were live outfits. In contrast, Elvis did not start out by playing clubs for money in a touring or house band. He had played his guitar to friends, and occasionally even to strangers, but before 'That's All Right' took off Elvis had not been paid to perform live on a professional basis. In effect his career therefore began in a "manufactured" group that had a hit record.

On the strength of interest in the WHBQ interview, Sam Phillips organized some of the trio's earliest promotional breaks. Elvis started this professional live career on July 17, 1954, at the Bon Air Club, a country music venue in Memphis where Scotty's band the Starlite Wranglers had a regular Saturday night slot.[112] The Tipler family, Elvis's employers at Crown Electric, came to cheer him on, but he had a relatively unsympathetic audience and suffered stage fright.[113] Although Sun was primarily a blues label and Elvis got his break on DJ Dewey Phillip's R&B show, his live performance was *packaged for the country music circuit*: the most lucrative and established form of live music promotion in the South. As well as Dewey's WHBQ show, Sam also knew about Bob Neal, a country promoter and emcee famed for his local WMPS show *High Noon Round Up*. Neal was a popular disc jockey who had a strong following on the country circuit.[114] Sam persuaded him to add the trio to the bill at the "Folk Music Show", an event headlined by country singer Slim Whitman and planned for the Overton Park Shell.[115] Memphis's smaller version of the Hollywood Bowl, the Shell is an outdoor venue with a capacity of around 4,000 people. After another engagement at the Bon Air club, on Friday July 30, the team tried the Overton Park Shell event—perhaps as a way to encourage attendance the next night at the Bon Air. The Overton Folk Music Show actually consisted of two sets: an afternoon and evening performance. During the afternoon show, Elvis only sang ballads and did not win the crowd over, which made him nervous. In the evening, he played his local hit and more up-tempo numbers, shaking his leg in time to the music.[116] According to Scotty:

> Elvis, when he played his guitar standing up, he'd just come up on the balls of his feet, and with the big breeches back then—big pants leg—when he'd do that and playing, well the things would start shaking. That's what the little girls started [enjoying]; they thought he was doing that on purpose. When he came off stage he said, "What did I do? What's going on?" Me and Bill started laughing. "Well", we said, "When you started shaking your legs they started screaming". He said, "I wasn't doing anything on purpose", which was true, but he was a fast learner.[117]

Not all of Elvis's most exuberant fans were teenagers; Marion Keisker also screamed when she saw him. After his wiggling ignited the crowd, he played two songs and an encore. It was country crooner Hank Snow—not Slim Whitman—who had trouble following him as the next act.[118] Elvis's reputation as an *electric* live musician was sealed. He recalled in August 1956, "I was scared stiff. And it was my first big appearance in front of an audience".[119]

While Elvis Presley's leg shaking has been framed as accidental, some have suggested that he learned it from Big Chief of the Statesmen: a commanding gospel quartet singer who had a sexy, refined, electric stage presence.[120] Indeed, credit for inspiring Elvis's performance style has been claimed by a wide range of people, notably Mae West. What is interesting here is that it links notions of Elvis *feeling* the music with his nervousness about performing, in a way that would please the audience: the shaking leg as nervous twitch that incidentally appealed to women. In other words, rather than—as his detractors and parodists suggested—manipulating his audience with gestures of seduction for his own narcissistic pleasure, his leg shaking was a way to *disarm* the anxiety arising from his *unstable* position as an emergent star. Elvis is therefore portrayed as a shy country boy—worried about performing—who becomes liberated by the music and automatically ignites his fans. It worked in his favour. If, later on, it might have felt scary to meet a person as popular and important as Elvis Presley, knowing that *he also seemed afraid of meeting you* offered great relief. Although he soon became confident of his stage role as a sexual persona, right the way through to the end of his unfortunately short life he retained an appealing humility. His nervousness positively informed his sexual chemistry. At live shows, eliciting squeals of approval from female fans, he would admit, "If you think I'm nervous, you're right".[121] Elvis both extended the commodification of male sex appeal, and retained a genuine sense of humility. He appealed as an icon, in part, because of *both* those things.

The following Saturday the trio switched to a different venue which became a weekend home for Elvis until tour commitments took him on the road in November. In the late summer of 1954 Elvis played in the Eagle's Nest, a nightclub above the Clearpool entertainment complex on Lamar Avenue with music nights hosted by the disc jockey Sleepy-Eyed John. One reason, perhaps, for Elvis's early live success was that his gigs were advertised as ladies' nights. Local patrons were more attuned to traditional country sounds, so Elvis's audience was simply bemused by him. His immediate problem was that the place served alcohol and there were very few teenage girls in the audience.

As their popularity grew, Elvis, Scotty and Bill began playing at more events and making more recordings for Sun. In October, they played at country music institution, the *Grand Ole Opry* in Nashville. The Opry had been going for three decades at this point and country was often pitched as a nostalgic "old time" style. When Sam Phillips found him a break on the *Grand Ole Opry* radio show, Elvis hardly stirred traditionalists in the country crowd. His next major opportunity was highly fruitful. The avuncular Bob Neal took over Elvis's management because he had skills and contacts as a promoter in the South. Because Elvis was too young for his signature to be legally binding, his early business contracts had to be co-signed by his parents.[122] Neal helped place Elvis on a very good radio show. Broadcast on weekly KWKH in Shreveport, then syndicated across both the mammoth CBS network, *Louisiana Hayride* was the *Opry*'s biggest competitor. The trio's first performance there was in October 1954. On account of noisy crowds of youngsters who loved him, Elvis was invited back, and soon acquired a 12-month deal to perform on the show. Introducing 'I Forgot to Remember to Forget' on one of Elvis's *Lousiana Hayride* radio shows, presenter Horace Logan described, "modern day type—well, you couldn't call it hillbilly exactly, I guess you'd have to call it bop-type Western ... this is the new look in Western music".[123] Pictures of Elvis's early live act indicate a marked contrast between the young singer (in flashy, *aspirational* clothing: suits, ties and sports jackets) and his two backing musicians (in traditional country shirts). Elvis differentiated himself, then, as a hip young kid *within* the country music scene. For example, Lamar-Airways was the first modern shopping centre in Memphis. WHBQ's disc jockey George Klein was hired to help open the complex in 1954 from a booth next to Katz Drugs store. Elvis and his Blue Moon Boys played for free that day on the back of a flatbed truck.

Presley became known as "the King of Western Bop" or "the Hillbilly Cat" (where "cat" was the Texan word for a lively, bopping musician). At engagements where young people were generally absent from the audience, his live act conspicuously *failed*. By contrast *Louisisana Hayride* allowed Elvis to become famous across a swathe of Southern states and took his professional career to a regional level. With the Hayride contract in place, Scotty and Bill resigned from their previous band and Scotty began to arrange live dates for the trio. As well as allowing them to start touring professionally and drop their day jobs, *Hayride* gave Elvis, Scotty and Bill an opportunity to work beyond the structure of a trio and include additional musicians. By March 1955, Neal was on 15% of the take, and Scotty was on a 2% road manager fee.[124] Bill Black sold Elvis merchandise in the intermission at his shows.[125]

From Sun to RCA

Virtually everything that the public knew about Elvis's personality was developed in the first instance by a range of key individuals who made decisions about his music and image. The musical persona emerging from Sun was not simply Elvis, it was *Sam Phillip's* Elvis. Sam had to *un-tutor* Elvis as he had *too many* influences, from Arthur Crudup to Bing Crosby. The Memphis producer once claimed that he only let Elvis record ballads at the first Sun sessions because he did not have the heart to stop him.[126] What he released, however, were up-tempo cuts exclusively from the rock'n'roll side of Elvis's studio output.

Elvis sang on just a handful of professional recording sessions at Sun. In August 1954, his second captured only a haunting version of the Rogers and Hart ballad 'Blue Moon', though Sam decided it was not a single.[127] The third Sun session in September 1954 included various rocking numbers such as 'I Don't Care if the Sun Don't Shine', 'Just Because', 'Good Rockin' Tonight' and 'Satisfied', but it began with the slower, 'Tomorrow Night'.[128] Elvis's version of 'Just Because' was recorded at both slow and fast tempo; RCA released the latter version on his first LP.[129] It contained fretwork by the Starlite Wranglers' singer, Doug Poindexter, who put paper between the strings of his guitar to create a chik-a-chik sound.[130] As key Elvis historian and catalogue curator Ernst Jørgensen claimed about the third Sun session, "There may have been many more [songs], as Sam Phillips recorded over many of the Presley tapes. The Sun tapes that RCA did receive from these sessions were lost in a vault clean out in 1959".[131]

Sam had such faith in his new charge that he released no other acts between the first and second Blue Moon Boys single. He realized that he had a star performer and did not want to compromise public attention.[132] Pressed under the catalogue number Sun 210, Elvis, Scotty and Bill's second single was 'Good Rockin' Tonight' / 'I Don't Care if the Sun Don't Shine'. Tin Pan Alley was a place in New York where professional songwriters crafted pop hits and sold them to publishing houses. The single's second side, a number by the Tin Pan Alley songwriter Mack David, had been performed by the Italian-American entertainer Dean Martin on his 1953 Paramount comedy

Scared Stiff. Sun Records assistant Marion Keisker had apparently added an extra verse to the version that Elvis recorded.[133] What was interesting is that while Dean Martin had characteristically performed the number as a flashy cabaret tune, Elvis's version was more folksy and styled as a breezy, up-tempo ditty. One of his key skills at this point was to convey commercial musical forms as though they were original and had arrived from outside of the heart of the music industry; he "unglossed" and radically rejuvenated material from various sources.

The Elvis who came roaring out of Sun Studio was entirely a rock'n'roll singer. As label owner Sam Phillips once said, "If I had released a ballad I don't think you would have ever heard of Elvis Presley".[134] The Sun rock'n'roll singles, however, had variable sales. With its deconstructed, tempo-changing introduction—surely one of Elvis's clearest articulations of the appeal of youthful abandon—'Milkcow Blues Boogie', for example, remains a classic Sun recording. However, 'Milkcow Blues Boogie' and 'You're a Heartbreaker' were probably not part of Elvis's live set and their Sun double A-side sold even fewer copies than 'Good Rockin' Tonight' / 'I Don't Care if the Sun Don't Shine'.[135]

Elvis was a regional celebrity by 1955. His trio had started augmenting their limited number of singles with contemporary covers: the Clovers' 1951 hit 'Fool, Fool, Fool', Big Joe Turner's 1954 song 'Shake, Rattle and Roll' (which had instantly been covered by Bill Haley), LaVern Baker's recent 'Tweedle Dee', the Charms' 'Hearts of Stone', the Drifters' 'Money Honey' and Ray Charles' 'I Got a Woman'.[136] Elvis thought that 'Tweedle Dee' would be a single at one point, though he never recorded it.[137] At the penultimate Sun session, Sam suggested covering the 1953 Sun hit 'Mystery Train' as he shared the copyright on it with Little Junior Parker.[138]

Elvis was by now entertaining capacity crowds on the country circuit. His future manager Colonel Thomas Andrew Parker first became his promoter, putting him on Hank Snow's tour.[139] Parker claimed that in the period of 1939–40 he worked with the entertainer Gene Austin, who had already been highly successful on the Victor label and in Hollywood, but lost a fortune after ballad crooner Bing Crosby emerged as a new phenomenon.[140] According to biographer Alanna Nash, "Whether Parker actually became Austin's manager during those years, as he later claimed, is open to dispute".[141] The Colonel nevertheless managed Eddy Arnold from 1944, and by 1947 had promoted him to the top of the country charts. In 1953 Arnold amicably ordered a split. Parker then switched to become a live music promoter who specialized in creating concert packages. Initially, his Jamboree Attractions turned down a booking inquiry by Scotty Moore. At the end of October 1954, Oscar Davis, a Nashville promoter who worked as the Colonel's advance man, met Presley at a show in Memphis. Jørgensen suggests that Parker may have read *Billboard* reviews of Elvis's singles and associated reports of him taking east Texas by storm.[142] In fact, Tommy Sands, one of Parker's own acts, had been a disc jockey and also a participant on the *Louisiana Hayride* radio show. He had seen girls rush the stage when Elvis played Houston, at the Eagles Hall, on New Year's Day in 1955.[143] Quite possibly at Bob Neal's invitation, two weeks later the Colonel then visited *Hayride* to see Elvis perform live and watch audience responses. The radio disc jockey Tom Perryman has claimed that he introduced Elvis to Colonel Parker by saying, "Elvis, that fellow over there will make you a million dollars in a year, but he will get at least half of it".[144]

Before he managed Elvis, Colonel Parker began by booking him on the Hank Snow tour, but he had, even at that point, already mentioned the singer to RCA's country-and-western A&R man Steve Sholes.[145] The second jamboree left New Orleans for three weeks from May 1, 1955. It featured Hank Snow, Elvis Presley, Faron Young, the Wilburn Brothers, Mother Maybelle and the Carter Sisters, the Davis Sisters (Skeeter and Georgie), Onie Wheeler and Jimmie Rodgers Snow.[146] RCA's country-and-western promotions manager Chick Crumpacker saw Elvis steal the glory from Jimmie Rodgers Snow in Richmond, Virginia. In the summer of 1955, the Memphis singer returned to more local venues, often accompanied by the new Sun star, Johnny Cash. Elvis's band by then included D.J. Fontana on drums, Floyd Cramer on piano, and sometimes Jimmy Day on steel guitar.[147] Fontana and Cramer in particular stayed with the act to become part of Elvis's studio sound following the Sun era.

After the summer tour, the Colonel and his assistant Tom Diskin obtained exclusive booking rights and began promoting Elvis more aggressively. At this point Parker charged $500 for his main act or $1000 for his whole package of artists.[148] The Colonel quickly set up an audition, which the band failed, for the long running CBS radio show, *Arthur Godfrey's Talent Scouts*. Parker also got Elvis a non-singing walk-on spot on Jimmy Dean's WMAL-TV show *Town & Country Jubilee* in Washington.[149] In a bid to increase national recognition, Elvis was booked on rock'n'roll disc jockey Bill Randle's radio show in Cleveland, alongside Pat Boone and Bill Haley.[150] At the event on October 20, 1955, Elvis lip-synched both sides of his first single to an unsuspecting crowd. His performance was filmed for a documentary called *The Pied Piper of Cleveland: A Day in the Life of a Famous Disc Jockey*. Unfortunately, contractual disputes kept the film from being released.

Music journalists Burke and Griffin have suggested, "Bit by bit, Parker undermined Neal's position".[151] Perhaps the Colonel used Neal to test the waters with Elvis, then plucked control of the singer from him before major rewards ensued. Neal put it more charitably, citing his own reluctance to travel: "I didn't want to get into the picture of being out of town all the time … it was a friendly relationship all the way".[152] The Colonel levered his place as Elvis's primary promoter to begin to manage the artist: on August 15, he instituted a contract that meant he became "special advisor" to both Neal and Presley, allowing him to legally take on a management function and negotiate on Elvis's behalf. Specifically, the contract gave the Colonel exclusive rights to a hundred shows for which he would give Elvis and his band $200 per show, and for coverage of 40 cities in which Elvis had proven popular. More importantly, it entitled him to negotiate all renewals on existing contracts and charge a penalty if Neal took his business elsewhere. Despite this, Neal initially contradicted the Colonel and negotiated the one-year renewal of Elvis's Hayride contract.[153]

Jimmie Rodgers Snow delivered the Colonel's first contract to Elvis in February 1955.[154] According to Elvis himself, Parker took over on March 15, 1955, and "We more or less picked each other ... I was makin' quite a bit of money, but I wasn't as nationally known as I am now. 'Cause the Colonel has a lot of friends in the entertainment business. He has a lot of connections".[155] Elvis may have asked many others—mostly disc jockeys—to manage him *before* asking the Colonel. As Parker gradually assumed the role of full manager, one of his initial moves was to wrest merchandising of Elvis's photos away from Bill Black's cottage operation, removing one of Black's sources of income.[156] In another move quietly instituted by the Colonel, Scotty and Bill were placed on salary: $200 per week on tour, and half that at home.[157] This was indicative of Parker's general approach. His aim was to put his client on a new stratum of popularity, professionalism and profit, but also to organize the whole process in favour of both Presley and himself.

Sun had cash flow problems. It was over-stretched trying to promote and distribute Elvis's singles across its independent network. The label could only pay a royalty rate of 3 cents per record.[158] By reminding everyone that Elvis needed proper management to become a major artist, Parker gained an advantage. Part of his plan was to provide the professional backing that would support a career in show business at a national level. The strategy included organizing Elvis's client status with both a major agent (William Morris) and publisher (Hill & Range), but first it meant placing him on a major record label. Since Elvis was already contracted to the Sun label, any change of record company would have to be negotiated with Sam Phillips. The Colonel therefore needed to find out what size of sum Sam might want in order to release his main act. Parker already had a track record of success with RCA: he placed the country artists Hank Snow and Eddy Arnold with the label. For months before the contract was finally signed, he had been promoting Elvis to representatives of the company, framing Presley as a dynamic young country artist. Mitch Miller at Columbia and Ahmet Ertegun of Atlantic Records had also been interested in Elvis, but they dropped out of the bidding at $20,000 and $25,000 respectively. The Colonel seemed to be asking for too much money. According to Guralnick, Parker "bamboozled" RCA, misleading the label by giving the impression that their competitors were seriously interested when his aim always was to place Elvis with them.[159] After a period of stand-off, negotiations got much hotter at the end of October 1955.[160] Talking with Parker on the telephone, Sam Phillips finally offered the option to sell Elvis's contract to another label. He asked for $35,000, plus $5000 to pay off the back royalties that Sun owed Elvis.[161] It was an unprecedentedly high figure at the time, but within two weeks the Colonel managed to broker a deal. Elvis signed the contract a week later in a special meeting at Sun Studio. RCA's 14-point contract was also signed by Vernon Presley because his son was so young. It demanded a minimum of eight record sides each year and said, "We shall at all times have complete control of the services to be rendered by you under the specification of this contract". In return it contained the condition that the record company be granted two successive options to renew for one year each time. The contract was signed by H. Coleman Tily for RCA. John Burgess Jr, a Sales and Promotions manager at RCA, immediately wrote a staff memo saying, "The NAME: Elvis Presley, one that will be your guarantee of sensational plus sales in the months to come!"[162]

Elvis's first contract included the purchase of all his Sun tapes, to prevent competition from Sun re-releases and allow RCA the right to release or re-package any spare material. In order to immediately start recouping their money, one of the first things that the record company did was to re-press Elvis's fifth and final Sun single 'I Forgot to Remember to Forget' / 'Mystery Train' and to send out 4,000 promo copies to larger country and pop radio stations.[163] Not everyone at the label, however, appreciated Elvis's musical reputation. RCA was used to dividing its output between adult music and pop; older and more conservative staff did not appreciate rock'n'roll.[164] Ironically, although such tunes were initially perceived as the lucrative side of his catalogue, Elvis knew that his move to a major label might spell an opportunity for him to pursue softer sounds, such as the mainstream ballads ignored by Sam Phillips. His own role models were people like Perry Como, Eddie Fisher, Dean Martin, Tony Bennett, Frank Sinatra and Vaughn Monroe—conservative, middle-of-the road ballad singers who had tremendous popular support and commercial success at the time. In March 1956, Elvis told one interviewer that Frank Sinatra was his favourite singer.[165] Sensing problems ahead, Sam decided to offer some advice:

> I told Elvis one thing. I said, "Elvis, don't let them change you". And I told Steve [Sholes of RCA], "Steve, I really would let Elvis do what he wants to do". I don't know how it was influenced, but they added a piano player before you knew it and then they added the Jordanaires—who, you know, were a good group—but we needed to keep away from sounding like anybody else.[166]

Taking to the studio on January 10, 1956, Elvis delivered his first tunes for RCA. Chief amongst them was a song offered to him by songwriter Mae Boren Axton called 'Heartbreak Hotel' that he had been interested in recording for a while. The latter number, which was also released in the UK, charted at number 15 and peaked at number two—competing against Elvis's own cover of 'Blue Suede Shoes'.[167] With both 'Heartbreak Hotel', and later 'Don't Be Cruel' and 'All Shook Up', Elvis was credited as a songwriter, thereby picking up part of the revenue stream. This practice, called "cutting in", was already common in show business. It was a way for stars to lever their position as gateways to much larger audiences and incomes than songwriters could ordinarily imagine. When the writer was Black and the singer was White, however, it contributed to the perception that racial appropriation and exploitation was happening. Elvis and his publishers ended the practice early in 1957 because they feared public criticism.[168] In the meantime, he had taken on America, and the world, with a range of new songs and a controversial new style.

Existential Elvis

Existentialism is a strand of European philosophy that argues the predicament of the individual is the starting point for any meaningful discussion about life. In some forms it becomes an exploration of the psychological entrapment and melancholy that can form part of the human condition. While Elvis's plaintiff vocal style was audible as early as his first Sun demo, it hit a new peak with his RCA debut, 'Heartbreak Hotel': a dark tale of broken relationships, alienation, depression and suicide. According to voice scholar John Potter:

> Elvis' singing enters an entirely new rhetorical domain. He sings with a menacing aggressive restraint, which at times has the vibrato and lyricism of Crosby and then suddenly switches into barely-audible muttering. The references to loneliness are sometimes actually spoken, or as close as the singer can get to pitched speaking. He forces language to accommodate his thoughts: the tension between what he is thinking and what he is singing can almost be felt by the listener. The artificial reverberation (the only remnant of country music to survive the song) often seems to blur the words, the sentiments of which seem to be so shocking that the singer can hardly get them out.[169]

Potter added that Elvis's "visceral and erotic" style on 'Heartbreak Hotel' "challenges his listeners to enter his world, or reject it, or to invent one of their own".[170] 'Heartbreak Hotel', and by proxy, songs like it, therefore used notes and forms from the blues to draw listeners into the emotional world of individual characters who expressed their angst and mental isolation. Potter was not the only critic to notice the emotional turmoil in Elvis's music. For Greil Marcus, Presley's blues were a set of sexual dramas so it "made sense" to make movies out of them.[171] This is important because it connects Elvis to broader themes that were prevalent in postwar American culture. Historian George Cotkin, for example, starts his book on the subject by saying, "Nearly everyone, it seemed, coming of age in 1950s and 1960s America danced to the song of French existentialism".[172] Although it would be a mistake to say that Elvis directly or single-handedly turned America on to the philosophy, his emotionally urgent music chimed with its concerns.

The idea of an existential Elvis enables us to perceive him at first as an *innate* rebel—a figure whose concerns were beyond those of his time—and later as a tragically *isolated* figure; it was this image that triumphed in some posthumous appraisals of his life. For example, in his 1973 book—one of the few volumes available about the star at the time outside of fan club releases—Favius Friedman asked: "Was Elvis one of the luckier ones, who came along at just that one enchanted moment? Perhaps. But there was also something else—his driving ambition to '*be* somebody, to *feel* like somebody while I'm alive'".[173] Friedman suggests that Elvis viewed stardom as a kind of existential affirmation. He casts his subject as an ego affirmed by successful participation in the American dream. Later writers tended to understand Elvis by focusing on the idea that he was trapped by fame: that his stardom was an unsatisfactory compensation for existential turmoil following the passing of his mother and failure of his marriage. However, justifications for Elvis's troubled side have gone as far back as his birth, and the effect on his immediate family of losing his twin brother Jesse Garon.

Televisual Controversy: Male Sensuality in the Public Sphere

> Hollywood beckoned and the singer quickly became a movie idol. Yet not all were happy with the Presley juggernaut. Furor mounted over his sexually aggressive stage routine.
>
> Michael Bertrand, Southern historian[174]

From the late 1940s onwards, ordinary Americans began adopting the medium of television as a domestic fixture. By 1955, well over half the households in the country had a TV set.[175] The Colonel groomed Elvis for stardom by having RCA write a series of national television appointments into his recording contract. His strategy of levering the media significantly raised the star's profile beyond the regional, country circuit. It instantly exposed Elvis's characteristically animated style of performance to a national audience. Elvis is remembered as a rock'n'roll artist because people saw him from the comfort of their living rooms. There were dynamic performers of various sorts in popular music before him. However, the novelty of Elvis Presley was also a product of an age in which moving visual imagery on the small screen was exciting and new. In the early days of television, broadcasters searching for a family audience adapted the variety show format from its roots in music hall. Elvis's performance did not correspond to traditional styles. In that sense, John Lennon's famous comment, "Before Elvis, there was nothing" flagged up the lack of exciting youth culture, of male sensual expression, of vernacular music, but was partly also a statement about the impact of television as a medium.[176] Elvis's major television appearances are listed in the fourth appendix of this book. His first ones were on Jackie Gleason's *Stage Show*. Since Elvis had been in Bill Randle's ill-fated live performance film, the forward-thinking disc jockey appeared in the studio to endorse his initial appearance. As if to hint at a comparison, Randle also mentioned Johnnie Ray. Accompanied by Scotty, Bill and D.J. Fontana, and wearing a signature dark tweed jacket from Lanskys—his favourite Memphis clothing store—Elvis took over the stage and performed with all guns blazing. One of the interesting things about his television performances is the rapid growth in audience approval. In the weeks to come, Elvis "cut up" to numbers like 'Blue Suede Shoes', and performed his slinky signature song, 'Heartbreak Hotel'. The start of 'Tutti Frutti' alone prompted screams from his audience, perhaps because it could recall Little Richard's recent chart version. While the first show had gained an 18% audience share, it was overshadowed that evening by viewing figures for Perry Como's NBC show. Over the course of Elvis's engagement, however, *Stage Show*'s ratings climbed 2%. Not only had the youth of America a chance to see Elvis; he had also said a few words between songs, clearly establishing his Southern persona on a national stage.

Midway through the run of *Stage Show* appearances, RCA released Elvis's first album. Bob Neal's contract ran out the next day, leaving the Colonel to fully pursue his own plans. Following the Gleason appearances, Elvis was offered a slot on *The Milton Berle Show*. Berle had begun in Vaudeville theatre, but later exploited his reputation as a snappy, charismatic comedian to become television's first fully-fledged star persona. Parker went through the William Morris Agency to suggest Elvis might audition to appear as a guest. His client's first appearance on the show was broadcast live from the deck of the *USS Hancock* while it was docked in San Diego. Susan Doll has argued that to understand Elvis, one must consider wider perceptions of his identity as a Southerner.[177] As part of the proceedings, Elvis performed a comedy skit that parodied his rootsy image. Berle played his twin brother, Melvin: a slow-witted lookalike who needs to have the notion of television explained to him.[178] Melvin explains, "I taught him [Elvis] his singing style: I used to drop grasshoppers down his pants". The hints at retardation and inbreeding allowed Berle to negotiate the rest of the union's stereotypical ideas about Southern identity.

Orientalism is the idea that a society in one geographic place exoticizes far-off foreign territories and projects on to them its own desires and fears. To different degrees, America has always understood its internal North-South divide through the lens of orientalism: locating the South as primal, backward, uncanny and marginal to modernity.[179] Southerners who entered the arena of the national media developed a kind of double consciousness: they knew that their identity was partly defined by how outsiders perceived their region.[180] The "rube" or dumb Southerner was an engrained stereotype by the time that Elvis started to seize the nation. When he played in Cleveland and was filmed by Bill Randle on October 20, 1955, Pat Boone—who was on the same bill that day—later recalled:

> He just went into some rockabilly type song. He looked like he was laughing at something all the time—like he had some private joke, you know? The audience started to get with it ... the song had a kind of raw energy to it ... Then he said, "Thankyuvirmush... Murrrbbllee"—that same hillbilly mumble again—and you could see the girls' faces fall a bit and almost hear them thinking, "Oh no, he's a hillbilly rube".[181]

There was significant prejudice against Southern states at that point in history. On the far side of the Mason-Dixon line, which divided the cultures of the North and South, working-class Southerners did not make good boyfriend material. Elvis's speaking voice, characteristic genre (country), and style (hillbilly), marked him out as Southern, and therefore culturally inferior in the eyes of some Northern, middle-class commentators. His national media phenomenon and hold on the youth market could only add to their concerns. On the second Berle show, the host continued his comic assault by creating a sketch in which fans misidentified *him* as Elvis. Boosted by national chart success, however, Elvis upped the stakes with a riské performance of 'Hound Dog' that involved him moving—this time with no guitar.

Early in January 1956, Elvis recorded the first of many RCA sessions in Nashville and produced 'Heartbreak Hotel'. At the end of the same month he switched to their New York facility due to his television commitments and began four days of East Coast sessions that captured a dynamic new rock'n'roll style that was less folksy or hillbilly than his Sun offerings. The collection included a song by Sun's new hope, Carl Perkins, called 'Blue Suede Shoes', Little Richard's 'Tutti Frutti', more Arthur Crudup material ('My Baby Left Me' and 'So Glad You're Mine') as well as 'Shake, Rattle and Roll', the Black songwriter Otis Blackwell's classic 'Don't Be Cruel' and 'Hound Dog'. According to Jørgensen:

> Those eight rock'n'roll cuts they cut in New York, they fit together. They are a style. It's a tough style, it's a fast style, it's an aggressive style, but it's also an exciting style. It's almost like he came to the big city. It's a city sound. It's a little bit brutal, actually.[182]

Sun Records never released any albums by Elvis. It is important to understand that in the mid- to late 1950s, the music industry's focus was on singles rather than albums, since hit singles were the key way to acquire profits. The era of art music and the concept album was a decade away. In the youth market, record labels tended to release albums to further capitalize on the singles success of their artists, almost as after-thoughts. RCA recouped their signing fee by releasing many different singles and EPs of Elvis's material. EPs were relatively inexpensive and were viewed by record companies as an important way to tap into the teenage market.[183] Revenue from singles and EPs was substantial and the label believed that few teens would buy the same material twice. Album releases were therefore not initially Elvis's central focus.[184] His first album, *Elvis Presley*, was an extremely diverse collection assembled by RCA from five unused Sun tracks plus more recent material, including songs from the New York sessions.[185] Jørgensen described it as "twelve different Elvises on one album showing each step of the development into, suddenly, the biggest star in America".[186] RCA's Chick Crumpacker agreed:

> If you look at the first album there's all different styles in there: pure country, not so pure, there's blues material, there's rock material, and he's doing it all with virtually no effort. Elvis would fine tune as he went along, but what came across in any take was this seamless stylistic delivery. And that was astonishing. And I don't think anybody was really ready for it.[187]

The monophonic album was released in March 1956, each side leading off with a storming rock'n'roll number: 'Blue Suede Shoes' and 'Tutti Frutti'. An image from the previous year, featuring Elvis in Tampa, Florida, was used by the Colonel for the first album cover. In August, as part of the saturation campaign to exploit its new artist, RCA released every track from the album as a single. The record went on, not only to become the first million selling LP; it set a precedent at RCA too, by making the company over $1 million.[188] Its picture cover has become iconic and been recreated by acts from Tom Waits to the Clash.

Characteristic of his post-Sun rock'n'roll style, 'Hound Dog' was one of a number of songs that Elvis had cut in New York. In April 1956, during the downtime from his relatively unsuccessful stint at the New Frontier hotel in Las Vegas, he had been impressed when he saw Freddie Bell and the Bellboys perform the song during their show at the Sands Hotel. Approached in a similar style, Big Mama Thornton's bluesy 1953 hit became a show stopper in Elvis's live set.[189] In his fourth session for RCA in July 1956, he also recorded songwriter Otis Blackwell's 'Don't Be Cruel' and Aaron Schroeder's tune 'Any Way You Want Me'. Jørgensen suggests that it was at this session that Elvis's studio perfectionism started to become more obvious. 'Hound Dog' made the Presley camp aware of the songwriting skills of Jerry Leiber and Mike Stoller. RCA's Steve Sholes and the Colonel persuaded Elvis to release the song and not just use it as a novelty number.[190] 'Hound Dog' appealed on stage because it involved a kind of game: Elvis went from lambasting the audience to being controlled by his own song, communicating to them not only with gyrations but also with flash and tease. He would point straight at the audience and say, "You..." then stand forward on the balls of his feet with knees bent, juddering and scissoring his legs in time to D.J. Fontana's machine-gun beats. Once he finished one version of the song, Elvis struck out with his arm back for the band to stop, then launched into a slow coda, continuing to scissor his legs and lock his hips as he jerked forwards in time to the music. Then he knelt down, kicking each leg out immediately after every drumbeat. The camera also cut to girls in the audience who bounced up and down with excitement.

As Elvis rose to national prominence, he came to personify rock'n'roll, a musical style that rapidly became associated with expressive sexuality and the issue of juvenile delinquency. One female journalist said in her article, "I don't know what it is, but he's got it. He moves. He struts. He shakes. He's mean. He's sweet. He's sex".[191] In his biography of Paul McCartney, Peter Carlin said that in the 1950s Elvis "not only sounded like a sexed-up riot, but looked like one too".[192] Talking to CBS veteran journalist Charles Karult, the advertising and seduction expert Vance Packard summed up in 1977 that Presley's key role had been to facilitate the public expression of female sexual desire.[193] Elvis was *the* performer that demarcated a significant social change. His stage performances associated him with the conjuring of sexual desire, something in the 1950s that was largely seen as exploiting female audiences or debasing civilized culture, but a decade later became understood as expressing personal truth and liberating society from repression.[194]

Presley's first appearance on *The Milton Berle Show* is a good example. Though the impact of his performance was diffused a little by laughter, when Berle arrived at the end to do a dance of his own, it had, nevertheless, sent shock waves through the national television audience. Berle recalled:

> Ten days later I got about 400,000 pan letters, not fan letters, *pan* letters, blaming me, [saying], "We'll never watch you again, Uncle Miltie, when you put that vulgar man that jives and wiggles his backside and his butt. It's disgusting!" Oh. The pan letters get worse, and they're blaming me ... I called Colonel Parker ... saying, "All I called you up for is to tell you this, Colonel: You have a star on your hands".[195]

After that, reactions to Elvis were far harsher than his music warranted.[196] Officials in a number of towns and cities accused Elvis in 1956 of causing young hoodlums to riot and "sexually setting young American womanhood on fire".[197] Initially, such controversy was not necessarily bad for business as it generated publicity. Colonel Parker may even have stoked the firestorm.[198] Nevertheless, unsympathetic commentators interpreted the performer as a low-class Southerner peddling a nightmare cocktail of racial miscegenation (race mixing), illicit culture, and sexual vulgarity to a vulnerable mainstream youth market. Knowing and experienced critics have also later played on this.

Robert Christgau, for instance, said that Elvis offered "inflections that shook teenagers out of their White-skin gentility ... rhythms that aroused their sexuality and aggressiveness".[199] A religious newspaper also claimed, "Presley and his voodoo of frustration and defiance have become a symbol in our country".[200]

Elvis was not alone in publically reflecting the beginnings of a shift in approaches to sex at the time. The men's magazine editor Hugh Heffner published the first edition of his *Playboy* publication in December 1953, featuring future Hollywood star and sex symbol Marilyn Monroe as its nude centrefold. Even if Heffner, Monroe and Presley started it rolling, however, the wheel of social change turned rather more slowly than we might recall. Not all of Elvis's audience took him in an erotic way. Sexual liberation—even on male terms—did not happen for almost a decade *after* Elvis was crowned the King of rock'n'roll. What Carlin was discussing was the frisson associated with Elvis as an *object* of desire. The stage show was controversial not just because Elvis teased his (female) audiences, but because in doing so he evoked shared expressions of female desire. He connected with the concerns of a new generation. Several commentators have noted that he only prompted significant critical complaints when he ventured beyond the South. However, it was the boldness of his performance *on national primetime television* and *family shows*—where audience members may have previously been unfamiliar with his music—that was upsetting. In an interview with a *TV Guide* journalist in Florida, Presley addressed his critics head-on in August 1956: "I'm not trying to be vulgar, I'm not trying to sell any sex, I'm not trying to look vulgar and nasty".[201] This response was characteristic. Elvis argued that it was the *music* that moved him, not any intention to arouse women. He explained in August 1956:

> When Mr Phillips called me to make that first record, I went into the studio and started singing ... My legs were shaking all over, mostly because I was so nervous and excited, but also because I can feel the music more if I just let myself react ... Because all that motion was just as much part of the music to me as the words I was singing.[202]

Historians have rarely offered such innocent readings of Elvis's stagecraft. The evident excitement of his female audience has been enough to convince most commentators that his success was *solely* a matter of sexual magnetism. One critic claimed, for instance, "It can't be said often enough that the source of Elvis's on-stage power was not his vocal performance but his erotic pantomime".[203] According to a commentator on CBS's *Special News Report* when Elvis was buried, "The shaking voice and hips offended parents no end. Presley didn't invent rock any more than he invented sex, but kids seemed to think he'd invented both".[204] Ironically, Elvis never *saw himself* as a seductive dancer.[205] He was, instead, a mover. In an interview for *Elvis Answers Back: The Truth about Me*, the singer explained: "Some people tap their feet. Some people snap their fingers. And some people just sway back and forth. I sort of do 'em all together I guess. Singing rhythm and blues really knocks it out".[206]

Steve Allen had already booked Elvis for his variety show before the second Milton Berle engagement. He had seen the singer's first performances on *Stage Show* and thought he was interesting. Although Allen may not actually have seen Elvis's televised rendition of 'Hound Dog', he was aware of the media controversy around it. In the wake of the Berle performance, Allen opted to present Elvis in a tuxedo and as a wholesome family entertainer. On the show, Elvis was set up to sing 'Hound Dog' to a basset hound that wore a top hat and perched on a pedestal. According to Guralnick, "If Allen was experiencing extreme pleasure, it was clear that Elvis was experiencing the opposite".[207] The audience response was both nervous and minimal. Elvis's supporters have often criticized Steve Allen for restricting their hero and making a mockery of Presley's edgy style. However, before Allen got to the basset hound sequence, he introduced Elvis by revealing an 18,000 signature petition collected by a disc jockey in Oklahoma in which fans said they wanted to see the star back on television. Presley then came out to perform 'I Want You, I Need You, I Love You' accompanied this time by gospel singers the Jordanaires, who were hardly visible on camera.[208] After the break, the show's guests—including Andy Griffith—came back to offer a "Range Roundup" country comedy sketch routine that opened to the tune of 'Turkey in the Straw' and featured Elvis as "Tumbleweed Presley".[209] It was another case of using comedy stereotypes to explore North-South differences, with Elvis sportingly complicit in his role. Following the show, live on television from the Warwick Hotel, Elvis explained to interviewer Hy Gardner that he had never worn a tuxedo before in his life and also that he had amassed a large car collection.[210] His star persona was taking shape as a young man who was starting to enjoy emergent fame and wealth, but doing so by embracing rather than rejecting his roots.

Variety show host Ed Sullivan had been a vocal critic of Elvis Presley and his rock'n'roll style, perhaps because the singer had appeared on various competing television shows. Elvis's immense popularity tempted Sullivan to find a slot for him, at which point the Colonel requested a very high fee. CBS paid the money. The first of Elvis's three engagements was introduced by the accomplished actor Charles Laughton who substituted for Sullivan. At the tail end of October 1956, on Elvis's second *Ed Sullivan* appearance, the Memphis rock'n'roll star set a new record by attracting just over 80% of the national viewing audience.[211] Months later, in the third *Ed Sullivan* performance—Elvis's final national television appearance before entering the army—during 'Don't Be Cruel', he was, famously, filmed from the waist up. While Elvis's whole body was visible in the two other episodes, Sullivan's decision was designed to keep things clean: "as for his gyrations", he said, "the whole thing can be controlled with camera shots".[212] Nevertheless, not only was Elvis still able to convey some of his smouldering performance style, he also began to show his "sacred" side by singing Thomas Dorsey's gospel standard '(There'll Be) Peace in the Valley (For Me)' on the same episode.[213] Reportedly made at the Colonel's request, Sullivan's endorsement of Elvis as "a real decent fine boy ... thoroughly alright" seemed to ring rather hollow. Ironically, as the national marketplace shifted, the aging presenter followed suit and embraced rock'n'roll as part of a changing youth culture. Within a few years he could be seen smiling and playing himself on the Elvis-inspired spoof biopic *Bye Bye Birdie* (Sidney, 1963), and inviting the Beatles and the Rolling Stones on to his show. Furthermore, Ed Sullivan no longer subjected his young guest to any "rube" type comedy sketches.

It is worth considering the role of clothing. As part of his incendiary package, Elvis wore clothes in mould-breaking style. When he was young, he was known as "Squirrel" in reference to the way that he backcombed his hair. Soon after he arrived at Humes, he was befriended by an active and sociable student named George Klein who recalled:

> Elvis did his own thing. He dressed differently. He'd wear a black pair of pants with a white stripe down the side. He'd wear a sports coat to school and turn the collar up; nobody wore sports coats to school. Elvis had long hair. Elvis's hair was longer graduating from high school than the Beatles' were when they came to America in 1964 ... He was nice to everybody.[214]

Even before Elvis became a professional musician, he started to differentiate himself from those around him by wearing items that stood out—a skill that was to prove an asset later when he became a popular centre of attention. Klein was not alone in noticing Elvis's dress sense. Billy Smith was a cousin on Gladys Presley's side of the family. Smith's wife Louise recalled the first time she saw Elvis, before he found fame. She was working in a local clothing store and he said to her, "Good gosh, I guess these shoes that I have on would make ol' man Crump sick!"[215] The fascinating thing about this statement is that it can be read as a reflection of generational rebellion or—given Crump's segregationist stance—perhaps a form of racial "cross-dressing" where someone from one race wore the clothes of another.

Elvis's act involved dressing up in loud clothes, wearing light stage makeup and jewelry to capture more attention. His flamboyant dress style was both part of his on-stage act and off-stage public persona. He also moved his body with a certain sensual abandon in time to the music. Perhaps because of this, academic and popular commentators have tended to question his manhood or virility in various ways. Their comments include Marjorie Garber's claim that Elvis was an "unmarked transvestite".[216] Proposing a more measured compromise, David Shumway has argued that Elvis was *not* camp or effeminate, but *feminized* because he adopted a mode of stage performance that encouraged audiences to objectify him.[217] Shumway's approach, however, confuses a historically specific mode of bodily display with one gender. His claim needs further elaboration, because White men outside of the emergent field of rock'n'roll did not generally move sensuously to music. The descriptions used by reporters *likened* Elvis to women and children in ways that downplayed the threat of his unconventional masculinity. According to dance history scholar Maxine Craig, "Reporters struggled to find the words with which to describe a *man* who moved sensuously".[218] However, feminizing approaches are also a way to *question* Elvis's level of adult responsibility, or to suggest that there was no "real" delivery behind his sexual promise.[219] For many female fans, the sensual response to Elvis was somewhat diffuse; rather than a gyrating phallic dynamo, he appealed as a *whole package*. Often, his looks were what women noticed first. When June Juanico of Biloxi first saw Elvis in concert, "My heart just jumped into my throat when I saw how gorgeous he was".[220] Those millions of female fans, however, were not wrong; Elvis was an eligible young *man*. He was a man who rebelliously donned outrageously flamboyant clothing and seduced his audience at a time when muted colours and conservatism dominated male dress.

Elvis can be seen as part of a continuum of peacocked and preening self-fashioned males, including royalty and aristocrats like Lord Byron as well as late nineteenth-century dandies. However, even to describe Elvis in this way misses some of his most appealing qualities. As a rock'n'roll performer, Presley was, as the cultural historian Leerom Medovoi has suggested, associated with subordinate social identities: his music style was part-inspired by "race music", and he teased his audiences, using his body like a woman.[221] In other words, at least in the loose sense of the term as referring to race mixing, Elvis *creolized* himself. As Potter claimed:

> He surely succeeded because he was not Black, not a blues singer, not a country purist, but a dynamic performer who could make something new from those ingredients that was at once uniquely his and at the same time was able to articulate the commonality of desires shared by a substantial number of those who had previously been satisfied (or not) with something less.[222]

Beyond this, it is also crucial to note that Elvis's persona was always *more* virile than the angelic Johnnie Ray or RCA's next discovery, the cherubic Neil Sedaka. Elvis's performance had an exciting edge, a rockabilly wildness authenticated by his Southern identity. There was a quality in his personality that, while not at all cross-gender, was highly distinctive and added to his *masculine* appeal. He was openly sensual, given over to flashes of temper, characterized by a kind of macho insecurity and feline feistiness; he was perceived as vulnerable and *only partially tamed*. These aspects, which gave

Elvis a kind of off-edge masculinity, were tempered by his Hollywood roles, but from the start they were always part of his image, and audiences knew that. Even when he played a teen angel, his untamed tendencies were always there, ready to come out. To put it another way, he had *claws*. His image was therefore characterized by a *drama of domestication*. This drama was multi-layered because it simultaneously explored how Elvis could become a family man without being fully emasculated, how he could retain a cultural stance that was racially mixed without being whitewashed, how he could stay vital without becoming suburbanized.

A sexualized reading of Elvis imposes a constraining framework on the responses of his fans and ignores the sweeping range of his wider audience, including children. Affect is an academic term for the social movement and intensity of emotion. Part of the thrill of Elvis's appeal was that he embodied *contradictions* in his image that affectively *framed* his fans.[223] For example, even though they are less fortunate than a superstar, fans understand that that they are inevitably more materially fortunate than the humble poor boy from Tupelo, and that helps them feel a connection to Elvis.[224] This meant that although he was a sex symbol, he was available to other audience identifications and more diverse readings. Asked in August 1956, "Do you have any tiny children [in your audience]?" Elvis replied, "Quite a few of 'em. In fact, I guess I get more real tiny ones than I have adults".[225] Children could easily understand his charm as a wiggling, singing centre of attention. Elvis was pictured holding children during and after the 1950s shows, but it was in movies like *It Happened at the World's Fair* (Taurog, 1963) and *Change of Habit* (Graham, 1969) that his publicists really drew on his natural affinity with tots.[226] One reason that Elvis appealed to children could be perhaps that he moved like a marionette, giving himself over to the music. Everybody, children included, thinks of themselves as more empowered than any puppet. Moving to the title song of *Jailhouse Rock* (Thorpe, 1957), and in *Loving You* (Kanter, 1957), Elvis did a kind of drum walk, a stiff, clicking march towards the audience in which he pointed his knees individually with each step. At other times he would scissor his arms and legs as if they were attached to strings. One radio commentator introduced Elvis by saying, "He's winding up his leg!"[227] Others said Elvis looked rubber-legged.[228] This is not to say that audiences *consciously* acknowledged the puppetry, but instead that Elvis's performance style was a compelling open secret, innately understood without needing to be explicitly defined. His lexicon of moves greatly influenced later performers.

Just after his first *Ed Sullivan Show* appearance, on September 26, 1956 Elvis Presley returned in triumph to play at the Mississippi-Alabama Fair and Dairy Show in his home town of Tupelo, Mississippi. Not long after his home-coming, Elvis dropped by Sun Studio to jam with Carl Perkins and Jerry Lee Lewis, already successful rockabilly acts on his former label. Sam invited a *Memphis Press-Scimitar* journalist to write up the proceedings and also persuaded Johnny Cash to arrive for the photo opportunity. In what later became known as the "Million Dollar Quartet" session, on December 4, 1956, they played a series of over thirty gospel, country and rock'n'roll numbers. According to Cash:

> Carl Perkins, Jerry Lee Lewis, Elvis and myself all became like one big family. We'd all know what days we were recording and we'd go and sit in on each other's records, usually having jam sessions after the records had been cut. I remember one time in about 1957 when Elvis was already with RCA he came back and the four of us sat around the piano and sang hymns. Elvis was playing and we were harmonising with each other. That record was never released, although Sam turned the tapes on and took two hours of tape.[229]

The Million Dollar Quartet was proof-positive that Elvis had not forgotten his start at Sun and was willing to endorse a clutch of talented new artists who, in his wake, had arrived at its door.

Although 1956 had become a year of national controversy, it was also one of record-breaking releases. Towards the end of the year, Elvis settled into a productive three-day studio session at Radio Recorders in Hollywood, aided, in part, by veteran house engineer Thorne Nogar. His new batch of fresh material included another Otis Blackwell number ('Paralyzed'), a cover of 'Long Tall Sally', the classic weepy 'Old Shep', plus Leiber and Stoller's plaintive, doo-wop styled 'Love Me'. That year Elvis had four RCA singles which had shifted a combined total of eight million units in the USA, with many more sales coming from his Sun single re-issues, two chart-topping albums, eleven television appearances (including twice, so far, on *The Ed Sullivan Show*), foreign successes, and a role in *Love Me Tender*, his first major Hollywood movie. As the year drew to a close he had ten titles in the *Billboard* Top 100 singles chart and a new release, 'Too Much', that had pre-sold around half a million copies.[230] He had discovered his place as a recording artist of global standing.

Musical Creativity: The Fan as Auteur

> I work strictly on instinct and impulse. My taste might be a little different because I choose songs with the public in mind. *I try to visualize as though I was buying the record myself.*
>
> Elvis Presley[231]

Elvis's story positioned him as an extraordinarily talented *ordinary* person. In one way he represented the ultimate fan turned music producer. The Million Dollar Quartet recording captures Elvis saying, "That's why I hate to get started in these jam sessions. I'm always the last one to leave".[232] The young star also had a photographic memory.[233] He could hear a demo and sing it word-for-word straight away from previous renditions. According to his backing singer, the gospel tenor Gordon Stoker, "We worked with many, many stars and still do, but none of them got up to the microphone and sang without using a word sheet ... He never used a word sheet with anything".[234] More concisely, Sherman Andrus of gospel group the Imperials said, "He literally loved music".[235] Elvis's interests extended well beyond obscure vernacular sounds and mainstream, American artists. This section will explore what he did with his fandom.

Partly because he caused social controversy and never claimed to have any formal musical training, Elvis provoked criticism over both his musical ability and creativity. He was a competent and versatile player, but his skills are not entirely to be found in musical virtuosity. Kern Kennedy, a pianist for Sonny Burgess and the Pacers (who opened for Elvis in Arkansas) said, "I thought Elvis was going to be big, but I never, ever thought he was going to be as big as he was ... to me he always appeared to be a three-chord musician and that was about it".[236] However, it would be fairer to say that Elvis Presley was a "good enough" player. In *Elvis Answers Back* magazine from 1956, under the subheading "Do I really play the guitar?" the singer explained to fans:

> I read in one magazine that I can't play a note on the guitar, and in another, in the same week, that I'm the best guitar player in the world. Well, both of those stories are wrong. I've never had music lessons, like I told you ... Then I went out on stage in my first personal appearance, I just naturally took my guitar along with me, to sort of keep me company ... There's always another fellow in the band who does most of the playing, and if you watch me real close in a performance sometime, you'll see how it works. He follows my motions and hits the chords at just the right time.[237]

Elvis was being relatively modest here. He learned piano and was practised by the time he lived at Graceland. He would play for two or three hours at a time, though he always had doubts about his own virtuosity. About his emergent piano playing, he explained:

> I also like the piano, though I guess I don't play it exactly the way you're supposed to. I just hit whatever keys look good to me. It's a lot of fun, and sometimes I'll play along while I'm singing. Never in a performance or on a record though. I'm not that good.[238]

In other words, at least in the 1950s, Elvis continually located his status as an *amateur* player. His musicianship, from that perspective, had folksy, democratic quality, marking it out against the highbrow approach of classical musicianship. Nevertheless, when Bill Black struggled to lay down the electric bass part for Leiber and Stoller's '(You're So Square) Baby I Don't Care' at Radio Recorders in the spring of 1957, Elvis jumped in and played the part himself, leaving Jerry Leiber to create a scratch vocal.[239] What is interesting about this is that Elvis's real interest in actually playing the bass did not occur until several years *later*, around the time he met the Beatles.

Elvis Presley had a superb musical ear, dexterity and timing. If he was a "good enough" musician on a range of instruments, the one that he triumphed over—spectacularly—was his own voice. What is interesting about Elvis is that he made his mark with an instrument that everyone possesses. As Theodor Adorno knew, music can be sonically trade-marked, branded so that listeners can distinguish material and become fascinated with its makers.[240] The voice is a *primary* way to do that.

Compared to other rock'n'roll singers like Bill Haley, Elvis's vocal style is sophisticated, heightened, inflected, versatile, empowered, mature and personal, colouring his words with additional implications and dimensions of meaning.[241] In *Elvis Answers Back*, Elvis reassured his fans in August 1956, "Like I told you with my singing, I don't want to copy anyone".[242] His style was thrilling and unique: powerful, gentle, haunting and melodramatic. As popular music scholar Simon Frith explained, Elvis was a profoundly creative singer. The Memphis performer had a diversity of inspiration. Another popular music writer, Jason Toynbee, has developed the cultural sociologist Pierre Bourdieu's ideas to talk about how musicians have a "radius of creativity" based on their musical influences.[243] Elvis had a vast radius of creativity, one that spanned several genres. He loved gospel, pop, country, blues and even "old time" genres and popular opera.[244] Scotty Moore was a conduit for jazzy guitar licks even in Elvis's early music; the recording of the *King Creole* (Curtiz, 1958) soundtrack bought Elvis into even closer contact with Dixieland jazz.

With his wide range of influences, Elvis could mix and match to create his own unique musical style. According to Jørgensen, "He stole those vocal tricks from all the heroes, and since the heroes came from so many different areas, it was a funny mixture of all these little mannerisms".[245] Music scholar Richard Middleton argued that this creativity, which extended vocality into arranging and, in effect, rewriting material, was characterized by "romantic lyricism" and "boogification". Simon Frith summarized Middleton's position:

> In giving Presley's singing a close musical analysis, Middleton makes three significant points. First, Presley was a self-conscious technician—the choice of vocal attack, the making of musical decisions, the playing of genre games, can be heard in the songs themselves; this is not a matter of "instinct". Second, Presley was well aware that pop songs are implicitly about their performance—and their own performers; his "narcissism" as a singer always had an ironic inflection. And the force and effect of that inflection—the rhetorical devices of embarrassment and seduction, sincerity and

flippancy—were a key aspect of his appearance. Third, and perhaps most importantly, Presley's musical gifts were not momentary or accidental, something he "had" in the Sun or early RCA days and then lost (or had stolen from him). He was always a vocal artist, a vocal technician, a vocal craftsman...[246]

According to Elvis's musical assistant, Charlie Hodge, Presley had a voice stretching above and beyond the average one and a half octaves, to manage a three octave range.[247] The singer also constantly attempted, and sang, notes that were out of his normal range. As an "untrained" singer, or rather as someone who taught himself to sing "from the gut", Elvis attempted things that trained professionals would not try.[248] Sherman Andrus of the Imperials gospel quartet noted, "You usually do things that are easy for you to do every night, and this guy tried things that were just hard".[249] On May 16, 1971, Elvis sang an ad-libbed version of 'The Lord's Prayer' in RCA's Studio B in Nashville.[250] Although it was just a short, throwaway piece, he pushed his voice to a point where it soared acrobatically beyond what other singers could do. Those who listen to the recording might almost be embarrassed for Elvis: embarrassed at what he risks, at how far he viscerally dares, at the way he manages to eclipse technique to find such emotional rawness. Beyond performances demonstrative of Elvis's vocal prowess ('Lonesome Cowboy'), purity ('Milky White Way'), gentleness ('You Asked Me To'), bravado ('Hound Dog') and passion ('If I Can Dream'), 'The Lord's Prayer' shows exactly *where his voice can go*, just what more it can do, both technically and emotionally.

A key issue for Elvis was that he sat oddly with the notions of popular music authenticity that emerged during his era. Folk authenticity is the idea that artists are authentic if they begin *before* or *outside of* the commercial marketplace and modern society. Unlike, say, Sun artists the Prisonaires, Elvis could not initially claim that mantle. He drove a truck and lived in a city, had worked in a cinema and collected records. Sam Phillips understood and marketed him as the face of modernity coming to vernacular music, a young artist refashioning the output of Arthur Crudup and others for the jet age. From the start, therefore, Elvis's image and up-tempo music became an arena in which the folk and the modern could enter into a dialogue.[251] His Southern identity and working-class accent positioned him outside of the polished norms of metropolitan show business. When Elvis became a national figure, RCA marketed him as a country act. From that perspective, rockabilly *was* the folk strand of rock'n'roll. Yet folk music commercially renewed itself, finding large sales in the 1960s. While Elvis had been a rockabilly, a rock'n'roller, a youth artist—at least in public—he ventured to take sides only implicitly as a supporter of Black civil rights. He did not fully locate himself as an artist who deliberately represented a community or spoke for a constituency that shared specific values or oppositional politics, as Bob Dylan had done. If rock was about self-expression, songwriting, making statements and taking sides, Elvis, in his iconic ordinariness and tremendous popularity, represented something larger. His constituency was a vast, relatively apolitical fan base: people who, for the most part, were concerned simply to support him.

Perhaps the critical problem with Elvis comes because, as a singer who naturally added a rootsy edge to his work, he was, however, willing to embrace folk's supposed opposite: commercial mass marketing. In the interview for *Elvis Answers Back*, Elvis was asked if he called his performance singing. He laughed and replied, "Do I call it singing? Well, I've sold five million records! Somebody calls it singing".[252] The singer was seen as a diamond in the rough: not so much a creative individual who had to be given space to do his own best work (though elements of that are there too), but an artist who needed the help of others who could ignore immediate constraints in their mission to produce something that unleashed his full potential. From that perspective the Colonel's help was viewed frequently as a tragedy, and Elvis's 1968 NBC TV *Comeback Special* director Steve Binder's involvement, a triumph. Elvis's embrace of mass marketing both reproved his folk status (as a poor boy looking to make good financially through the American dream) and denied it (as a gun for hire, willing to rent his vocal talents out to Hollywood). When the music industry maintained a division between commercial folk (such as the blues singer Leadbelly) and show business (say, when dancer Fred Astaire sang show tunes by Irving Berlin), existing estimations of authenticity were easier to maintain.

By adding mainstream and vernacular music together, Elvis raised new questions about what or who was authentic and why. Ironically, Leiber and Stoller became positioned as creative geniuses for adopting a Tin Pan Alley approach to R&B, while Elvis was criticized as an appropriator for taking a cut of songs offered to him when show business stars like Al Jolson had previously done so without controversy. In other words, Elvis upset the popular music apple cart, not just as a blender of racialized genre traditions, but as a mixer of music conventions. New forms of authenticity emerged later to adroitly segregate rock from pop and clarify the cultural field.

Songwriting was not Elvis's province.[253] He could not be credited with the kind of honesty of self-expression that was now attributed by audiences to the range of individual singer-songwriters who came around that time of the Beatles. From that perspective, Elvis faced *potential* criticism for being unoriginal and insincere.[254] A critique along such lines did not immediately materialize, however, because he arrived at a time when artists were praised for *a number of musical skills* including cross-genre adaption, arrangement and performance. It was partly because of the emotional expressiveness that he contributed that, only well after his debut, songwriting became seen as the master skill. After rock'n'roll had subsided from the mainstream and rock culture had slowly emerged, contemporary popular music was positioned as an art form, with prominent acts writing their own material. Even during this period, Elvis was understood as expressing soul and credited with inspiring social change through music. He was more likely to be criticized for accepting poor material than failing to write. To talk of his limitations as a songwriter is ultimately to focus *only* on composition and its claim to novelty when there are evidently other modes of musical creativity.

Part of Elvis's skill was in radically *reinterpreting* songs. 'Trouble' offers an example of his great skill as an arranger, as he effortlessly transformed it from a parody cabaret number to something that seemed more serious. He orchestrated the Jordanaires on 'Good Luck Charm'. Partly because of his profile, but also because of his musical skills, he sometimes made successful versions of the same songs that others had trouble selling. 'Bossa Nova Baby', for instance, had been a flop for Tippy and the Clovers before Elvis recorded it for the *Fun in Acapulco* (Thorpe, 1963) soundtrack early in 1963.[255] Such success was not just down to Presley's immense stardom, as some of his records did poorly on the charts. He also knew his limits. Elvis never covered any Roy Orbison songs, for example, claiming that he could not improve on their perfection.[256]

Despite becoming the best-selling individual music artist in the world, alongside his unbridled popularity, Elvis encountered controversy in equal measure. It was not simply that his fame made him become iconic: a discursive resource, a stake in wider discussions about America, commerce, race, class and taste. He was hard to pin down and fully comprehend in relation to a key aspect of creative culture: originality. Elvis was profoundly talented and yet could be challenged as dependent on others' authorship.

Having no credentials as an *author*, Elvis ultimately represents a kind of blind spot and *bad object*: present as a wonderful voice, a performative trace, a commercial entity, but broadly ignored or rejected by academia and the critical field. He could not be dismissed for standing in someone else's shadow; he had no singular source of inspiration. *He eclipsed all that he adapted: first by his own distinctiveness and second by his immense fame.* Yet neither has Elvis been fully embraced as a true original. He was always a stylist—a covers artist, even if an extraordinary one. The perception that Elvis was not an original source for the culture that he evidently created blinds us to what he actually did. Gospel quartet singer Gordon Stoker explained, "He once said, 'I can't sing, I can't dance, I can't play the piano—what do they want me for?' We said, 'You've got what it takes—give it to 'em'".[257] Other than good looks and on-stage charisma, what did having "what it takes" actually mean? Elvis offered something radically novel: an ability to charge his numbers with a kind of haunting intimacy and urgent passion quite unlike any previous performers. He effortlessly rebranded songs with his own unique arrangement and performance style. Auteur is a term developed by French film critics in the middle of the twentieth century to describe directors whose creative visions repeatedly defined and marketed their films. The term is useful, because it shows how the vision of one individual can lead a collaborative process of cultural production. Elvis was, in effect, *an auteur in music* who orchestrated a vision based upon *feel*. According to Dixie Locke, a girlfriend from his formative years in Memphis, "He had the most innate sense of rhythm and motion of anybody I've ever seen. It was totally natural to him".[258] Biographer Peter Guralnick observed:

> The [Sun] sessions are these kind of concentric circles where the musicians wander around, and wander around, and basically the whole idea is for Elvis to get to that point where he's free. He'll be honing in on something that he can't really define and yet when he gets it, the feeling is what defines it. It has nothing to do with the technical perfection ... the feeling was that feeling of loose spontaneity.[259]

Charles Keil has argued that engrossing popular music has to be a little out of time. He described these very human, perfect imperfections as "participatory discrepancies".[260] They seem to characterize Elvis's music, a body of work where *soul* was much more important than technical accuracy. Discussing the Sun singles 'Baby Let's Play House' and 'Mystery Train', Guralnick suggests, "What each of them has to offer is just a sense of irrepressible joyousness and the feeling that they must have been created on the spot".[261] According to Elvis's drummer, D.J. Fontana, the Memphis singer often countered studio professional listeners who heard "mistakes" in his takes by saying "Why go over it again? You're going to kill it".[262]

With his capacity to enter into a place of musical feel, Elvis had a series of skills and aptitudes that helped make him a great musician. He quickly emerged as a confident and able leader in recording sessions. Because he knew what to do, he got his way in what he wanted. His leadership of studio sessions was manifest in various ways. While he was scheduled to record particular numbers, Elvis often played unconnected songs in the studio to warm up his vocal chords. When he was supposed to be recording the soundtrack for *Jailhouse Rock*, for instance, he spent part of the session singing gospel around the piano with the Jordanaires.[263] Once his RCA sessions got underway, he emerged as a perfectionist in the studio.[264] Again, according to Gordon Stoker of the Jordanaires, "He'd take all night for one song, many times".[265] In the December 1961 session for *Kid Galahad* (Karlson, 1962), for example, on the first day Elvis recorded 31 takes of 'King of the Whole Wide World' to get it right.[266] Part of this propensity for re-takes can be attributed to studio technology, which initially would not allow for over-dubs and other cosmetic fixes to songs. It also reflected Elvis's training at Sun, where musicians were given ample opportunities to get it right because they did not have to rent studio time. Elvis's inclination towards communal singing, and his training in the intimate environment of Sun Studio, meant that he generally preferred smaller locations for making music. He also had the ability to adjust the tempo of his songs in tune with audience desires. According to Ray Walker of the Jordanaires, "He was a master at tempo, a master at knowing the feel of a song".[267] Elvis sped up the tempo of 'I Don't Care if the Sun Don't Shine', a tune used in the Dean Martin and Jerry Lewis movie *Scared Stiff* (Marshall, 1953). Martin had sung it as a smooth, jazzy, cabaret number. Elvis raised the tempo, transformed the vocal, and created a more innocent ditty. He also, for example, suggested changing the middle of 'I Was The One' to a country shuffle.[268] It is crucial here that his manager Colonel Parker always stayed out of the way and did not interfere with immediate processes of recording or the social energy in the studio. The Memphis singer was free to re-word material. Just as he had done with 'That's All Right', in different ways, Elvis reworked many of the songs that he used. He changed a line in Arthur Gunter's 'Baby Let's Play House' from one about his partner getting religion to her buying a pink Cadillac—as if, in modern society, consumerism had *replaced* religion.[269] He also lightly modified the lyrics of 'Heartbreak Hotel'.[270] Elvis would sometimes abandon songs half-recorded in the studio just to keep RCA from releasing them.[271] Elvis's records may have been overseen by Sam Phillips, Chet Atkins, Felton Jarvis and Chips Moman (though some of these were uncredited), but to different degrees, the singer was always at the helm. According to Gordon Stoker of the Jordanaires, "He was the producer of his records, but somebody else would get the credit".[272] Elvis Presley was also in charge of choosing the singles from amongst his material.[273] He was on a mission to get things spot on.

Elvis and Gospel Music

> Part of the strength of Elvis is his faith and his belief spiritually—that's what attracts a lot of people to him. People can talk about his swivelling hips or his wonderful voice and then the sexual attraction he had, but the biggest attraction of Elvis in my estimation was his spiritual strength and his faith, and his being plugged into the power source—so to speak—plugged into God, and people are always attracted to that tremendous energy.
>
> Elvis's friend Christine Ferra[274]

At least in a musical sense, Elvis Presley had two first loves: gospel singing and romantic ballads. This section will discuss his gospel style. Elvis had been raised in the First Assemblies of God church in Tupelo. The church had been one of the first places where he experienced community through singing. On the radio from the *Grand Ole Opry* in Nashville, Elvis heard gospel group the Jordanaires sing occasional spirituals. Sun's roster of hillbillies had almost all been to Pentecostal churches.[275] Sacred vernacular music was, in fact, divided between two types of singing. Gospel songs tended to be slower and on the beat, sung in a way that emphasized vocal harmony. Spirituals, on the other hand, were more associated with Black traditions. They tended to be based on stories and could contain spoken word motifs. They were also associated with hand clapping, finger snapping types of performance. Elvis liked both traditions. According to Joe Moscheo, for instance, who sang with a gospel group that worked for Elvis (the Imperials), Presley loved Black groups like the Harmonizing Four, a quartet formed in the late 1920s that became Sister Rosetta Tharpe's backing band and started recording in the 1940s. Their song 'Let's Go to that Land', with its delightful bass singing, had its place amongst his favourite records.[276]

Gospel appealed to young people in 1940s and 1950s Memphis because it combined spiritual practice with show business. In the South it was thoroughly implicated in other genres and forms of singing. The genre effortlessly bridged the divide between amateur and professional music making, offering a route through which dedicated and talented, but otherwise ordinary singers could enter Southern show business. Although gospel was a racially differentiated tradition, White groups such as the Blackwood Brothers, who worked in Memphis from 1950, drew their repertoire and audiences from both races. Elvis would travel across town to South Memphis early in 1954 to visit the First Assemblies of God church, because it was where the Blackwood Brothers had a teen apprentice gospel quartet called the Songfellows. Presley failed an audition with them, however, as he could not blend in his voice.[277] Nevertheless, the Blackwood Brothers hosted all-night shows at the Ellis Auditorium. This famous auditorium held a special place in Elvis's memory: in his teenage years he had regularly watched gospel quartets perform there to packed crowds. He performed at the auditorium in 1955, 1956 and 1961.

Elvis had first seen the gospel bass singer J.D. Sumner in an early 1950s act called the Sunshine Boys. Once Presley became famous, he called on Sumner to sing for him. The bass singer eventually became a fixture in Elvis's live act. Sumner's daughter said her dad always said that Elvis really wanted to be a gospel singer.[278] He would occasionally say, "I know every religious song ever written".[279] According to J.D. Sumner's daughter, he listened to 'He Touched Me' over and over, at least fifty times; he was obsessed to learn it.[280] During the *How Great Thou Art* sessions, Elvis told Ray Walker of the Jordanaires, "You know, Ray, the Lord really messed up on me when he didn't make me a bass singer".[281]

Presley was a lifelong and highly dedicated fan of commercial sacred music. It was hardly surprising, then, that gospel would become a central part of his stage act and gradually help to define his celebrity persona. He began to reflect on his connection to religion during his first phase in the national spotlight. Explaining his style, Elvis said in May 1956, "I just landed upon it accidentally. More or less I [am] a pretty close follower of religious quartets, and they do a lot of rockin' spirituals".[282] By the time of his final *Ed Sullivan* appearance, Elvis showcased his passion for gospel singing to an unsuspecting public. When asked about why he did not include gospel in his live set, in March 1956, he said that he did not have the time. He had talked to RCA about doing a gospel album, but, he said, "I think I might get a completely different following if I did".[283]

Expressing his love of gospel in public was a way for Elvis to show his conservative side and to tone down the apparent threat of his rock'n'roll persona. In *Elvis Answers Back* magazine, he explained that, unlike his critics suggested, he had not forgotten religion, and had stayed dedicated. He added, "I believe all good things come from God".[284] As the national controversy broke over his supposedly suggestive rock'n'roll style, however, he could not sustain the link. Four months later, discussing a piece which said that he got his moves from church singing, Elvis told a *TV Guide* interviewer, "My religion has nothing to do with what I do now, because, the type of stuff I do now is not religious music. My religious background has nothing to do with the way I sing".[285] To the older generation, a young rock'n'roller was the last person who should have been allowed to record sacred music.

The Jordanaires already knew Colonel Parker though their work with Eddy Arnold, Hank Snow and Tommy Sands. Elvis first met the group backstage at a show in Memphis in 1955 where they were backing Arnold. The young singer told them that he would employ them if he signed with a major label, and he kept his word. They performed as a backing ensemble on many of Elvis's records. In January 1957, he recorded the inspirational ballad 'I Believe'—a song already covered by Roy Hamilton—at RCA's Radio Recorders studio in Hollywood; he also recorded '(There'll Be) Peace in the Valley (For Me)' and 'Take My Hand, Precious Lord' in the same session, the idea being to release a gospel EP.[286] When the *Peace in the Valley* EP sold over half a million copies over the Easter season of 1957, it became the first of Elvis's gospel hits.[287]

Later in 1957, RCA decided that they wanted a Christmas album from Elvis, drawing on the success of his recorded gospel repertoire, so in September he went into Radio Recorders in Hollywood and cut a knowing cover of 'Blue Christmas'—which had been a country hit for Ernest Tubb—along with Leiber and Stoller's equally racy 'Santa Claus Is Back in Town' and more conservative classics like Irving Berlin's 'White Christmas' and the carol 'O Little Town of Bethlehem'.[288] This was a characteristic pattern in his recording career: sacred music alongside secular music, with considerable interchange—such as the use of the Jordanaires—between the two.

Late in 1960, Elvis returned to RCA's Studio B in Nashville and recorded a series of 14, mostly gospel, songs over the course of one night, including 'Milky White Way', 'Joshua Fit the Battle' and 'Swing Down Sweet Chariot'.[289] The session also included a 1949 Jordanaires hit, 'I'm Gonna Walk Dem Golden Stairs' which took Elvis and his fellow singers only one take to record.[290] His early gospel efforts were consolidated on his sixth studio album *His Hand in Mine*.

Just as Elvis's movie career was beginning to lose its spark, on the back of steady sales of *His Hand in Mine*, he was given a fresh opportunity to make another gospel album. This time he enlisted one of his heroes. Jake Hess had been in White gospel quartet the Statesmen from 1948 onwards. In 1954 his quartet was one of Elvis's favourite acts. They performed in Memphis at the monthly all-nighters at the Ellis Auditorium. In the 1960s West Coast contemporary Christian music took over from gospel. Hess had recorded for Benson Records from 1964 onwards and founded a new vocal group called the Imperials which toured and released a couple of albums per year. Beyond their solo success—particularly the contemporary-sounding 1967 Christian music album *New Dimensions*—the quartet had also accompanied the charismatic country crooner and TV presenter Jimmy Dean. 'I've Got Confidence' was contemporary Black gospel. Elvis was thrilled to secure the services of Hess and his group for the May 1966 recording session for 'How Great Thou Art'. As Marsh noted, it was the first time that Elvis had recorded at RCA without Chet Atkins and his first non-soundtrack recording for over two years.[291] Early in 1967 'How Great Thou Art' became the centrepiece of Elvis's second gospel album. Ten years after he first recorded gospel, in September he continued the tradition by tackling 'We Call On Him' and 'You'll Never Walk Alone' (though the latter was not successful in sales terms).[292] A third studio gospel album followed in April 1972, named after its lead-off track, 'He Touched Me'.

Gospel was central to Elvis's later live music. The Jordanaires had a good relationship with Colonel Parker, who gave them royalty points on Elvis's records, yet when the singer assumed his residency in Las Vegas they did not take up his invitation to perform. At that point the quartet had a number of lucrative studio bookings with other acts and it could not squeeze in an additional two live shows per night. The Imperials were a natural replacement on stage for the Jordanaires. Within two years, though, the group could not continue with their commitment. In 1958 Elvis had asked J.D. Sumner to sing at the funeral of his mother Gladys. From the mid-1960s onwards, J.D. had worked with the Stamps and was well known for having the lowest bass voice in gospel music. Elvis saw J.D. Sumner as a father figure and considered him a bigger celebrity than himself. J.D. Sumner and the Stamps were enlisted by Elvis in 1971, in part to procure the services of their leader. Elvis hero-worshipped Sumner, sometimes thanking him for sharing the same stage. Another skilled gospel singer that Elvis enlisted was the tenor Sherrill (Shaun) Nielsen. Nielsen had performed with the gospel groups the Songfellows, the Speer Family, and an early incarnation of the Imperials. He moved to Nashville in 1973 to organize a gospel outfit that would eventually open for Elvis. The star adopted the group and called them Voice after a name he saw on the cover of a religious periodical.[293] On tour, Elvis would get Nielsen to perform a solo version of 'O Sole Mio' to showcase his powerful yet haunting style. The pair also performed a showcase duet on stage of the heartbreakingly sad 'Softly As I Leave You'—a traditional Italian song previously popularized by Matt Monroe and Frank Sinatra—with Elvis speaking the lyrics and Nielsen singing backing.

By turns, gospel served a variety of functions for Elvis. First, it was the music that expressed his faith. To one magazine journalist he said, "I never expected to be anyone important. Maybe I'm not now. But whatever I am, whatever I will become, will be what God has chosen for me. I feel he's watching every move I make".[294] The values expressed in gospel were part of his explanatory framework. When Sherman Andrus told Elvis that he was in a unique situation and really blessed, he replied, "You know, I know that and I couldn't have done it without God".[295] Second, gospel was, in effect, Elvis's version of both folk (pre-commercial) and soul (deeply expressive) music. Perhaps for this reason, historian Charles Reagan Wilson has located Elvis's use of gospel music as part of a uniquely Southern tradition of spiritual practice.[296] It put his mind at ease, connected him to his roots and to a mother who also had a strong faith. The gospel genre was also one where Elvis was not pressured to create hit singles. He would sing gospel in pop recording sessions, using up expensive studio time. It is important to note, here, however, that his indulgent pursuit of the genre was sometimes falsely positioned *against* the imperatives of commerce. Gospel was Elvis's warm-up music, a way to get his voice ready to attempt various vocal feats. Gospel was also Elvis's "party" music, in so far that it connected him to a certain kind of communality. He rarely performed up-tempo gospel on stage, but often sang it back in his penthouse, joining together with his friends into the early hours of the morning. He used gospel when he wanted people to bond together. Performing the genre blended Elvis with those around him, linking all of them to a strong tradition of sacred music. It was a way to add spiritual mystery to his appeal as an entertainer.

Elvis eventually won three Grammy Awards for his contribution to gospel music. Ironically, these prestigious awards meant that he was more officially recognized for his gospel recordings than for his secular output. He was the star who did most to popularize the gospel genre and bring it to the mainstream during his era. He helped Christian music find a secular audience. Gospel was the musical style through which Elvis dreamed, and it also located him as a fan.[297] In the end, gospel became a way to authenticate Elvis. As Jordanaires singer Ray Walker once claimed, "Sometimes you can pretend that you have an emotion in a song. Almost every time he sang that song you could feel the spirit of him because that was his astral praise to God".[298] Gospel is the music that fascinates Elvis's most dedicated fans, precisely because it was his favourite music. It said a lot about him and the social environment from which he emerged.[299]

Totemic Elvis

With his exciting combination of vernacular music styles and appealing stage moves, between 1956 and 1958 Elvis won over audiences and dominated the rock'n'roll era. One newspaper headline noted, "He's Riding the Crest of a Teenage Tidal Wave".[300] Another exclaimed, "Elvis Presley Disturbances Surely Hit Seismic Scale".[301] Though they sometimes dismissed Elvis's concerts as a case of trickery or manipulation, the terms that journalists often used to interpret his energetic and riotous live shows could reflect natural forces. "Gothic" is an often-used label for atmospheres that seem to envelop receptive individuals and lead them in non-rational directions. While the term is often associated with horror or dread, it can arguably reflect other, more positive emotions. Some of the 1950s news stories were, basically, gothic or kinetic in tone. They featured riots, eruptions, earthquakes, waves or floods—a case of the singer's sensual passion crashing against his audience like wave on wave. The language was poetic, but it also emphasized that what was going on was irrational and emotional enchantment. Stars become icons when they achieve vast levels of popularity and start to be perceived as representing profound ideas. By his death, Elvis had become an icon—in rock critic Greil Marcus's words, "a supreme figure in American life"—the most famous performer to represent his nation.[302] According to *Rolling Stone*, by 2005 the "Memphis Flash" achieved sales figures of over a billion records worldwide, with an estimated 40% from outside of the USA.[303] Cultural history has been powerful in explaining how Elvis assumed his role as the King of rock'n'roll, but his ongoing celebrity has inevitably also shaped our understanding.

Talking about another King, and American bestseller—Stephen King—fellow horror writer Dale Bailey argued that commercial success has made him difficult to accurately interpret:

> He has become a popular culture icon and virtual cottage industry, churning out fiction in a variety of media; but this success has made it difficult to assess his work. If the keepers of our culture have been too hasty to dismiss him, his apologists have proven over-fond of hyperbole in his defense.[304]

One might say that the same is true of Elvis Presley. Popular accounts place Elvis as pure talent mishandled by his manager and the music industry. In these narratives Elvis is over-hyped and undersold, reduced to pure product and parcelled off to legions of indiscriminating consumers. However, there are some problems with this view. If popular culture is about the way that audiences champion particular objects from the media marketplace—all sorts of things including real celebrities, fictional characters and their stories, songs, recordings, and feature films—then Bailey, as a cultural critic, is attempting to create a separate conceptual space. His claim assumes he can use this space to get some perspective and make fair judgements. With popular forms, critics do not have the last say, but even more importantly, vast sales figures do not exactly *distort* our perception of the work of iconic figures, especially ones like Elvis. Instead, they *shape* our perception of them and can therefore be taken as *part of their creative contribution*. Elvis's significance cannot be measured by extraordinary sales figures alone; they play a role in helping to shape perceptions of his phenomenon. This book argues that is not just that Elvis made some truly great music, but also that we can understand it better if we take different aspects of this phenomenon into account.

It is worth considering whether there are sound explanations for the unspoken *emotional rationality* of Elvis fandom. From the Sun days onwards, Elvis's relationship with his audience was sincere. Historian and biographer Joel Williamson recently described the "incredible spectacle" of Elvis's 1950s shows as something that built a "bubble" containing both the singer and his female audience:

> It was as if each girl and Elvis had created a magic space, a huge bubble in which they existed alone together, isolated, ecstatic, and exclusive of the dreary world. Increasingly, the girls sent up such a roar that Elvis's voice and music could not even be heard. His performances became totally visual, and the girls responded to his every move as he sang audibly, visibly, physically and without inhibition. Their performance became the dominant performance. The girls might as well have been on the bill. It was a collaboration.[305]

Where Williamson arguably misses the mark a little is in quite so emphatically assuming that his fans were and are female. Nevertheless, his concept of the "bubble" captures both the excitement of Elvis's live concerts and the way that fans stayed in the frame of them.[306] Building on this, the section will conclude by exploring how Elvis's phenomenon can be understood with the help of Emile Durkheim's ideas on religion. Saying as much does not mean that Elvis was a "god" who is "worshipped" by his fans, but rather that Durkheim offers us a window on *human* interactions and helps to illuminate the electric thrill of Elvis as a celebrity.

In his 1912 book *The Elementary Forms of Religious Life*, Durkheim analysed the totemic religions of Australian clans. In his model, social groups share a set of beliefs that separate the sacred from the profane. This absolute cosmological distinction becomes represented in rites, myths and symbols. Totems are material objects (sometimes people) that are worshipped by the whole group because they focus and mediate the emotional force of social collectivity. The totem is a potent symbol because it determines what is sacred and what is profane. When clan members gather to worship their totem, it channels collective energy from the group back to the individual in a force that builds each follower's strength and confidence. Because followers feel connected through the totem, they are at the heart of the clan and feel empowered. This feeling emerges by a process of social electricity that Durkheim calls "effervescence".

While Durkheim's distinction between the sacred and profane is not very useful for commercial music, his specification of the mechanism of effervescence is relevant. His schema helps us to understand the social phenomenon that supports Elvis step by step. First, totems embody the collectivity of their following. Representations of Elvis constantly foreground his ability to attract a vast and dedicated audience. The Colonel promoted signs of commercial success and indicators of popularity as part of Elvis's image. A good example here is the practice of "shipping" vinyl records. According to Ray Walker of the Jordanaires, Elvis was marketed as a *popular* artist: at one point RCA was contracted to press a million copies of anything he recorded, which were sent to shops on a sale-or-return basis, allowing Parker to announce that his client had shipped a million.[307] Another example of the mass popularity strategy was the November 1959 greatest hits RCA compilation album release *50,000,000 Fans Can't Be Wrong*. The approach has found its echo in both the prolific graffiti on the wall outside Graceland and the invitations that Elvis Presley Enterprises makes to fans, asking them to participate in vast collective online photo mosaics.

Second, a totem is a focus of undivided attention. One of the Colonel's strategies to maximize Elvis's appeal was to cut other artists out of the spotlight in order not to marginalize his client. This approach relegated supporting musicians, avoided album sleeve credits, prevented Elvis from singing duets, and barred ensemble casting in his movies. As Durkheim says about the totem:

> This unusual surplus of forces is quite real: it comes to him from the very group he is addressing. The feelings provoked by his speech return to him inflated and amplified, reinforcing his own. The passionate energies he arouses echo back to him and increase his vitality. He is no longer a simple individual speaking, he is a group incarnate and personified.[308]

Durkheim's paragraph could just as well be a review of Elvis's *best live performances* as a statement on the sociology of religion.

Third, totems channel energy to individual followers. Music provides an ideal vehicle for the process, which is why it is often discussed in terms of energy and power. For Durkheim the voice allows a human connection because it creates a certain kind of intimacy: "the exhaled breath establishes a connection since it is part of us that is released to the outside".[309] As one fan explained, "Elvis's music is different. It's like it comes from inside him to inside you".[310] This deeply felt connection gives dedicated fans a form of personal support that can help get them through the trauma of illness, divorce or bereavement. They therefore relish the possibility of Elvis's attention. Reviewing a concert, one journalist reported, "When he starts to shake, the crowd bursts into a frenzy of squeals".[311] Fans always felt a great buzz from the thought of getting closer to Elvis. In Las Vegas, they would tip hotel staff in order to get seats as close to the stage as possible. Concert performances involved Elvis symbolically distributing his attention to fans in the form of scarves and kisses.

Finally, those individual feelings of empowerment established by focusing on the totem in turn engender a series of moral practices and obligations that sustain the life of the collective, including the observing of various prohibitions. Fans often maintain a strong sense of community and loyalty to Elvis. They carefully protect his reputation and aim to boost his fan base. In its manifesto, the Universally Elvis Fan Club of Memphis lists four specific aims: to return Elvis to number one, to bring him back into the public eye, to promote Elvis as a humanitarian, and to "be aggressive" towards all negative media by correcting or campaigning against them.[312] This charter is broadly typical of Elvis fan communities. "Boosting"—raising the public profile of the artist in order to increase his exposure and fan base—is a *central* practice of many Elvis fan clubs.[313] To use Durkheim's words, Elvis and his fans therefore "form an interdependent system in which all parts are linked and vibrate sympathetically".[314] Totemism is a *usual* element of music stardom, but Elvis and his phenomenon take it to an *exceptional* level.

2 Image

Elvis Presley's Hollywood films acted as showcases for his image and persona. He worked as an ambassador for Hollywood in the middle part of his career. This chapter considers Elvis's army service and Hollywood acting days in the wider context of his public image. Elvis's teenage years were shaped by his job as an usher at Loew's theatre in Memphis and he remained a film fan all his life. He talked in public about being in Hollywood as far back as 1955.[1] Once Colonel Parker took charge of his career and landed him a major record contract, the pair set their sights on the movie world. Hal Wallis, a veteran producer at Paramount, was persuaded to give Elvis a screen test. The Memphis singer posed with a guitar (without strings) and was rushed into his acting job in the film *Love Me Tender* (Webb, 1956). In August 1956, Elvis told an interviewer that his Paramount contract scheduled an annual picture for the next seven years.[2] The deal with Hal Wallis allowed him to make a movie with another studio every year.[3] It meant that the star and his manager were free to shop around and play off potential employers against each other. Between 1956 and 1969, Elvis had a lead role in 31 narrative feature films created to specifically target the American youth and family market. They are listed in the fifth appendix of this book. Some commentators have categorized these movies as a subset of the musical, but they do not fully conform to its traditional expectations. Elvis's films were never musicals in the classic, Busby Berkeley sense—namely, movies featuring a focus on set choreography, unmotivated singing, and themes of utopia and abundance. They represented a cycle, not a subgenre, one designed around an iconic performer.

Popular music has a political dimension, in part, because it can express the social changes to which politicians respond. Populism, a term from politics, means the approach taken by individuals who reflect the concerns of ordinary people. Societies are usually ruled by elite minorities, but in democracies, where everyone gets a vote, populist figures can gain broad public support. With his unique package of youth, looks and music, Elvis emerged as a prominent figure at a time when individuality was becoming celebrated by society, and populism emerging within electoral politics. Even as Elvis's music implicitly questioned social conventions—perceived sexual repression, a lack of inclusion—he embraced the consumer boom and enjoyed a life of leisure activities, flash clothes, fast food and faster cars. For some, Elvis's fusion of roots music genres located him as a traitor to his race and its codes of propriety. His personal approach, however, was to disown the "rebel" label, constantly show deference to family, and accept the commercial process as a way of pleasing the people. Elvis's general refusal to enter the fray of political causes *was itself political*, and gradually located his image as the ambassador for an inclusive form of universal humanism. In effect, he was a young populist who spearheaded a wave of mass culture.

In the twentieth century, some commentators in the United States hoped that people of different national backgrounds and races would unite in the "melting pot" of the nation. So much more interesting than any of the bland characters who inhabited his Hollywood features, Elvis was a walking contradiction—a figure who not only embraced and embodied generational shifts in American popular culture, but who also demonstrated that his nation could begin to achieve its "melting pot" aims. What the debate about his Hollywood output asks is whether he could fully express his gift in a highly commercial, collaborative environment where he was basically used as a gun for hire. For many, his acceptance of conscription marked the end of his time as the unwitting leader of a youth rebellion. Such accusations provide a good example of how Elvis was made to carry the weight of social change. His return to performance in a tuxedo on Frank Sinatra's television special, and his return to cinema screens in *G.I. Blues* (Taurog, 1960), are often said to mark the start of a new phase in his constantly changing career. In the 1960s, his efforts to sidestep the controversies surrounding rock'n'roll and become a family entertainer finally succeeded. The decade has been presented as a period in which he lost his edge.

Supposedly, and despite a wealth of information to the contrary, Elvis simply joined the army and acted in bland and uninspiring movies. Presley's Hollywood years, however, ultimately *extended* his appeal. The critical discussion about his less appreciated Hollywood output is not just about the industry or the fans; its root lies with our ambivalent relationship to Elvis himself as a representative of social democracy through the imperfect means of the marketplace. His career began with a translation of marginalized cultural formations into the mainstream, so his image became associated—almost accidentally—with democratic ideals. It was not just that Elvis was offering low culture. His Hollywood output showed that he was rather a translator of *all* forms into, as his 1961 RCA studio album put it, *Something for Everybody*. From this perspective, Elvis was never likely to please all the people all the time—and yet, more than any other popular music artist, he defined a musical centre ground by reflecting a majority following. It was no wonder, then, that his later experiments with social consciousness—embodied in message songs like 'In the Ghetto', 'If I Can Dream', and 'Walk a Mile in My Shoes'—were themselves limited by a certain unwillingness to mark his cards and take a firmer stance on issues such as civil rights.

At least according to early girlfriend June Juanico, Elvis hated the idea that he would star in musicals.[4] In April 1956, he explained to an interviewer from KMAC in San Antonio, Texas, "I've had people ask me was I gonna sing in the movies ... I'm not, I mean as far as I know, 'cause I took strictly an acting test and I wouldn't care too much about singin' in the movies".[5] Elvis's career in the 1960s has therefore been understood as descending into mediocrity, compromised in a search for short-term profits. In part, this explanation frames rock'n'roll as a revolutionary youth movement that paved the way for civil rights protest and the counterculture.

At the time of the original theatrical releases, audiences simply did not have access to the amount of information that we now have about Elvis. Douglas Brode has ventured the only book-length academic analysis of Elvis's movie features. One of the few apparent problems with Brode's analysis, however, is his tendency to read Elvis's screen image in relation to the "real" Elvis, a figure who we only *now* know about through various factual nuggets. Brode argues that life imitates art in Elvis's celebrity profile, and that there are many parallels between Elvis's biography and film work. Some connections can be seen, but we must not make the mistake of reading too much of the star's life into his music or film output. As a Hollywood actor, one problem that Elvis had was that everyone watching him already knew he was a star musician. This made the idea of Elvis constantly becoming a new character something that lacked full credibility. His immense popularity as an iconic performer effectively eclipsed his on-screen characters, preventing audiences from fairly assessing him as an actor. For this reason, when Elvis's film roles are discussed here, he is conjoined with them, as Elvis/Clint or Elvis/Vince, etc. After all, we are seeing Elvis on screen *first* and his character *second*.

Rather than attempting to critically rescue Elvis's narrative features, the aim in this chapter is to understand the extent to which those seemingly apolitical moments of entertainment spectacle reflected the concerns of their time. While it is possible to quibble with the edges of the Elvis cinema canon and its borderline cases, this chapter does not aim to critically rescue Elvis's blandest fare. Instead it will suggest that the critics have got it wrong in a different way. The 1960s Hollywood years should not be consigned entirely to what one bootleg album sarcastically categorized as *Elvis's Greatest Shit* (RCA Victim, 1982). At least in a sociological sense, Presley films remain worthy of attention precisely because they were so permeable to the social and commercial concerns of their era. Though Elvis films explored a series of perennial Elvis-related topics, their themes were much broader in scope. The films began to reflect a transitional period of American history—a time that marked the emergence of high modernity and was defined by the gradual, somewhat fraught integration of the melting pot. The films drew upon Elvis's image to carefully address changing gender and class relations. They reference both past roots—cowboys, communities, steamboats, carnivals—and future technologies—helicopters, racing cars, jet airplanes, media industries. Through the soft focus lens of family entertainment, Elvis's Hollywood features chart the changing social relations of a particularly tumultuous era of American history, one characterized by the struggle for racial equality, growing independence of women, rise of the baby boomer generation, and emergence of the permissive society. The movies frequently portray Elvis as a carefree Southerner who is comfortable in a new society. There might therefore be *sociocultural* reasons not to ignore the films, even ones as aesthetically limited as *Kissin' Cousins* (Nelson, 1964) or *Harum Scarum* (Nelson, 1965).

Upon close inspection, Elvis's films were all different. As this chapter will show by analysing a sample, their thematic DNA recombined in ways that constantly updated Presley's image in a new era. My argument is that the ways in which Elvis was *already* apprehended constantly guided his screen image. In turn, his Hollywood persona has shaped our understanding of him as an individual. The best approach to his movie years is therefore not so much chronological as thematic.

Evolutionary theory provides suitable concepts to explain the interaction of the different threads. Its emphasis on experimental variation, competition and natural selection neatly summarizes the concerns of Hollywood scriptwriters who compounded different elements of Elvis's image in their attempts to weather a rapidly changing social environment. More specifically, to begin with, Elvis was a star that achieved the American dream. When he first walked into Sun Studio he had *two* discernible ambitions: to be a romantic ballad singer and to be a film star in the style, perhaps, of the actor James Dean. Instead he found himself bringing musical excitement to a new generation interested in bopping country and blues. Elvis was therefore known as an artist who came from the Southern margin of his nation and represented its hopes for assimilation. As a young rock'n'roller, he was framed as a troubled outsider—a delinquent. He was criticized for igniting female lust, but scriptwriters implied that beyond his sensual abandon lay a refusal to fully grow up. When youth culture moved into a new phase that was both saucy and innocent, Elvis embodied the zeitgeist. In the context of a changing marketplace, the different strands of his screen image gradually diversified and began to accommodate more adult complexity.

Country Cousin

Elvis's first film, *Love Me Tender*, was a western in which he played in a supporting role as one of the Reno brothers. The film made a movie hero of him, but that was primarily because he was already a star recording artist. His debut picture was controversial both because Elvis was reduced to a supporting role and because his character died at the end of it—a move that some thought would damage his reputation with fans. Several of his early film roles, in different ways, also painted him as a *country cousin*: an innocent unaccustomed to the slick ways of modernity and bright lights of the city. In Paramount's *Loving You*, from 1957, Elvis played the upcoming country singer Deke Rivers. About two-thirds of the way through, on a country ranch, Elvis/Deke accompanies himself on acoustic guitar as he sings the title tune to his belle Dolores, played by Susan Jessup. Their family picnic is disrupted, however, by the noisy arrival of sassy Ms Glenda Markle, played by Lizabeth Scott, in a shiny, new $10,000 Crown Convertible. After standing up and staring, one of the family quips, "Wow! The flying saucers have landed at last!" Elvis/Deke exclaims, "Boy! Where did this come from?" Glenda replies, "Right off the drawing board and into your life. It's all yours!" By negotiating between the old ways of the rural South and the glamorous and lucrative, but insincere business of country music, Presley's struggle became an indicative microcosm of the journey of his young and still growing country. Elvis's existing image was already consistent with the "country cousin" idea. His real birthplace in Tupelo had two rooms, no electricity or running water. His lifetime spanned roughly from the coming of the modern era to the rural South through to the middle class, high modernity of the 1970s—from the emotional prosperity of small town and extended family to a comparatively decadent and sterile era of disposable living and alienation. Elvis returned to different Hollywood versions of the countryside in *Wild in the Country, Follow That Dream, Kissin' Cousins* and other films.

Presley's "country cousin" image can be related to racial issues. Scholars such as Peter Nazareth have begun to understand Elvis as an intercultural figure.[6] Directed by Don Siegel and shot in Utah and California, *Flaming Star* (1960) was a western that became seen as one of Elvis's dramatic offerings. With Frank Sinatra and Marlon Brando originally considered for the lead role, it had some weighty elements of racial drama. According to Elvisologist Adam Victor, "Many critics and fans consider the movie to be one of the finest Elvis ever made, along with *King Creole*".[7] It was rather unfortunate, then, that the studio premiered it just a month after the Los Angeles debut of Elvis's other post-army feature *G.I. Blues*. With its constant atmosphere of tension and hostility, *Flaming Star* was less popular with the female audience. Its violence was more than fist fights. In the role of a half-breed native American, Elvis (as Pacer Burton) is torn between the contrasting cultural worlds of the Texan frontier. The film's tagline exclaimed, "CHOOSE! ... Between your White father and your Kiowa mother!" In revenge for some Indian attacks a White settler mortally wounds Elvis/Pacer's mother and he finds that racial prejudice stops people from helping her. In response, he joins her Indian tribe. He then returns home only to be told that Kiowa native Americans have killed his White father. Finally, he turns on his adopted tribe and, mortally wounded, rides off into the hills to face his own fate. Elvis/Pacer sides with factions of neither racial group, but instead with the humanitarian value of peace. *Flaming Star* peaked at number 12 in *Variety*'s box office survey on its week of release. Musically, Elvis was joined off-screen by the Jordanaires. At a surprise birthday party for his half-brother Clint, he opens the film with acoustic guitar in hand, reciting the folksy but kitsch ditty 'A Cane and a High Starch Collar'. Elvis and the director both fought to keep songs out of the movie, and one ('Summer Kisses, Winter Tears') was removed when a screen test audience laughed. *Flaming Star*'s lack of box office success guided the Colonel towards lighter fare.

While he had already assumed something of a half-breed role in the 1950s on the national stage as a Southerner performing a racially hybridized music genre, Elvis extended that aspect of his image in the 1960s as Hollywood continually presented him as a character who helped to defuse and consolidate the American melting pot. After *Flaming Star*, for instance, he was made a member of Los Angeles first nations Indian Tribal Council. Elvis's films suggested that if charm and music could help a token humble Southerner become so well integrated in mainstream society, there might be hope for all the marginalized people in America. Movie soundtracks significantly expanded Elvis's palate of musical styles beyond American vernacular genres. The safely hybridized identity of many of his Hollywood characters was reflected in a rapidly expanding film music catalogue as he sang Hawaiian music, reworkings of European folk tunes, Dixieland jazz, Neapolitan ballads, marching songs, bossa nova, and children's ditties.

Although Hollywood showcased Elvis as a mass entertainer, commentators understood that he promised something more. While he always embraced racial integration in his music, as an icon, Elvis gradually developed an image that was characterized by a focus on pleasure, an all-embracing universality and a refusal to take sides. Ironically, however, time proved that if Elvis was a country cousin, he was one at home with high technology, hedonistic sensuality and New Age philosophy. In real life, he might have eaten meatloaf, but he also wore *Super Fly* clothes, read the *Physician's Desk Reference* and dreamed of being a narcotics agent. In other words he represented a living connection between the old and the new.

Juvenile Delinquent

Directed by Richard Thorpe, Elvis's first film for MGM, *Jailhouse Rock*, brought together the same narrative that propelled *Loving You*—achieving the American dream through folk music—with the fashionable 1950s trope of existentially troubled youth. Leiber and Stoller were now centrally involved in constructing the musical version of Elvis as screen icon. For the *Jailhouse Rock* soundtrack, Jean Aberbach of Hill & Range encouraged the pair, along with a series of other writers—including Aaron Schroeder, Sid Tepper and Roy

Bennett—to come in with fresh material. Their offerings were circulated to MGM, then RCA, but it was Elvis who made the final choices.[8] He decided to record several of Leiber and Stoller's strongest tracks: 'Jailhouse Rock', 'Treat Me Nice', 'I Want to Be Free' and '(You're So Square) Baby I Don't Care'. The pair met Elvis in person for the first time in May 1957 at Radio Recorders. Thoroughly expecting a culture shock, the songwriting duo was pleasantly surprised to discover common ground with him when discussing rare R&B singles. They also learned that he was a hard-working perfectionist in the studio.[9]

In *Jailhouse Rock*, Elvis stars as the feral Vince Everett, a singer who ends up in jail for his propensity towards violence. He befriends two parental figures—Peggy Van Alden (played by Judy Tyler) and prison insider Hunk Houghton (played by Mickey Shaughnessy)—who guide him through the music industry in ways that border on exploitation. Like *Loving You*, *Jailhouse Rock* portrayed Elvis as a poor boy who eventually managed to sing in a plush sound studio surrounded by movie cameras. The film's most iconic dance scene featured its title song performed in a stylized Jailhouse. Mexican choreographer Alex Romero arranged this dream-like sequence around Elvis's own gestures, because the star did not easily take choreographic direction.

Already known as a rock'n'roller, Elvis was soon framed by Hollywood as a troubled outsider. As youth culture became prominent and controversial in the mid-1950s, its most significant Hollywood representative, James Dean, personified the idea of the tragic teenager. Although Elvis seemed somewhat less internally tortured than Dean, he aspired to play the same kind of tragic hero.[10] A key aspect of the singer's image is the question of his control, or lack of it, as an individual. In tune with the intellectual currents of his time—currents that were having a profound impact on society—Elvis was increasingly positioned as a troubled and rebellious hero.

As a *collective* culture, the hurricane that was rock'n'roll arguably marked the start of a gradual social shift towards sexual liberation. Those who spearheaded the music provoked anxieties that led to them being framed as deviant in the media, and the music becoming a kind of permissive soundtrack to delinquency. One convenient explanation for delinquency was the idea that deviant young people came from difficult, unbonded or overly bonded family backgrounds. This promoted the explanation that there might be psychological issues behind casual attitudes to sex. Elvis's seductive teasing on stage incited female audiences. Given what else people knew about him, movie narratives could easily frame his motivation as a refusal to grow up. In his studies of psychological maturation and the human mind, drawing on the classic play *Oedipus Rex*, the famous analyst Sigmund Freud argued that male children go through an Oedipal stage of male psychosexual maturation as they grow. Briefly, Freud argued that when young boys bond with their mothers, they reach a point of wishing to be "romantically" bonded in a couple with them, and it means they can see their father as an obstacle or threat. Oedipal desire emerges after the child realizes that he is a separate individual, but lasts only as long as his "first love" is not revealed as a product of immature thinking. To mature, boys have to get beyond their Oedipal desire and grow up, and find a partner around their own age. Society helps them by making mother-love a taboo, at least in its sexual form (incest). Nevertheless, for Freud, the Oedipal stage of maturation frequently leaves unfinished business. In his 1926 essay *The Question of Lay Analysis* he explained:

> With the end of the early sexual period [of psychosexual maturation in childhood] it should normally be given up, should radically disintegrate and be transformed; and the results of this transformation are destined for important functions in later mental life. But as a rule this is not effected radically enough, in which case puberty brings about a revival of the [Oedipus] complex, which may have serious consequences.[11]

The Oedipal stage, for Freud, is thus a *typical* phase of individual personal development that is entered into and then abandoned. It represents part of growing up, but what is also normal is that the process is not perfectly completed. While individuals face residual challenges from this stage of psychosexual development in adulthood, a minority experience "serious consequences" when they try to form stable adult relationships.

Whether one believes in the "truth" of Freudian ideas or not is irrelevant: they were in circulation as a common theory of human psychology in the 1950s and 1960s. Freudian ideas were in the air. They functioned as generative frameworks for myth-making in popular culture and were referenced by various image shapers: scriptwriters, journalists, commentators and other professionals who critically interpreted individual identity. Epitomized by parental abandonment issues, Oedipal patterns were already a common explanation for behaviour in popular fiction. Consider, for example, Elia Kazan's 1955 film *East of Eden*, where James Dean plays the troubled son of a brothel owner who struggles with his father, a righteous preacher. Then, of course, there was Alfred Hitchcock's 1960 film *Psycho*, a film in which the Oedipally-arrested Norman Bates keeps the corpse of his mother in his basement and kills a girl from his own generation. While Elvis was nothing like Norman Bates, given the prominence of Freudian thinking, it is hardly surprising that his closeness to his mother became part of his image, both as a singer and movie actor.

As the celebrity spotlight rapidly widened beyond Elvis and included his immediate family, he became known as a young man who was unusually close to his mother. It was well known in his era and almost inevitably lent itself to a particular reading. In Freudian terms, Elvis exhibited Oedipal characteristics and appeared to fit the template. One aspect of such a reading is the idea of the mother that retains an abnormally close connection with her son. Elvis's mother encouraged her son by transmitting her ethics.[12] They had a very close relationship. According to Alan Fortas, Elvis loved his mother "like no one on this earth".[13] Elvis famously recorded one of his Sun vanity discs as a present for her. Recalling his first visit to the Memphis Recording Service, Elvis explained, "I made it to surprise her. When she played it, it was me singing ... I never did sing that much in my life".[14] Equally, a young Elvis explained to an interviewer in 1956 that he constantly telephoned his parents:

> Well, my mother ... especially my mother ... she is always worried about a wreck, or something ... me getting sick... so I have to let 'em know, 'cause she's not in real good health anyway. And if she worries too much it might not be good for her. So I make it a habit of callin' every day.[15]

In *Elvis Answers Back* magazine the star announced that people loved the swimming pool at his house on Audubon Drive, "And momma, *my best girl*, is learning to swim, too".[16] According to one writer from the *Memphis Press-Scimitar*, Gladys was "very possessive".[17] After describing Southern matriarchy, biographer Elaine Dundy said of Elvis's mother, "In short, she was the person [in the Presley family] with the greatest power".[18]

During the rock'n'roll era, Elvis's mother-love, it could be argued, was a way to relocate his sexual availability as something that suggested he was socially safe, not an indication of an identity or attitude that was deviant or threatening.[19] Since he loved and obeyed his mother, the story implied, he might not follow through to consummate any sexual come-ons. Moreover, mother-love proved he was not *unloving*. He might be able to transfer that love to an appropriate woman if she came along. Elvis's on-screen stage performance of the song 'Got a Lot o' Livin' to Do' as Deke Rivers in his 1957 film *Loving You* is interesting in that respect. In a film often taken to be the nearest thing to a "real" Presley biopic, a key scene shows Elvis/Deke moving charismatically on a fictional television show. Amidst the young crowd a small group of older ladies watches Elvis/Deke perform. One initially disapproves, but she is soon won over by the crowd's response. His gyrations may be potentially interpreted as sensually exciting, she realizes, but they are *just for show*. It is notable that Elvis's actual parents also appeared on screen in the crowd. In other words, mother-love helped to position Elvis, not as a "damp squib" on the youth market, but as a dynamic performer who, when he did sing rock'n'roll, could be accepted by parents. His greater social acceptability could only serve to enlarge his audience across different geographic regions, taste brackets, age groups and classes. While the familial bond between Elvis and Gladys Presley was real—her support sustained him in the early years, and her loss was evidently catastrophic to his life—at the same time, it became a part of his legend. For some years there was a sense in which Elvis enjoyed life and yet appeared vulnerably arrested, never quite assuming mature adulthood. His youthful image united teenage rebellion with boyish charm. When Gladys died in her early forties from heart failure after being hospitalized for hepatitis, Elvis's grief was deep, sincere and palpable. Photographers captured the moment in the summer of 1958 as Elvis sat on the steps at Graceland with his father. Perhaps even more than news of his army service, such photos reminded audiences that there was a normal person behind the image.

Fan communities for contemporary artists often write fictional stories around male characters entering into periods of emotional turmoil. One fan fiction genre is known as 'hurt/comfort' or 'H/C' for short. 'H/C' is arguably as much a form of identification as a genre. It is notable that Elvis fans very rarely, if ever, write amateur fan fiction. One explanation might be that Elvis's estate might not approve, but another is that he already has a very full story. His life, at least as fans perceive it, functions as a kind of soap opera in which a real extended Southern family—the Presleys—has become extraordinarily public due to the success of one member. Seeing a popular figure facing personal loss in public allowed many viewers to feel empathy. Gladys's passing presented itself as both a tragedy and an obstacle for Elvis: something that, like the death at birth of his twin Jesse Garon, had to be overcome. The idea that he had an extended emotional struggle with his mother's loss offers an argument that complicates the notion that he was simply worked into oblivion by his own capitulation to commercial pressures. Once Elvis's mother died, however, a door was left open in his public image that suggested he might mature more smoothly by transferring the energy of his remaining attachment on to a partner. Reflecting the view of a range of writers, Brode said of Elvis, "He projected emotions associated with his own deceased Gladys onto Priscilla".[20] He also noted that Elvis gave both women the same nickname ("Satnin").[21] Somewhat debatably, Brode goes on to explain how Elvis's lack of sexual intimacy after the birth of his daughter can be read as a kind of Priscilla-as-Gladys incest taboo.[22] Together with his isolated celebrity status, the way that Elvis's perceived Oedipal struggle generated emotional distance in his relationships has been read as a cause of his personal downfall. Commenting on a telephone call made toward the end of Elvis's life, Red West described him as, "A boy in a man's body who could not handle the celebrity that he had now become".[23]

Beyond any question of its truth, the Oedipal pattern has significant explanatory power as a frame through which to interpret Elvis's celebrity image. In 1956, the singer supposedly quipped about marriage, "Why buy a cow when you can get the milk through the fence?"[24] The line might have been read as a clarion call to free living, but the fact that it came in the context of Elvis being especially close to his mother gives it an Oedipal hue. Freudian explanations could easily be transferred to the youth market to justify the acts of real or fictional delinquent villains and anti-heroes. In July 1956, Hy Gardner gingerly asked: "What about the rumour that you once shot your mother?" Elvis replied, "Well I think that one takes the cake, I mean [laughs]. That's about the funniest one I've ever heard".[25] Of course Elvis never shot Gladys, but the myth frames rock'n'roll as a kind of symbolic violence, a limited attempt to break away from Oedipal bonds. Struggles against the pattern therefore got mixed up in the idea that the music was about breaking away from parental stricture. Furthermore, Elvis's relationship with Gladys makes him seem vulnerable and appealingly childlike. Mother-love guaranteed the social conservatism that marked Elvis out as no threat to the modern family—what Ed Sullivan called "a real decent, fine boy"—but it also made him tantalizingly *less available* to female fans. In other words, a true lover would have to *seduce him* into growing up.

While his loyalty towards his mother had been a prominent part of his image in the 1950s, Elvis's boyish charm came to the fore as his career progressed on to the terrain of family entertainment. *Loving You* was the first film in which Elvis played the lead, and it was one of the earliest films to play up the Oedipal side of his image. In the film, as Deke Rivers, he is an orphan who succeeds on the country circuit with the help of a sassy older woman called Glenda, played by Lizabeth Scott. Glenda encourages Elvis/Deke to call her "Mama". Such women, and the relationships they evoke, are akin to *femme fatales* in Elvis's films. Before he can fully grow up and find the energy to commit to a partner of his own age, any potential of a sexual or romantic entanglement with these surrogate mother figures has to be resolved.

Perhaps because it so naturally included great music *and* located Elvis's image within existing co-ordinates (as both existential, Oedipal and intercultural), *King Creole* has been seen by many as Elvis's finest feature film. Before shooting, it was already a successful novel and off-Broadway play called *A Stone for Danny Fisher*. Seamlessly directed by veteran Michael Curtiz, the film emphasized its New Orleans locations. Somewhat in the sultry style of a Tennessee Williams play, it opened with ballad-singing traders wandering down an early morning street. Bereft of his parents—just like he was in *Loving You*—and working hard to help his father keep the family afloat, Elvis/Danny finds expression in both violence and music. His school principal, Mr Evans, says, "You have all the earmarks of being a hoodlum; a hoodlum or a hustler or whatever you call it". Elvis/Danny replies, "I'm not a hoodlum. I am a hustler". He is streetwise. After he has beat up one boy in a fight, the boy's brother tries to attack him in a local back alley with a knife. When Elvis/Danny defends himself, the mobster says, "Good boy—he fights real dirty".

King Creole contains some excellent music. More and more songs were added to the film script until there were 11 in total. Nevertheless, the music emerged relatively seamlessly from the story, with Elvis/Danny gaining greater control over his musical numbers as he achieves mastery of his life. When he sings 'Trouble', he is backed by Black jazz musicians who are dressed in bowler hats. Elvis/Danny the nightclub singer here is jerky and jiggy, clicking his fingers and moving forward in a stylized side-to-side walk, as if his energy is held in check but barely contained by the music. During 'Dixieland Rock' he is energetic, clapping and in control of his band. By the time he sings 'New Orleans' he is in a club that is lit more like a television studio. The style is Vaudeville meets Dixieland and his on-screen audience is noticeably more adult than in earlier pictures like *Loving You*, with no screaming girls in evidence. 'King Creole' functions in a similar way, with Elvis on guitar. The film ends with two more traditional ballads—'Steadfast' and 'As Long As I Have You'—complete with the Jordanaires accompanying Elvis on backing offscreen. Beyond Elvis's own involvement, *King Creole*'s stomping, up-tempo title track was an amalgam of Leiber and Stoller's finely-honed song craft, the Jordanaires' urgent vocals and Scotty Moore's jazzy fretwork. In the end, though, RCA decided to release 'Hard Headed Woman' as Elvis's next single.[26]

Beale Street in Memphis has long been known as one where Black visitors enjoyed themselves in bars and clubs, a street associated by some with illicit activity such as gambling. *King Creole* portrays Elvis/Danny as smouldering and internally troubled. He operates as a stray cat in a town where Bourbon Street was the allegorical equivalent of Beale. Medovoi has taken this further, noting that Elvis/Danny was both associated with subordinate identities (prostitutes, ethnic minorities) and critical of his impotent, downwardly mobile, White middle-class father. As Medovoi notes, *King Creole* therefore relocates *Elvis*'s Oedipal struggle by situating it as part of a class struggle too.[27] The feisty Elvis/Danny fights to assume his manhood against forces that aim ultimately either to emasculate him—his father's safe, but spineless middleclass idealism—or exploit him (Walter Matthau's gangster commercialism). His journey reflects the fraught narrative of America itself, struggling to bring marginalized citizens into the heart of the melting pot without either homogenization or exploitation. It is Elvis's story too, as a *creolized* performer who represents the symbolic potentials of that project.

An Oedipal narrative is prominent in *King Creole*. The film references Elvis/Danny's absent mother and portrays him as an abandoned man-child character that has had to grow up fast, because his father is inadequate. Elvis/Danny chastises him for not fighting back, for his past lack of assertiveness in life. At one point when his father urges him to return to education, Elvis/Danny angrily says, "You go to school—I'm going to make a buck". *King Creole* also offers older characters that Elvis/Danny can project on to as substitute "parents", figures who must dispatched in the plot as part of his Oedipal maturation: the gangster Maxie Fields (played by Walter Matthau) and his bad girl moll Ronnie (played by Carolyn Jones, who later starred as Morticia in *The Addams Family*). After they are introduced bickering in a club, Elvis/Danny sings 'Steadfast, Loyal and True' to them, and leaves by defending Ronnie with a pair of broken bottles, saying, "Now you know what I do for an encore". Eventually, Elvis/Danny's "bad" father substitute—the nasty, over familiar and objectifying Maxie—gets his thugs to beat Elvis's inadequate "real" screen father. Perhaps through guilt, Maxie then relents and pays for the old man's hospital operation. The surgeon says, "Maxie Fields—strange man, isn't he? Very coarse, vulgar, and very powerful". Angered by Maxie's violence, Elvis/Danny beats him up in return and the gangster's boys then take revenge. Meanwhile Elvis/Danny's career is blossoming under the guidance of his "good" father: the nightclub owner Charles Le Grand. Elvis/Danny's screen sister, who looks very similar to his lover, ends up with Le Grand. After Maxie's moll Ronnie has seduced Elvis/Danny, Maxie kills her, and is then drowned by a mute mutineer from his own mob.

Innocent Hedonist

Filmed on location in Florida, *Girl Happy* (Sagal, 1965) had been lined up as *Girl Crazy*, indicating its focus on riotous young lust. The movie represents an example of Elvis's contribution to the beach party cycle. The cycle was inspired by Columbia Pictures' CinemaScope offering, *Gidget* (Wendkos, 1959). Starring Sandra Dee and spawning two sequels, the film was also remade for television. Associated with the famous youth exploitation independent studio, American International Pictures, the beach party cycle proper started in 1963 with *Beach Party*, directed by William Asher. By that point, of course, Elvis had already appeared in *Blue Hawaii*. Beach party films tended to mix the sexy innocence of musicals with the fun of Doris Day capers. In 1965 the genre was at its height, with several bikini films hitting the box office. MGM executive Joe Pasternak, a Hungarian-born Jew, had dabbled in the trend. First he expressed interest in producing *Gidget*. Next he got involved in producing *Where the Boys Are* (Levin, 1960), a film that portrayed Fort Lauderdale as a hedonistic student paradise. It was Pasternak who produced *Girl Happy*.

When Elvis returned from the army, the society he re-entered had changed significantly. Films like *Girl Happy* were indicative of a significant shift in society. Young women began to find more confidence, question tradition, seek more choice, and to determine how they should live. Some were deciding to define themselves less around their potential place as wives, and to stay in work and postpone marriage. Within mainstream society, sex before marriage was becoming increasingly acceptable even though it had been framed as delinquent, foolish or deviant a few years earlier. In 1960 a female contraceptive pill branded as Enovid was introduced on to the market. It allowed women to control the possibility of their pregnancy, a change that would eventually help to define the looser sexual habits of the permissive society era. Initially, however, popular culture actually became less radical. The tide turned significantly against rock'n'roll. The mainstream of the pop charts appeared more conservative. Elvis was, of course, a leading figure in this shift: between the mid-1950s and early 1960s he moved from fast, edgy numbers to ballads like 'Love Me Tender' and gospel material. In that sense, he was ahead of his time both for being racy and for then being conservative.

Presley's original pursuit of rock'n'roll was a way to address a growing female youth market. From that perspective, his turn to softer sounds was entirely consistent with the marketing styles that emerged to address that audience. Chart analyst Joel Whitburn listed singers like Frankie Avalon, Paul Anka, Del Shannon and Bobby Vinton leading the American hit parade during the era. As Whitburn explains, "Pop music mellowed with the infusion of strings ... then was enlivened by the California harmonies of the Beach Boys and their New York counterparts, The Four Seasons".[28] Elvis was often marketed alongside younger teen angels of the era in girls' romance magazines like *Valentine* and *Mirabelle*.[29] As early 1960s youth culture moved through a more conservative phase, Hollywood used Elvis to reflect a time that was initially both saucy and innocent. Shifts in transport technology and the tourism industry in the late 1950s and early 1960s facilitated a shared fantasy of luxurious global leisure. The idea of taking vacations in exotic places gained popularity as advances in air travel cut down flying times and costs. New technologies allowed audiences to imagine new realms of glamour, exoticism and sophistication. The emergent era of leisure was reflected in adult styles of popular music centred on sounds like Brazilian samba.[30] Films like *Blue Hawaii* set in exotic locations capitalized on the growth of tourism and fitted in with these romance narratives.

Douglas Brode's work has done much to capture the permeability of Elvis's cinema to issues from the era of rapidly changing sexual politics. The gender ambiguity of Elvis was not so much *within* his own image—he was always framed as a seductive heterosexual male—but in *how* his seductiveness should be interpreted. As Brode put it, "Whether Elvis Presley was pro- or anti-feminist depends on how one chooses to read his work".[31] Commentators such as the Marxist folk historian Dave Harker argued that Elvis's popularity with women reflected a distinctly *macho* ideal: that Elvis was a skilled seducer who aggressively achieved a series of conquests.[32] However, feminist sociologist Sue Wise noted that not all fans shared the stud or "butch god" reading of the singer. In fact, Harker assumed that Elvis revelled in his own image in order to manipulate vulnerable admirers. Wise suggests that there is an alternative reading that frames Elvis as a "teddy bear": a relatively benign and non-sexual friend.[33]

In contrast to the work of Harker, there is also another perspective on Elvis that sees him more as a "U.S. male". While not all of his audience may have taken him that way, Elvis "the pelvis" was marketed as an objectified commodity for female consumers: a ladies' man successfully groomed to serve a marketplace governed by female desire. From that perspective, the singer is potentially sexual, but on terms that suit women rather than disadvantage them and ignore their dignity. The rise and consistency of Elvis's *female* audience from the mid-1950s onwards formed a bedrock of continued support that underpinned his success. In this paradigm, *both* the rocking "butch god" *and* the crooning "teddy bear" Elvis were, in a sense, different sides of the same coin. Throughout his career, his edgy, seductive and pleasing styles ultimately served the same purpose. Rather than a simple case of subdued edginess, the fluctuations in his musical output represented complementary aspects of his consistently masculine appeal. Furthermore, from the "U.S. male" perspective, Elvis is not simply fodder for teenage girls' *sexual* fantasies, he is also pitched at their *romantic* ones: growing up, finding a boyfriend, having a romance, and potentially settling down. Certainly, once Presley entered Hollywood he served *its* ideological concerns, but his output also had to shift with a rapidly changing marketplace.[34] "Early Elvis films", claimed Brode, "argued against the dichotomization of women into good and bad girls; [Elvis's last fictional feature] *Change of Habit* takes that idea to its extremes".[35] To read Elvis as objectified by a female gaze does not entirely suggest that he led the headlong charge towards sexual liberation. Instead it implies that, as gender norms shifted, he constantly reflected girls' concerns about appropriate men.

    Fun in Acapulco is an interesting addition to Elvis's hedonistic films in that it includes intercultural themes. While Elvis was finishing *Girls! Girls! Girls!* Hall Wallis and writer Allan Weiss were planning the feature. With its exotic, picture-postcard mise-en-scène, the movie was a classic example of the travelogue category, though, characteristically, Elvis did no location shooting. Biographers have suggested that he was not welcome in Mexico after passing comment on the local women, although an alternative explanation might be the Colonel's now-known reluctance to go abroad.[36] Ironically, Paramount distributed fake passports as promotional material for the film. Elvis's movie characters often have casual labouring occupations. In *Fun in Acapulco* he plays an ex-trapeze artist called Mike Windgren who finds work as a boat hand. After the opening credits show romantic beaches at dusk, he gets accosted, first by a drunken party of singing Mexicans, and next by an adventurous young blonde. Elvis/Mike brushes her off as under-age, recalling a moment in *Follow That Dream* where, as a romantic object, he acts as arbiter of womanhood. Next he enters a smoky club in a favela, where he sings 'Vino, Dinero y Amor' with a whooping party of Mexicans in sombreros. When the under-age girl's father—a "bad" father figure, like Big Frank in *Girl Happy*—catches up, he confronts Elvis/Mike for leading her astray. Before pacing off in anger, the accused singer snarls, "She was a delinquent long before anyone contributed anything".

    Fun in Acapulco contains a love-triangle plot where Elvis/Mike is torn between two women: a female bullfighter (played by Elsa Cárdenas) and Marguerita (played by Ursula Andress, fresh from the James Bond feature *Dr. No*). Will he go for the Latina or the White girl? At this time, except Conchita Cintrón, there were very few well-known real-life female bullfighters, but the character's key quality (as the discussion about marriage just before the sports car song attests) is that she is an *independent woman*, just as uncomfortable with the idea of marriage as any man. Meanwhile, Marguerita's "bad" father discusses national differences and their need to acquire American visas. When the two men meet, to discuss the idea of marrying for her visa, her dad snaps, "Peasant!" At one point Elvis/Mike says, "You can always rely on a foreigner to point out your faults". Marguerita's father replies, "You are a foreigner here". Intercultural themes were foregrounded in such ways. Elvis/Mike soon gets entangled with a jealous rival: a diving champion who, confident in the knowledge that his rival has a fear of heights, challenges him to the famous Acapulco high dive. The feat is especially difficult because Elvis/Mike's brother died when he fell off a high trapeze. The idea of a dead brother is a common trope in Elvis movies and it has been read as reflecting the loss of Jesse Garon Presley. *Fun in Acapulco* climaxes with Elvis/Mike successfully facing the dive as the ultimate test of his masculinity. In one of the last scenes before Elvis/Mike jumps, he genuflects at a Catholic shrine. After he emerges successfully from the dive, he talks about going home to Florida, and then sings a celebratory song *in Mexican* to the Mexican crowds—before the old men throw their sombreros in the air. During this thoroughly intercultural ending, while his rival greets him warmly, there is no clear sense that he is going with any of his two girls—although the matador has worn Ursula's red bikini and the film implies that Elvis/Mike is leaving with White Mexican Ursula (as he jumped for her sake).

The music of *Fun in Acapulco* exemplifies its festive atmosphere. After performing 'Vino, Dinero y Amor', Elvis/Mike develops a career as a nightclub singer, a role that echoed *King Creole* and was a convenient way to include performances naturally in the script and explore the exploitation of talent. *Fun in Acapulco* also has a plucky child character, an eight-year-old called Raoul Almeido, played by Larry Domasin, who becomes Elvis/Mike's "manager" and—as we now know, paralleling the demands of Colonel Parker, like some kind of cruel joke—demands half of the singer's earnings. At one point he says, "Girls are trouble, Mike, and if I'm your partner the trouble is half mine too". Elvis performs 'Mexico' with Raoul, continuing the theme of singing to children. Elvis also sings a Neapolitan ballad, 'El Toro', complete in a mariachi outfit. The Mexican theme continues when Elvis sings 'Marguerita' at an outdoor party with an eight-piece mariachi backing band. Later, introduced as "The North American with an exciting voice", he sings, 'The Bullfighter Was a Lady' in a Mexican cummerbund with a nightclub mariachi band. After singing the tawdry 'No Room to Rhumba in a Sports Car' *in a sports car*, he resumes his nightclub act, wearing a sharp cream 1950s suit and black tie. Backed by his dynamic band, he plays the keyboard and dances an electric, hip swivelling on-stage dance. At points in this film the directing is daring too: when his manager deals with clubs on the telephone, there is a trendy split-screen scene, the first in an Elvis film—perhaps in the wake of the Doris Day romcoms. While *Fun in Acapulco* peaked at number five in the *Variety* chart it failed to make its $3 million costs back in the home market, though international receipts put it in profit.

U.S. Male

First titled *Christmas in Berlin*, then *Café Europa*, *G.I. Blues* began location shooting eight months before Elvis finished national service. With its wooden puppets, the 1960 film suggested to American audiences that Europe was a quaint, romantic location. *G.I. Blues* was the first of nine films Elvis did with Norman Taurog. The Hollywood veteran, who was now in his sixties, had started as a child star before winning an Academy Award in 1931 as the young director of *Skippy*. He had continued as a studio workhorse, overseeing a string of Dean Martin and Jerry Lewis comedies in the 1950s. The *G.I. Blues* soundtrack album debuted at number six and hogged the top of the chart for six weeks, eventually selling over 3.5 million. Despite songwriters Leiber and Stoller's withdrawal from the project, *G.I. Blues* was packed with catchy numbers. RCA arranged with the Colonel to put 'Wooden Heart' out as a single in Europe.[37] Indeed, the *G.I. Blues* soundtrack LP was the commercial peak of one of Elvis's top years. In 1960 he made three films, recorded 51 sides, had three number one singles and scored a million-seller in the UK alone with 'It's Now Or Never'. The song slowly ascended the charts and stayed at the top for over a month. In continental Europe, because the melody was still under copyright, RCA compensated Hill & Range and released 'The Girl of My Best Friend' instead.[38] At that point Elvis represented 20% of the label's turnover and the *G.I. Blues* album eventually became his biggest-selling LP.[39]

G.I. Blues drew on Elvis's army duty and levered it as something that the public knew about him. To begin to understand its full meaning, that phase of his life needs analysis. This section will begin by thinking about his real army years. Back at the end of the 1950s, Colonel Parker had a policy of reducing audience contact with Elvis once a fever pitch of excitement had arisen. He surmised that over-exposure could easily ruin his artist's career. While working with country star Eddy Arnold, Parker forged a relationship with William Morris Agency president Abe Lastfogel.[40] Because of its great reputation, the talent agency was a good vehicle for promoting Elvis in the national media. After the third *Ed Sullivan* appearance, Parker withdrew Elvis from television and live touring, telling Harry Kalcheim of the agency in December 1957 that over-exposure would only harm his client.[41] The withdrawal policy helped to upgrade Elvis's celebrity status from popular music star to Hollywood icon.[42] Editing a compilation of early interviews in 1981, Mick Farren noted, "Elvis Presley's personality was virtually a closed book".[43]

There were exceptions to the blackout, of course, such as Elvis's tour of duty with the US army. Elvis's period in the forces as a model soldier shaped his image. He received his draft notice on December 19, 1957.[44] Induction involved a series of decisions that had to be carefully calculated on the part of both the US Army and on Elvis's side. In the wake of the Korean conflict, inducting one of the most popular music performers was a great coup for the army, because everyone knew he would act as a role model for thousands of working-class

Americans. Extending a pattern that emerged from the gospel releases, Colonel Parker knew that revealing Elvis's conservative side could only serve to endear the young man to parents in what might now be called middle America. The move into the army was partially designed to position his charge as a patriotic, clean-cut boy—a "peacetime war hero" not delinquent rebel.[45]

The decision to induct Private Presley as normal soldier rather than a special entertainer was a way to show audiences that the singer would get no special treatment for his celebrity. He entered the army on March 24, 1958, several months before his mother's death on August 14 that year. After completing basic training at Fort Hood, Texas, he was posted to Friedberg, Germany with the Third Armored Division. Elvis Presley served with the division from October 1, 1958, until March 2, 1960. Three days later, he was discharged from active duty with the rank of sergeant.

While he was in the army, Elvis was not worried that he would lose his status as a rock'n'roll rebel—personally, he never wanted the initial controversy—but he was very concerned that he might be deserted by his fans and lose his livelihood. The Colonel therefore made efforts to see that his charge would not be forgotten by the American public. There was the issue of finding new material. Stationed in Friedberg, Elvis's priority was now his army duty rather than singing career.[46] However, RCA had already kept plenty in storage from his previous recording sessions. The label kept up a steady stream of single and EP releases which included *Elvis Sails*, a profile-raising spoken word interview EP that sold around 100,000 copies.[47] The first army period musical release was a single featuring the blistering ballad 'One Night'. In March 1959 the label released '(Now and Then There's) A Fool Such As I'. 'A Big Hunk O' Love' followed in July.[48] After the Colonel suggested that he use home recording equipment, Elvis also taped a few songs while he was stationed in Germany, like the Drifters' 'Such a Night'. His home recordings in Bad Nauheim included versions of 'Danny Boy', 'Que Sera, Sera' and 'Hound Dog'.[49] None of this material was released by RCA at the time.[50] The label told the Colonel that singles sales were generally declining for all artists during this period.[51] Nevertheless, Elvis's sales were relatively buoyant; according to his manager, his music income topped $2 million within a year when he was away.[52] While the singer was abroad in Germany his films and records acted as a forum for fans to feel closer to him.

Elvis's spell in the army led to a significant extension of his retinue of male aides and bodyguards. By the time of his death, journalists had dubbed them the Memphis Mafia. Some of the earliest members, George Klein and Red West, were his friends from L.C. Humes High School. Charlie Hodge met Elvis in the army and was a significant musical influence. Other key members of the circle included Joe Esposito, Jerry Schilling, Marty Lacker and Alan Fortas. Another inner circle member, Elvis's friend Lamar Fike, said that the singer did not trust people or make friends easily; his entourage allowed him to feel comfortable. As *The Independent* put it in Fike's 2011 obituary:

Lamar Fike was one of Elvis Presley's career-long entourage who became the singer's friends, foils, scapegoats, bodyguards, road managers, lighting technicians, punch bags, babysitters (for the singer himself) and procurers of girls, pills or sweets. Or, as Fike put it, "his buffer zone".[53]

The Memphis Mafia created a kind of semi-permeable social barrier around their employer, inviting female admirers and staging parties. They maintained his mood in the state of equilibrium required for his personal and professional life. While their critics have viewed them as sycophantic and parasitic, it is evident that they were partially star-struck but individually talented people who gave up aspects of their ordinary lives to participate in a lifestyle that was both glamorous and fun. It is notable, too, that some of Elvis's retinue used their skills and connections to pursue successful careers in their own right, both before and after their leader passed away. Marty Lacker ran his own record label and at one point Jerry Schilling managed the Beach Boys. Beyond his macho persona, Memphis Mafia insider Red West also proved extremely versatile. Once Pat Boone had cut one of his songs in 1961, West began pitching material to Elvis.[54] He wrote the ballad 'Separate Ways' and the funky 'If You Talk in Your Sleep'. The former bodyguard found work as a character actor and stuntman after his friend died.

As Elvis neared the end of his tour of duty, plans were already in place for what was to be the first "comeback" of his career. Almost every teen magazine had featured Elvis while he was away. Some of the parents who had been concerned at his stage act now began to respect him. There was a pincer movement from the Colonel and publishers Hill & Range to tie up Elvis's first post-army single ('Stuck On You'), first TV appearance (Frank Sinatra's *Special* on ABC) and movie deal (Paramount's *G.I. Blues*).[55] Elvis returned from Germany on March 3, 1960 to pursue these various projects.[56] The Sinatra show was properly called, *The Frank Sinatra TIMEX Show: Welcome Home Elvis*. The Timex show attracted 65% of the evening's national audience and gained $125,000 for Elvis and his manager. Presley and Sinatra exchanged songs—and audiences—on the show, with Frank swinging his way through 'Love Me Tender' while Elvis tried his hand at 'Witchcraft'.

Elvis's initial studio output during this period was diverse. When he came out of the army, three-track tape technology had arrived, offering the possibility of post-session mixing.[57] Once Elvis returned from Germany, it was the Colonel who suggested that he record 'Are You Lonesome Tonight?', a staple popularized by Al Jolson.[58] The lilting ballad which was a little reminiscent of his first film score number, 'Love Me Tender', allowed both Presley's bold and gentle sides as a vocalist to shine through. He began recording material from his own record collection too, rather than exclusively using Hill & Range finds. At his first session back in RCA's Nashville studio, in April 1960, Elvis recorded Peggy Lee's smouldering arrangement of 'Fever' and a reworded version of the Neapolitan ballad 'O Sole Mio'. Sung, famously, as 'It's Now or Never', the song was captured in just four takes.⁵⁹ As part of his outstanding promise to Scotty Moore, when he got out of the army, Elvis also recorded 'Girl Next Door Went A-Walking', a song written by Thomas Wayne from Scotty's Fernwood Records label.⁶⁰ Scotty and D.J. Fontana resumed their places on Elvis's team and stayed in his pool of studio musicians for the next eight years.⁶¹ Bill Black, however, had a successful career with his own live combo and did not wish to return.

The sixth appendix in this book lists many of Elvis's key live and studio albums. Some of the post-army material was released on a new LP called *Elvis Is Back!* One of the interesting things about the album was that Elvis had begun to reduce his quotient of country and gospel in favour of a more polished, mainstream and inclusive, pop and Broadway style. Jørgensen reads this sound as a continuation of Elvis's ethos of racial integration, arguing that *Elvis Is Back!* represented the best album release to date:

> There was a new depth to his voice; his interpretations were increasingly sophisticated; the group was probably the best studio band in the business; the song selection was imaginative and varied, the technical quality excellent ... There was no strong country flavor, and only a hint of gospel in the voices of either Elvis or the Jordanaires. It was as if Elvis had invented his own brand of music, broken down the barriers of genre and prejudice to express everything he heard in all the kinds of music he loved.⁶²

What Jørgensen does not mention in this particular passage is that Elvis's image as a singing Hollywood star was rapidly overshadowing his popularity as an established recording artist. RCA had inadvertently become their own competitor by releasing both *Elvis Is Back!* and the *G.I. Blues* soundtrack in close proximity. Promoted by the film, sales of the latter significantly outsold the more acclaimed studio release, sending a message to the Colonel about where to concentrate his efforts. It was obvious that Hollywood was an invaluable tool, a form of marketing that made the team money rather than lost it. Once *Elvis Is Back!* ascended the charts, RCA also stopped releasing non-soundtrack EPs as the format had gone out of style.⁶³

Many music critics have painted Elvis as a phallic figure, erect for rock'n'roll, but "castrated" by mother-love, working-class deference, or his work on tame movies. Music writer Richard Meltzer follows this trope. In 1970, Meltzer described Elvis's April 1957 hit 'All Shook Up' as "the last of his important songs".⁶⁴ He argued that questions arose once Elvis included a traditional ballad like 'Love Me Tender' in his repertoire:

> Could Elvis now be considered a popular musician in the "adult", Muzak-oriented sense? Was rock'n'roll, not yet too many years old

as an identifiable movement, on the verge of fusion with the popular mainstream? Or was Elvis about to lose his designation as a rock'n'roll singer by flaunting "legitimate" popular music?[65]

In a musical sense, Meltzer's dilemma is problematic as Elvis was never *simply* a rock'n'roll singer. Songsters were the wandering blues minstrels of the early twentieth century, people who borrowed the songs they performed from widely shared collections. Elvis operated like a songster insofar as he also drew on a range of material for his repertoire. While Presley created some of the finest examples of rock'n'roll, his first ever (non-commercial) recording at Sun in 1953 was a cover of the Ink Spots' low-key ballad, 'My Happiness'.[66] Although his first four Sun releases only featured up-tempo material, his early stage sets also included slower numbers. When *Billboard* reviewed his second single—'Good Rockin' Tonight'—late in 1954, its writer claimed, "His style is both country and R&B, and he can appeal to pop".[67] If Elvis "turned" from making pure rock'n'roll records, it therefore happened much earlier than 'Love Me Tender'. Equally, his up-tempo music never fully went away, although, of course, rock'n'roll was a reduced element in the mid-period repertoire.

As soon as Elvis started active service, his army duty was associated with him *growing up*, something that was only compounded by the loss of his mother, befriending his future wife, who was called Priscilla Beaulieu back then, and expanding his musical repertoire. John Lennon's most famous dictum about his hero's changing career offers a way to further this discussion. Often slightly misquoted, the ex-Beatle's famous lines come from a BBC Radio 1 interview conducted two days before his own untimely death. In context, it was about the press framing Lennon as having gone "underground" because he did not speak to them in the late 1970s: "When Elvis died, people were harassing me in Tokyo for a comment. Well, I'll give it you now: he died when he went in the army. You know—that's when they killed him. That's when they castrated him, so the rest of it was just a living death".

In Lennon's reading, running scared that his stardom will melt away, "Elvis the Pelvis", the Hound Dog rock'n'roller, foolishly accepts the lucrative burden of family entertainment—signified by army photoshoots, bland ballads and formulaic movie roles—in exchange for losing his life-affirming rebelliousness, gyrating sexual potency, and personal freedom. There are bigger issues than Elvis at stake here. Lennon's choice of terminology was, perhaps, not simply a personal choice on his own part: it reflected the era of the permissive society, an era in part *shaped by rock'n'roll* where sexual activity, sometimes located under the banner of "free love", was politicized in ways that equated it with personal and social liberation. From this perspective, growing up and creating the nuclear family is viewed as a mechanism that entraps individuals in a repressive and regressive social system. From this perspective, in Elvis's case, Uncle Sam does the job of enforcing his social conformity by perceptibly ending the possibility that he can be understood as a genuine rock'n'roll rebel. Sexual promiscuity can itself be seen as symptom of Oedipal arrest, however, because it appears to block monogamous adulthood by substituting one lover with many. This formulation suggests that rock'n'roll was not dangerous because it represented the potential chaos of free living, but instead it positioned the promotion of casual sex as a symptom of Oedipal entrapment that also marked an emergent historical period of extended adolescence. One thing that the "castration" argument does is to draw a link between "Elvis the Pelvis", a person whose Oedipally-arrested adult character cannot quite place him inside a "normal" family, and Elvis the icon: an allegedly passive, working-class Southerner whose desperate gratitude for the material rewards of working in the entertainment industry becomes his downfall. Even that narrative is, however, not quite true. The "castration" argument ignores the creative freedom Elvis continually had when recording gospel music. Towards the end of the 1960s, furthermore, it was not any simple refusal to accept the obligations of commerce that helped him rejuvenate his creative role as a singer, but, initially, his decline *as a bankable Hollywood asset.* Hollywood and the army helped Elvis to become seen as a family entertainer, but he did not enter either to get over his mother, and, at least initially, his Hollywood and army success destroyed neither his popularity, creativity, nor social relevance. In some ways, films like *Jailhouse Rock, King Creole* and perhaps even *G.I. Blues* arguably helped him *attain* those things.

"Castration" is the term selected to drive home Lennon's critique, and is worth considering in more detail. Freud's views of castration were complex and developed over time. However, it is *fear of* castration, for him, that is actually associated with the *end* of the Oedipus complex. In other words, if a small boy understands himself as anatomically male, desires his mother, plus hates and wishes to eliminate his father, he may well begin to believe that his father will pre-emptively strike by emasculating him:

> In boys ... the [Oedipus] complex is not simply repressed, it is literally smashed to pieces by the shock of threatened castration ... its objects are incorporated into the ego, where they form the nucleus of the super-ego and give that new structure its characteristic qualities.[68]

In other words, childish fear of castration forces each boy, to some extent, to put aside his Oedipal yearnings and make further progress towards growing up. If one way to shift perceptions of Elvis's rock'n'roll persona from randy to respectable was to promote his evident love for his mother, his army duty could be perceived as threatening a kind of "castration" that took him away from both arrested Oedipal yearnings and adolescent sexual displays. In a 1958 news story called, "The Army Makes a Man Out of Elvis!" Jack Good wrote, "Well paralyse my pelvis! ... Now that Presley has gone into the Army it is possible that the most exciting phase of his career has come to a halt".[69] However, this reading is not quite correct, insofar as the drama of struggling to fully grow up continued to shape his music and screen career. The Oedipus complex was a flexible ingredient of Presley film plot structures that in retrospect helped audiences gauge the state of both changing gender relations and his transforming image. From that perspective both the rocking Elvis and the crooning Elvis were two sides of the same coin, the pivot of which was his female audience. He was always *marketed* as a ladies' man. From the mid-1950s onwards, the rise and consistent support of his *female* audience formed the bedrock that underpinned his success. In that sense, throughout his career Elvis served the same purpose, albeit in different ways. This "U.S. male" reading would imply that we should pay attention to two aspects of Elvis's Hollywood movies: the changing of his character, and those of his leading ladies. Rather than a simple case of "castrated" edginess, the fluctuations in his musical output represent *complementary* aspects of a consistently masculine appeal. Most focus, however, on Elvis's changing genre output attempts to locate a shift in his *perceived degree of social relevance*, framing rock'n'roll as a revolutionary youth movement that paved the way for civil rights and the 1960s hippie counterculture, and arguably ignoring the complexity of both Elvis and his changing era.

What is interesting is that when Elvis was first repackaged in *G.I. Blues*, his post-army feature, he evidently lost some of the adolescent dilemmas that shaped his earlier roles. Consider, for example, the way that Elvis/Tulsa and his fellow soldiers struggle with maturity. Such struggle formed a dramatic dimension of Elvis's screen personae for years to come. Rather than reflecting the taming of a rebellious delinquent, however, *G.I. Blues* amplified the conservative side of Elvis's image in the service of a new cohort of female spectators aiming to marry the ideal man, but also beginning to find equality on their own terms. Director Norman Taurog helped shift Elvis's image from troubled hillbilly delinquent to mainstream potential husband. While Elvis, as an adult, always embodied the more benign and utopian aspects of masculinity—affability, availability, humility, tenderness—his screen roles changed considerably to reflect the evolving pattern of gender relations of his time. *G.I. Blues* also promoted his image as a popular and potentially "tame" sex symbol. It put him firmly into boyfriend territory in a light romantic comedy that demonstrated how a good man might transition from the masculine world of army banter into a more balanced and functional family environment. All dressed up in his army uniform, as GI serviceman Tulsa McLean, Elvis pursues, dates and babysits in the film. He is an active member of his sexually obsessed peer group until he meets the elegant and independent Lillie (played by Juliet Prowse), a dancer who initially refuses to date GIs. Lillie is a capable and sympathetic person. She has confidence in the power of her sexual allure, knows what she wants, and is willing to proactively propose marriage. Elvis/

Tulsa begins by treating Lillie as a sex object, then sees her as a mother, before finally accepting her as a full woman. *G.I. Blues* implies that a man can sleep with a girl *and then* marry her.

If *G.I. Blues* showed that women could avoid playing to the objectifying stereotypes of immature men, then *Viva Las Vegas* took female autonomy up another notch. Written by a woman (Sally Benson) and filmed partly on location in Nevada, the movie took two months to shoot. Its credits feature the bright lights of the city's strip and set the film up as a celebratory spectacle of America's capital of leisure. In the role of Lucky Jackson, Elvis is introduced as a car mechanic working opposite a suave, European-accented rival Count Elmo Mancini (played by Cesare Danova, who closely resembled his counterpart from the previous film, *Fun in Acapulco*, Paul Lukas). In between them is the feisty, red-headed Rusty Martin (played by Ann-Margret), a children's swimming coach in hot pants who needs assistance with her car. After she drives off, the male leads head to Las Vegas to sample the stage shows and high life. After meeting the Count, Elvis/Lucky is soon introduced to his second obstacle in the movie, Rusty's father. The plot moves forwards when the Count attempts to seduce Rusty while Lucky/Elvis comically disrupts their meal in his role as waiter. As the Count laments, "Potato chips and champagne don't go too well together". His line quietly echoes Marilyn Monroe's classic *The Seven Year Itch* (Wilder, 1955).

Viva Las Vegas (Sidney, 1964) was patterned on the romcom tradition, yet it was also clearly a musical—a real celebration of dance—featuring Elvis paired with his strongest, most energetic female co-star. Indeed, Elvis was awarded third prize at the 1965 Laurel Awards for best male musical performance. *Viva Las Vegas* was also the movie that made driving a racing car a test of Elvis's masculinity and associated him with the glamour and pleasure of Las Vegas. In the movie Elvis/Lucky courts Rusty at the swimming pool and in the dance studio. Sharing the ultimate, extravagant, exuberant leisure fantasy date, within the first half hour they have danced, play-acted a shootout, water-skied and flown in a helicopter. Both clearly love every moment.

Whilst Elvis's characters assumed playboy-type roles in some of his early 1960s pictures, in *Viva Las Vegas* he stars opposite a fully rounded and vivacious woman who is willing to humiliate men for treating her like a sex object, who conforms to none of the stereotypical roles (mother figure, good girl or bad girl), and who wants marriage but only on *her* terms. As Steve Pond said, Ann-Margret was Elvis's equal in every scene. The pair actually sang Leiber and Stoller's 'You're the Boss' as a duet but it was left out of the movie.[70] Referencing an ascendant sense of female empowerment, in production the film was first named *Mister Will You Marry Me*.

As had already been the pattern for several years, highlights from the film's soundtrack music were released in EP form, then other tracks appeared much later on a double LP (with music from *Roustabout*). As the film progresses, a string of strong numbers comes on thick and fast: 'The Yellow Rose of Texas

/ The Eyes of Texas' in a Las Vegas cabaret, 'The Lady Loves Me' (a romcom duet with Rusty which ends with her pushing Lucky off a swimming-pool diving board—referencing the recent *Fun in Acapulco*) and 'C'mon Everybody' (in the dance studio, with Ann-Margret gyrating as much as Elvis). After Lucky meets Rusty's father he slows the pace down with the piano duet 'Today, Tomorrow and Forever'. This is one of the first film scenes where Elvis is sat at a piano. The movie immediately cuts into a floor scene where the dance style is surprisingly energetic and contemporary.[71] Both dressed in yellow, Elvis/Lucky jives with Rusty as a Black R&B vocal quartet called the Jubilee Four (backed off-screen by the Jordanaires) sing 'The Climb', a Leiber and Stoller number designed to capitalize on an era of dance crazes. A jiggy Elvis then launches into a memorable up-tempo guitar cover of Ray Charles's 'What'd I Say' featuring Rusty as his jiving partner and some acrobatic dancers.[72] The later numbers include solo songs by Ann-Margret, though her relatively weak vocals meant she did not want them released on record. Her vocal track was also stripped from 'C'mon Everybody'. Such practices may have related to keeping the film an Elvis picture.

Elvis's evolving Hollywood image slowly began to include a certain kind of male maturation and acceptance of adult complexity. Even in the mid-1960s, he did not look quite right in mature roles. Off-screen he was still boyishly at play, learning martial arts, postponing marriage and playing practical jokes on set, or at home in Graceland. His public image reflected some of his cheeky sense of humour too: he starred in light romantic comedies. Such films were, in effect, for Elvis, romantic rites-of-passage movies. Although he had outgrown the troubled delinquent roles that characterized his earliest film career, as a young adult, Elvis never seemed quite at home (despite his powerful voice) in virile roles, like playing the cowboy Jess Wade in *Charro!* (Warren, 1969). It was as if, for the sake of the drama, Elvis was simply not allowed to *start out* as a man. Instead he had to *become* one. Part of the reason for this is that Hollywood producers soon realized that Elvis could competently perform fist fights on camera, and the "mild peril" associated with them could also make spectators root for him. Aimed at a young audience, Elvis's feature films therefore involved pivotal tests of masculinity. In *Kid Galahad* for example, as Walter Gulick, Elvis's skills in fist fighting were tested in parallel with his ability to stand up to his love interest's father. At one point Elvis/Walter tells the man, "I'm a grease monkey that won't slide so easily".

Some of Elvis's later films subtly but significantly updated and complicated his existing gender image. Consider two particularly interesting late movies: *Frankie and Johnny* (de Cordova, 1966) and *Change of Habit* (Graham, 1969). *Frankie and Johnny* is intriguing not just because its play-within-a-play scenario makes prominent its own artifice, but because it does this as a parody of the romanticized history of Elvis's own region: the Deep South and Mississippi river. It positions Elvis/Johnny as an unfaithful rogue whose philandering is open to questions of moral judgement. The young Elvis played innocent and rebellious delinquents. A tarnished persona was never one that would have been open to him back then. In the context of the swinging sixties, *Frankie and Johnny* carefully exposes limitations of the carefree, playboy side of Elvis's image.

Elvis Presley's last narrative fiction feature film represents a "clever mistake" in his career. Coming at a time when the permissive society era was reaching new heights, *Change of Habit* begins with a cheesy exploitation scene as the camera invites us to voyeuristically survey nuns getting changed out of their habits and into street wear. As we soon discover, they are preparing to visit the inner city. In its own compromised, family-friendly way, the film attempted to explore serious ills associated with urban poverty, such as mental illness, poor health care, loan sharking and racism. Elvis plays John Carpenter, a streetwise doctor who has, in a sense, achieved the trappings of lower middle-class life—he works in professional health care, understands pediatric therapy, wears a University of Memphis sweatshirt—and is dedicated to helping those around him. *Change of Habit* ended Elvis's run of narrative feature films, as part of his final commitment to the TV show and film deal that also prompted the *Comeback Special*. In effect it is a coming-of-age film in which female innocence and idealism are continually challenged by the painful injustices of the ghetto, notably the racket of a Colonel-like loan shark called The Banker (played by Robert Emhardt). Elvis/John has a mediating function in the film: he is streetwise enough to know about the horrors of the ghetto—and of American society in general at the time—and yet responsible enough to care for children, and ready to stop his female charges from letting their idealism destroy them. The film gently departs from the dreamy and hokey character roles Elvis had played in the past. It presents a sentimentalized, 'In the Ghetto' vision of urban deprivation, but, through the notion of the virginal sisterhood, also raises the issue of female (spectatorial) projection.

After they help to rescue a traumatized young girl (with some rather dated therapy techniques), Elvis/John and Sister Michelle bond with the child to create a surrogate family unit when they visit the park. The film climaxes, however, when Julio—a troubled local delinquent with a speech impediment—tries to rape Sister Michelle. Elvis/John comes to the rescue. *Change of Habit* thus broaches some weighty, dramatic issues, but not in a style that would have allowed Elvis to express his full range as an actor. Nevertheless, he tangles with some funky Black power supporters in the film and generally has a good time playing songs like 'Lawdy Miss Clawdy' and 'Rubberneckin'. After its extended inner-city caper, as the film ends it knowingly alludes to the idea of Elvis *as God* by asking Sister Michelle to choose between him and her more tranquil vocation. *Change of Habit* remains an interesting curio for the way that it injects gritty subject matter into the extremely safe Hollywood formula that was created for Elvis. One wonders precisely who the producers saw as its primary audience, since some of the themes were too heavy for family viewing and unlikely to engage existing fans. Indeed, fans and critics tend to celebrate neither *Frankie and Johnny* nor *Change of Habit*. They usually prefer the early films or *Viva Las Vegas*. Nevertheless, the two movies indicate the flexibility of Elvis's star image and its openness to the concerns of dramatically changing times.

Exploited Entertainer? *Kissin' Cousins*, Vernon and the Colonel

Kissin' Cousins (Nelson, 1964) was Elvis's first low-budget quickie. Written in the wake of the Cuban Missile Crisis and released in theatres back in 1964, the light-hearted comedy saw Presley playing *two* different lead characters: an army general Josh Morgan and his fair-haired country cousin Jodie Tatum. Elvis filmed each scene twice, swapping wigs with his body double Lance LeGault. *Kissin' Cousins'* tagline read, "Elvis feudin'. Elvis lovin'. Elvis swingin' ... as he joins his mountain kinfolk for a hey, hey, hayride to good ol' mountain music!" Elvis's movie schedule moved so fast that *Kissin' Cousins* was his fifteenth feature. By 1961 a pattern had emerged: Paramount musicals had become more popular and profitable than Elvis's "serious" Fox pictures.[73] After *Wild in the Country* (Dunne, 1961), a serious character drama, failed to ignite the box office, Elvis's team realized that the public wanted to see him in exotic locations and breezy, carefree roles. With its large box-office takings *and* soundtrack sales, *Blue Hawaii* (Taurog, 1961) set a template for later movies.[74] From the mid-1960s, however, in many cases their sets were cheap, schedules rushed, production budgets minimal, and location shooting was avoided. Because RCA would automatically promote each project as a soundtrack with title singles pushed to radio, the total budget had sometimes been as low as $2 million, with half going straight to the star.[75] Audiences got tired of the frequency, similarity and superficiality of Presley pictures.

Kissin' Cousins is generally remembered as the watershed in Elvis's painful descent into Hollywood mediocrity. After the costs of Elvis's previous film, the spectacular *Viva Las Vegas*, had eaten into profits, Elvis's manager Colonel Parker had asked for the budget of the new feature to be kept low. Sam Katzman, the famous quickie director, oversaw production. Katzman was fresh from his stint making *Hootenanny Hoot* (which had featured Johnny Cash). He also made a low-budget Hank Williams biopic for MGM that year starring George Hamilton called *Your Cheatin' Heart*.[76] Katzman worked fast. *Viva Las Vegas* had taken three months to shoot. By contrast *Kissin' Cousins* was filmed on the MGM lot and wrapped in just 17 days. As an entry into Elvis's catalogue, it was only a modest success. MGM made it for a tiny $300,000, with Elvis getting a salary of $400,000, another $100,000 for expenses, and a further share of the profits.[77] Exploitation films are simple, cheaply made, youth pictures sold by using easily understood, appealing marketing concepts rather than high production budgets. *Southsploitation* films are exploitation movies that stereotype the American South. As a Presley

Southsploitation feature, *Kissin' Cousins* grossed $3 million after it peaked at number eleven in the National Box Office survey.

Elvis himself reportedly said, "The only thing worse than watching a bad picture is being in one".[78] This statement allows fans to side with both their hero and those who dismissed his blandest movies. Indeed, the contradiction between Elvis performing formulaic songs for children on the movie lot and then meditating off-stage allows fans to see him as a figure bored by his own media output; a perspective that enables them to collude with Elvis himself in ignoring the worst of his catalogue during this period. This reading locates Elvis's 1960s as a matter of genius constantly compromised by commerce.

Kissin' Cousins' soundtrack was characterized by relatively unmemorable material from staff writers Bernie Baum, Bill Giant and Florence Kaye.[79] Gene Nelson and his fellow screenwriter Gerald Drayson Adams were nevertheless nominated for the WGA best American musical award. The film is so dismissed as an item of mass culture that even Brode's book on Elvis cinema devotes few pages to it. As Guralnick said in the second volume of his definitive Elvis biography, *Careless Love*, "*Kissin' Cousins* marked a turning point in Elvis Presley films".[80] Gradually, the movies became roundly dismissed—by critics, fans and even the star himself—the argument being that they were badly-made, formulaic features exploiting a gifted singer but a limited actor. *Kissin' Cousins*' may have begun a period where profit was prioritized over quality, but its reputation is not just based on its production ethos or aesthetic value. What the film did was to *replicate* Elvis, offering a double helping of the star as if to say that more was better. We might therefore ask how such products reflected on Elvis's own reputation. It seems a little absurd to ask whether *Kissin' Cousins* should be selected for preservation by the US National Film Registry, as *Jailhouse Rock* was in 2004. The film was fifty years old in 2014. Given its poor critical reception, the appropriate question may be to ask who cared. So how *should* Elvis's less appreciated films be remembered? To what extent can he be rescued from the worst of his proliferating Hollywood output?

It would be easy to dismiss *Kissin' Cousins* precisely because it epitomizes questions of compromise raised by commercial pressures, yet the film is worthy of analysis because it seizes Elvis's universalist image as a premise to consider America's heritage of internal orientalism. *Kissin' Cousins* demonstrates that its star could be financially rewarded while being artistically stifled. This can be related back to issues of both provincial Southern identity, reflecting on Elvis as a supposed country boy who knows or deserves no better, and perhaps onwards to the Oedipal dimension of his supposed artistic impasse.

As Freud explained in his 1926 essay *The Question of Lay Analysis*, "The first object of a boy's love is his mother … The other parent is felt as a disturbing rival and not infrequently viewed with strong hostility".[81] This leads to the father figure becoming understood as an obstacle.[82] Each boy's mother-love may be accompanied by perceptions that repress the notion that his father is an object of competition for his mother's attention. The father can become seen as a figure of blame, hatred or pity. Mother-love effectively makes him superfluous: either inadequate (unsatisfying to her) or evil (she needs rescuing from him). His inadequate masculinity is understood as the main reason that the mother has turned to her son for loving comfort in the first place. At an extreme, Oedipal trauma can evoke a desire to eliminate the father. Since the father is a placeholder and site of projection, more than one figure can occupy the role. Jealous projections that emerge from those arrested at this stage of psychosexual development are therefore likely to find fulfilment in the image of "bad" father figures: the monstrous cargo of the family romance.

Elvis's father Vernon Presley was portrayed as an illiterate "bible belt Hillbilly" and framed as borderline "White trash", with all its negative connotations, at worst suggesting an inadequate man who was mean, lazy, shiftless, quick-tempered, criminal, tasteless and sexually immoral.[83] Vernon's image was positioned as that of an inadequate father: childish, unable to provide for his family. He was supposedly weak—his wife called him "steercotted" (castrated).[84] Of course there is plenty of evidence countering the negative portrayal of Elvis's father. For a shiftless man he had been remarkably stable, working at the United Paint Company for five years in Memphis, for instance, before Elvis made the big time.[85] Although Vernon was supposed to be subordinate to Elvis and therefore way below the Colonel, at first he bucked Colonel Parker by re-signing the Hayride contract.[86] Yet that was not the way it would usually be described. At best, Vernon has been portrayed as the dumb butt of Elvis's practical jokes; fooled by his son's bogus plan to release an X-rated version of the song 'Hurt'.[87]

As Memphis writer Jackson Baker noted, "No one connected with the Elvis Presley phenomenon has undergone such drastic ups and downs on the reputational flow chart as 'Colonel' Tom Parker".[88] Some Elvis fans have accused him of over-working and exploiting his client.[89] The Colonel increasingly became seen as a nightmarish burden to Elvis, to the extent that when Parker died in 1997, he received vitriol from some quarters. Upon hearing the news, Elvis's early lover June Juanico told one interviewer, "That really does prove one thing; only the good die young and he was not a good man".[90] Parker is therefore positioned within Elvis's drama as an Oedipal phantom. For music critic Dave Marsh, for instance, the singer's central dilemma personified a seemingly passive-aggressive "employee mentality".[91] Biographer Elaine Dundy suspected Colonel Parker may have blackmailed his charge, humiliatingly forcing him to act out his father's story in *Jailhouse Rock*.[92] The public did not know Elvis's father Vernon had been in jail for forging a cheque years earlier; that scandal broke in *The Midnight Globe* after Elvis died.[93] Dundy's scenario seems outlandish. Singing prisoners already existed: a few years earlier the Sun label had hits with the Prisonaires, a group of inmates from Nashville State Penitentiary.[94] Elvis and Vernon also told at least one friend their family secret. Such portrayals draw attention to questions of Elvis's sense of control and his relationship to the Colonel. The story portrays Parker as a kind of over-grown, non-contributory and parasitic figure: a "bad" father figure who exploited Elvis's vulnerability and unduly constrained his career. This aspect of Elvis story is therefore more than just Oedipal (a young man's passive-aggressive struggle to break free from the grip of an older, father figure). It also acts as a means by which fans can discuss issues of free will, employment, control and exploitation. As a source of mass commodities, Elvis was indeed exploited by the Colonel.[95] His story dramatizes an issue we all face as individuals who sell our labour power in a marketplace: the possibility of exploitation.

While the Colonel helped Elvis enter Hollywood and Las Vegas, two of the singer's career highlights—the *Comeback* and American Sound sessions—would have had a different outcome if the manager had not deferred to his charge. After Elvis returned triumphantly to command a live audience in Las Vegas, the two embraced, overcome by emotion. As Susan Doll remarked:

> People have told countless stories about Colonel Tom Parker over the years, many of them illustrating his shrewdness, his greed, his mistakes, or his ruthlessness. Yet no story reveals the complexity of the relationship between Elvis and the Colonel like this one.[96]

The point is that Elvis's rise to global fame did not simply make him a superstar. When he sky-rocketed to international success in the 1950s, a coterie of people became celebrities in his wake. With his carnival background, honorary rank and mystery origin, Colonel Thomas Andrew Parker of Virginia, *née* illegal Dutch immigrant Andreas Cornelis van Kuijk, was already a dubious performer.[97] According to Elvis historians Burke and Griffin:

> As has been documented by every music journalist from Albert Goldman to Alanna Nash, Parker was a crafty, if not downright devious, character. A cigar-chomping vulgarian with no particular sense of taste, he was also the hardest-working guy in his end of the business. One oft-repeated tale is that Parker ran an animal act called Colonel Parker's Dancing Chickens.[98]

Colonel Parker knew that his reputation as an uncanny character preceded him. He would recount tales of his own past, act out daft scenarios, and dress up in various costumes.[99] One of the first times that Elvis discussed the role of the Colonel was in March 1956. He said, "I don't think I'd have ever been very big if it wasn't for him. He's a very smart man".[100] In other words, on the back of Elvis's rise to fame, though one might stop short of using the term "star", it would be fair to say that Parker became an infamous celebrity in his own right. The manager of the world's most famous music act had inevitably developed an image for himself.

Parker developed his own legend and shared the spotlight as part of his client's story. In 1956, after MGM signed Elvis, one of the stranger press stories read that the studio wanted Presley to star in a biopic called *Right This Way Folks* about the life of his manager.[101] At the end of Elvis's 1972 Madison Square Garden press conference, the Colonel finished a question and answer session with the dry comment, "I'd like to live up to my reputation for being a nice guy: this is it folks". He revelled in the negative caricature that the public had of him. In short, Colonel Tom Parker played up his greedy image. Jackson Baker therefore rightly claimed, "To call Parker a con man is merely to give him his due".[102]

It was primarily after Elvis died that more negative readings of the Colonel began to dominate.[103] One grey area concerned Parker's approach to Elvis's funeral in 1977. Writers have made much of the fact that Colonel Parker came to Elvis's wake dressed in a Hawaiian shirt and admiral cap and never cried or looked inside the casket.[104] Yet Elvis's nickname for him was "the Admiral" and the singer told friends he did not want his mourners to wear black.[105] Some others avoided funeral garb; some never went at all.[106]

Two crucial things logically follow from framing the Colonel as a villainous "bad" father. First, he is posited as a disturbance in the balance of familial relationships. One thing implied by Parker's portrayal is that the Colonel replaced Elvis's strong, supportive mother—he "stole her baby"—while Elvis's ineffectual father Vernon did nothing about it.[107] In this reading Gladys mistrusts the Colonel and his contracts.[108] After she died, nobody could restrain Elvis.[109] Second, Parker is symbolized as a drain on Elvis's vital energies.[110] In the obituary written by Chris Hutchins for *The People*, Colonel Tom "bled Elvis dry ... [because Parker was a] cut throat wheeler dealer".[111]

Several commentators have lamented how much Parker treated his client only as a source of profit, so it seems appropriate to again consider issues of commodification. The movies were lucrative financial vehicles for Elvis and the Colonel: as well as record royalties and publishing revenue from soundtracks, eventually the pair collected a $1 million flat fee and up to 50% of the profits. Movie songs also filled the quota of the RCA contract; although the label prized good sound on its releases, studios like MGM wanted to separate the lead vocal, instruments and backing vocals on different tracks.[112] In effect, at this point, Elvis was making more from Hollywood than his usual popular music sales and royalties.[113] His hallmark became romcom caper movies that veered rapidly in the same film between generic markers. Just like his career as a rock'n'roll singer, however, Elvis's Hollywood career was haunted by a kind of bad faith that implied that his success could never last. Joe Esposito claimed that Colonel Parker secured a customary lump sum in each film contract because he did not trust long-term streams of income.[114] The movies represented a rapidly evolving genre that greatly extended Elvis's musical reach, audience base and global brand. As a singer, Elvis made a number of changes during the period, adding a variety of musical styles to his catalogue. He also made his interest in gospel more prominent and gradually shifted into a revamped, funkier, more soulful sound that reflected the changing preferences of the period. However, his film cycle was roundly dismissed at the time as trashy and vacuous mass culture.

In 1963, Andy Warhol produced a series of artistic images of 32 cans of Campbell's soup. The famous images—which went on to become iconic in their own right—were Warhol's comment on the artistic tradition of the readymade or found object, a tradition started by Marcel Duchamp's famous 1917 "Fountain" urinal. Warhol recreated the soup cans as if to say that everyone could have access to art because it could be found in everyday commodities. Of course, the painted soup cans hid their own kind of elitism. Warhol was both making an artistic case for graphic design and commenting on consumer society. He was also drawing on his status as an artist to designate what counted as aesthetic beauty and what did not. Warhol also had a lifelong interest in celebrity. He had begun his cultural interests as a young fan of Shirley Temple. In 1963, he exhibited a series of screen prints of Elvis which cloned a publicity shot from *Flaming Star*. Plasketes described Warhol's Elvis as "vulnerable, androgynous" and "disguised".[115] Prints such as *Eight Elvises* raised issues about the meaning of celebrity in an age of cloning through mechanical reproduction on record or screen. Indeed, Warhol had also silkscreened a composite in 1962 called *Campbell's Elvis* which super-imposed a horizontal close-up of a red soup can label with six identical 1950s publicity shots of the singer.[116] Raising the spectre of what Adorno called "pseudo-individualization", Warhol seemed to be saying that by submitting to consumer choice and offering themselves up as commodities, modern celebrities were as varied but ultimately similar as soup cans. One point here, however, is that Elvis did *first* what Warhol did *next*: traversed the American dream from super fandom (as a consumer and collector) to super stardom—as a controversial innovator who challenged the boundaries between art and commerce—then himself became a kind of *medium*: a branded conduit for a range of content (in Elvis's case an avalanche of distinct recordings, movies and merchandise).

In November 2009 a piece in *The Economist* relayed that Warhol's *Eight Elvises* was sold by Italian Annibale Berlingieri to a private collector, in a deal brokered by a French art consultant for $100 million, making it one of the most expensive paintings ever sold. Should the painting be remembered *because* it secured such a high price tag? Is it that what Warhol had to say about commercialism remains relevant? Does *Eight Elvises* still matter, ultimately, because of Elvis's continuing iconicism? Or, more relevant here, does Elvis matter because of his Hollywood replication?

A crucial point is that Elvis's early films frequently explore the process of media production. *Jailhouse Rock* is sociologically significant because it parodied the music industry for a public audience. It showed new tape-based recording practices, independent labels and buy-outs, the importance of television and movie exposure, as well as the seedy side: payola, alluring females misused to plug records, the star as prima donna and, above all, a greedy, corrupt manager. Riddled with song theft and trading on pity, the music industry, it claims, is worse than being in jail. Elvis/Vince's manager is his most expensive flunky and when the star is muted by a punch from him, he faces the trauma of a lost voice. Plots like this encouraged fan audiences to see the industry and manager in a certain way that gave them further opportunities for empathy. Colonel Parker had a hand in Elvis's films and approved of such scripts as technical advisor.[117] In reality, he also tended to prioritize commerce above creativity.

Elvis Presley's film music was based on a 1950s model—Tin Pan Alley—but when the Beatles were filmed from 1963 onwards performing material they had written, the quality of Elvis's professional opportunities only got worse. Both songwriters Otis Blackwell, and Leiber and Stoller, created versions of the title track for *Girls! Girls! Girls!* (1962). Blackwell's effort won out over the duo's version, which had been written in 1960 for the Coasters.[118] As the music business shifted, good songwriters soon demanded that they keep their own royalties. By 1962, Leiber and Stoller would only donate songs that they had written for others, while the Doc Pomus and Mort Shuman partnership was not producing great material.[119] Top songwriters had become reluctant to work for Elvis by 1965, not just due to the reduction in their royalties, but also because the contests established by Hill & Range often rejected their efforts. Movie score material could rarely be recycled for use elsewhere.[120] As Elvis's record sales declined, the prospect of writing for him also became less lucrative.[121] The soundtrack for *Stay Away, Joe*, for example, had only four songs, including 'Stay Away' from the title credits, 'Stay Away, Joe', and 'Dominic'.

It became common practice for Elvis's songwriters to adapt traditional folk tunes in order to acquire royalty revenue.[122] Hill & Range adapted Offenbach's public domain tune 'Barcarolle' as 'Tonight Is So Right for Love'.[123] In April 1960, Elvis recorded songs for the *G.I. Blues* soundtrack, including 'Wooden Heart', a number that Fred Wise and Ben Weisman developed from the German children's tune, 'Muss I Denn'. Weisman was a versatile and assertive songwriter who had already placed songs with Roy Hamilton, Patti Page and Ernest Tubb. He worked carefully within the parameters set by Hill & Range and had quality vocals recorded on his demos supplied by Jimmy Breedlove. In the end, his approach paid off and Elvis eventually recorded over 50 Ben Weisman songs, more than any other songwriter.[124] The almost equally prolific New York City-based staff writers, Bernie Baum, Bill Giant and Florence Kaye, formed another unit who wrote movie music for Elvis. They delivered a steady stream of soundtrack material between 1962 and 1968. The most prominent number, '(You're the) Devil in Disguise', scored a hit for Elvis outside of his film career.

By the early 1960s, RCA had settled into a quota of four Elvis singles per year.[125] His studio work fell into a pattern of equal parts specially written material, existing Hill & Range numbers, and songs from Elvis's memory, the aim being to balance up-tempo numbers (often rock'n'roll covers) with slower, specially written love songs.[126] The Colonel had also established a strong formula for releasing Elvis's music: scout singles six weeks before each movie release and no separate release for any material that was already available on album.[127] In the summer of 1961, seeking out a new single for his client, he demanded no covers or public domain songs, only fresh, strong rock'n'roll numbers.[128] However, since RCA's Steve Sholes and Paramount's Hal Wallis had competing demands for what they wanted to hear on Elvis's soundtracks, the Colonel kept RCA out of the studio after the *Loving You* sessions while film music was being recorded.[129]

Parker worked out a system for new material: songwriters had to submit their compositions to Elvis's publishing companies (Gladys Music or Elvis Presley Music). Failing that, they at least had to agree to a third of their royalties going to the Presley camp. The singer and his manager would then decide upon releases. RCA would finally press and distribute the product with no earlier input in the process.[130] When songwriter Jerry Leiber pitched a film version of *A Walk on the Wild Side* featuring Elvis directly to Elvis's publishing administrators, the Aberbach brothers at Hill & Range Music, he was warned off by the Colonel. Leiber and Stoller were also annoyed that Hill & Range controlled publishing rights even to material that was cut from soundtrack albums. They soon stopped writing specifically for Elvis and the Colonel made sure that their material was rarely taken up on soundtracks again.[131]

There was some truth in the idea that Elvis was becoming more and more exploited by both his manager and his label. In addition to flat fee contracts that promoted exploitation filmmaking, we might add the urge to create a repeatable formula and the insistence by his publisher Hill & Range that they control any soundtrack material. The publisher, who supplied demos to Elvis's RCA sessions, had an office in the famous Brill Building and worked with in-house songwriters such as Aaron Schroeder and Ben Weisman; the pair's lively faux rock'n'roll number, 'Got a Lot o' Livin' to Do' was recorded by Elvis at the same session that he took on 'All Shook Up' in January 1957.[132] Freddy Beinstock of Hill & Range was attuned to Elvis's rock'n'roll style and also commissioned Brill Building songwriter Claude DeMetrius to write 'Mean Woman Blues'.[133] In June 1961, Elvis recorded 'Kiss Me Quick', 'Little Sister', plus Doc Pomus and Mort Shuman's '(Marie's the Name) His Latest Flame'. The latter song went through a lot of different variations before it came into focus.[134] Songwriters initially competed for film title songs, because they knew he would quite likely record their material.[135] His band would work out a chord chart and play just in case he wanted it and he would also consider how they dealt with it. Following the pattern set by the commercial success of the *G.I. Blues* soundtrack, Presley's pop albums could not compete with his movie soundtrack material. Although *Something for Everybody*—Elvis's thirteenth album since his March 1956 debut—topped the *Billboard* album chart in 1961, it was outsold by the *Blue Hawaii* soundtrack.[136] At least one 1963 studio album project was also shelved in its original form in favour of soundtrack and greatest hits LPs; the album was released in 1990 as *The Lost Album / For the Asking*.[137]

The movie years were a time when Elvis appealed to a range of audiences including younger fans. As the first generation of teen fans began to settle down and have families of their own, his features reflected their circumstances and appealed to their concerns. The cohort of female fans who supported Elvis grew older and many had young families of their own. As Elvis shifted into his role as a family entertainer, his films began to feature more children, and eventually cater to them. From this vantage point, the perceived indignity of the world's premier rock'n'roller reduced to singing comparatively infantile songs like 'Sound Advice' just five years after he broke nationally is explicable in terms of his repositioning in the marketplace.

Elvis's second project with producer Sam Katzman for MGM was a clumsily intercultural children's film called *Harum Scarum*. As matinee idol Johnny Tyronne, Elvis is introduced watching a preview of his own movie *Sands of the Desert* where he stars as an Arabic seducer who sings the ballad 'My Desert Serenade'. Later he is ordered, "On your feet American unbeliever!" He soon quips, "I'm the Sheik of Araby" then says to a capering local, "What about the American embassy ... You mean Lunarkand hasn't been receiving any American foreign aid?" The backing music resembles an Arabic snake charmer's dirge. After a couple more songs Elvis/Johnny watches a girl child dance and starts lip-synching the funky, sassy 'Hey Little Girl', complete with a bongo drummer. The star is wearing Arabic garb: embroidered shirt, beige leather cummerbund and green pleated leggings. He has to become a hit man to protect threatened orphans. Elvis then appears as a spectre in a princess's bath singing the lilting number 'Golden Coins'. Soon the king arrives, talking about cod-Arabic culture: "At sunset the fast of Ramadan ends and the feast of Byron begins". Elvis/Johnny goes incognito to see the king's entertainments where he watches an acrobatic dwarf and a troop of dancing girls putting on a bare-midriff formation dance—as if the Elvis film format was now incorporating the TV variety show. Through the bars of his jail cell, Elvis/Johnny is caught and sings 'So Close, Yet So Far (From Paradise)'—with its military drum pattern and rising and falling vamp.[138] "The American infidel swore he was going to kill the king", explains an assistant. Some of the dialogue seems too serious for a children's film. The film climaxes limply with 'Harum Holiday', with Elvis singing in a black suit jacket, on a casino stage with a lot of harem girls. While he began enthusiastically, thinking that he was following the footsteps of Valentino, he soon flagged. The film borrowed its set, costumes and props from previous epic movies. It was, essentially, a pantomime. When it looked like the movie was over budget, its producer Sam Katzman reputedly ripped four pages from the script. Released at Thanksgiving, it debuted at 11 in the box office chart, making 40th for the year. Sadly, after the movie wrapped, Elvis gave director Gene Nelson a signed photo inscribed, "Maybe one day we'll do one right".[139]

The children's movies are taken to epitomize what made Elvis's Hollywood career "bad". It is not so much that the films were kitsch as that they appeared bland, but part of the reason is that they were, in effect, like children's television: simply not marketed at a teen or adult audience. Indeed, many of Elvis's seemingly less dignified soundtrack songs were actually designed for the children's market. One of the low points of Elvis's recording career was singing Ben Weisman and Sid Wayne's 'Dominic' in October 1967, a song for the *Stay Away, Joe* (Tewksbury, 1968) soundtrack that Elvis had to sing to a bull: "Elvis hated the song—no surprise—and made [his producer] Felton, who was in complete agreement, promise it would never appear on a record".[140] He insisted that the weakest material that he had to record for the movies be omitted from the soundtrack releases.[141]

Elvis received little recognition from his industry peers for movie work. He won a Golden Laurel Award for best male musical performance in *Tickle Me* (Taurog, 1965), a second prize award for *Girls! Girls! Girls!* (Taurog, 1962), and a third prize for *Viva Las Vegas*, but none of his performances received an Oscar. Ultimately, many entries in the Elvis Presley feature film cycle are, like so much mainstream culture, slowly receding from popular memory. In the context of this imperfect scenario, fans do not just crave a series of memorials to their cultural interests, but support approaches which emphasize that attention to the worst of Elvis's output should not blind us to the best. This, of course, relates to canonization: the process whereby superb examples of a media form or genre are recognized and celebrated. In some ways, the object of the fans' interest has already got the legitimacy they desire. Sympathetic critics like Peter Guralnick and Greil Marcus tend to share a sense of Elvis's Hollywood canon that reflects their views. Films outside of this canon are kept alive by Elvis's continued circulation as an icon and remembered simply as mainstream movies from Hollywood studios. They can therefore be discussed as part of a "faded mainstream" of popular music culture: a past about which many know and to which many have access, but one that includes products about which audiences might not presently care.[142] Reduced to an afterimage, such products nevertheless still have their place in history.

3 Comeback

> Oh, when are some stupid kids going to realize that Elvis, a twenty-eight-year-old ADULT, cannot be expected to come onto stage with sideburns meeting under his chin, and wiggle his hips and mumble and growl, wearing a black leather suit? He would probably get locked up! Also, it would be a waste of his truly beautiful voice.
>
> Jane Wright in *Elvis Monthly*, 1963[1]

Published in England from February 1960 to March 2000, *Elvis Monthly* was one of the longest running fan magazines of its era. After a 14-year-old reader heard someone say on *The Public Ear* radio show, "Where are all the leather-jacketed, hip-wiggling pop idols of the past? Even Elvis", she sent a letter in to explain that her hero had outgrown that "black leather" image. Considering her letter in retrospect raises some interesting points. The first is that Elvis never really adopted the iconic black leather back in the 1950s. The second is that five years after Jane's letter to *Elvis Monthly*, her hero *did* actually don a black leather outfit and gave the greatest performance of his career. This chapter discusses Elvis's music from 1968 onwards and explores the way in which he became an icon. The chapter begins with Elvis's NBC TV *Comeback Special*, which was both a career retrospective, a coming of age, and a way to subtly place social issues in the heart of the mainstream. It explores Elvis's subsequent triumphs at American Sound studios, in Las Vegas, and on global television in *Aloha from Hawaii*. The chapter ends with the final years of Elvis's life and career. By focusing on music, not cinema, the manager, record label and star all helped Elvis Presley achieve unimaginable success. In the end, though, all three parties arguably squandered his immense potential.

Many commentators have suggested that despite his love of rock'n'roll, Elvis was a relatively conservative individual who loved his family, country and religion. Two things, perhaps, above all else, contributed to the wider perception that he was never a radical figure. The first was his patriotic engagement with military service. When Vietnam became a ground war for American troops from March 1965 onwards, many young people joined the pacifist movement to oppose the draft. Elvis was already associated with patriotic duty, but not the lethal risks of active service in a war zone. In relation to such roles, it might seem logical to cite his "employee mentality", because it represented a stance that prized social deference above rebellion. In the late 1960s, Elvis seemed at odds with tendencies in the new generation that seemed to be unpatriotic, anti-establishment, pacifist, sexually aggressive, drug-orientated, non-Christian, politically radical and racially militant. When the charts had been awash with the Beatles in 1966, he released the sedate and sentimental 'Love Letters', a song utterly out of step with contemporary trends.[2] His conservative reputation was consolidated when it was found much later that he had secretly visited President Nixon at the White House.

The horror for many writers was that Elvis *appeared* to use his movie years to tread a path from young rebel to old conservative. Yet at any one time a large part of him was actually opposite to the image that his cultural output suggested. To the president he had written: "The drug culture, the hippie elements, the SDS, Black Panthers, etc, do not consider me as their enemy or as they call it The Establishment. I call it America and I love it!"[3] This statement reads as if Elvis was volunteering to become a double agent within radical youth culture, but he wrote it specifically to persuade the president to donate a badge from the Bureau of Narcotics and Dangerous Drugs. He was neither the inert, arch-conservative Republican that some suggested, nor the political radical that protest singer Phil Ochs might have liked him to have been. Instead, he *began* as a comparative conservative *playing* a rock'n'roll rebel, and ended as a unique figure within the mainstream. Rather than a rebel who became a conservative, Elvis might be better interpreted as a progressive assimilationist: open to the potential of new influences, but also true to his roots, conservative (with a small "c") and at odds with radicalism in either direction. He was primarily "apolitical", compassionate and humanitarian: an individual whose private views melded conformity to social progressivism. Indeed, while Greil Marcus has suggested that Elvis was trapped in his own world, and made sense only *within* his own iconicism, it is also true to say that Elvis used his role as a singer to *not* speak at certain times and therefore refuse to take sides or draw lines. The result is that he could be a catalyst to assimilation because he functioned as a universal inspiration. His image suggested good things remained possible in a fraught era of social change. For that reason he was able to take up a mantle of heroic subjectivity in his later career.

Beyond the movie soundtracks, Elvis never lost an understanding of contemporary music and constantly enlarged the possibilities of his repertoire. He also changed producers. Chet Atkins had worked on the previous RCA sessions. Before he met Elvis, he already had a reputation as a smooth country musician and executive at RCA's Nashville operation. Atkins—who was rarely credited on recordings as Elvis's producer—tended to take a passive, observational approach to the sessions. In May 1966, Elvis started working instead with Felton Jarvis. Jarvis was an Elvis fan who had recorded an early tribute ('Don't Knock Elvis' in 1959) and had since worked with Fats Domino and Gladys Knight as staff producer at ABC-Paramount.[4] He had a more contemporary ear and was able to supportively push his client to do even better. The baton of rebellion had been taken up by young protest performers like Bob Dylan. Nevertheless, Elvis started to return to rock'n'roll. For music critic Dave Marsh, the shift of style was gradual and perhaps imperceptible.[5] After the mid-1960s, the singer became interested in Bob Dylan's style and sang 'Blowin' in the Wind' when he practised at home in Hollywood.[6] Assisted by Jarvis, he immediately started recording Dylan numbers with 'Tomorrow is a Long Time'.[7] In September 1967, Elvis cut Nashville session guitarist Jerry Reed's 'Big Boss Man', Tommy Tucker's 'Hi-Heel Sneakers' and 'You Don't Know Me' by Ray Charles. 'Big Boss Man', and another Reed composition, 'Guitar Man', became Elvis's biggest hits since 1966. He returned to the studio early in 1968 to cut another Reed number, 'U.S. Male', which entered the top 30 and acted as a sister piece to 'Guitar Man'. Already, there were signs that Elvis was back.

The NBC *Comeback Special*

> The second-generation rockers were self-conscious rebels. Elvis had been a rebel by definition, never by choice; he had no taste for the mass bohemianism that followed Beatlemania. The Beatles' long hair, the Stones' dirty sneers, Dylan's polysyllabic verbal obtuseness: All these were a response to things people had seen in Elvis but they had very little to do with how Elvis saw himself. In the end, Elvis was still too big to join forces with any trend or movement; such alliances could only diminish him.
>
> Dave Marsh[8]

Elvis Presley was 33 in 1969. He still had a degree of youth. On June 25, two days before the taping of his NBC *Comeback Special* show, wearing a light blue shirt, he held a press conference with 45 television news editors from across the country.[9] Marking out his continuing alliance with youth culture, he explained that he wanted to do the show "before I got too old".[10] Marsh summarized this view in his discussion of Elvis's predicament before the *Comeback*. While Marsh's claims were broadly correct, what his discussion ignored was the way that Elvis's approach to the rock'n'roll side of the *Comeback* was actually *made possible* by the contemporary *music* of the mid- to late 1960s, particularly the British Invasion and blues rock revival. It was ultimately Elvis's audience— not its servants in the industry—that prompted his change of career. Elvis's films were a way for his fans to see him when he appeared nowhere else in the public sphere. One of the problems with his worst films, however, is that they are seen as the result of misguided pandering to an indiscriminate paying audience. This reading confuses mass marketing, movie revenue and public endorsement.

Henry Jenkins has argued that media fans are stereotyped as brainless consumers who will buy anything connected with their passions.[11] What is interesting is that as the 1960s rolled on, Elvis's fan base evidently began to take issue with cardboard characterizations and flimsy plots. The box-office intake for Elvis pictures went down, and with it the quality of the music pitched by available songwriting teams. It was the relative decline of Elvis's value to Hollywood that in 1968 paved the way for his *Comeback Special*. More precisely, his manager Colonel Parker could not obtain the usual $1 million flat fee for Elvis and had to settle for an enlarged two-project deal featuring a film and TV show for $1,250,000. Marsh has argued that Elvis was struggling so much in Hollywood at the time that the industry may have wondered why NBC was prepared to invest so much in him at all.[12] Plans for the TV special were announced in January 1968 by Colonel Parker and NBC's Tom Sarnoff. Elvis had not appeared in a TV show since 1960 and had not performed for a live audience for seven years. When he used the show to reconnect himself to his rock'n'roll roots, it effectively rekindled wider interest. The 1968 *Comeback Special* was all the more spectacular therefore for being a career resurrection *within* the mainstream.

Parker offered up a previous Elvis radio broadcast as a template.[13] For the Colonel, the *Special* was supposed to be a Christmas show in the style of Perry Como or Andy Williams: a smooth, adult, conservative affair that would continue the mission to locate Elvis as a conventional family entertainer. By the time the *Comeback Special* was recorded, after all, Elvis Presley was a married man with a young daughter. NBC had hosted the Williams' show on a weekly basis from 1962 to 1967 and revived it from 1969 to 1971. The network understood the format. Ironically, the same NBC executive producer who had worked on the Como and Williams' shows, Bob Finkel, was responsible for shifting the ethos of the Elvis TV project and gradually persuaded both his network, the sponsor (the Singer Sewing Company) and the Colonel to move away from a sedate yuletide celebration.[14] Once Finkel had sufficiently convinced all interested parties, he met Elvis several times and relayed that the performer was "not interested in what Colonel Parker has to say about this show; he 'wants everyone to know what he really can do...'"[15]

Finkel commissioned Steve Binder to produce and direct the show. Binder was fresh from creating a TV special for Petula Clark.[16] According to Jørgensen, the television director was just 23 at the time—ten years younger than Elvis.[17] His televisual pedigree was firmly in 1960s popular music. Ironically, Binder began his directing career working on projects for Steve Allen, a fact forgotten to the Elvis story.[18] In 1964 he had also staged *The*

T.A.M.I. Show, a concert film that featured James Brown and the Rolling Stones. More recently he had directed some episodes of NBC's rock party show, *Hullabaloo*. Based on Binder's experience, Finkel recalled, "I thought this was a guy who knew and understood the new music, so I decided. This is the guy for the job".[19]

Binder ran his production company with Bones Howe, one of the best sound engineers in Los Angeles. After graduating with a degree in electronics from Georgia Tech, Howe, who was just two years older than Elvis, started work as an assistant at Radio Recorders in Hollywood, where he developed skills in tape editing and worked alongside the star on early RCA hits. Howe had also been there when Elvis returned from the army to record material for *G.I. Blues*. He was already a familiar face to the singer. Howe was able to bring in some top LA session players—notably pianist Larry Muhoberac—to update Elvis's sound. The singer was able to work on songs out of sequence and harmonize with horns and strings for perhaps the first time in his career.

Parker persuaded NBC to finance the recording of the *Comeback Special*'s accompanying RCA album. He put Billy Strange in charge of creating song arrangements. Strange had previously worked on the music for *Speedway* and *The Trouble With Girls* (Tewksbury, 1969). From the NBC side, however, the Broadway-trained Billy Goldenberg had already been hired to orchestrate Elvis's music; in the event, however, he seemed to have little to do. When Goldenberg complained, Binder considered firing Strange, who in turn said he was too busy working on arrangements for the film *Live a Little, Love a Little* (Taurog, 1968). Hearing news, Parker predicted that Elvis would walk out, but the star just carried on and the Colonel made no attempt to interfere. Harassed by Elvis's middle men, Goldenberg called Finkel to arrange to work directly with the star himself. When they met in person, he found Elvis playing the first movement from Beethoven's 'Moonlight Sonata'. Goldenberg recalled his surprise, telling Guralnick that although some in the Memphis Mafia hated classical music, their boss "had class" and "was an incredibly quick study".[20] It was a typical instance of Elvis demonstrating ability to create rapport through music.

The *Comeback* was developed in a very specific way. The show began life with the simple title of *Elvis* and was then aired as *Singer Presents Elvis*.[21] The *Comeback Special* was taped inside NBC's vast studio complex at 3000 West Alameda Avenue in Burbank, California, a studio that had just been used for three seasons of *The Dean Martin Show*. Together with Allan Blye and Chris Bearde, Binder, Howe and the Colonel "wrote" the *Comeback*, but the central creative choices remained, in effect, down to Elvis.[22] Together they re-examined Elvis's old catalogue constructing a show around his existing musical image and past output.[23] Binder conceived the *Comeback* as a rare opportunity for Elvis Presley to express his true identity as a singer and tell the world who he really was.[24] The director said, "I mean, I didn't care about ratings. I didn't care about my relationships with the network or with Colonel

Parker. I cared about doing the greatest special I could possibly do."[25] After his previous experiences, Elvis associated television with entering alien cultural territory and not having much control. Binder put him at ease by explaining that he would not so much make a TV show as primarily *make a record* that would have pictures added to it.[26] In other words, Elvis was given musical control, but would not have to struggle over its visual portrayal all by himself.

While the *Comeback Special* is primarily remembered as a return to rock'n'roll splendour, it was never entirely conceived as such, and was actually designed to showcase *different* sides of Elvis's career: Sun *and* Hollywood, rock'n'roll *and* romantic ballads. The show was eventually built around several distinct segments which alternated between career highlights from the 1950s (with Elvis in black leather, jamming with his old band mates or standing alone on the "boxing ring" stage) and portrayals of Elvis in the 1960s (the opening and closing sequences, the gospel set, and filmic, secular, 'Guitar Man' sequence). These segments were respectively designed to reflect the two career phases that the American public already knew: the rock'n'roll rebel and the Hollywood icon. Elvis's clothing choices—black leather contrasted to softer fabrics—clearly helped to demarcate the two.[27] What is interesting, however, is that the show's opening medley—'Trouble' and 'Guitar Man'— was re-performed towards the end, this time with Elvis in black leather (in fact the shots of 'Trouble' segue between both styles and stages as if to merge the two aspects of his image).

In its entirety, the *Comeback* was a mixture of various performance styles in different segments: lip-synching, live vocals over pre-recorded instrumental backing ('Memories') and live jamming in the boxing ring. The gospel segment was included because Binder knew that Elvis loved gospel and had won Grammies for his sacred music. To Binder's regret, the segment was lip-synched. Reflecting a similar sense of diversity, Elvis was choreographed in the *Comeback* by at least three people: his friend Lance LeGault, Jaime Rogers and Claude Thompson. LeGault had arranged some of Elvis's steps in *Viva Las Vegas*, so he was a natural choice for the role.[28] Thompson, on the other hand, had a more high cultural pedigree. The production numbers were taped first.[29] According to Guralnick, it was a careful balance:

> The idea was to pre-record everything except the last two live performances (the concert and the informal segment with Scotty and DJ) that remained at the centre of the show. That way they would be able to use a pre-recorded instrumental track as the backing for a live vocal wherever possible, but if Elvis appeared in a choreographed segment or was captured in a long shot in which the presence of a microphone might be visually obtrusive, they could simply plug in the vocal track at that point.[30]

The first segment of the show celebrated Elvis's success to the sound of Jerry Reed's 'Guitar Man'. Its cellular stage set referenced the jail sequence from *Jailhouse Rock*. Marsh noted that the singer's dynamic performance in front of many choreographed, Elvis-like silhouettes—each equipped with a guitar—indicated the star's universality, multiplicity and iconic status: "In that moment, Presley is like Melville's whale in the first moment that we see him, glimpsed not in terror but in awe ... we feel how special and precious he is".[31] To exploit Elvis's Hollywood side, one of the choreographed numbers, 'It Hurts Me', even featured a mock karate fight. According to Guralnick, this segment had a narrative loosely based on Belgian playwright Maurice Maeterlinck's 1909 staple, *The Blue Bird*—the idea being that a poor boy set out to travel the world looking for fame and fortune, only to find that true happiness lay in his back yard.[32] With its combination of hunger for a new life and faith in the comforts of home, the concept resonated with Elvis's existing image. Part of this segment showed Elvis entering a theatrically-staged bordello, populated by scantily-clad female dancers dressed in pink, as if to indicate the extent of his distraction from the right path. Unfortunately, Binder had announced his plan in advance, so it caused controversy at NBC and the segment was removed from the show's initial broadcast. Binder recalled, "That scene was taken out in editing. It happens to be the best scene I've ever been responsible for".[33]

Despite being younger than Elvis, because he helped the singer so much, Binder has been positioned, like Sam Phillips, in the role of the "good" father: someone who looked out for his charge and sent him on a beneficial journey. According to Marsh:

> To put it plainly, Steve Binder wasn't the guiding genius behind Elvis in 1968 any more than Sam Phillips had been in 1954 or Col. Parker had been in 1958: What carried the show was Elvis and his music, which transcended every obstacle it faced, every shred of mediocrity ... Binder did play a crucial role in the *Special*: He filled a spot that had been too long missing from Presley's creative environment. He was the instigator, the man who pushed Elvis to the hilt.[34]

The gravity of this stimulating challenge was famously bought home to Elvis when Binder goaded him during rehearsals in his office to visit an ordinary Los Angeles street by saying, "This is 1968 ... nobody's gonna tear your clothes off. Nobody's gonna hound you for autographs ... These are different times, you know".[35] A few days later, Elvis decided to test Binder's assertion and he walked downtown with the director, but nobody seemed to pay any attention to him. Most discussions of the *Comeback* begin with that story: to a celebrity, of course, public appreciation is a career asset but everybody can associate with the horror of being utterly ignored. Binder said those famous, furtive ten minutes of loitering took place at about 5pm in front of the Classic Cat topless lounge. The place was located at 8844 Sunset Boulevard and apparently had a large car-port in front.[36] It was owned by the actor Alan Wells and was a haunt for Hollywood celebrities.[37] In that sense there were multiple reasons for passers-by not to linger, or quite believe they were seeing Elvis there, or perhaps to take him for granted. Marsh called it "the most important moment" in the whole of the *Comeback* and added "He could not bear the thought of anonymity".[38] The story functions not so much to suggest Elvis's narcissism, but as a dire warning about the fragility of his career. The totemic foundation of his stardom was at stake because the public had, Binder suggested, already begun to forget why he mattered. Elvis responded to the challenge. In interview Binder concluded:

> And then, the irony of the thing is I was convinced if anybody had a sign out on Sunset Boulevard saying, "This is Elvis Presley, not some Hollywood impersonator" or character or whatever, he would've been mobbed and they would've torn his clothes off and so forth but he never knew that and I never mentioned it to him.[39]

Ironically, then, the Sunset Boulevard incident actually re-inscribes the idea of Elvis's *isolated stardom*, an idea that in turn supports the thrilling notion that the *Comeback* was a rare, intimate moment.

In effect addressing the problematic expressed in *King Creole*, the *Comeback* triumphantly moved Elvis from a *creolized* performer to an iconic one, someone who symbolically *embodied* his nation's unity in the face of potential sabotage in all its dimensions: existential and totemic, commercial and Oedipal. To put it another way, America would be existentially threatened without "melting pot" unity that came about through universal democratic support achieved and signified through market prosperity reflecting a modern society that had put aside its adolescent angst—and Elvis arguably signified that by portraying it in his own journey to achievement. If the first two threats (existential and totemic) were tested by his lonely visit to Sunset Strip, the last two (commercial and Oedipal) were reflected in the way his team ignored opposition from the Colonel. Parker constantly continued to attempt to police the show, pricing out the suggestion that Elvis do a walk-on on another series in order to cross-promote the show and reminding the production team about publishing priorities.[40] Howe, meanwhile, was frozen out when he started to suggest that his colleagues might claim producer's royalties for the soundtrack record. To the Colonel, Elvis's recordings *did not have* a (named) producer.[41] The two live shows conceived for the *Comeback* were arranged to have audiences of less than 300 each. Binder recently estimated that he could have sold the tickets for $1000 each, even at 1968 prices, for such a rare and intimate show with such a huge icon.[42] The Colonel, however, said that he had to distribute all the tickets if the show was to benefit from an appreciative crowd of hardcore fans. Binder said that he also called local radio stations to distribute tickets on the air and a messenger was sent to Bob's Big Boy 1950s diner to entice customers.[43] Ironically, the audience for the *Comeback* was in part a hastily convened crowd composed of *both* fans and the general public:

> No one understood the Colonel's rationale. Evidently he had given out batches of tickets to [NBC Burbank studio] gate guards and waitresses, along with the usual fan club presidents, and just assumed that the crowds would follow … in the end he and Finkel rounded up an audience.[44]

Ultimately, the *Comeback* is known as a time when the Colonel fronted up *and backed off*. Binder said, "He could've fired me in a minute".[45] Yet two of the show's writers, Allan Blye and Chris Bearde, penned a special version of the song 'It Hurts Me', which Elvis sang on the set at a birthday party for his manager; it lambasted the Colonel by complaining about Binder, the show's growing budget, and the need to include a Christmas number.[46] Jerry Schilling claimed that Parker "still wasn't won over" by a private screening of the finished show at NBC.[47] Binder explained that, "With all his hollering and threats and the rest of it, the Colonel let the show be done. He's a sly old fox. He is the wizard in *The Wizard of Oz*".[48] The Colonel finally revealed that he was an impotent hoax. Particularly in its rock'n'roll numbers, the *Comeback Special* has thus been interpreted as a kind of *coming of age* for Elvis.

Binder wanted the "boxing ring" segment to increase audience access to Elvis and create a voyeuristic moment that would reveal a different side:

> These are moments where'd you get to look through keyholes and see things that you're just in awe of because you're not supposed to be seeing this stuff. I said I got to get a camera in there and got to film this.[49]

Binder and Howe had to fight both NBC and Singer, who objected to any visible wiring, camera work, or even the star sweating, as too informal and unprofessional for primetime viewing.[50] When they won, Elvis was given a hand microphone for much of the show, because Howe believed that he would respond more naturally to its presence. Part of the show's construction also featured a small, "boxing ring" stage. Its role changed one day during rehearsals, when Binder realized that he wanted to feature a kind of documentary piece reflecting the energy of Elvis fooling around, joking and bantering with his entourage in the dressing room.[51] The *Comeback* showcased an informal Elvis *at play*: goofing around and forgetting lyrics during 'Heartbreak Hotel' (in effect prizing entertaining informality over serious "professionalism"), or liberating himself by standing up in the middle of his set. The achievement of the *Comeback* was that it re-introduced the star to a broadcast audience specifically as a humorous tour guide to his own myth, while at the same time providing a taste of the musical excitement that made him popular in the first place. The rawness of his vocal on songs like 'Saved' and 'One Night' demonstrated that he was not merely an anachronism, but still a vital performer who knew how to ignite a young audience. Such moments expressed the potential of a man who now both looked at his physical peak and sang in a way that was utterly unrestrained.

The *Comeback* was planned to maximize intimacy. Nevertheless, Binder had his work cut out, as the NBC contract initially stipulated no live audiences would be involved with the show.[52] The Colonel also forbade it, but after some discussion with Elvis and the Colonel, Binder got permission to use the "boxing ring" stage in an informal way to simulate a backstage environment, with Elvis's early musicians Scotty Moore and D.J. Fontana flown in to help him feel at home.[53] They were joined by Charlie Hodge, Alan Fortas and Lance LeGault. The net result, however, was more like a studio warm-up session than a dressing-room exposé. The whole idea was to get him talking.[54] However, according to Jørgensen, "When Binder suggested that he tell stories about his early years, Elvis hesitated—'I'm not sure it's gonna be a good idea for me to go out and do this ... What if I can't think of anything to say?'"[55] The jam segment of the *Comeback Special* was *not* an insider confessional but offered a scripted framework for Elvis's spontaneous recollections of his *public* life.[56] According to Guralnick, "These things were essential, Steve said, to re-establish the rebel image".[57] In the context of old friends, it was almost inevitable that Elvis would interrogate his own past. In that sense, the *Comeback* is the nearest that Elvis ever came to public career therapy. 'Baby, What You Want Me to Do', functioned as a matrix within which he could discuss controversial events like his *Ed Sullivan Show* appearance. It was less an insider account than an off-edge but shrewdly arranged rehashing of popular memory. As a writer for *Record World* noted, the star was trading on nostalgia.[58]

Any idea of a *carefully constructed* "return to roots" raised a contradiction that was symbolized by costume designer Bill Belew's special black leather outfit. Elvis had rarely worn leather earlier in his career.[59] Indeed, it was fictional characters like Marlon Brando's Johnny Strabler and his gang the Black Rebels in *The Wild One* (Benedek, 1953) that popularized the leather look and had associated it with juvenile delinquency.[60] In popular music, it was actually Elvis's peers, disciples and imitators who had adopted the look, notably Gene Vincent, the early Beatles, and Vince Taylor. By the early 1960s it had already become a clichéd way to market "bad boys" in opposition to teen angels. Belew decided to create an outfit that combined black leather—plus all its implications—with the rough-hewn tailoring of a denim jacket.[61] Ironically, then, the result clothed Elvis with connotations that a decade earlier, during the controversy over rock'n'roll, he would have done anything to avoid.

If other parts of the *Comeback* framed Elvis as a family entertainer, by presenting his masculinity in a way that had not been seen before, the urgent rock'n'roll segment masterfully recouped generational memory in *his* favour. As Susan Doll said of Elvis's black leather suit, "it recalls the past but doesn't emulate it".[62] The same, of course, could be said of the show itself.

The timing of the *Comeback Special*'s recording can be seen in the seventh appendix of this book. For Billy Goldenberg, the show's aim was to reflect the same existential eroticism that represented the darker side of Elvis's image and had surfaced in 'Heartbreak Hotel'. To Jerry Hopkins he explained:

> "The one thing I've always felt about Elvis is that there was something very raw and basically sexual and mean", says Billy. "There's a cruelty involved, there's a meanness, there's a basic sadistic quality about what he does, which is attractive".[63]

Over two decades later he elaborated on the same position to Guralnick:

> I wanted to tune in to Elvis underneath ... there was no question that he tuned in to the darkness, to the wild, untamed, animalistic things ... He was blatantly sexual, and that was something that I wanted in the music. And if I could get that, I felt I was getting closer to the raw Elvis. Not the Elvis that came in the room to talk to you, because he was the sweetest person in the world, I mean, he was the [good] son—I think that was a lot of Elvis's problem.[64]

Goldenberg's discussion of Elvis as "butch god" indicates both the unique image and the seismic shock of the singer in his prime. It refers to Elvis as both feral *and* civilized, a force of sexual liberation *and* a sweet, dutiful son. Because of such complexity, Elvis's persona is like a proverbial onion skin that can be peeled back layer by layer, exposing a more complex individual than the "dumb Southerner" stereotype assumes. Goldenberg's version of Elvis is a figure who reflects a sexual dark side and is edged with the risk of violence. His words squarely define the existential Elvis, locating his musical vitality as the conduit of a perverse eroticism: mysterious, twisted, passionate, resentful, sadistic. Goldenberg's Elvis is an amalgam of the sensual yet suicidal protagonist of 'Heartbreak Hotel', the troubled delinquent Danny Fisher in *King Creole*, and the criminal Vince Everett in *Jailhouse Rock*. (Hence the *Comeback*'s opening sequence, which merges a song from the first of those two films with a stage set reminiscent of the latter.)

The *idea* of the black leather Elvis, epitomized by the metaphor of the caged panther, exoticizes him in ways that connect to his momentary descent onto Sunset Boulevard and the racial connections of his image. As this passage by Marcus about the pivotal song 'One Night' indicates, the notion of

Elvis as a prowling, big cat conjoins aspects of gender, sexuality, authenticity, memory and agency:

> In Smiley Lewis's original, it was about an orgy, called 'One Night of Sin' ... Elvis cleaned it up into a love story in 1958. But he has forgotten—or remembered. He is singing Lewis's version, as he must always have wanted to. He has slipped his role, and laughing, grinning, something is happening ... suddenly the band rams hard at the music and Elvis eats it alive. No one has ever heard him sing like this; not even his best records suggest the depth of passion in this music ... Shouting, crying, growling, lusting, Elvis takes his stand and the crowd take theirs with him. No longer reaching for the past they had been brought to the studio to re-enact, but responding to something completely new ... It was the finest music of his life. If ever there was music that bleeds, this was it.[65]

Marcus's notion of Elvis "eating the music alive" combined primitivist and erotic assumptions in ways that recalled the singer's Hollywood image as an instinctual talent and troubled delinquent. When Elvis/Vince kisses Peggy in *Jailhouse Rock*, for instance, he justifies his passion in a Freudian way by saying, "That ain't tactics, honey—that's the beast in me". The beast within Elvis also came across in his short temper, and the occasional flashes of violence in his early public life, when jealous men challenged him to fights. These different sides of his image gradually became conflated in the popular imagination. The "boxing ring" segment therefore locates Elvis as a totemic figure (a star) through the idea of him being like an animal in captivity: a big cat pacing round his cage and demonstrating his prowess by defending his space from the encroaching, desiring audience.[66] It is this that connects the existential *and* totemic Elvis: our knowledge that he is under threat gives us an opportunity for empathy that can actually increase the strength of fannish connections and therefore boost the star's popularity.

Goldenberg and Marcus's discourse uses Elvis's existential dimension *in service of* his totemic mandate. Free of the "bad" father and compromise of Hollywood, Elvis can finally fully *express* himself in a sensual way. This idea reverses the generalized Freudian equation around rock'n'roll. In the 1950s, Elvis's urgent music was said to move *female audiences* beyond their sexual repression; he was accused by city officials of "sexually setting young American womanhood on fire".[67] Male sensual expression was associated with delinquency and deviance, a move that also potentially placed it in the province of Oedipal inadequacy: a girl might replace a young man's mother in bed, but marriage was not an option if his mother still ruled his heart. In that context, epitomized by songs like 'Hound Dog', rock'n'roll functioned as a *game to tease the audience*. The 1968 *Comeback*, however, suggests that it is *Elvis* who needs encouragement to publically express his erotic potential: even though

Gladys has been dead for a decade, the star's supposed mother-love (or at least his will to please his parents) is so engrained that it has to be overcome *in order* for him to get down and dirty with his audience. In a back-to-the-future reboot of the 1950s, only Elvis's more adult *post*-Oedipal incarnation could lead the way forward to contemporary sexual liberation, expressed in his exceptional potential for human contact through *musical* sensuality.

The *Special* unleashed an Elvis sheathed in leather so dark that it matched his black hair. Speaking to Guralnick, Goldenberg said:

> But Elvis just kept rehearsing this 'Guitar Man' sequence, and when he got through for the evening, it was like he had just fornicated. I mean he was on such a high, he was so involved and excited and emotionally charged—I don't remember anything in my life like that, frankly. It was a high point.[68]

Biographer Gillian Gaar also noted:

> There was just over an hour to the next sit down show at 8pm. As Steve was preparing for the second show, Bill Belew came running up, exclaiming, "You're never going to believe this! Elvis's own excitement during the show had been raised to such heights, he'd actually ejaculated". "That was true!" says Steve.[69]

These sexual interpretations locate the *Comeback Special* as a satisfying moment for Elvis. The performer constructed through the *Comeback* is primarily an *uncastrated* one: paradoxically a 1950s Elvis, resurrected (or perhaps "re-erected") within the concerns of late 1960s counterculture: permissiveness, authenticity and rebellion. Rather like some of his other live performances, apparently Elvis was so nervous beforehand that on June 27, 1968 he almost never went on stage.[70] Indeed, his hand shook visibly on camera when he reached for the microphone.[71] However, what is perhaps more interesting than knowing Elvis was nervous—he frequently was before *any* live performance—was the devilish sense of confidence that surged into him once he knew that the live audience was on his side. Through a commitment to vocation that sees the *social* as a forum for rebellion, the *Comeback* therefore arguably fulfils the implicit promise of his rock'n'roll period: sex with the audience, at least through music. Symbolically, the *Comeback* has thus been historicized as a story in which Elvis Presley achieved his masculine balance. The existential-erotic interpretation thus makes the *Comeback* a *coming-of-age* ordeal: a musical version of the high dives, boxing matches or car races so familiar from the movies, moments in which Elvis finds his masculinity by facing the ultimate challenge. The *Comeback* is framed as a moment of both therapy and ordeal in which Elvis—a trapped star risking his career / captive animal facing his death—*achieves the promise of his identity* above and beyond social controversy and its internalization as reflection of parental disapproval. It is no wonder that the *Comeback* is also mythologized both as the moment when Elvis bucked the edicts of the Colonel and found a kind of orgasmic musical experience. According to Marsh, "He was that boy who had climbed on the mystery train and returned home as an adult, ready to tell tales and spin yarns of adventure".[72] He concluded, "With the *Special*, Elvis had finally found a vehicle that claimed his place in the world".[73] As Guralnick observed, "Each wildly unpredictable element [that] seems only to encourage Elvis to forget himself all the more, encourages him, paradoxically, to find himself".[74]

In some moments of the *Comeback*, Elvis's performance became more tender and gentle. In one he recorded a ballad from songwriters Mac Davis and Billy Strange called 'Memories'. Such songs were arguably some of the best examples of Elvis showcasing his soft and gentle side. Unlike many other songs in the *Comeback*, that particular ballad was shown in its entirety. Two months after the show aired, it became a single but peaked at only number 35.[75] Nevertheless, Elvis used 'Memories' a lot in his first Las Vegas season as a live performer in 1969. It became the closing theme on his feature documentaries, *Elvis on Tour* (Abel and Adidge, 1972) and the posthumous *This Is Elvis* (Solt and Leo, 1981). What is interesting about this number is the way that Elvis and others around him ignored the limited success of 'Memories' as a single in order to induct it into his catalogue, eventually as a classic item: a case of short-term commercialism being over-ridden in the name of good taste. This was not entirely atypical of the way that new numbers entered Elvis's canon of 50 or so "signature songs" known even to non-fans.[76] Crucially, he sang the ballad in his black leather outfit. 'Memories' therefore gently merged the "butch god" and "teddy bear" sides of his image.

The *Comeback* showcased the extent to which Elvis was adored. When the live audience arrived for the "boxing ring" performance, the Colonel arranged it so that the most enthusiastic female fans came to the front, prompting a similar response to the ones Elvis achieved in 1956 and 1957.[77] His ploy worked. Positioning the guys on stage and female fans so near them also organized the genders in a way that reflected the excitement around Elvis back in the 1950s. It was a replay of the famous Frank Sinatra show appearance and made some sense: the fans got what they wanted and in turn they connected with Elvis in a way that explained to anyone else watching exactly why he mattered and how important he could be. During the *Comeback*, these fans screamed regularly through the "boxing ring" segments of the show. There was also a moment, after 'Tiger Man', when his female fans screamed when he threw a tissue out that he used to wipe his face. Between 'Lawdy Miss Clawdy' and 'Santa Claus Is Back in Town', when Charlie Hodge brushes a piece of lint off Elvis's cheek, a female fan slips it in her handbag, as if to demonstrate the immense power of his stardom. Indeed, many *male* commentators have talked about Elvis's physical attractiveness during the *Comeback*.⁷⁸ Binder once explained:

> I mean, I'm heterosexual. I'm straight as an arrow and I got to tell ya, you stop, whether you're male or female, to look at him. He was that good looking. And if you never knew he was a superstar, it wouldn't make any difference if he'd walked in the room you'd know somebody special was in your presence.⁷⁹

Watching the footage, Elvis's star aura and radiant masculinity *work hand in hand* in the *Comeback* to hold the attention of both sexes in the audience.⁸⁰

The *Comeback Special* defined Elvis *alongside* his movies and reflected mainstream American entertainment at a time when the country was divided by the struggle for civil rights. By 1968, the trauma of race was not just felt in the South: riots exploded across Newark and Detroit. The "Mississippi Burning" trial attempted to bring murderers of three civil rights activists to justice. Black power had emerged as a prominent stance on racial issues. The Supreme Court over-ruled the Virginia legislature when it attempted to outlaw mixed-race marriage. Two months after Martin Luther King had been in Memphis at the start of 1968 supporting the painful African American sanitation workers' strike, he returned to the city and was shot dead on his balcony at the Lorraine Motel. Elvis entered into talks about the *Comeback Special* the following month. During rehearsals for the show, news also came through that New York senator Bobby Kennedy had been shot in the kitchen of the Ambassador Hotel in Los Angeles. It was becoming evident that assassination was becoming a political tool, one that reflected the immense social tensions of the era. In his biography of Elvis, Guralnick notes how aware the singer was of these issues:

> He was practically beside himself on June 5 [1968], the day that Bobby Kennedy was killed, and could talk of nothing but the conspiracy against the Kennedys and the assassination of Martin Luther King two months earlier. It was all the more terrible that Dr King should have been killed in Memphis, he said, thereby only confirming everyone's worst feelings about the South.⁸¹

Part of *Comeback* director Steve Binder's project became reflecting Elvis's sense of compassion: "I wanted to let the world know that here was a guy who was not prejudiced, who was raised in the heart of prejudice, but who was really above all that".⁸² The real question was therefore how to broach the notion of race in the heart of conservative mainstream American media without losing anyone in the audience.

The *Comeback* has been seen as a response to its era. By the early 1960s, the Stax label was bringing musicians of different races together and releasing the recorded results. In 1963 Bob Dylan's classic song 'The Times They Are a-Changin' used popular music in a way that explicitly drew a line between the older generation of conservatives and those who supported a civil rights agenda. Dylan's work was a clarion call to youth culture, but its impact was limited. One of the issues for civil rights supporters was to erase divisions and engineer a progressive inter-racial majority. The endorsement of prominent Whites, especially conservative ones, was part of that process. Bands of the British Invasion had explicitly endorsed Black artists. Both Elvis and Binder had previously sparked controversy in relation to race and yet been commercially popular. Elvis established his musical success for daring to mix vernacular genres associated with distinct racial traditions. In the 1960s, Binder had engineered on primetime television what Elvis had done with vernacular recorded music. Finkel almost certainly chose Binder *because* of his reputation for creating interesting, edgy, music programming. Inter-racial couplings were still defined as taboo for family audiences in *mainstream* American culture. Binder's Petula Clark special had ignited tremendous controversy because it ended with an inter-racial touch as the female host duetted with her African American guest, RCA artist Harry Belafonte during a pacifist song. The Black singer had been a prominent civil rights activist. While Binder may not have *deliberately* staged the inter-racial moment on the *Petula* special, he had been held responsible for *not editing out* the controversial portion of the show.

So how did Binder and Elvis negotiate race? Marsh described one of the dance sequences of the *Comeback* as "deracinated".[83] Though various Black supporting singers and dancers were included, on the surface it appeared true that Elvis's songs and stage sets were given a Hollywood treatment and the *Comeback* seemed relatively unruffled by dilemmas of social identity. Rather like the films that followed—*Charro!* and *Change of Habit*—adult *themes* were evoked while steering well clear of adult *content*. For example, as Marsh described the set for the show tunes part of the programme, "It wasn't all that far from the hackneyed melodrama of the Elvis movie but ... put him down amid the hustlers on a honky-tonk strip, Beale Street gone Vegas".[84] The process of setting Elvis in an uncanny, dream-like environment also broadcast a message that the *Comeback* was acting out his myth. One example of this was the 'Sometimes I Feel Like a Motherless Child' segment of the show. The song was not sung by Elvis—who never recorded it—but by a member of the Blossoms, the *T.A.M.I. Show* (Binder, 1964) graduates who were gospel backing singers for the *Comeback*. The "motherless child" described by the traditional spiritual was, of course, America's Black population, descended from slaves. 'Sometimes I Feel Like a Motherless Child' had already found its place as a civil rights number performed, for instance, by the Black folk singer Odetta, just before 'Ain't No Grave Can Keep My Body Down', on her 1960 album for the Vanguard label, *Odetta at Carnegie Hall*. On Elvis's *Special*, the tune became the soundtrack to the art of a wistful Black male dancer from the Claude Thompson troupe. The *Special* therefore raised the issue of the predicament of Black America in a symbolic way without associating it too closely with Elvis himself or otherwise causing controversy. It was essentially a softly, softly approach. Something a little stronger and more direct was needed.

Binder wanted Elvis to offer an informal closing speech, though the Colonel put pressure on him to end the show with a Christmas song.[85] In the end, the main references to the festive season in the *Special* were the slinky R&B numbers, 'Blue Christmas' and 'Santa Claus Is Back in Town'. However, rather than give up, Binder got W. Earl Brown to write a song that would work as a political monologue but escape the Colonel's censorship.[86] The result, 'If I Can Dream', featured an almost verbatim quotation from Martin Luther King's famous 'I Have a Dream' speech, delivered in 1963 at the Lincoln Memorial in Washington:

> We cannot walk alone. And as we walk, we must make the pledge that we shall always march ahead. We cannot turn back. I have a dream that ... *all* of God's children, Black men and White men, Jews and Gentiles, Protestants and Catholics, will be able to join hands and sing in the words of the old Negro spiritual: *Free at last! Free at last! Thank God Almighty, we are free at last!*[87]

As an intense and earnest show tune, 'If I Can Dream' was more mainstream in style than rock'n'roll. With its dream of a multiracial America, it squarely aligned Elvis with King's assimilatory project.[88] The song was simultaneously a comment on social turmoil, a plea for peace and statement of profound commitment to the dream of social harmony. Its all-encompassing, utopian stance did not ignore race, but instead connected it to humanitarian ideals. Elvis's profound commitment to racial integration in a sense paralleled the emotional intensity with which he delivered that urgent rendition. Jørgensen said that Elvis "sang as if he were pleading for his very life".[89] What is interesting in terms of authenticity here is that the version Elvis sang was lip-synched by him the day *before* he had recorded a live vocal for it, making perhaps the most important performance of Elvis's career a kind of convincing composite.[90] Nevertheless, 'If I Can Dream' reflected Elvis's humanitarian ambition. The white suit that Belew made for Elvis to wear for that number was, according to Guralnick and Jørgensen, "designed as if presenting the star as a Southern gentleman of unassailable purity".[91] The commitment he poured into it also reflected his own sense of determination to grasp the reins of his career.[92] He told Binder, "Steve, I'm never going to sing another song I don't believe in. I'm never going to make another picture I don't believe in".[93] Binder challenged him, "Maybe you'll go back to making another twenty-five of those movies". Elvis replied, "No, no, I won't. I'm going to do [other] things now".[94]

The *Comeback Special* helped to re-establish Elvis in the public eye as a recording artist in his own right, rather than the front man for Hollywood comedies. It was broadcast at 9am on the evening of Tuesday December 3, opposite *Red Skelton* and *Doris Day* on CBS, and *It Takes A Thief* and *NYPD* on ABC.[95] NBC followed the show that evening with a Brigitte Bardot special and took an impressive 42% share of the national audience—the network's biggest ratings winner that year.[96] After the show aired, the *New York Times* called the Memphis singer "charismatic".[97] In 1996 *TV Guide* ranked the *Special* in the top 10 of its 100 most memorable television moments.[98] Within weeks, the single 'If I Can Dream' had reached number 12 and the associated soundtrack album reached number eight. The *Comeback Special* may have introduced the idea of intimate, in-the-round star performance into the cultural lexicon of post-war popular music broadcasting and offered a prototype for *MTV Unplugged*.[99] More immediately, Elvis said that his experience with a supportive live audience on the show made him eager to go out and tour again.[100]

Elvis Presley was now charting his own path as a popular music icon. His direction as a popular musician was unique because his team rightly conceptualized his talent and potential on a different level to other performers. After listing a series of contemporary rock practices in which Elvis *did not* participate—making festival appearances, pursuing collaborations, dressing down, adopting a four-piece band, playing the live circuit—Ian Inglis argued that "his life after 1968 was not defined by the history he experienced, but rather by the history he rejected".[101] With Bill Haley, Jerry Lee Lewis and Chuck Berry amongst several classic acts still touring, the late 1960s and early 1970s saw a new wave of nostalgia for 1950s rock'n'roll. Elvis's *Comeback* catalysed the trend, which was consolidated by a series of fictional films and television shows such as George Lucas's *American Graffiti* (1973) and the ABC series *Happy Days* (1974–84). Another generation of rock'n'roll-inspired artists exploded in the wake of that boom to create glam rock. David Bowie, Alvin Stardust and Suzi Quatro all had a passion for Elvis. In 1975 Bowie—who emerged as RCA's second most popular artist—offered the nostalgic 'Golden Years' to his hero. From the *Comeback Special* onwards, Elvis clearly in part *burlesqued* his own past. For Marsh, "He was presenting a man-monument, a candidate for Mt. Rushmore. He was enacting the living legend, a tribute to his own glory".[102]

American Sound Sessions

As the 1960s came to an end, America continued to change. Gradually, the nation assimilated its Southern states to the point where comedy sketches about rustic hillbillies would have seemed impossible. As vernacular music historian Bill Malone explained, "By the decade of the seventies the rube parodist had virtually vanished from country music".[103] Christian music had fused with an easygoing pop mainstream. Popular culture gradually gave the South a cache of cool. Jimmy Carter declared a state-wide "Elvis Presley Day" in 1974 when he was Governor of Georgia. At a show in 1976, the singer quipped that he was "Jimmy Carter's smarter brother".[104] After Carter was elected President in 1977, the two talked on the phone. Carter wanted to recruit Elvis as an advisor on youth culture and music.[105] He was the first elected Southern president in over a century to assume office without first moving north. Elvis played a role in that social transformation. According to Brode, the Memphis singer symbolized social stability in the turbulent times and paved the way for a Southern president.[106] Describing the Presley phenomenon, Brode claimed, Elvis had "countrified the entire country" and could therefore return triumphant to Las Vegas without changing himself.[107] One aspect of Elvis's decision to *keep things local* was where he chose to record.

American Sound was located at 827 Thomas Street in run-down North Memphis. George Klein and Marty Lacker both independently suggested to Elvis that he should record at the studio. Chips Moman, its strong-minded house producer, was a noted guitarist and songwriter who had helped set up Stax on McLemore Avenue, then moved in 1964. He had helped create over 100 hits, mostly released on the Atlantic label, by a range of artists, including Neil Diamond. When Elvis recorded with Moman, the American Sound LP *Dusty in Memphis* was released to great acclaim.[108] Elvis's escape from the Hollywood treadmill was already catalysed by the support of Felton Jarvis, by the success of his gospel material, by his association with Jerry Reed, and finally by the *Comeback Special*. If he aimed to tour again, he would need plenty of strong, secular recorded material. The American Sound session marked Elvis's time to "come home" and fully reclaim his roots.

Using new recording equipment funded by Jerry Wexler, the American Sound house band summoned up a country rock sound with a prominent rhythm section. More than ten instruments were used on the sessions: guitar, bass, drums, steel guitar, piano, organ, harmonica, trombone, trumpet, French horn and saxophone. They created a full, orchestrated mature music with a harder, funkier edge than RCA's Nashville studios could muster. The musicians were all Southerners of Elvis's generation. Many either knew him or had connections to his career. Moman tended to oversee different aspects of the recording process, and unlike the RCA staff, he insisted that Elvis participate in multi-track music making: a modern approach that resulted in a tighter, cleaner sound.[109] When Elvis arrived on Monday, January 13, 1969, he set to work on a country ballad called 'Long Black Limousine' which came his way when his publishing house acquired another company.[110] Working with Moman and his regular session musicians, the sound was superb.[111] Although the Colonel's team offered Elvis a wide variety of material, some of which was from songwriters who had supplied movie soundtrack material, he decided to go his own way.[112] Even though Elvis had a cold, he worked the next day, and returned the following Monday to record a Mac Davis song called 'In the Ghetto'. According to Jørgensen it was "another step forward" in Elvis's "development as a serious contemporary artist ... an inner-city morality tale that pointed the finger at social (and, by extension, racial) injustices..."[113] The following day Elvis recorded a range of songs including the Beatles' number 'Hey Jude'. He arrived early the next time to meet one of his heroes, the Black R&B artist Roy Hamilton. The last song of the session was completed in four takes that night. It was offered by staff writer Mark James and called 'Suspicious Minds'. Elvis returned to American Sound for six days in the middle of February to record more material. These sessions produced a wealth of great tracks from the bluesy and spacious 'Stranger in My Own Home Town', to the mellow country of 'Kentucky Rain'. In an unusual move, early on his last morning of recording Elvis accepted an interview with local newspaper, the *Memphis Commercial Appeal*. With great pride he said, "It all started right here in Memphis for me, man".[114]

Moman fought to retain production credits and publishing rights for all his songs, and Elvis agreed. Fulfilling his promise to Binder, he actually ejected Hill & Range representatives from the studio upon Moman's advice and continued to record.[115] His publishing houses (Hill & Range Songs, Elvis Presley Music and Gladys Music) were co-credited with publishing rights to only some of the songs. After Moman helped Elvis create what was arguably his best music, however, the pair never worked together again, perhaps because Chips had been disillusioned by having to haggle over royalties.[116] In the summer the album *From Elvis in Memphis* nevertheless reached number 13 and sold half a million. Its scout single 'In the Ghetto' also did well, quickly selling over a million copies and making the top five.

Describing its sound as "blue-eyed soul or swamp pop", Susan Doll noted, "*From Elvis In Memphis* became Elvis's biggest critical and financial success since 1960 ... In the United Kingdom, the LP actually topped the charts".[117] Guralnick and Jørgensen suggest that it completed the job that the *Comeback* had begun: offering Elvis to a new generation, restoring his music to a position of popularity and artistic credibility.[118] Certainly, the album played upon the publicity generated by Elvis's *NBC Special*. It used a cover shot from the opening of the show. With its funky, gospel arrangement, urgent and soulful rock vocals, the opening track 'Wearin' That Loved-On Look'—written by two country musicians—clearly referenced the *Special* as a musical melting pot. The album's second side started with the slow, forceful, syncopated majesty of 'Power of My Love'. As Jørgensen noted, "The upfront sexuality of the cut was underscored by the sharp horn arrangement, Ed Kollis's wailing harmonica, and a set of orgasmic counter-vocals from the girl singers".[119] Elvis's confident style was now expressed by the prominence of *female* backing singers, who added a smooth supporting vocal and made a significant contrast to the male gospel quartets who usually augmented his sound.[120] After a haunting and whimsical cover of 'Gentle on My Mind', Elvis delivered the nostalgic country ballad 'After Loving You' with heart-wrenching sincerity. Following the warm, mellow, 'True Love Travels on a Gravel Road' and a Burt Bacharach number ('Any Day Now'), the album reached its climax with 'In the Ghetto'. Jørgensen framed Elvis's American Sound sessions as a kind of studio equivalent to the ordeal of the *Special*: "he knew he was being challenged, and was challenging himself, in a way he hadn't since perhaps the days of Sam Phillips".[121]

Return to Las Vegas

After the success of the NBC television *Comeback Special*, the Colonel did again what he had done a decade earlier. He withdrew his star from the medium and refused all offers for more appearances. On Tuesday December 10, 1968, Parker told talent agent Abe Lastfogel of the William Morris Agency that Elvis would consider a Las Vegas engagement for $500,000 for a month if he could play a show each week night, two per evening on weekends, and rest on Mondays. Just over a week later, the Colonel accepted an offer from Kirk Kerkorian, though the terms were less ideal: twice-nightly shows and no free days. Elvis Presley would perform at Kerkorian's planned International Hotel in the 2000-seat show room the following summer.[122]

Back in the 1950s Elvis had worked a relatively unsuccessful stint at the New Frontier Hotel. His triumphant return to Las Vegas showed that he wanted to be taken more seriously as an artist. In the middle of July 1969, Elvis asked James Burton to lead his Vegas backing group. The guitarist made weekly appearances as leader of Ricky Nelson's house band on *The Ozzie and Harriet Show* in the late 1950s, and had since become a top session player. Burton enlisted keyboardist Larry Muhoberac, who in turn suggested Dallas drummer Ronnie Tutt. He also brought in Jerry Scheff on bass and John Wilkinson on rhythm guitar. Elvis, meanwhile, contacted gospel quartet the Imperials (who had sung on *How Great Thou Art*) and a soulful Black female quartet called the Sweet Inspirations.[123] Together with Charlie Hodge—who acted as arranger—Elvis put together a varied show, rehearsing a repertoire of well over one hundred songs. According to Guralnick and Jørgensen:

> His articulated idea for the [live] show is that it will encompass *all* of the diverse strands of the American vernacular tradition, Black and White, sacred and secular, bringing together on one stage all the music that has influenced him.[124]

The American Sound material was not only popular on record; it also suited Elvis's live act. Indeed, when 'Suspicious Minds' was released the following summer, its style had been altered, perhaps in reference to Elvis's Las Vegas live set. American Sound's arrangers, Mike Leech and Glen Spreen, changed its ending to include a false fade and the addition of a repeated horn backing motif.[125] The October 1969 RCA double album *From Memphis to Vegas / From Vegas to Memphis* combined the remaining American Sound recordings with live material. In order to test the International Hotel for teething issues, Elvis's team decided to allow Barbara Streisand to open the new venue. After rehearsing with the 30-piece International Orchestra led by Bobby Morris, on Thursday July 31, 1969, Elvis finally took to the stage for an invitation-only opening night that included a gala audience made from journalists and celebrities. That evening, a spellbound and appreciative host of prominent figures that included everyone from Cary Grant to Sam Phillips gave him an immediate standing ovation.[126] Having not yet consolidated his 1970s set list, he began with 'Blue Suede Shoes'.[127] The singer jokingly introduced 'Hound Dog' by saying, "This is the only song I could think of that really expresses my feeling toward the audience".[128] Rock'n'roll provided Elvis a safety net, allowing him to repeat the kind of games he played in the 1950s. Yet he also played two Beatles numbers ('Yesterday' and 'Hey Jude') plus 'Suspicious Minds', which had yet to be released but still received a standing ovation of its own. Elvis closed the set with 'What'd I Say' and used 'Can't Help Falling in Love' as an encore.[129] While his movie tunes have often been maligned, 'Can't Help Falling in Love' became a show stopper and clear audience favourite. At a press conference held later that evening, Elvis discussed his nerves and praised his supposed rivals the Beatles by saying, "I mean, you can't compare a song like 'Yesterday' with 'Hound Dog', can you?"[130] According to Guralnick and Jørgensen, both the mainstream *and* alternative press wrote rave reviews of the show.[131] On the strength of it, the Colonel immediately renegotiated a Las Vegas contract that paid his client an annual $1 million minus expenses for two months' work per annum through to 1974. Elvis's Las Vegas performances not only broke attendance records; they also doubled the hotel's income from other operations.[132]

To untrained observers, Elvis's 1970s live shows appeared to feature similar set lists, instrumentation and activities. Indeed, Susan Doll has emphasized their ritualistic nature.[133] There was, however, some variance of the material.[134] Towards the end of January 1970, Elvis returned to the International in Las Vegas with a 40-minute set concentrating on his American Sound numbers and fresh covers of contemporary music. His rock'n'roll material had largely been reduced to medley form. It was here that he pioneered the white jumpsuit look, complete, at first, with a macramé karate belt.

Live work became a way for Elvis to fulfil his annual commitments to RCA without having to hire a studio. The *On Stage* album in particular captured the quality of his early 1970 Las Vegas residency, so its set list will be discussed in more detail. The album begins with the show's instrumental primer, 'Also Sprach Zarathustra', which prompted fans to ready themselves for the excitement of seeing Elvis in the same room. Next, the customary up-tempo, rock'n'roll opener, 'See See Rider', audibly heralded the spectacle of his appearance on stage. It usually ended with Elvis thrusting out his acoustic guitar and triumphantly posing. Sometimes listed as 'CC Rider', the old blues tune dated back to the early years of the twentieth century and may have referred in the title to a sexually liberated character. Song historian David Neale noted that Big Bill Broonzy recorded and claimed ownership of the tune as early as the 1920s, but Ma Rainey, Leadbelly and a range of other blues players and later singers also covered the tune.[135] What is interesting is that Elvis had probably never performed the song before. Its inclusion represented another accommodation of history on his part.

'See See Rider' was delivered as a very fast number. Some sources claim Elvis's rock'n'roll tunes were 'thrown away' in his 1970s live show: performed because the audience wanted them, but discarded as quickly as possible in the set. There is, however, a different argument to be made. In part due to their urgent pace, Elvis's 1950s rock'n'roll numbers were always known as 'hot' records. In comparison to previous versions, the beats per minute were raised, marking the energetic excitement of the moment in which Elvis appeared. The change within 'Milkcow Blues Boogie', for instance, connected an acceleration of tempo to hedonistic abandon. Raising the tempo had also been a key tool used in the *Comeback Special*; consider the elastic sequence leading up to the gospel standard 'Saved'. It was also a hallmark of Elvis's post-*Comeback* sound. Increasing the tempo not only linked the music to a form of emotional liberation;[136] it also reflected the exponentially increasingly, frenetic speed of modern life.

Less hard-edged but just as full and mature as Elvis's American Sound session material, the *On Stage* album's full, smooth, orchestral approach demonstrated that Elvis was on a winning streak in the charts. It placed at number 13. After its adrenaline-fuelled opening, the album included the forlorn 'Release Me (And Let Me Love Again)'. In the later 1950s and '60s, Elvis recorded previously unheard material supplied on acetate by songwriters. After his rock'n'roll debut, he did not *cover* very much until the 1970s. *On Stage* is all covers. Elvis tackled Neil Diamond's 'Sweet Caroline', Del Shannon's 'Runaway', and finished the LP's first side with a show-stopping ballad, 'The Wonder of You'. The mesmeric, narrative rock number 'Polk Salad Annie' began the second side of *On Stage*. Elvis usually re-arranged, re-worked and altered his cover versions. He would re-imagine them to suit his own unique style. 'Polk Salad Annie' was exceptional because it closely followed Tony Joe White's original. Safe in the knowledge that the South was no longer openly despised or dismissed but had become a key element of the new liberal, cool, swinging America, Elvis could now act alongside country rockers like Lynyrd Skynyrd as a curator of the region's myths for a wider audience. He continued *On Stage* with a melancholic and mature 'Yesterday', as if to remind critics of his newfound seriousness, and then delivered a showy, big band version of Creedence Clearwater Revival's swamp rock classic, 'Proud Mary'. Before ending the album with the almost cinematic 'Let It Be Me', Elvis Presley presented the most startling and swinging track on what was essentially a live covers record: Joe South's plea for empathy, 'Walk a Mile in My Shoes'. Compared to South's original, Elvis's version is tighter and contains fewer lyrics; his vocal delivery, smoother and more on point. The song choice was interesting because back in the late 1950s Harry Belafonte had been RCA's second biggest artist and sold calypso to a slightly older audience.[137] In the wake of the *Comeback*, Belafonte and Elvis were in effect doubling each other more closely. Belafonte's ABC special, *Harry & Lena*, aired a month after the Las Vegas live LP was recorded. It not only started with 'Walk a Mile in My Shoes' but contained songs by the Beatles and Creedence Clearwater Revival. Belafonte also included Ewan MacColl's tender ballad, 'The First Time Ever I Saw Your Face', which was already a hit for Roberta Flack and was covered by Elvis in 1970.

Once Elvis began to play Las Vegas he was hungry to hit the road and serve his fans. On August 14, 1969, just after he began his Vegas residency, the Colonel struck a deal for his act to appear early in the following year at the Houston Livestock Show and Rodeo. Although the concerts were characterized by terrible sound problems, this first stint at the Astrodome (he came back in 1974) showed yet again that Elvis could embody the different constituencies of the melting pot. He knowingly took Black female backing singers the Sweet Inspirations into a venue that was known for its White, provincial, Southern, country music audience. According to their most prominent member, Myrna Smith:

> When we decided to take the gig with Elvis, we had no idea that there would be any racial flack regarding it. Our first racial encounter was when we went to Texas. Elvis was told by his people that, "Well, you can leave the Black girls home—you don't have to bring them". So Elvis wasn't going to do the Astrodome unless his girls could be with him and he demanded that we be given the "star" treatment. We had to be in a convertible where everybody could see us and our little blonde could drive us. That was his statement: "You don't like it? Deal with it or I'm not going to be there". And I thought that was very big of him.[138]

What it proved was that Elvis was following through on his commitment to engineer racial equality. For the weekend engagement, February 27 to March 1, 1970, he was paid a one-off sum of $150,000. Doll suggested that the Colonel booked the Astrodome—which sold tickets for as little as a dollar—because an audience was already there for the rodeo: Elvis could therefore resume touring without risking rejection.[139] Demand for tickets, however, proved phenomenal. Just the Saturday show sold over 43,000 and set a new record for the venue.[140]

The release of *On Stage* in the summer of 1970 was followed by an MGM in-concert feature documentary towards the end of that year. Featuring performance footage from Elvis's summer residency in Las Vegas, *Elvis: That's The Way It Is* also contained rehearsal sequences that gave fans a clear picture of exactly how their hero commanded his band and put together his music. The Vegas set list now mixed up Sun, early RCA, movie and American Sound material, as well as contemporary covers of songs like 'Bridge Over Troubled Water' and Neil Diamond's 'Sweet Caroline'. Clad in a white "concho" jumpsuit, Elvis was celebrated for being at his most magnificent and dynamic in *That's The Way It Is*. The film has constantly remained a firm favourite amongst his fan community. Another success from the early 1970s was Elvis's first proper concert engagement in New York—he had only come for television shows in the 1950s. A recording of one evening was rush released as the summer 1972 live LP, *Elvis: As Recorded at Madison Square Garden*. MGM produced a second successful feature documentary that year, *Elvis on Tour*. While visually it did not show its subject at his best, it remains a significant autobiographic study.

Aloha from Hawaii and Final Years

Elvis's most famous concert from the early 1970s was his January 1973 satellite broadcast, *Aloha from Hawaii*. While the *Aloha* show represented a phenomenal triumph, it is crucial to note that its legend contains no "good" or "bad" fathers—no Steve Binder or Sam Phillips. Perhaps that was because Elvis's image and music had matured to an extent that the need for such roles became irrelevant. In fact, the event developed after a suggestion from the Colonel, who for many years had aimed to exploit the new possibilities of satellite broadcasting and was reminded when he saw satellite pictures of President Nixon's historic visit to China in February 1972. *Aloha* represented an Elvis who flatly refused to make statements or draw lines. At the press conference beforehand he described it as "pure entertainment. No messages, and no this and that. Just trying to make people happy".

Starting with footage of Elvis arriving by helicopter, the broadcast showed a concert that began with 'See See Rider' and kept the tempo going with the funky, blues rock cabaret sound of 'Burning Love'. After that, Elvis—who appeared nervous as he spoke to the crowd—brought down the tempo and offered a cover of George Harrison's 'Something', a number that the Beatles made famous on their 1969 album, *Abbey Road*. His next choice was an epic by Marty Robbins, made a hit by Frankie Laine in 1969, called 'You Gave Me a Mountain'. Whereas Laine's version was straight country, Elvis pushed the song towards a kind of pop centre ground, using it as a vehicle to express his vocal force. The band then segued into the swinging cabaret number 'Steamroller Blues', a tune that actually began as James Taylor's playful spoof of the genre. There was a new power, range and possibility in Elvis's vocals and he was by now visibly enjoying himself. His next choice was to showcase Paul Anka's staple ballad, 'My Way'. Frank Sinatra made the song a hit early in 1969 and the next year it was covered again by Dorothy Squires. Elvis recorded a studio version in 1971, but outside of *Aloha*, no recording of the song was released until after he died. His in-concert version started in a subdued mode, accompanied by slight, melancholic strings, but burst into a powerful ending.

After announcing that he wanted to sing a medley, Elvis then offered 'Love Me', a classic of the rock'n'roll era, before delivering the gentle ballad 'It's Over' with a characteristic virtuoso ending. Next in the medley was 'Blue Suede Shoes'. Elvis was visibly sweating by this point, his face contorted into an effort by the tune. His next choice was a maudlin 1949 Hank Williams' standard, 'I'm So Lonesome I Could Cry', followed by a quick version of 'Hound Dog'. After that, Elvis tackled 'What Now My Love', a grandiose French tune that had been a hit in the previous decade for Sonny and Cher, then Herb Alpert. Its solemn ending squarely demonstrated the potential of Elvis's vocal delivery. Almost immediately he switched tack and offered the erotic crowd-pleaser 'Fever', a track with a walking bass line that allowed Elvis to roll his shoulders and tease his audience. During the gentle 'Welcome to My World', made popular a decade earlier by country star Jim Reeves, Elvis dispensed a white silk scarf to a highly appreciative front row of female fans. 'Suspicious Minds' began with greater adulation from the crowd—indeed, Elvis almost lost one of the large rings on his fingers—and built up to a spectacular ending.

An interesting thing about the way *Aloha* was filmed was that Elvis was very much *the* centre of spectacle. Neither his band nor his audience is prominent for most of the show. He alone is pictured, from all angles, in the white American Eagle jumpsuit, and he looks adult and masculine. It was as if just to see him is enough to understand his music. At this point in the broadcast, however, Elvis introduces the different members of his extended band and mentions that the event is a benefit concert for the Kui Lee Cancer Fund. As a tribute, he sings Lee's bittersweet ballad 'I'll Remember You', something of an easy listening classic popularized in Hawaii by Don Ho and covered by Andy Williams.

Having celebrated the talent of a native Hawaiian, Elvis unleashed his monumental ode to American patriotism, 'An American Trilogy'. Mickey Newbury had originally arranged it as a composite of three songs that represented different aspects of the nation's fraught past: a Confederacy anthem named 'Dixie' that originated in the days of blackface minstrelsy, a lullaby called 'All My Trials' associated with the spiritual and folk revivalist tradition, and the Union Army's rousing civil war anthem, 'Battle Hymn of the Republic'. Newbury delivered his version in a gentle and haunting country style. Elvis changed the medley's pace, volume and instrumentation in a way that transformed it into the affective tidal wave. Its final crescendo began with a trembling kettle drum roll and reached a crescendo reminiscent of the blast-off from a NASA space rocket. Discussing *Aloha*, Esposito said that his boss was extremely patriotic and loved the American Eagle cape.[141] A voice-over to the documentary *Elvis: True Stories* explained, "Elvis never lost faith in his country, his flag or his God. He was proud of his Southern heritage and Memphis, which forever remained his home. Everything he believed in is in the 'An American Trilogy'".[142]

Elvis's 1970s concerts have been interpreted as moments of supreme triumph. In his review of one, Marcus reflected the giganticism that came with Elvis's iconic position:

> Performing a kind of enormous victory rather than winning it, Elvis strides the boards with such glamour, such magnetism, that he allows his audience to transcend their desire for his talent. Action is irrelevant when one can simply delight in the presence of a man who has made history, and who has triumphed over it.[143]

As the *Aloha* set ran its course, Elvis and his band returned to Earth with the swinging 'A Big Hunk O' Love'—a song by Aaron Schroeder and Sid Wyche, released as a single over a decade earlier while Elvis was still in the army. Playing the 1959 version alongside its 1973 rendition shows how much his voice had matured to create a tone that was thicker, richer and deeper. Before the closing vamp recalled 'See See Rider', the final song of the broadcast was 'Can't Help Falling in Love'. The song gave Elvis, after he was dressed in an American Eagle cape by Charlie Hodge, a last chance to pose triumphant for a global audience.

Aloha was not Elvis Presley at his rawest, but it represented the singer at what was perhaps his most securely charismatic and totemic moment. More than any of his other performances, it affirmed him as an icon. The show fully displayed his maturity. Any extended adolescence reflected in his movie music had already been shaken off in the *Comeback Special*. By the *Aloha* period, the singer appeared to be in a post-Oedipal phase. Elvis's immense charisma finally came from a place of innate confidence; he revelled in his own virility and took his level of popularity almost for granted. This is not to say that Elvis had no humour or humility, or that he could not still be nervous, but rather that he was thrilled by the knowledge that such a vast audience was firmly behind him.

One crucial question about Elvis Presley is how a poor boy from Tupelo, Mississippi used popular music to become, in Marcus's words, a "supreme figure" in American life. It also, however, has an inverse: what did Elvis do *to* and *for* America?[144] *Aloha* was filmed in between the breaking of the Watergate scandal and impeachment of President Nixon. In many ways, it appeared purposely designed as Elvis's coda to the monumental human triumph of the moon landing: the concert was framed as a supra-planetary broadcast. It began with a literal landing (as a helicopter touched down on non-mainland territory), continued with the theme from Stanley Kubrick's 1968 film *2001: A Space Odyssey*, and climaxed with the shiver-inducing 'An American Trilogy'—a kind of ritual planting of the national flag. In that sense, on a global stage Elvis proudly asserted his country's musical diversity at the very time that its reputation was most tarnished. As Medovoi noted, "Elvis Presley represented the lowest possible class of [White male] person out of the most stigmatized region of the country".[145] In the 1950s, the singer had *achieved* the American dream. Now he *embodied* it, showing that such a person could represent his nation as a superpower. At a time of disillusionment, Elvis forwarded America's national project by asserting a vision of its ideals. Vast in his legend, he finally came to fully represent the country that made him.

At roughly an hour long, *Aloha* is a thrilling document of one man at the height of his musical prowess: a charismatic icon and versatile rock singer who could command his vocal talents to achieve operatic feats that were well outside the range of any of his contemporaries. In an insightful piece on the *Aloha* show, Lisa Parks and Melissa McCartney suggested that Elvis had become an *agent* of global modernity:

> *Aloha* functions to establish continuities between an "eternally primitive" Hawaii and the "fully modern" American nation, and it does so in a way that elides the social struggles that necessarily attended such transformation. The figure that negotiates this cultural alchemy—that mediates this tension between an ahistorical idyllic past and a technological global future—is Elvis.[146]

Elvis's show *simultaneously* advertised Hawaii to American tourists, homogenized a territory characterized by divisions, promoted local creativity (giving Kui Lee international recognition), and offered a bridge to a wider vision of global modernity. While its notion of planetary harmony was organized on distinctly American terms, *Aloha* operated as much as a moment of unity as of imperialism. In other words, it *was* indeed like a popular musical version of the moon landing: not so much a global cultural invasion (a charm offensive) as a triumphant humanitarian spectacle achieved by an exceptional and patriotic American. Perhaps because his immense appeal transcended the borders of so many imagined communities, Elvis could make such a global spectacle work more than any other single artist. Parks and McCartney claim that *Aloha* set a benchmark for televised charity concerts before Live Aid.[147] They also note that satellite TV allowed further market penetration, since global superstars could now get beamed to living rooms and serve conglomerates, advertisers and concert promoters. The two researchers concluded:

> As one of the earliest [global] live satellite concerts, the *Aloha* show is symbolic because it offered a formula for interweaving

pop music, television, charity, and tourism. As such it serves as a site through which we can begin to understand how these industries helped to develop the global music television economy even before MTV.[148]

Parks and McCartney saw Elvis as the charismatic poster boy for a period in which satellite broadcasting helped knit together a global media village. In that sense, Elvis and other stars of the era—notably the Beatles—acted as appealing content for each new wave of technology that caused shifts in the pop marketplace. This effectively reversed the smaller equation of the star's rise to fame. In the 1950s, television sold Elvis as a national figure. In the 1970s, he helped to sell television as an international medium. In between, Hollywood had made Elvis a global icon. What *Aloha* did was capitalize on and consolidate Elvis's stardom, drawing the 1960s lead from *Blue Hawaii* into alignment with the jumpsuit-clad Las Vegas musician of the 1970s.

Aloha was, in a sense, a lap of honour: a moment of profound totemic triumph. However, readings of Elvis as an individual suggest that he had nowhere else to go after meeting his greatest challenge. Elvis the individual remained a paradox because everyone in his audience felt that they knew him, yet some aspects of his private life remained unknown for years and seemed opposite to his stage act. In the 1950s, he was an edgy rock'n'roll star who loved his mother. After she died, he made shallow movies but found a deeper and more exploratory spirituality. His iconic status as a singer became more secure after he succeeded again, live in concert: the Presley stage persona became too regal for Oedipal strife and too popular for existential struggles. Elvis's public obligation was simply to reign triumphant. Throughout his career he had also shaped his act by covering songs written or performed by women. In the 1970s, such songs were typically sentimental ballads. Existential Elvis showed up on stage in a range of renditions, from the sultry 'Fever' to the operatic 'Hurt': songs previously associated with strong *female* vocalists expressing powerful emotions. A good example was singer-songwriter Buffy Sainte-Marie's haunting 'Until It's Time for You to Go'.

Elvis's divorce was public knowledge. Both critics and those around him said that rather than the singer accidentally *reflecting* his personal life, he *actively* dramatized it, capitalizing on the assumptions of his audience.[149] Repeating a pattern from 1957's *Loving You*, in the 1970s he performed his most heart-wrenching numbers *as if* they were works of autobiography.[150] Such numbers ranged from mellow country rock to dramatic ballads, including 'Good Time Charlie's Got the Blues', 'Hurt', 'You Gave Me a Mountain', and 'Bridge Over Troubled Water'.[151] Writing in 1979, for example, Robert Matthew-Walker took the song 'Separate Ways'—recorded in Nashville, March 1973—as a reflection of the singer's separation and looming divorce. Yet Elvis recorded it at that particular time because his bodyguard Red West, who wrote the song, kept it back until the right moment.[152] That way perhaps everybody got the most satisfying result. Disappointments in Elvis's private life could have caused him to lose enthusiasm in the studio and give poorer performances. On the other hand, he was a professional singer. He had sung a very melancholic version of 'That's When Your Heartaches Begin' when he had first entered Sun Studio. If his later life hit rock bottom, the question becomes why he could occasionally record upbeat songs like 'Way Down'. If any singer felt their song too deeply, they could only perform it at every show the way they felt at the time.[153] Speaking at the *Conversations on Elvis* event in Humes high school during Elvis Week 1997, one thing the Jordanaires said that they admired about their leader was his polished approach to singing material he did not like. Nevertheless, it is interesting that much of the studio output after 1975—heard on the albums *From Elvis Presley Boulevard*, *Welcome to My World*, and *Moody Blue*—includes material that supports a tragic reading. The established Oedipal and existential aspects of Elvis's public image helped commentators eventually frame his deteriorating life off-stage.

4 Phenomenon

This final chapter will discuss Elvis's last musical ventures and posthumous phenomenon. Elvis Presley's final years have often been characterized as a time when he once again lost focus and direction. After the departure first of his wife Priscilla and then his mainstay girlfriend Linda Thompson, his personal life seemed less fulfilling. Binder recalled, "I didn't know if he had a lot of real close personal friends. I equated him to Hamlet, who was afraid to go out into the real world because he was sort of insulated and isolated".[1] Elvis's commercial operation suffered too. He was reduced to touring secondary markets (smaller, interstitial US cities) and taking along 100 staff for shows that might sell 10,000 tickets at just $10 per seat. By today's hyper-commercial, colossal standards, the singer was playing a small game. As Elvis's general health deteriorated, the Colonel kept live dates coming and arranged for a CBS TV special to boost his client's career. There was also an increasing challenge of filling his record company's annual quota of recordings. As early as 1961, RCA and the Colonel agreed to build a recording studio at Graceland, but the label re-negotiated and backed out.[2] In the final part of Elvis's career a mobile recording truck was sent to Graceland, and, in February and October 1976, he laid down what was to become the second side of his final album, *Moody Blue*. Much of the first side of the record, which was released in July 1977, was compiled from recordings made on tour, making *Moody Blue*—which included a virtuoso cover of 'Unchained Melody'—a semi-compilation album.

At this point, it is relevant to talk about the personal habits that marked Elvis's 1970s decline: his tendency to over-eat and gain weight, and associated use of prescription drugs. Sometimes these habits interfered with his live performance. Undoubtedly they contributed to his untimely passing, but how has public knowledge about them shaped what Elvis means? That last part should be rephrased as: what Elvis means *to who*. Elvis's more self-destructive personal habits have been read differently by people with different forms of identification, levels of knowledge and kinds of empathy. Some have seen his human failings as a case of indulgence, mental laxity or excess, and others as a case of tragedy. It is hard to disentangle the relationships between Elvis's work life, personal life, and predilections. There is no definitive reading of Elvis's demise. The approach of many commentators to framing Elvis, as usual, depends on the story they want to tell.

A first reading of the negative perceptions of his weight gain is simply that Elvis just became less active as he aged and succumbed to the delights of the Southern diet. As he gained weight, his larger appearance became a cause for commentary that ranged from sympathy to scorn. *Variety*, for instance, called him "paunchy" in its review of a Baltimore show in 1977.[3] An associated argument here, perhaps, is that as rock'n'rollers get older, they lose the rebellious agency of their youth, this being signified by their increasingly decaying bodies. Yet this reading does not *quite* explain the sustained level of interest in Elvis's size. Victor Livingston, for example, writing about a 1975 show in the *St. Petersburg Times*, explained:

> The King of Rock 'n' Roll has grown puffy-faced, pale and paunchy in this, his 40th year ... The 8000 mostly White, middle-aged fans didn't mind a bit that their idol just stood there clutching the microphone and crooning most of the time, or that his belly bulged out at times making him look something like a chubby penguin.[4]

The description of Elvis here is one of a number of instances in which he was cruelly likened to overweight animals. In another, cultural studies writer Lynn Spigel compared him to Jumbo the elephant.[5]

For sociologist Pierre Bourdieu, because a class-based diet creates a class-bound physique, "the body is the most indisputable materialization of class tastes".[6] As Bourdieu observed, "Having a million does not in itself make one able to live like a millionaire".[7] Consider, for instance, the time in 1976 when Elvis flew his private jet to Denver while looking for a specially made "fool's gold" sandwich, a treat consisting of grape jelly, peanut butter and bacon. His cook Mary Jenkins Langston's *New York Times* obituary read, "She cooked the meals in king-size proportions: cheeseburgers, chicken-fried steaks, hamburger steaks, caramel cakes and family-size bowls of banana pudding".[8] These foods differ significantly from the gourmet meals usually associated with affluent Americans. Along with Elvis's deferential lack of ego, his dietary preferences fixed his class position. His habits reflected a form of culinary and therefore social stasis. Elvis food stories mark the singer as both an excessive eater and a person who preferred cornbread to caviar, someone who never got above his (culinary) raising. He was a singer who had more than a million, but he retained the dietary habits of a truck driver and thus reduced his affinity with middle-class commentators. In 1996 a BBC *Arena* documentary called *The Burger and the King* (dir. James Marsh) joyfully described how the original Presley family might have hunted squirrels and eaten them fried in a pan. Even his famous peanut butter and banana sandwich had gained popularity as a cheap way to acquire calories in the Depression era.

Elvis's continued lack of culinary sophistication distinguished him as someone who gained the material wealth of a different class, but not its cultural trappings. In 1955, he claimed in the magazine *Country Song Roundup* that he could eat eight deluxe cheeseburgers, two BLTs (bacon-lettuce-tomato sandwiches), and three milkshakes in one sitting.[9] His enthusiastic boast captured the attitude of a new generation entering an era of conspicuous consumption, a process that celebrated mass-produced cars, flashy clothes and precooked food. As some theorists have suggested, consumer culture has an impact on the bodies of its participants. Just as the burger marked a new era of mass consumption for Southern youth, in the next two or three decades it became passé, "junk"—a symbol of tasteless working-class pleasures. Class-based readings of Elvis dismiss his lack of songwriting talent and emotional performance style, like his beloved burgers, as all calories and no content: the fatty junk food of popular music.

One indication of this class-based reading is that occasional commentaries about Elvis's weight and taste also extended to descriptions of his fans. As Presley gradually changed from a dynamic young rockabilly to a mature act, he was squarely *accepted* by a middle-aged, middlebrow audience. In the Canadian magazine *Maclean's*, Heather Robertson pointedly describes a 1975 show in Niagara Falls, New York, by drawing attention to the sartorial tastes and bodies in the crowd:

> People start coming in half an hour before show time, married women mostly, with their husbands, some with their kids, plain, White women in their thirties with thick waists and fat asses bulging out of drip-dry wash 'n' wear pastel slacks, bleached hair teased into Tammy Wynette curls, women with lots of make-up and jewelry, all dolled up, strutting down the aisles like queens, their husbands, dumpy sunburned men in seersucker, shuffling along embarrassed and inadequate.[10]

What is interesting here is that Robertson begins the article by describing herself as a fan. Her shock at seeing Elvis's audience can be interpreted on different levels, superficially for its support of the rock'n'roll ethos—that the music is for nimble youth, not those with middle-aged spread—but also for its questioning of working-class taste and perhaps anti-Americanism.

Elvis's weight represented an Achilles heel in his image, a perceived point where his resources (talent, fame, money, respect) were inevitably squandered because they were not worth having without the control that would come from emotional happiness. His weight became a focus for commentary because it represented a point of social division: if the journalists who wrote about Elvis's shows cared, there was much less evidence that his audiences shared their views.¹¹

Many of the body-focused readings of Elvis miss out on his vocality. In the modern era, all celebrities, especially singers, are not just faces or bodies, but are understood as faces, bodies, voices and stories *all at the same time*, a point neglected by many writers. What if we simultaneously consider Elvis's voice and take it seriously? Those attracted to Elvis's voice, however, reframe his obesity, placing a different meaning on it. In one article on the 1977 CBS television special *Elvis in Concert*, a fan who called him or herself the Phantom said that the show exposed the first flaw in Elvis's perfect image, that, like any other human being, "Elvis Presley could actually become middle-aged, overweight and ill".[12] The Phantom continued:

> Yes! Elvis is carrying extra weight but take a good look at the distant shots, his arms and legs are quite slim compared with his upper torso and face that really shows the weight gained. But does Elvis really look like the 18 stone balloon which some critics described him as? Then take a good look at the audience's reaction to "The King" … Not once do I see, as the cameras pan into the audience, anyone sitting in a state of shock.[13]

Turning attention to the show's presentation, the fan continued, "It seems as though the CBS camera team were set on emphasizing Elvis' ill health which added even more fuel to an already burning fire". For the Phantom, the public's general disgust at seeing *Elvis in Concert* revealed "the sad fact that through the eyes of the public and media, sex symbols just cannot age".[14] Offering a different interpretation, Guralnick saw this degradation of Elvis's body as a cause for concern, yet at the same time he registered that the audience could feel empathy for the singer's plight and vocal accomplishment:

> Hunched over the piano, his face framed in a helmet of blue black hair from which sweat sheets down over pale, swollen cheeks, Elvis looks nothing so much as a creature out of a Hollywood monster film—and yet we are with him all the way as he struggles to achieve grace. It is a moment of what can only be described as grotesque transcendence.[15]

The implication here is that Elvis had, through his vocality, emotionally escaped—overcome—his own body, not just because he had struggled to do so, but also because audiences empathized with his struggle. As the Marxist cultural critic Theodor Adorno recognized back in 1938, the voice is a trademark; it reflects the individuality of the performer.[16] Vocally, beyond the ways Elvis *used* his voice—beyond his technical learning, active performance style, plurality of registers, musicality, beyond even his *sheer vocal power*—is what we might call a perceived *body-in-the-voice*. This heard "body" is different, but related to, the embodied voice (i.e., the voice within the body), as this "body in the [singing] voice", as Simon Frith called it, is both constructed and reinforced by the identifications of listeners.[17] In Elvis's case, the singer's body-in-the-voice connects with our own. For, as Frith explained, the voice seems particularly expressive of the body; it gives the listener access to it as if without mediation.[18] From its early incarnations, as something perceived as a hillbilly cat howl, Elvis's body-in-the-voice was understood as animalistic. It was sometimes gendered feminine, as "voluptuous" or purring. For Frith, the "young Elvis Presley, for example, seemed to bask like Swift's cantors in the sheer voluptuousness of his own vocal noise".[19] Such comments can be read in relation to the sensuality of Elvis's performance that both seduced and troubled different sections of society. As the media studies scholar Stephen Harper has shown, if the public already has sympathy for a celebrity, then stories about their difficulties are met with support.[20] For Elvis, in particular, that support has sometimes failed to extend beyond the fan base. Because they remained transfixed by his still-powerful voice, fans either pitied or ignored Elvis's body. In turn, that response allowed commentators outside of the fan community to question its tastes.

Obesity is often framed in our society as an individual's lack of willpower and discipline. Unlike thin bodies, fat bodies are portrayed in contemporary culture as either something to be struggled against or accepted in comparison to thin bodies, which are in no need of acceptance.[21] If Elvis had truly been happy, the theory asks, would he really have ballooned out so much? Perceptions of abjection guarantee romantic interpretations of a *real* private self longing to be free. They instruct us to see overweight celebrity bodies as a kind of physical baggage. To quote feminist Katariina Kyrölä:

> It is almost impossible to see a representation of fat embodiment in popular media these days without fatness being portrayed as something extra surrounding the body, a closet of a kind that can be peeled off or stepped out of to show the "real", normal and attractive slim body under the layer of fat. The fat body is almost always represented as something that includes, not is, a person.[22]

Some fans believe that the tragic aspects of Elvis's personal life, which included the death of his mother and his later divorce, led him to binge on unhealthy food to escape. Their interpretations make his excessive eating all about pain—some trauma, some former experience—that he was burying underneath the fat.[23]

We might even argue that because of the continued adoration of his followers, Elvis began to use his weight as an oscillating point of defiance. It allowed him both to lever his value as a commodity and to resist his exploitation. During the movie years, Hollywood's representative Hal Wallis sometimes wrote to Colonel Parker, asking him to make sure his client was slim, rugged and on top physical form for his upcoming movie roles. The Colonel tried to control Elvis's weight in later years, but eventually became philosophical about it.[24] Guralnick chronicled the advent of Elvis's final tour:

> Elvis told everyone he was looking forward to the tour; he said to Dr Nick he thought it was going to be the best one yet, but at the same time he did nothing to get ready for it—he rarely exercised, he never put together any new material he continued to talk about introducing into the act, and he kept putting off the diet that he claimed he was going to begin on any day, if only to silence some of those damn critics who couldn't talk about anything but his weight. He alternated between bouts of depression and moments of defiance: What was a forty-two-year-old man supposed to look like anyway?[25]

As Elvis's celebrity-sign found new popularity after his death, a legion of impersonators, or "Elvis tribute artists" as they are now known, exploded across the media and performance spaces of a market-driven society increasingly concerned with looks as a measure of self-worth and social acceptability. Elvis's weigh gain, and pill use for that matter, *might appear* to challenge his place as a commodity, to dent the fantasy that he might be an ideal, and idealized boyfriend figure. Spigel saw his tribute artists, however, as celebrating the rule-breaking possibility that he might also be a lovably fat, cuddly sex symbol. In that sense, for some, Elvis appeared as similar to Black singer Barry White or other men who had been seen as sex symbols *despite* their build. Again his changing—now re-imagined—body was used to symbolize his changing agency:

> The men, who are often overweight and middle-aged, adopt the look of the 1970s bloated Elvis and, in a sense, invert traditional standards of male sexuality. It is a mark of distinction in this profession for a male impersonator to display his beer gut in a cling-fit white jump suit studded with jewels and held in place by a flashy, oversized belt.[26]

Elvis's overweight body is framed here as demonstrating the power of his celebrity-sign to contradict the superficial approach of show-business entertainment, and the emphasis it places on youth and cosmetic perfection. The key here is that Elvis's weight is read in relation to his emotional struggle. A plus-sized Elvis is a flawed image, a flawed commodity, but within limits—along with his voice—the flaws *humanize* that image and *serve to guarantee its authenticity*: the man struggled, he was real. Ironically, then, escaping the cultural expectations of his changing social station is perceived as part of both Elvis's making and undoing as an icon.

Consider the parallel and associated case of Elvis's connection to pills. Though the drug found inside country star Hank Williams when he died too young in 1953 was medicinal morphine, other drugs may have been a part of the country music circuit. Writing on the history of amphetamines, Mick Farren claimed, "Before cutting his first record for Sam Phillips at Sun Records, the young Presley had a reputation for dressing 'colored' and always having a supply of uppers".[27] Quite how Farren knows such information is hard to fathom. Elvis encyclopedia author Adam Victor has created a more comprehensive and grounded account, noting that *No-Doz* caffeine tablets and Benzedrine were legal, non-prescription remedies and at least one Sun artist said everybody was taking them. He also notes that members of Elvis's entourage said he borrowed Dexedrine diet pills from his mother, and may have used them as stay-awake pills in the army.[28] There is an easy slide from here, however, to larger claims based on less grounded speculation. For instance, according to Bobby Gillespie, the singer of the rock group Primal Scream, "The drug behind the Sun sessions—Elvis, Jerry Lee Lewis, Johnny Cash, Sam Phillips—was amphetamines. They were speed freaks".[29] In 1956, one newspaper even claimed that Elvis had a "$100-a-day dope habit".[30] In other words, drug intake can easily become a source of unproven speculation.

There are further things to be said about the mythic resonance of Elvis's drug intake, too, insofar as it holds up a mirror to his place in history. In Elvis's mind, his use of prescription drugs separated him from the next generation. Where they used recreation drugs seemingly to "opt out" of society, he stayed within its parameters. Yet this was not quite true, as he both occasionally tried recreational drugs, and, through his use of prescription medication, had moods that were not within the realm of everyday experience for most people. This duality can be traced back to rock'n'roll. Elvis's ascent in the 1950s was aided by the music genre which itself represented a new meeting point between vernacular styles and the mainstream of show business. In that sense, Elvis was a bridge figure. His interest in drugs seems to reflect that, too. If they represent a kind of illicit, "underground" cultural phenomenon, it is one that helps a modern industry to function. Equally, they arguably indicate a kind of provincial approach to modernity: a naïve trust in the authority of contemporary medicine as a tool that can offer solutions to life's problems. Elvis's supposed use of his mother's diet pills and uppers in the army is interesting in that respect, as they frame his drug use not so much as personal choice, but rather as a *family tradition* or *means of public service*. The former story, in particular, links Elvis's personal struggle back to his commodification. If his physical regime in the 1960s aimed to keep in shape for Hollywood, then diet pills were part of it: a way to conform to his place in the commodified world of entertainment and presentably "be himself" in public.

If the beginnings of Elvis's drug intake are a place of speculation and myth, the extreme intake of uppers, downers and painkillers at the end of his life is easier to prove. They can be framed as a way to cope with the emotional and physical exertions of a punishing work schedule, associated sleep problems, or with a sense of emotional loss, that got out of hand and became an addiction. There is evidence that other individual artists, from Hank Williams to Amy Winehouse and Justin Bieber, have faced similar temptations and difficulties. In relation to Elvis, however, prescription drug abuse has become framed as signifying a horrifying descent into the living hell of mass commodification. For some critics, Elvis, in his later, Vegas years, is a symbol of entertainment capitalism taken to its absurd conclusion. In this formulation, the singer rode commodification until it destroyed him. Supposedly, he was indulged to the extent that the boundaries around appropriate thinking and behaviour were erased, and in response, he could only enter into excess, addiction and denial. The denial frames Presley as a hypocrite, dissociated from himself. This reading not only shows limited empathy with Elvis as a person, but also forgets two key issues. The first is his agency.

The tragedy-of-capitalism reading is a formulation of the crass commercialism argument that assumes Elvis's affliction is *entirely* a side effect of his being exploited by the industry and made to tour too often. It suggests that there is nothing in Elvis's psyche or personal life that might also have sent him down the wrong path. Another rock star, David Bowie, makes an interesting comparison here, as his career extended three more decades than Elvis. Bowie was a singer, songwriter and actor whose creative agency is widely recognized. He had a rather different level of fame, tour schedule, and drug intake, so any comparison is limited. Nevertheless, at times Bowie's drug consumption was excessive, but, relatively speaking, he survived. Discussions of Bowie frame drugs as a source of creativity, and temptation to chaos, but rarely are they positioned as ways to cope with capitalism.[31] Equally, Elvis's own admission to his girlfriend Linda Thompson—"I'm self-destructive, but there's not a lot I can do about it"—indicates that his inner beliefs played a more important role in his life than his work predicament.[32] Those who do show little interest in fully acquainting themselves with Elvis's story, however, fail to see such evidence. Instead they prefer to stereotype the singer, locating him as a fool who ignored the emotional costs of making a pact with capital, and thus became a dissociated and hypocritical victim. Second, the tragedy-of-capitalism reading forgets a central aspect of Elvis's appeal: his ability to vocally *perform* popular music. While Elvis's drug intake contributed to his temper, and had a variable influence on his working life, he retained the ability to perform vocal feats and made some significant accomplishments even in his final phase of touring.

Around the time of Elvis's demise, tabloid newspapers fuelled perceptions of him that ignored his music and focused on his drug intake and diet as signs of personal laxity. These, in turn, informed accounts made by middle-class detractors that framed the singer and his fans as absurd and tasteless. It is important to understand, however, that this has not meant that Elvis's fans have themselves chosen the path of hypocrisy and denied his drug intake. Both supporters and detractors have portrayed Elvis as an existentially trapped and isolated figure.[33] Elvis's estate and fan base have pursued a dualistic strategy: emphasizing the music and downplaying the drugs issue to outsiders, so that they are not off-putting to new fans, and more fully exploring Elvis's prescription drugs habit amongst themselves. For instance, the 2005 book *Elvis by the Presleys*, which was designed by Elvis's estate to include "intimate stories" from his immediate family for fans, contains a two-page pictorial spread showing Elvis's copy of the 1972 *Physician's Desk Reference*, itself open on a page about methamphetamines.[34] Pills were part of Elvis Presley's history and downfall. Writing in a book targeted at fans, Elvis's hairdresser Larry Geller recalled visiting his friend backstage before a show in Louisville in May 1977, and waiting in another room before the Colonel appeared and barged in to see his client:

> He threw open the bedroom door, and in the instant before it closed behind him I caught a glimpse of the horrifying scene inside. There was Dr. Nick kneeling next to the bed, holding up Elvis's unconscious body and working frantically to revive him. He kept dunking Elvis's head into a bucket of ice water … Less than two minutes later the Colonel emerged, slamming the door. He stalked over to me, pointed his cane heavenward, looked coldly into my eyes and declared, "The only thing that's important is that he's going on that stage tonight. Nothing else matters!"[35]

Geller's story appears similar to the tragedy-of-capitalism reading here, but the psychological causes of Elvis's drug-induced coma cannot be deduced from the quotation alone. While the Colonel comes off as uncaring and tyrannical, the story at least hints that he feels a duty of responsibility towards the show's promoters and audience. Elvis is portrayed as a victim, patched up enough to work, but not really helped in his time of need. The market for new Elvis commodities, however, constantly generates speculation which makes it harder to definitively decide whether he was simply a victim or why he might have slowly self-destructed. Marcus's *Mystery Train* portrayed him, in his later years, as a docile icon, someone who was lost in the inhuman magnitude of his own legend. For Marcus:

> It is as if there is nothing Elvis could do to overshadow a performance of his myth. And so he performs at a distance, laughing at his myth, throwing it away only to see it roar back and trap him once again.[36]

This reading suggests that in the 1970s Elvis gradually found himself isolated by his own stardom. His predicament, the theory went, fed his ego and bank balance, but it also encouraged others to see *his image only*. Supposedly, by preventing genuine human communication, in some ways the situation indulged Elvis, but in others it rendered him out of control. Eventually, this story goes, it paved the way for the singer's lapses of judgement and tragic demise. Serge Denisoff and George Plasketes labelled the vernacular theory that Elvis could not escape his self-made superstar lifestyle as the "prisoner in the mansion" hypothesis.[37] In fantastic versions of the story, any possible tendency that Elvis might have had towards self-destructiveness—including the notion of slow suicide by prescription pills—is formulated as the idea that his death had actually enabled a "release" into anonymity.

Geller's horror story, Marcus's account, and *Elvis: What Happened?* raise the question of who was responsible for Elvis's demise: his audience, industry backers, entourage, family, or the star himself. Could he really have been taken in hand and helped? Would he have allowed that? Those around him suggested he would not. What is interesting about the question is that it pits Elvis's rights as a free individual, albeit one who at times may not have been fully in control of his mental faculties, against a social duty to save him. The question takes a specific hue, however, when the vast extent of his commodification is considered.

On August 16, 1977, Elvis Presley was found dead, aged just 42, in his bathroom at Graceland. Much speculation has surrounded the cause and immediate aftermath of Elvis's death. Occupational therapy researcher Irene Ilott has, for example, explored the question of whether "Elvis died of boredom": not so much a medical condition itself as an abdication of spirit.[38] The issue with this, of course, is that although Elvis evidently felt somewhat alone and perhaps jaded in his personal life, he always said that he enjoyed live touring. It may have been stressful, but it was hardly boring. He had stressed his body by worrying about work, keeping odd hours, gaining and losing weight, and becoming a heavy user of prescription medication. It is important to note, too, that Elvis played an extended racquetball session at Graceland from 2am to 6am that morning. His death was reported early the next afternoon.[39] In a sense, Elvis both opted out of the pressure of his life and stayed working at the same time, and eventually that dualistic choice killed him. His death certificate, however, simply recorded cardiac arrhythmia. After a lifetime of music, his heart had skipped a beat.

Elvis's tragic passing catalysed immense and self-amplifying public interest. In the midst of a ratings war, public demand forced America's news networks to make it the top story.[40] Fans lost in grief converged on Memphis. As the wake and funeral were held, his Graceland home became a focus of public spectacle. A whole generation of Americans began considering exactly what they had lost. Simultaneously, there was a rush on Elvis's commercial products. Popularized by the Russian literary scholar Mikhail Bakhtin, the chronotope is an idea that explains how we imagine the world in language. It suggests that when we talk or think meaningfully, we do so by considering specific unified portions of time and space, or more accurately, time-places. So, say, for example, that a person becomes fascinated with the life of William Shakespeare. Their chronotopic imagination will be centred around southern England, particularly Stratford-upon-Avon and London, between the years of 1564, when the playwright was born, and 1616, when he died. This idea relates to perceptions of Elvis. If commercial, totemic, existential and Oedipal elements help us to understand his success while alive, then to understand his posthumous phenomenon we have to substitute the last two elements for others: a shared chronotopic imaginary based on Elvis's lifetime, a living culture of fandom, a musical heritage industry, and his timelessly appealing voice.

Record labels faced a crisis of stagnation in the 1970s, but things went haywire when Elvis died.[41] In Britain the singer had already been relegated entirely to back-catalogue status. Growing interest caused his label to simultaneously bring out all previous number one singles in May 1977 and five soundtrack albums were scheduled for re-release.[42] RCA's County Durham pressing plant was on strike at the time of his death and they had to compete with Presley product from subcontracting labels. There was also a rush on his 16mm movie reels.[43] Shelby Singleton, who owned the revamped Sun label, tried to bring out whatever he could find. He had not released Elvis's material before, "Because he didn't mean anything to us and he didn't mean that much to RCA. His product did not sell on RCA until after he died".[44] Early in October, *Elvis in Concert* topped TV ratings and got a rush-released maximum pressing.[45] Thirteen RCA LPs and 50 bootleg albums appeared within two years after his passing.[46] Membership of his biggest fan club rose in the same period by three hundred per cent.[47]

Keeping His Memory Alive

Elvis has retained a worldwide family of fans. At the root of the critique of his iconic status is an experiential impasse. To fans, Elvis had an enduring gift. Those who do not understand that are liable to misinterpret the nature of his phenomenon. "Elvis world" forms a living culture with shared pleasures, debates and news stories centring on Graceland, but uniting a communal network of fans. Elvis fans do not display *cultural capital* by their passion for an obscure artist. Instead their display of obscure knowledge about Elvis and his world constitutes a form of capital *within* their fan community. The Elvis Presley Fan Club of Great Britain is still one of the biggest ever offline fan club for a single artist. It has chapters throughout the UK and many members in Europe and elsewhere. Since Elvis thrived as a populist performer, those fans were always interested in boosting his public profile and gathering more recruits into the fan base. Now they feared that he would become forgotten. They had lost their hero in person and now their deepest desire was to "keep the memory of Elvis alive".[48] However, fans alone could not fully "boost" Elvis as a totemic entity without industry support. While most members of the general public knew about Elvis's music, in the formatted environment of commercial radio or MTV they rarely heard it.

Elvis's personal absence in death highlighted the nature of his role as a totem. He had always been both an industrious individual, a cottage industry and widely followed star. Michael Bertrand has suggested that Colonel Parker was cruel for his virtual denial of Elvis's death, but from another perspective Parker was just taking care of business.[49] Until power was wrested from him, however, he was also its main beneficiary. Elvis Presley Enterprises had been set up in 1954 by Bob Neal to exploit Elvis's merchandising. When the Colonel took over, it quickly became subsumed into Parker's operations. His client's will left his grandmother Minnie Mae, daughter Lisa Marie, and his father as beneficiaries. Vernon was the executor. Lisa's share of inheritance was to be held in trust until 1993 when she would be 25. Vernon died in 1979. His own will passed on executor status to Priscilla Presley.[50] When Minnie Mae died in 1980, Lisa became sole heir to the Presley estate.

After his death, it was discovered that Elvis's finances were in disarray. Like most singers, his record company RCA financed his studio sessions, so it owned the rights and revenue streams specifically accruing to his sound recordings. He did have publishing interests and was co-credited as a songwriter on many songs, but Parker had never encouraged him to join ASCAP or BMI. Elvis therefore never took his full income as a credited songwriter. He also collected revenue on mechanical royalty payments as a performer. In 1973, however, the Colonel made a badly judged gamble and waived Elvis's future rights to the inevitable stream of royalties from previous recordings. The singer's estate still had some rights income from his post-1973 output. Meanwhile, when Elvis had found national fame back in 1957, Parker had started a merchandising company with Hank Saperstein called Factors Incorporated. Late in 1977, he started Factors Etc, to capitalize on Elvis's posthumous merchandise boom. Parker himself took a 56% cut, while Elvis's estate took 22%; the remainder was split between other businesses. Priscilla and the estate's Trust were happy to let the Colonel take care of business, but by 1980 the estate owed $15 million in back taxes and faced a $500,000 annual bill for running Graceland. A judicial investigation appointed attorney Blanchard Tual to examine Parker's financial activities on Lisa's behalf. The Presleys had been advised to sell Graceland, but instead Priscilla hired a Missouri investment counsellor called Jack Soden to give it a $50,000 facelift and open it to the public the following summer. After the estate turned from a Trust into an active economic entity, Elvis Presley Enterprises (EPE) was incorporated. Since then the estate has successfully increased its net worth. In August 1981 it was ordered to sue Parker for financial mismanagement.

Ironically, Parker also sued out of court in 1983 and pocketed an extra $2 million from the estate. A stipulation, however, was that he was banned from interfering with Elvis's posthumous business for five years. In effect, Parker was forced to hand control of Elvis's name and likeness over to EPE.

In death, Elvis again became associated with mass culture and merchandising. News stories of hawkers in the crowd at his wake were verified when *People Weekly* ran a cover in October 1977 which featured a fan who was adorned with trinkets. Its headline read, "Remembering Elvis: Imitators, fans & rip-offs launch a billion dollar industry".[51] The piece noted that Alan Meyer, a leading Elvis impersonator, was contracted to earn $100,000 per week and it profiled Harry Geissler of Factors Etc, the firm given the rights to merchandise Elvis's image. As one fan wrote on the wall at Graceland, "Elvis is undead".[52] He ceased to exist as a person but continued as an icon through commodified traces and shared memories.[53] After re-opening Graceland, EPE, the corporation that oversees Elvis's estate, made it an ongoing mission to address the festival of unlicensed merchandising that characterized the periphery of the Elvis tourism industry—a matter all the more urgent because Elvis's posthumous income from music was so limited. The mansion was located opposite a strip mall on Elvis Presley Boulevard that had, after the star died, been a home for unauthorized merchandising operations. In 1983 EPE acquired rights to manage the plaza. It finally had the power to police unruly retail tenants and strategically replace properties when their leases expired. By 1987 all the stores were part of its own operation and it relaunched the mall as Graceland Crossing.

In the first two decades after Elvis's death, his estate's corporation pursued an active protectionist strategy by filing over a hundred lawsuits against unlicensed interests, from merchandisers to tribute artists to fans. It used its growing economic force to secure legal representation and even managed to change US copyright and trademark legislation in its favour. EPE was not initially successful everywhere, however. When the corporation attempted to contest merchandiser Sid Shaw in the UK, back in 1999 there was no clear precedent in British law to support the trademark exploitation of a celebrity's name. A court decided that EPE had no unique right to Elvis's name or signature likeness, noting that "Elvis" was an ordinary, if rare, name, and that consumers bought merchandise on the basis of its visible connection to the star rather than its manufacturing source. Since then in the UK other celebrities have gone further in trademarking their names to protect lines of goods connected with their specific fields of expertise.[54]

In an insightful article about Elvis's posthumous predicament, David Wall has noted that star images are multi-authored, social spaces. Public participation is both encouraged and policed in order to maintain the star's continuing profitability. Celebrity image assets are therefore arenas of cultural conflict: they simultaneously emerge from both the creativity of their makers (Elvis), wider social conversations and activities (fans), and legal protection as intellectual property assets (EPE). They inevitably become legally contested spaces.⁵⁵ EPE's active licensing strategy was about *both* directly profiting from commerce that had an Elvis connection *and* policing "inappropriate" representations (like Barry Capece's Velvet Elvis nightclub in Houston); in effect the two went hand in hand.⁵⁶ This created some unusual situations because EPE strategically both outlawed *and* embraced fan activities, for example addressing fans for making items like t-shirts but using fan-artist Betty Harper's pencil sketches on Graceland postcards. It also effectively airbrushed away images the overweight Elvis and used favoured tribute artists to momentarily replace him on music videos and at live events. Meanwhile, at least until the internet era, certain archival representations of Elvis (such as his 1977 CBS TV Special) effectively remained contraband: exchanged and enjoyed by fans, but kept under wraps, away from official release for mass audiences.⁵⁷

While academics have often painted the history of relationships between EPE and Elvis fans as a series of flash points, the two parties have *colluded* for much of the time, with the fans squarely recognizing the good that EPE was doing for Elvis's memory.⁵⁸ One example of this is the estate's philanthropic activity. Elvis himself regularly gave significant sums to different causes, but many of his contributions were low key. Every Christmas he would send cheques to a range of Memphis charities. His supporters collected donations as acts of fan philanthropy. EPE continued the tradition by operating the Elvis Presley Charitable Foundation. In 2001 it funded the construction of Presley Place, a 12-unit housing community for Memphis residents on the edge of homelessness. Lisa Marie Presley also revisited 'In the Ghetto' in 2007 to create a duet with her late father, releasing the result as a download to help victims of Hurricane Katrina.⁵⁹ In Elvis's wake, Lisa and her son are now recording artists. The Presleys have become a kind of show-business dynasty.

For EPE, Elvis culture primarily operates as an economic interest: a brand and heritage concern. The corporation neglects aspects of Elvis history that cannot easily function as economic assets. In a recent piece on Elvis heritage in the Memphis area, sites were distinguished that were preserved, renovated, decaying and disappeared.⁶⁰ Graceland and Sun Studio (which is not owned by EPE) are examples of the first category, whereas the old Memphian Theatre is an example of the second. Until it was re-opened as apartments in 2015, the Chisca Hotel was an example of the third category: it was perhaps the most important location in the history of postwar popular music—the place where 'That's All Right' was given its first public airing—but it spent years as an abandoned building. Poplar Tunes record store and American Sound studios are examples of the "disappeared" category. Even in Memphis, it is not viable for EPE to save all those sights. Dedicated fans have tried to raise money to rescue some of them—notably Elvis's honeymoon ranch, the Circle G—but they effectively constitute a numeric and economic minority.⁶¹ Instead of "real" heritage, EPE has instead attempted to float Elvis-themed businesses such as Elvis's Presley's Memphis (a restaurant and bar facility that opened in 1997 in the Lansky's building on Beale Street), and a hotel near Graceland renovated in 1999 called Heartbreak Hotel.

Contested Hero: Elvis Biographies, the 1980s and 1990s

What follows in this section locates Elvis's changing reputation in relation to his presence in print media, and debates about crass commercialism in the 1980s and 1990s. In the mainstream of popular music, the shock of punk was gradually absorbed at that time. Focus moved to a new generation of young pop stars. The MTV era marked a time when, perhaps more than ever before, mainstream music became led by its own marketing. Voices of social rebellion could only speak ironically by addressing the commercial sphere *from within*. Musicians were once again losing their rebellious edge and focusing on becoming multi-skilled entertainment entrepreneurs. Greil Marcus's 1991 book *Dead Elvis*, Gilbert Rodman's 1996 volume *Elvis After Elvis* and George Plasketes's 1997 meditation on, in his words, "the mystery terrain" provide comprehensive examinations of the free play of Elvis's signifier in popular culture. What they show is that after Elvis died, as an individual, he remained, to use the words of John Fiske, a body of controversy.[62] The posthumous image of Elvis Presley rapidly became a flexible and fictionalized placeholder for wider conversations within popular culture, not just because he no longer, in death, had the legal status that would have made a libel campaign effective: it was also because, in an era that favoured the free market, Elvis was a way for commentators to talk about the pressing dilemmas of commercialism.[63]

In death Elvis could be used to symbolize the dangers of indiscriminately embracing the concerns of commerce. His sign hitched a ride on debates about personal control in an era of exponentially increasing commodification, a time when previous spheres of social life—welfare, national industry, the academy— were being turned (back) into privatized businesses. Individualist attitudes that prioritized self-interest above collective responsibility gained ground in society. They paved the way for greater deregulation of business. During this era, especially as lurid biographies proved best-sellers and royalty payment disputes between RCA and the Presley estate limited the promotion of his music, the crass commercialist reading of him gained significant new ground.

To understand how this came about, it is worth considering how the Elvis book market gradually evolved. Back in the 1950s, some of the earliest biographic material emerged from extensions of Elvis's press and magazine publicity stories. Robert Williams of the *Memphis Commercial Appeal* released the magazine *Elvis Presley Speaks* in 1956 and several other magazines offered similar material.[64] Elvis's biography played out in girls' romantic publications. Charlton Comics' *Young Lovers* issue 18 in May 1957 claimed to show "The real Elvis Presley life story". Into the next decade, the singer pursued his private life with his bride-to-be in Memphis. He developed a cosy relationship with the local media: periodic world-exclusives in exchange for secrecy most of the time.[65] Aside from fan club publications like the *Elvis Special* annual series, the 1960s were a relatively meagre time for Elvis publications. A trickle of books emerged in the wake of the *Comeback*. Favius Friedman's slim biography *Meet Elvis Presley* was published by Scholastic Book Services and marketed at US high school students through mail order book clubs. Inspired by a suggestion from the singer Jim Morrison and supported by *Rolling Stone*'s Jan Wenner, *Elvis*, by Jerry Hopkins, was the first substantial biography published in both the US and UK. It ran to almost 450 pages. It was based on extensive interviews with many of the most important players in Elvis's life story—except the star, his family and manager. Promoter-turned-superfan Paul Lichter also began a series of books in 1975 with *Elvis in Hollywood*.

A new trend was set in Elvis publishing by the sensationalist 1977 exposé *Elvis: What Happened?*, written by three of his former bodyguards—Red West, Sonny West and Dave Hebler—and ghost-written by Steve Dunleavy, gossip columnist for Rupert Murdoch's tabloid *The National Star*. The authors said their book was a plea asking Elvis to curb his lifestyle, written to avoid his "path to disaster".[66] Its authors even claimed to have "underplayed" the facts.[67] If Memphis Mafia members could not control Elvis from the inside, they reasoned that maybe he could be levered by public shame.

Elvis: What Happened? started its narrative in the confines of a Las Vegas suite where an out-of-control superstar issued death threats against the man who seduced his wife. Dunleavy wove rambling recollections from three bodyguards into a seedy tale of guns, drugs and selfishness. He created a *narrative* that allowed readers to feel more dignified than the star. It was a portrayal that was selected, slanted and designed to shock. Since information came from the private sphere, it could not be fully neutralized by the singer's public appearances. After Elvis died, *Elvis: What Happened?* was still being sold, reframed as a cautionary tale.[68] The Wests held a Beverly Hills press conference to regretfully say co-writer Dunleavy made the story too sensational.[69] According to Red, the book persuaded Rod Stewart and Tommy Chong to clean up their acts.[70] Very few of the readers, however, were rock stars. *Elvis: What Happened?* was a highly commercial product: copyrighted to World Media Incorporated, excerpted by the *Ladies Home Journal*, and serialized in Murdoch's tabloids: the *National Star*, and, in Great Britain, the *Sun*. The Wests' book must therefore be seen in a wider context of scandal as an approach to entertainment. Its account of the star's private life proved that there was a trash market for stories that stretched well beyond his fan base. In fact, the book sold over three million copies.[71] *Elvis: What Happened?* thus set a commercial template for books that linked Elvis to vulgarity.

Print was not the forum where Elvis Presley left his greatest gifts. Yet it has, beyond his music, become one of the most significant domains for the recollection of his life. Books are the medium in which Elvis seems to have been treated the worst and where he had the least agency to answer back. He was never a prolific writer. Apart from a handful of personal letters, he rarely put pen to paper.[72] There were rumours that he was planning a book whilst in the army, then later an autobiography called *Through My Eyes*, but it was going to have contributory chapters from friends and never happened.[73] After his death, Elvis re-entered the print medium in a variety of ways, including popular paperbacks.[74]

The most significant effort to scandalize Elvis Presley was Albert Goldman's Presley biography, *Elvis*. The book was not initially conceived by Goldman, but by the music entrepreneur Kevin Eggers.[75] Goldman had received a doctorate at the start of the 1960s for questioning the originality of writing by Thomas De Quincey. He then embarked on a career that included teaching popular culture at Columbia University, writing for *Life* magazine and writing a biography of the controversial comedian Lenny Bruce. Goldman's opinions on pop culture varied widely. On the strength of his Lenny Bruce book, he received a $1 million advance from McGraw-Hill to write a biography of Elvis Presley. In the meantime, he published books on the carnival in Rio, marijuana and disco. Elvis's friend Lamar Fike did the legwork and all three men shared copyright. The book was a well-researched piece. Compared to 75 interviews Jerry Hopkins conducted for his second biography *Elvis: The Final Years*, Goldman claimed that he managed 600, a figure not to be approached again until Guralnick's first book in 1994.[76] Despite this, Goldman missed several key players including Elvis's main doctor (George Nichopoulos), Charlie Hodge, Joe Esposito, Vernon, Priscilla and the Colonel. Yet somehow assessing Goldman's *Elvis* by its groundwork seems the wrong way to adjudicate it. Its author's 1994 *New York Times* obituary summed up:

> Mr. Goldman's *Elvis* (1981), an epic-length work written in a supercharged, impressionistic prose style, provoked howls of outrage from fans of the rock legend, who saw their idol portrayed as a self-indulgent, barely talented rube with perverse sexual inclinations and enormous (and enormously vulgar) appetites, including a gargantuan [prescription] drug habit.[77]

Goldman had essentially acted like an enemy agent on the terrain of another man's life with a mission to sever all empathy with his victim. His special method was to find rock stars large enough to attract public curiosity beyond their fan base, then craft a hatchet-job biography and become infamous in the process. He deductively pushed a figment of Elvis Presley's image so far beyond its source that he came up with something different altogether. Elvis was portrayed through contradictions as a living corpse with a morbid grasp on his girlfriend's arm, a Frankenstein's monster. This approach was not new; for instance in 1956 a reviewer of the film *Love Me Tender* at *The Reporter* said Elvis Presley "resembled an obscene child".[78] Goldman elaborated upon such strategies. He also claimed that Elvis was a sham:

Elvis Presley never stood for anything. He made no sacrifices, fought no battles, suffered no martyrdom, never raised a finger to struggle on behalf of what he believed or claimed to believe. Even gospel, the music he cherished above all, he travestied and commercialized and soft-soaped to the point where it became nauseating.[79]

Southern gospel music was, of course, always commercial. Quite beyond Goldman's misinterpretation of it, his claims strategically ignore Elvis's deep love of music, his use of it as a way to draw races together and bring pleasure to millions, his patriotism and love of family, his philanthropy. He ignored the way that Elvis sincerely served his fans. The slippery logic of Goldman's claims are that they lever *our* assumption that Elvis's mission was not *about* drawing lines or taking sides, and artificially extends it to *ignore* his social contribution and perceive his life and work as an exercise in futility. For Goldman, Elvis's unique voice is meaningless.[80] He locates the singer, like the rock'n'roll genre itself, as a *con trick*.

Goldman's sensationalist biography was big business. After Penguin's first edition, McGraw-Hill published a hard-cover version. Then Avon Books bought the reprint rights for $1 million.[81] Sales rocketed on the back of controversy that the book created. Marsh called the author "the master of a fact that is not quite a fact".[82] Musicologist Charles Hamm wanted Goldman's work reclassified as fiction.[83] It could be argued that all biographies are interpretive part-fictions, however, as there is no life story without some sort of theory.[84] Nevertheless, Goldman's reworking seemed an *extreme* misrepresentation. Elvis's friend Larry Geller said the book revealed more about its writer than about Elvis.[85]

Goldman's book came, of course, at a time when Elvis could not respond. His character-assassinating biography was perceived as an assault on a living legend. On a 1990 *Geraldo* TV show debate, Esposito exclaimed, "Albert Goldman lives off people that are dead. He assassinates people after they die".[86] Every person, and especially every celebrity, has a reputation. Discussing the political philosopher Slavoj Žižek's work, Tony Meyers suggests that "after our bodies have died, people remember our names, remember our deeds and so on".[87] The posthumous celebrity or "afterlife" of popular musicians is maintained by the peaks of their fluctuating reputations, and by circulating or celebrating their recordings. Goldman's sustained attack on Elvis indicated a pitched battle against something much larger: the star's totemic edifice and what it represented. In his book *Mystery Train*, Marcus had previously argued that Elvis was an icon who embodied hopeful possibilities for America. He described Goldman's biography as "cultural genocide" in a review for *The Village Voice*.[88] In an insightful commentary, the science fiction writer J.G. Ballard, meanwhile, concluded that it remained a mark of Elvis Presley's immense talent—and perhaps therefore what people believed it might mean—that the singer could "transcend everything", including Goldman's vituperative assault.[89]

In the 1980s, Elvis continued to be a controversial figure precisely because his image so readily lent itself to reflecting upon the anxieties of American society. The idea of him as a mass-marketed phenomenon—a critique that rejected his blander films in the 1960s *and* sentimental music in the 1970s—became implicitly focused on a new avalanche of book publishing. At its centre, Goldman *reductively equated* Elvis with meaningless commodification. This idea formed a seedbed for representations that presented fans as deluded fantasists governed by blind faith and conspiracy thinking. A concerted effort to erode Elvis's popularity focused not just on the star but also on his fans, asking why anyone would want to join such a seemingly misguided rabble. His fans aimed to "keep his memory alive" in respectful ways, but—especially in the wake of Goldman's book—a grotesque and scandalous version of Elvis began to colonize popular imagination through a virally expanding set of puns and clichés. The singer's image was under siege. Taking their cue from the 1950s, commentators equated his story with the excesses of mass culture. A set of stereotypes was erected to contest his memory across a broad field that included art, cartoons, stories, TV comedies, merchandising and even sport.[90] Detractors argued that although Elvis *appeared* to be someone who had everything—a superhero—his success came because he had so readily embraced the commodification of his gift. He supposedly never resisted capitalism. It was no substitute for (self) love. Commercial exploitation had supposedly hastened his mortal demise. Now that he was "immortal", as only a commodity can be, his private life was being posthumously colonized. Biographies and buddy books became evidence that Elvis fans—or "Elfans" as they became known around this time—could not let go of their hero. They became framed as blind loyalists. My aim, briefly, is to deconstruct the multi-faceted critique at play here.

For those critical of the Elvis phenomenon, Goldman's work offered the foundation of a rapidly formed ordination system, a mental map that highlighted Elvis sightings (the idea that he was still alive) and impersonators (as possessed channels of his worst excess).[91] The first plank of the strawman idea questioning Elvis's cultural worth was that he epitomized pure-bred commerce as someone who had passively accepted his commodification but in doing so lost his own agency. Here Elvis was framed not only as cheap tat—gaudy and bad taste—but also as a hidden exploiter and racist thief. The next notion was that he was therefore part of a conservative plot to destroy radical impulses in popular culture. In this guise, he was rejected as both corporate and hypocritical: an insecure fame addict, fat karate exponent, secret pill popper. An associated foundation of Elvis's posthumous grotesque was that he represented, in effect, a graven idol: the commercial brand. As an emblem, he was therefore supposedly engorged, bloated, copied and cloned. The final foundation was that Elvis fans were those consumers foolish enough to misidentify their favourite brand as a religion. It marked Elvis out as a debased messiah and then argued that his fans were irrational, deluded and *fundamentalist*. These different ideas partly came into focus in discussions about Elvis's fan following.

While Elvis was becoming accepted as part of the cultural furniture of a nation whose collective memory he had helped to shape, middle-class commentators simultaneously rejected the deceased singer as the unwelcome face of unhip capitalism. One of their targets was the living culture of Elvis fans who regularly assembled every year at Graceland to mark the anniversary of his passing. The radio presenter Andy Kershaw recalled:

> It was the tenth anniversary of Elvis Presley's death, August 1987, and Radio 1 had dispatched me to Memphis, specifically to Graceland, to cover the maudlin ceremonies, the tribal tribute gatherings and city-wide shopping frenzy for truly shocking souvenir tat. Elvis fans must be the easiest consumers upon whom to offload tawdry, sentimental baubles: being an Elvis true believer is itself a measure of abysmal taste and poor judgement.[92]

Kershaw's flippant assertions quickly reveal some of the most widespread and misguided ideas about Elvis fans: that they are stuck in the past, that they follow their hero with religious fervour, and that they are gullible consumers who have little or no taste. While such thinking was prominent in the 1980s and 1990s, traces of it still linger in some quarters. To address the claims, Elvis fans are not stuck in the past, but instead form a *living culture* based around an ongoing celebration of their hero's performances. In other words, the process through which they create cultures and form social bonds uses Elvis as a shared theme, but happens very much *in the present*. The religiosity argument is also problematic. Although, when elaborated respectfully, it captures some of the totemic aspects of fandom, it nevertheless ignores and disrespects any organized religions that Elvis fans already have. It fails to specify a shared theology. It is attributed, by contrast, to *confuse* fandom with irrational conviction or blind loyalty. Ted Harrison's 1992 book *Elvis People: The Cult of the King* provides classic examples of metaphorical, anti-fan thinking. For Harrison, Elvis impersonators are the "high priests" of a supposed Elvis religion.[93] Asking whether fans pray to their hero he explained, "So it is that many Elvis fans will hotly deny any religious suggestion that they have turned their hero into a cult religious figure ... Yet from time to time a fan will 'come out'".[94] Harrison's metaphorical thinking is unscientific, but nevertheless engrossing in its cloying and rather distorted logic.[95] Such ideas became *the* context within which academic work of the era (particularly cultural studies, anthropology, folklore research and fine art) tended to talk about Elvis.[96] Yet Elvis fans were not pseudo-religious "true believers" any more than radio DJs like Kershaw, music writers like Harrison, or academics have been "true believers" in their own vocations. It is the pseudo-religiosity perspective, not actual fans, which misunderstands aesthetic judgements as spiritual beliefs.

Pseudo-religiosity arguments mention "sacredness", but are actually designed to reference *submission* (star "worship"): a process in which the rational self of the individual is to some extent abandoned. This is the point of perceived connection between religion and consumption. Elvis remains an extremely popular artist and has a base of collectors big enough for the release of many kinds of product. His fans do not, however, indiscriminately buy everything. The 1974 RCA concert outtakes album, *Having Fun on Stage with Elvis*, which included no actual music, for example, has been one of the poorest selling records in the Presley catalogue.

Andy Kershaw's critique of "abysmal taste" is really a show of *disgust at perceived excess*. What his argument fixates upon is an unholy marriage: an imagined meeting point between the excessive demands of commerce (which conceptually tends to exploit for profit) and the excessive demands of fandom (which conceptually doubles for obsession and addiction). Elvis is the symbolic meeting point here, so he can only be portrayed in such arguments through ideas about gluttony or depravity. It is important, however, to see such arguments from a different perspective. In a Freudian world, the perceived excess of both commerce and fandom represents the primal mind or *id*, out of control, indulging its appetites in an extended binge. In contrast, any commentators who spot this represent the voice of conscience, or *super-ego*: cautious, conservative, in control, not given to sensual or sensory abandon. They place themselves as displaying taste (not tastelessness), and therefore appear more middle class, more refined and more *civilized*. That mode of distinction has not just been applied to Elvis and his fans, but also to other fan cultures. As fan researcher Henry Jenkins noted in 1992, media fans have often been portrayed as "brainless consumers".[97] Kershaw's critique is arguably, therefore, not *just* against Elvis fans, but, by proxy, against mainstream music fans *in general*—Presley fans just being an embodiment of commercial music's "true believers". In effect, such mass-culture thinking creates a correspondence between fans and other identity groups who have been socially marginalized by being labelled as "brainless", "uncivilized" or "excessive". Such stereotypes have included blunt perceptions of females as hysterical; working-class whites as addicted; and Blacks as impulsive or licentious. These portrayals miss the complexity of individuals from the stigmatized groups. In relation to fandom they ignore both the multifaceted nature of consumption and *other concerns* associated with most fans' roles, including networking, tourism, sharing creativity and developing expertise. While fans participate in the process of consumption, in general, and with Elvis in particular, they do not resemble "brainless consumers" in reality.

Kershaw's stance allowed him to express his own cultural capital, as a seemingly hip music fan, but the irony is that he was a passionate follower of African guitar bands and other forms of world folk music. If Elvis and his generation had not embraced Black vernacular sounds, the path in society towards the celebration of African music may not have been so emphatically trod.

While Elvis had been controversial in the 1980s as a discursive resource in debates about America, in different ways he was increasingly legitimated in the 1990s as the country came to terms with him. It is important to understand that in 1992 the US public voted for its favourite Elvis from a choice of two commissioned competing stamps. Mark Stutzman's young Elvis won out over the Vegas version painted by John Berkey. The Smithsonian had also begun a gradual process of commemorating Elvis Presley as a great contributor to the country's heritage. In other words, Elvis's image became the arena in which some pressing struggles played out. This created a cultural backlash based on social anxiety about celebrating such an ambiguous hero. Much academic work from the era offers an example of the way in which the "trash" image of Elvis had taken a firm (but temporary) foothold over certain sections of the popular imagination. Marjorie Garber, a Harvard university professor whose work examines portrayals of sexuality, for instance, claimed that Goldman was an "Elvis debunker".[98] Another example was sociologist Peter Stromberg's article, "Elvis Alive?" which suggested that Elvis fans were nothing more than consumerists. When used as a term of academic critique, reductionism means the creation of explanations that damage understanding by oversimplifying complex phenomena. According to Stromberg: "Celebrities are deities because they are the most significant mediators of American consumerism ... at once human and God".[99] With this, Stromberg reductively and dismissively aligned fandom, consumerism and religion. His work was not based on first-hand contact with fans, but instead explicitly referenced only two secondary sources drawn from commercial media: a story about Elvis memorabilia in the *San Francisco Examiner and Chronicle*, and Elvis's obituary from *Time* magazine.

A further example comes from psychoanalytic scholar Stephen Hinerman's discussion of Elvis fandom *as a process of fantasizing*, which begins: "Although Elvis has been dead for more than 10 years, fans who believe he is alive send him an average of a letter a day".[100] Hinerman's sources are drawn from a highly commercial environment, where new books locate Elvis as a figure in popular culture without much respect for his story or regard for his fan base. Hinerman's first source of fan fantasies was Hanz Holzer's book *Elvis Presley Speaks*, a sensationalist account with a subtitle which Hinerman conveniently missed in his bibliography: "The Astonishing Evidence of Spiritual Contact with Elvis from Beyond the Grave". Later editions of the book were simply titled, *Elvis Presley Speaks from the Beyond and Other Celebrity Ghost Stories*. This first source was therefore commercial fiction; whether it contained genuine fan fantasies is another matter. Hinerman's next source was Raymond Moody's 1987 book *Elvis After Life*. Its own tagline read, "Unusual Psychic Experiences Surrounding the Death of a Superstar". These two sources demonstrate the ambiguities of the early years of posthumous Elvis publishing, where superstar sightings were floated commercially as ways to attract both cynical and a few sympathetic readers.[101]

A final example of academic work that questioned the cultural worth of Elvis as an icon is Erika Doss's 1999 ethnography, *Elvis Culture: Fans, Faith and Image*. According to bibliographer Mary Hancock-Hinds, it presented, "An example of the narrow-mindedness and stereotyping that Elvis fans endure. From a few examples, fans are painted as racists, with Elvis appearing to be a White supremacist icon".[102] Hancock-Hinds clearly shows the sense of betrayal that some fans felt over what remains the only published, book-length English language ethnography of Elvis fandom. While Doss's work sometimes framed the fan community unsympathetically, it was not entirely without insight or merit. If some academic interpretations in the 1990s emphasized, exaggerated or hallucinated various aspects of the Elvis phenomenon, part of their implicit aim was perhaps to register social anxieties about the public expression of emotion associated with media fandom *in general*. Beyond this activity, however, there was a fringe of sympathetic Elvis scholarship published both before, alongside, and after, the era, not least by popular music researchers.[103] Nevertheless, still smarting from the long shadow of Goldman's disdainful critique, the Elvis fan community was, broadly speaking, right to be weary of academia at the time, given the ways it selectively portrayed its hero.

Elvis's own popularity was significantly bigger than that of his critics; indeed, they were arguably exploiting his fame to raise their own profiles. The irony was not only that the discussion had little or nothing to do with Elvis's music, but also that the pendulum soon swung the other way. In an era where mediated entertainment was increasingly central to daily life, pop culture had become the terrain upon which national and international diplomacy was conducted. Dominating politics and other public discussions, the baby boomers gained increasing credibility by making references to their own generational fandom as a form of "common touch". Siding with Elvis had the potential to draw diverse constituencies of voters together. In June 1992, as part of his electoral campaign, future president Bill Clinton played 'Heartbreak Hotel' on his saxophone on *The Arsenio Hall Show*, a late-night chat show presented by a Black comedian. Writing at the end of that year, TV critic David Zurawick described how others perceived the event:

> It wasn't dignified. It demeaned presidential politics. It "coarsened" the discourse of democracy ... such media mockery only reinforced the overwhelmingly positive messages emanating to the larger audience of voters. Clinton as Sax Man. Clinton as Baby Boomer. Clinton with a sense of humor about himself. Clinton participating in a Southern-Black-and-White-folks' strain of music ... MTV and

The Arsenio Hall Show are part of a larger movement: the change from White-male hegemony to a multicultural America.[104]

Clinton was not the only person to play the Elvis card, however. Boris Yeltsin was the first president to oversee the transition to a post-Soviet Russia. He had become a committed fan after hearing the singer in the late 1950s, when Elvis was necessarily an underground phenomenon in the communist Soviet Union. After Yeltsin oversaw the transformation of his country from 1991 onwards, he told interviewers that Elvis had "a beautiful voice from God". He also located Elvis as a symbol of harmonious East-West understanding by explaining, "I would like to open up our trade relations with the West and Elvis is a good ambassador. It is a very good way for our people to understand and learn about the American culture".[105] In a sense, Yeltsin used his Elvis fandom to express his country's newfound embrace of Western values. Presley was, in effect, therefore located as the affable face of imperialism: America's biggest Cold War weapon finally coming home to roost; the bridge figure in a globalized world governed by *consumer sovereignty* as the concept that linked capitalism and democracy. At the end of June 2006, in the company of President George W. Bush and Bush's wife Laura, the Japanese Prime Minister Junichiro Koizumi visited Graceland. Koizumi's visit came in the wake of him supporting US foreign policy in Iraq and Afghanistan, and discussing North Korea and the resumption of beef imports to Japan with the president. The Japanese premier had actually been a long-time fan. Just after he assumed office in the summer of 2001, acting on a suggestion from a Japanese fan club leader, he had released an EPE-endorsed collection of his favourite Elvis songs, complete with commentaries. When he sang a few bars of 'Love Me Tender' in the Jungle Room, it was another sign that Elvis's music had become a way to cement international relationships. Elvis was a central symbol of America. America was central to the new world order. Declaring Elvis fandom consequently became a popular means by which world leaders could endorse American values.

Legacy Artist: Elvis in the 2000s

In recent years, the prominence of Elvis's music has helped to reclaim his reputation. The fans have continued to celebrate annually in Memphis as a means to show how much their hero is remembered. Early in January there is the annual celebration of what would have been Elvis's birthday. Elvis Week culminates every August with streams of fans visiting Elvis's last resting place as part of a candlelit vigil. The celebration has been an annual event from 1977 onwards. It greatly boosts Memphis tourist figures and has climaxed at five-yearly intervals. The Memphis Mafia have acted as ambassadors for their former employer and are curators of his legend. Elvis enthusiasts now have, in conjunction with his music, a wealth of fan club and heritage opportunities at their disposal, plus an avalanche of insider accounts and biographies. In a recent book, I described immersion in details of Elvis Presley's life as the enjoyment of "imagined memories" within a very specific *chronotopic* container. Dedicated fans are fascinated with the details of how Elvis lived in *a particular portion of time and place*, one that begins in Tupelo, 1935, and ends in Memphis, 1977.[106]

One indication of continued fan interest is the buoyant niche market for Elvis releases. Especially if marginal and bootleg releases are counted, Elvis's musical output actually became more frequent and prolific after his death. Though some of it has not always found the widest audience, Elvis's music has actually survived somewhat better than his physical heritage. Over 700 official and 1000 unofficial Elvis CDs have been released since the format was adopted in the 1980s.[107] After its burst of capitalizing upon the spike in demand precipitated by Elvis's death, RCA tended to repackage old hits. Mainstream *promotion*, however, was initially hamstrung, partly due to disputes between EPE and RCA over the allocation of royalty revenue.[108] Elvis's music did not get the promotion it deserved. His label initially lacked imagination in its efforts to revive his catalogue and tended not to fully exploit its potential.[109] An ongoing hunt was staged to find the full scope of his recorded legacy. Living on Elvis Presley Boulevard for the last few years of his life, it goes without saying that Elvis was highly cognizant of his own legend. In 1969, he bought a microfilm reader and had 4000 of his personal items archived.[110] Some of his effects included home recordings, but beyond those there were also live recordings (from sound engineers and audiences), studio outtakes, alternative versions, different mixes, radio broadcasts and other rarities. The immense value of this legacy has not always been recognized. When EPE called Binder in the 1980s, saying that it was planning another Elvis tribute and asking him if he had any ideas, he retrieved an unseen tape of the *Comeback*'s improvisational segments from NBC's Beacons vault, but was then asked, "Do you think anybody cares about this stuff?" The estate went on to sell the footage to HBO for a million dollars.[111]

Joan Deary joined RCA in 1955 and was based at its California office from the early 1960s, initially working under Steve Sholes. She was the first female Manager, Director, then Executive Director of A&R at RCA Victor. Deary had a strong relationship with the fan clubs and worked on creating some interesting Elvis compilations—notably the *Anthology* series and *Elvis Aron Presley* silver album set—which included outtakes, rarities and historical information. In 1984 *People* magazine called her "a kind of high priestess of Presleybilia, overseeing RCA's release of posthumous Elvis material ... whose official title is producer but whose de facto job is Presley curator".[112] In mid-1983, after Colonel Parker struck himself a lucrative deal for unreleased material and offloaded 300 reels of tape from his own collection, Deary searched

Graceland and found a further 29 tapes, which she "cleaned up" with the help of recording engineer Dick Bogert. Some of the results came out on RCA's six-LP *Golden Celebration* set, but Deary preferred to release rarities as part of a series of concept-based releases rather than selling them all at once. Her packages began the work of informing dedicated audiences about Elvis's recording practices. Fans also looked instead to the bootleg market for new releases.[113] A turning point occurred, however, when RCA changed hands in 1986. The struggling major label was bought out by General Electric, which then sold a controlling interest to the European conglomerate Bertelsmann. Bertelsmann's music operation was called BMG (Bertelsmann Music Group). More recently Elvis has posthumously become a Sony Music artist. Sony BMG was created as a joint venture between its two parties in 2004 and became defunct again when Sony bought out BMG's 50% stake in 2008, leaving its properties as part of Sony Music Entertainment. When Elvis Presley's recorded music became a BMG asset in the 1980s, one senior figure in the corporation's Danish operation, a former A&R man called Ernst Jørgensen, seized his opportunity to give the vast catalogue an overhaul.

Recent scholarship on fandom has suggested that fans are not simply consumers who exist *outside* of the media industries. They have also used their interests to find roles within it. Matt Hills, for instance, suggests that they can become textual "gamekeepers".[114] In the Elvis world, Jørgensen is, in effect, such a figure. After hearing his hero for the first time when RCA recordings reached Denmark in the 1960s, Jørgensen had been passionate about the music. To Elvis fans he has come to represent a kind of posthumous, contemporary "good" father figure: a man who has left his own almost auteurist stamp on Elvis's musical legacy through the careful husbandry of the catalogue. Under Jørgensen's stewardship, dedicated Elvis fans have been recognized as a niche marketplace and richly served with an ongoing series of new releases.

Working alongside another Elvis-supporter inside BMG, the label executive Roger Semon, Jørgensen secured a key role, helping to supervise Elvis's catalogue within the whole label, a job that drew on his forensic skills as a musical detective, archivist, historian and fan.[115] He had already done enough research to make a comprehensive Elvis sessions timeline, one that could be used as a map to locate any lost recordings. Jørgensen was charged with working alongside talented sound engineers to remaster Elvis's catalogue for the CD age and organizing new kinds of release strategy for the material that he had assembled. So far it has proved a gargantuan task. His first mission was to persuade RCA to orientate some of its Elvis output more squarely towards dedicated fan audiences and in that way claw back some of the territory ceded to the bootleg market. In doing so, he began to break down and replace some of the gender stereotypes that surrounded the label's perception of Elvis fandom:

The first thing I did was fly to New York and meet with RCA's marketing department. They told me they had demographic studies that proved the typical Elvis consumer was a woman between the ages of 35 and 55, who was married to a blue-collar worker and was unwilling to spend more than eight dollars on an Elvis album. They assured me this was true, but I was just as sure they were wrong. I suggested a box set at $80, *The King of Rock 'n' Roll: The Complete '50s Masters* ... Once they saw the sales numbers, the Americans all changed their ideas about Elvis ... their idea of who liked Elvis was absurd. It wasn't just older women who thought he was sexy. Mostly, it was men who lived all over the world, serious music lovers and collectors.[116]

From the start, Jørgensen pursued a dualistic strategy. Recordings likely to appeal to the wider public were re-mastered in a contemporary style. Meanwhile, those considered only to appeal to historical or fannish interest were given a sonic reshaping that aimed to deliver a faithful version of Elvis's own specifications—a process that involved cleaning up some of the Columbia-type reverb from the early RCA material.

Jørgensen is now at the helm of a kind of privately-funded community history project. His releases lever the fannish urge to share new material within the forum of a legal, industry operation. Jørgensen explained his concerns more fully to an audience of fans during Elvis Week in 2012, as he explained the redeveloped package of Elvis's famous Madison Square Garden engagement, *Elvis: Prince From Another Planet*.[117] As a fan, he wants to hear new material. As a record company executive, he cannot endorse illegal commercial recordings. In effect he is thus a professional über-collector, charged with researching and bringing more Elvis material within the boundary of the RCA catalogue, a role that means he serves a kind of *inverted* A&R function as someone who *already has* a lucrative artist but needs to find suitable material to serve the marketplace. If unreleased recordings cross his path, Jørgensen has to make financial calculations about their worth that rest on their exclusivity, quality and viability. He will not buy up poor quality recordings, no matter what rare moments they contain. Neither will he pitch for material that is already in the public domain. This means that many items, from audience-made recordings of Elvis's final concert to "unreleased" rarities posted up on YouTube, have not made it into Sony's expanding Elvis collection.

Jørgensen first oversaw a release schedule that concentrated on periodic compilations reflecting specific phases in Elvis's career beginning with *The King of Rock'n'Roll* box set. New collections of masters followed from the same series in 1993 and 1995. In 1999 Jørgensen helped to start the Sony Elvis collector's label, Follow That Dream (FTD). Although its curator is potentially interested in Hayride-era material, FTD releases have tended to consist of performances documented on cleaner audio recordings: later studio sessions,

1970s concerts and their rehearsals. While the label was initially uninterested in revising previously released material, it has also occasionally relented.[118] Sony's box-set release strategy culminated in October 2010 with a 30-CD set featuring all 711 known master recordings issued in Elvis's lifetime plus a further 103 rarities. Its current edition retails for just over $900 and, in effect, offers completists an instant collection.[119] The problem is, however, that more recordings are discovered all the time. In 2012, Jørgensen oversaw the release of yet another highly prized RCA/Sony limited edition book and CD set of Elvis's Sun years called *A Boy from Tupelo*: a set so sought after that some fans uploaded videos of them unwrapping it to YouTube. Capitalizing on the cache of rare recordings and limited-edition release events, what these—and bootleg—packages clearly prove is that there is still significant demand for new material from the specialist Elvis fan market.

In the era of social media Elvis is not just an absent individual. His name marks out a vast cultural constellation that circulates, in part, around a brand: a coherent and meaningful set of intellectual property interests. In 2005 the rights to his image and likeness were acquired by CKX Inc, a company that later became Core Media and owned the rights to *American Idol* and other properties. Core Media Group were bought out in 2011 by the private equity firm Apollo Management Group, who then sold the rights to Elvis's likeness to the Authentic Brands Group (ABG). Leaving National Entertainment Collectibles Association founder Joel Weinshanker in charge of Graceland, the move positioned Elvis alongside ABG's other iconic intellectual property assets, including his old friend Muhammad Ali. In other words, Elvis's image has been passed between a series of different corporations which specialize in entertainment heritage as a mode of investment. In 1993, Colonel Parker claimed that he probably never "exploited Elvis as much as he is being exploited today".[120] Parker's claim seems slightly disingenuous, because he "exploited" Elvis as a specific living individual. As a posthumous icon, "Elvis" is (as opposed to "was") a brand "exploited" as dead labour. Core Media Group's decision in the summer of 2013 to include Elvis on Buffalo Studio's *Blitz Bingo* online gaming platform seems as ill-advised as the worst of Elvis's tacky 1980s pirate merchandise. Although he performed in Vegas hundreds of times in his lifetime, to my knowledge Elvis never directly endorsed gambling and one wonders if he would have approved the invitation to "Play Elvis Bingo!"[121]

Although Priscilla and Lisa Marie Presley have so far acted as enthusiastic guardians overseeing his posthumous reputation, Elvis's having "left the building" means that he can no longer participate in the *authorized* configuration of his image. It is becoming increasingly divorced from his music and owned by organizations that had nothing to do with his living career as an individual. In this climate there has been some doubt about how long commemorative rituals might continue. In 2003, Marcus reported, "if Elvis Presley was indeed immortal, his fans were not".[122] One anxiety is that even if Elvis's music still stands, if his fans do not make more noise or if his brand is not subject to appropriate husbandry, then his music will begin fading from the public sphere. It is instructive that EPE did not allow any remixes of his music to hit the marketplace until 2002. To have Elvis's vocals reduced to cues for a dance track would have been to attack his star aura. Instead, the JXL track 'A Little Less Conversation' revamped its source material by keeping Elvis's vocal at the heart of the song and building a fresher, more solid and contemporary instrumental base. The JXL version included punchy drumming and lively, female backing vocals. As a result, Elvis's vocal presence was more reinforced than deconstructed. Elvis Presley's other mash-up albums have been *Christmas Duets*, which followed the recent tradition by pairing the singer with female country singers in 2008, and *Viva Elvis*: a fully remixed, but poorly received album from 2010, designed to accompany an EPE-endorsed Cirque du Soleil spectacular.[123] Any fragmented and repeated pattern turns its original sound into music. One of the issues here is that remixing causes a kind of decomposition of Elvis's vocal agency, reminding us of his passing into history in a way that the integrity of his recordings and their ritualistic replay constantly wards off.

Digital sound-mixing technology reached a point in the 1990s where ambient noise could be "cleaned up", allowing for the isolation of Elvis's vocal on his recordings. Two decades after Elvis died, EPE and Stig Edgren could therefore pioneer his "resurrection" as a video-screen performer at live concerts. They created a spectacle at the now-defunct Mid-South Coliseum in Memphis that featured Elvis on video backed by his original team. In the wake of its great success, its musicians began an annual international tour that continues to this day. In an age of video screens, *Elvis: The Concert* worked as a simulacrum. The only person who that was not actually there was Elvis. His fan audience was thankful to get a step nearer to experiencing his live show. Like the *Comeback*, *Elvis: The Concert* has become both a retrospective and an update for an age in which audiences have come to use video-screen images to verify the presence of their objects. Indeed, the characteristic hybridization of recorded medium and live event was taken a stage further in January 2013, when a full audience of fan-tourists assembled at the Neal S. Blaisdell Center (formerly the Honolulu International Center) to watch a "live" video screening of the original *Aloha* concert as the highlight of six days of celebration staged at the Hilton Hawaiian Village Waikiki Beach resort. While fans maintain a keen awareness of Elvis as an individual performer, such events also affirm him as an intellectual property and heritage commodity. The return to *Aloha* demonstrates that now Elvis is spearheading a phase of virtual celebrity characterized by a degraded boundary between the live event and mediated commodity. A further development in this direction is that holograms are now making tours, though so far an Elvis hologram has not yet appeared on stage. In the mid-2010s, his signature recordings have, however, been remixed into several new albums with input from the Royal Philharmonic Orchestra and sent out on an *Elvis: The Concert*-style video tour.

What Elvis left us with—beyond, of course, his hooded eyes, charming smile, jet-black hair, quick temper, profound grace, humility, and even his cheeky sense of humour—is the trace of a unique, powerful and commanding human voice. His greatest legacy is in sound. To understand the heart of Elvis's musical contribution, the uniqueness of his vocality must therefore be understood. In a 2013 piece on how listeners process musical recordings, the cultural commentator Mark Fisher drew attention to the way that Marcus's interpretation of popular music works. Fisher broached the idea that Marcus's writing "with its privileging of voice, live performance, spontaneity" might offer "rock writing's version of what Derrida calls the 'metaphysics of presence'... [with listening] secured and settled via an anchoring to a body".[124] In this formulation, the singing voice is authorized, embodied, authentic and present. It is *there* rather than produced by us hearing it, a perceived point of origin rather than a disembodied or ventriloquized effect. Elvis's unique voice has become a kind of fetishized guarantor of this "metaphysics of presence": not simply a justification for Marcus's approach, but rather a source of emotionally guaranteed certainty, a source that stops us from thinking. For Fisher:

> We live in a time when the past is present, and the present is saturated with the past ... What is mourned ... it often seems, is the very possibility of loss. With ubiquitous recording and playback, nothing escapes, everything can return.[125]

Such senses of time do not just reflect Elvis, but the state of music in a contemporary era. Fans know that unfortunately Elvis is dead and gone. Nevertheless, in an age of ubiquitous recording, precisely as a voice, Elvis remains unsurpassed: no one can quite replace him. Fans that lived through Elvis's career remember his many touching performances as events unfolding in the past.[126] For the rest of us, those recorded moments seem timeless; we might remember when we first heard them, but in relation to historic time, whether in relation to Elvis or to the society from which he came, they feel remarkably *unmarked*. We can place them academically, but not emotionally; they belong, instead, to our own perception of Elvis and how we feel about him. Even in his lifetime, the strange duality of presence and absence was a hallmark of his iconic celebrity. It is our fascination with him, with his personality and what he represents—not simply with the shape of modern media culture—that means that we both feel that we know him and experience a sense of time in free fall now that he is gone.

Michel Foucault describes writers who inspire an avalanche of cultural production in their wake as "transdiscursive": they create a body of work that "contains characteristic signs, figures, relationships and structures which could be reused by others".[127] Elvis is the archetypal "transdiscursive" popular musician. He did not just contribute to one particular genre. Instead he shifted and reworked genre configurations so radically that their foundations changed, new styles and traditions emerged, and an explosion of musical efforts followed in his wake. Pondering the impact of Elvis, you might wish to consider a world without his influence. Cultural phenomena would have come and gone, but would life have been quite the same? Without his "revolt into style", rockabilly might never have existed. Would there have been such rapid progress towards the end of racial segregation in music? Would there have been such intense popular expressions of desire, a youth culture, Cliff Richard or the Beatles? Would Dylan have had his sneer, the Stones had their swagger, or the Fonz combed his hair? Would Michael Jackson ever have made the transition from star to icon? Would hundreds of other artists— from Jim Morrison to Barry White—ever have gotten started? Could Bowie or the Sex Pistols actually have happened? What about the more immediate explosion of Elvis culture and his global legion of impersonators? Would our understanding of fandom or the pop commodity have been quite the same?

When George Klein asked the Everly Brothers about Elvis's influence on later musicians they explained, "No, Elvis didn't open the door; he kicked it down and we walked through".[128] After Elvis, the racial segregation of music genres could never be maintained in quite the same way. Any distinction between mainstream and vernacular genres, between showbiz and soul, was gone. Elvis Presley may have been "raised on rock", but his all-embracing integration of musical strands owed more to easy listening and pop. His incendiary style challenged the long-standing hierarchical divisions separating high art (classical music, opera), middlebrow commerce (Irving Berlin, Tin Pan Alley), and creolized, sexually permissive low culture (blues, rockabilly, rock'n'roll, exploitation cinema). Furthermore, "Elvis the Pelvis" did not simply shake America out of its funk of sexual and social repression; his image always mixed *together* abandon and restriction in ways that renegotiated the line in between. Sticking to one's roots and "selling out" were not mutually exclusive categories in Elvis's world: because he "bought in" (materially and politically but not geo-culturally), he accomplished both things at once.

Elvis Presley still matters because he shared his immense gift without taking sides and in doing so created a musical legacy that still reflects our dreams. In 1969 the pop producer Phil Spector said, "I can't tell you why he's so great, but he is".[129] Elvis was not simply the generational link between Frank Sinatra and Bob Dylan. His vocal presence and magnetic personality represent a field of influence that stretches far and wide across popular music culture. Elvis contributed a sense of *personality* to commercial music that had rarely been there before, and in some ways has not been seen since. He had the whole package—the voice, the looks, the story—and with it the means to deliver on everything that his musical talent could promise. In doing so, he embodied a transition from roots to modernity and spoke to the shared experience of his country. While everything about Elvis has been debated and disputed, his immense legacy lives on as a testament to what one man, given the right opportunities, could achieve. In that sense, he has become a stake in discussions about human agency in a capitalist world. To put it another way, Elvis was not just an individual who became an icon: to many he symbolized individuality itself. According to Brode, society "produced, adored, damned, accepted, then came to worship him".[130] It was a trajectory that started in his dreams. Elvis's teacher in sixth grade, Mrs Dewey Camp, was once interviewed about his childhood years. She recalled "Elvis sitting in the class at the back of the room, rather timid, until the day, she asked, 'Can any of you children sing?' His little hand flew up in the air".[131]

To mark Black History Month, in February 2012, President Barack Obama sang part of 'Sweet Home Chicago' with B.B. King at the White House. The White House blues jam session had come about in Elvis's *conceivable* lifetime. At least symbolically, it marked the continuing aim of equality *in* diversity for a troubled nation. Mick Jagger was present that day, but the vanishing mediator between the Black president and blues playing ex-Delta labourer, at least in a symbolic sense, was Elvis. The Elvis of rock'n'roll who faced opposition in the public sphere when he crossed a line as a colour-blind fan and musician a year and a half in advance of Rosa Parks' protest. The inspiring Elvis of the *Comeback*, who channelled Martin Luther King. The triumphant Elvis of *Aloha*, a self-made brother of Abraham Lincoln. In fact Obama's team had previously asked if they could use 'If I Can Dream' for the president's inauguration. As the most prominent figure of the rock'n'roll era and then as a charismatic superstar, Elvis raised questions in the public sphere that allowed a global superpower to explore the possibilities of its own project. Those questions concerned the relationship between the individual and society, how popular art might be assessed, whether it can be fostered by the marketplace, and the extent to which the Western world could fully accommodate social difference.

From the 1950s to the 1970s and beyond, Elvis helped to transform society. By delivering a certain style, with all its associated politics, *to the mainstream*, he assisted everyone in deciding what mattered. In effect, Elvis was made to carry the weight of contradictions of his own culture. His persona represented the shared journey of America from hope to the beginnings of a kind of fragmentation and disillusionment. It also marked its constant possibility of change and resurrection. We must not forget, however, that for Elvis the music came first. Other performers blended and mixed genres, but none quite touched people like he did. Consider, therefore, Buffy Sainte-Marie, who was born on the Piapot Cree First Nations Reserve in Canada, raised an orphan, and became a folk singer-songwriter and activist. At first sight, she appears to have the ethnic identity and political conviction towards which Elvis could only gesture. We should not, however, necessarily reject one kind of artist in favour of another. As Sainte-Marie once said, "I was a huge Elvis fan! ... Elvis Presley gave me the courage to be myself. If he could be unique, then maybe I had a chance".[132]

Appendices

Appendix 1:

Some Biographic Turning Points

1935, January 8	Elvis born in Tupelo, Mississippi.
1948, November 6	The Presleys move from Tupelo to Memphis.
1953, c. August 1	Elvis visits Memphis Recording Service and cuts 'My Happiness' / 'That's When Your Heartaches Begin' as a vanity recording.
1954, c. July 19	Elvis's first single, 'That's All Right' / 'Blue Moon of Kentucky' is released today by Sun Records.
1954, October 16	The Blue Moon Boys debut on the *Louisiana Hayride* in Shreveport, Louisiana. This series of engagements allows them to tour.
1955, November 21	RCA signs Elvis Presley.
1956, January 28	Elvis debuts on national television, from the CBS studio in New York on the Dorsey Brothers' vehicle, *Stage Show*.
1956, July 1	Elvis guests on *The Steve Allen Show* in tails and sings 'Hound Dog' to an indifferent basset hound.
1956, September 9	First appearance on *The Ed Sullivan Show* from the CBS studios in LA.
1956, November 15	Elvis's first Hollywood film, *Love Me Tender*, opens in New York and goes national almost a week later.
1956, December 4	Famous impromptu Million Dollar Quartet session at Sun Studio in Memphis.
1956, December 7	Presley puts in a guest appearance at the WDIA Goodwill Revue in Memphis; the Black audience loves Elvis's appearance.

1958, March 24	Presley reports to the draft board.
1958, August 14	Elvis's mother Gladys dies.
1958, September 22	Elvis stages a press conference and boards a ship bound for Germany to continue his army duty.
1960, March 5	Release from army.
1961, March 25	*USS Arizona* memorial press conference and benefit show in Honolulu.
1964, May 13	Elvis borrows a life-changing spiritual book, *The Impersonal Life*, from his hairdresser, Larry Geller.
1967, May 1	Elvis and Priscilla get married at the Aladdin Hotel in Las Vegas.
1968, December 3	The *Comeback Special* airs on NBC.
1969, January 13	Elvis enters American Sound studio in Memphis.
1969, July 31	Elvis returns to Las Vegas with a live show at the International Hotel.
1969, November 10	Elvis's final Hollywood drama, *Change of Habit*, screens in movie theatres across America.
1970, February 27	Houston Astrodome's *Live Stock and Rodeo Show* concerts mean touring resumes.
1970, November 11	*Elvis: That's The Way It Is* documentary opens in theatres across the USA.
1970, December 21	Elvis Presley meets President Nixon.
1971, January 16	Junior Chamber of Commerce of America's Ten Outstanding Young Men of the Year speech in Memphis.
1972, May 9	Madison Square Garden in New York plays host to Elvis press conference and concerts.
1972, November 1	*Elvis on Tour* documentary debuts in movie theatres across the country.
1973, April 4	*Aloha from Hawaii via Satellite* broadcast on TV to various nations.
1977, June 19	First live show filmed for *Elvis in Concert*, a CBS-TV special.
1977, August 4	*Elvis: What Happened?* 'bodyguard book' released.
1977, August 16	Elvis found dead in Graceland.

Appendix 2:

Elvis Presley Biographic Timeline

This section features highlights from Elvis's life and career. He spent part of his professional life in the 1950s and 1970s on tour. For brevity, however, only a handful of exceptional tour dates have been included.[1] The more significant entries are in bold type.

1935, January 8	**Elvis born in Tupelo, Mississippi.**
1938, February 6	Elvis's father incarcerated for forging cheque.
1945, October 3	Elvis comes fifth singing at the Mississippi-Alabama Fair and Dairy Show.
1946, January 8	Gladys buys Elvis a guitar for his birthday at Tupelo Hardware Store.
1948, November 6	**The Presleys move from Tupelo to Memphis.**
1948, November 8	Elvis starts at Humes High School.
1949, September 20	The Presleys are accepted into Lauderdale Courts housing project.
1951, c. June 1	Summer work at Precision Tool this month.
1952, c. September 1	Elvis starts work at MARL Metal Products this month.
1953, April 9	Elvis sings 'Till I Waltz Again with You' at Humes High's annual Minstrel Show.
1953, c. August 1	**Elvis visits Memphis Recording Service and cuts 'My Happiness' / 'That's When Your Heartaches Begin' as a vanity recording.**
1954, c. January 1	At Memphis Recording Service this month, Elvis cuts second vanity recording: 'I'll Never Stand in Your Way' / 'It Wouldn't Be The Same Without You'.
1954, February 26	Elvis attends All-Night Gospel singing session at Ellis Auditorium.
1954, March 19	Presley leaves his job at Precision Tool.
1954, April 20	Elvis starts work at Crown Electric.
1954, May 15	A young Elvis Presley fails an audition for Eddie Bond's band at the Hi-Hat in Memphis.
1954, June 26	Sam Phillips asks his secretary to call Elvis, to try singing 'Without You' at Sun.
1954, July 3	Guitarist Scotty Moore calls Elvis on behalf of Sam Phillips to arrange Sun audition.
1954, July 4	At Scotty's apartment, Elvis jams an audition of sorts with bass player Bill Black.
1954, July 5	**The trio record 'That's All Right' at Sun Studio.**
1954, c. July 6	They record a B-side: 'Blue Moon of Kentucky'.
1954, July 8	**Dewey Phillips debuts 'That's All Right' and interviews Elvis on WHBQ.**

1954, July 12	Scotty assumes management of Elvis to protect him.
1954, July 17	Elvis tries two songs live with Scotty's band the Starlite Wranglers at the Bon Air in Memphis.
1954, c. July 19	**Elvis's first single, 'That's All Right' / 'Blue Moon of Kentucky' is released today by Sun Records.**
1954, July 26	Bob Neal adds Presley to his live package coming up at the Overton Park Shell.
1954, July 30	Elvis performs at the Overton Park Shell in Memphis and audience responds to him shaking his legs.
1954, August 7	New trio, the Blue Moon Boys (Elvis, Scotty and Bill), play the Eagle's Nest in Memphis, and play there on occasion for the rest of the year.
1954, September 8	The trio play Katz Drugs Store at Lamar and Airways in Memphis.
1954, c. September 22	'Good Rockin' Tonight' / 'I Don't Care if the Sun Don't Shine' released as a Sun single.
1954, October 2	The Blue Moon Boys play the *Grand Ole Opry*. Bill Monroe and Ernest Tubb offer Elvis words of support.
1954, October 16	**The Blue Moon Boys debut on the *Louisiana Hayride* in Shreveport, Louisiana. This relationship allows them to tour.**
1954, December 28	'Milkcow Blues Boogie' / 'You're A Heartbreaker' released today as a Sun single.
1955, January 1	**Bob Neal becomes Elvis's contracted manager and Tommy Sands see the Blue Moon Boys play in Houston.**
1955, January 15	**Colonel Parker attends a *Louisiana Hayride* event and sizes up Elvis's show.**
1955, March 23	An unsuccessful audition for Elvis and his band today on *Arthur Godfrey's Talent Scouts*.
1955, April 10	'Baby Let's Play House' / 'I'm Left, You're Right, She's Gone' released as a Sun single today.
1955, June 5	Elvis's pink-and-white Cadillac catches fire as he tours Arkansas.
1955, July 24	**Colonel Parker's arrangement begins, at first to exclusively represent the live side of Elvis's career.**
1955, August 5	Elvis makes his second appearance at an Overton Park Shell concert event.
1955, c. August 6	What becomes the final Sun Records single release, 'I Forgot to Remember to Forget' / 'Mystery Train', comes out today.
1955, August 15	Elvis signs new, more encompassing contract, making the Colonel his 'special advisor'.

1955, September 15	Against the Colonel's wishes, Bob Neal arranges to renew Elvis's *Louisiana Hayride* radio show contract for an extra year.
1955, September 17	Under pressure from the Colonel, Bob Neal reduces his role as Elvis's manager.
1955, September 23	Elvis attends the Blackwood Brothers' All-Night Singing at the Ellis Auditorium in Memphis.
1955, October 1	Colonel Parker changes Scotty and Bill's salary from a collective 50% of Elvis's gross income to $200 each per week.
1955, October 20	Elvis is on the same bill as Pat Boone and Bill Haley at special showcase being filmed by Cleveland DJ Bill Randle.
1955, November 21	**RCA signs Elvis Presley.**
1956, January 27	**'Heartbreak Hotel' released. It reaches number 1 on the *Billboard* Top 100 singles chart, tops the Country and Western chart, and goes top 5 on the R&B chart.**
1956, January 28	**Elvis debuts on national television, from the CBS studio in New York on the Dorsey Brothers' vehicle, *Stage Show*.**
1956, February 23	Elvis is hospitalized for exhaustion from touring and television.
1956, March 2	Having pushed out Bob Neal as manager, Colonel Parker gets rid of his business partner Hank Snow.
1956, March 23	*Elvis Presley* album released. It reaches number 1 on the *Billboard* Top Pop Albums chart. Ironically, both an extended player (EP), and double EP, all with the same name as the LP, are shipped on the same day. They represent Elvis's debut on the EP market.
1956, March 26	Elvis does screen test for Hal Wallis at Paramount Studios in Los Angeles. Parker and Presley also create a signed letter that consolidates Parker's role as exclusive advisor, manager and representative.
1956, April 2	Colonel Parker buys Elvis out of *Louisiana Hayride* for $10,000.
1956, April 3	The Blue Moon Boys appear on *The Milton Berle Show* live from the deck of the *USS Hancock*.
1956, April 13	Flight problems experienced by Presley on trip from Texas to Tennessee.
1956, April 23	Elvis starts two-week live stint at the New Frontier Hotel in Las Vegas.
1956, April 25	Elvis signs non-exclusive movie contract with Hal Wallis.

1956, May 12	'I Want You, I Need You, I Love You' released. It reaches number 1 on the *Billboard* Top 100 singles chart.
1956, June 1	Non-singing guest appearance at another Overton Park Shell event alongside Johnny Cash, Carl Perkins and Roy Orbison.
1956, June 5	Elvis participates in a second *Milton Berle Show* appearance at NBC television in LA alongside Debra Paget.
1956, July 1	**Elvis guests on *The Steve Allen Show* in tails and sings 'Hound Dog' to an indifferent basset hound.**
1956, July 13	'Hound Dog' / 'Don't Be Cruel' released and reaches number 1 on the *Billboard* Top 100 singles chart.
1956, July 26	The Colonel arranges a deal giving Hank Saperstein exclusive rights to merchandise Elvis's image in exchange for $35,000 and a 45% royalty.
1956, August 20	Elvis begins working on the film *Love Me Tender*.
1956, September 9	**First appearance on *The Ed Sullivan Show* from the CBS studios in LA.**
1956, September 26	First gig of two days at the Mississippi-Alabama Fair and Dairy Show in Elvis's home town of Tupelo.
1956, September 28	'Love Me Tender' is released. It makes number 1 on the *Billboard* Top 100 singles chart.
1956, October 18	Update of the RCA contract includes 5% royalty rate and at least ten promotional radio or television appearances. Elvis has altercation with Gulf gas station attendant on the same day.
1956, October 19	The (first) *Elvis* album is released. It reaches number 1 on the *Billboard* Top Pop Album chart. *Elvis Vol. 1* EP featuring 'Love Me' is also released today; not his first EP, but his first one to top the EP charts.
1956, October 28	Publicity for *Love Me Tender* in New York includes a press conference, 40 foot cut-out, and the Colonel distributing 'Elvis For President' buttons.
1956, November 15	***Love Me Tender* opens in New York and goes national almost a week later.**
1956, December 4	**Famous impromptu Million Dollar Quartet session at Sun Studio in Memphis.**
1956, December 7	**Presley puts in a guest appearance at the WDIA Goodwill Revue in Memphis; the Black audience loves Elvis's appearance.**
1957, January 4	'Too Much' released and reaches number 2 on the *Billboard* Top 100 singles chart.
1957, January 22	Elvis starts filming *Loving You*.
1957, March 10	*Loving You* wrap party.

1957, March 22	'All Shook Up' released. It achieves number 1 on the *Billboard* Top 100 singles chart. Elvis also pulls a Hollywood prop gun on a marine who accosts him near the Chisca Hotel.
1957, March 23	Presley attends Ellis Auditorium again for an all-night gospel singalong.
1957, March 25	Graceland purchased for $102,500.
1957, c. April 1	*Peace in the Valley* gospel EP is released this month and makes top 40 singles chart.
1957, April 2	Elvis plays Toronto on tour, continuing on to Ottawa.
1957, May 6	Elvis turns up at MGM to start making *Jailhouse Rock*.
1957, May 14	Unfortunately, Presley inhales a tooth cap while working on the famous dance sequence in *Jailhouse Rock*.
1957, June 11	'(Let Me Be) Your Teddy Bear' released. It reaches number 1 on the *Billboard* Top 100 singles chart.
1957, June 17	Camera work completed on *Jailhouse Rock*.
1957, June 24	Elvis finishes his duties on *Jailhouse Rock* this week.
1957, June 26	*Loving You* EP released. It makes the top 5 of the EP chart.
1957, July 1	*Loving You* soundtrack album released. It will make number 1.
1957, July 19	A second *Loving You* EP is released, and tops the EP chart.
1957, July 30	***Loving You* opens in movie theatres across America.**
1957, August 1	*Jet* magazine interviews Elvis about his attitude to race. Colonel Parker rejects an attempt to get Elvis to play the UK.
1957, August 21	*Just For You* EP released, with more material from the *Loving You* soundtrack, and it makes number 2 on the EP charts.
1957, August 31	Elvis again ventures into Canada with a press conference and show in Vancouver.
1957, September 10	Colonel Parker arranges a deal for his client to profit from photos on record sleeves.
1957, September 21	Scotty and Bill depart from Elvis's employ.
1957, September 24	'Jailhouse Rock' released. It makes number 1 on the *Billboard* Top 100 singles chart.
1957, September 27	Elvis performs at Tupelo Fairgrounds to benefit a youth centre named after him.
1957, October 12	Elvis vacations in Las Vegas.
1957, October 15	*Elvis' Christmas Album* released and tops the *Billboard* Top Pop Albums chart.
1957, October 16	*Elvis Sings Christmas Songs* EP released today and dominates the EP chart.

1957, October 30	*Jailhouse Rock* EP released today and tops the EP charts.
1957, November 8	***Jailhouse Rock* debuts in movie theatres across the USA.**
1957, November 10	Show at the Honolulu Stadium in Hawaii, and another one for both servicemen and the public the next day at Schofield Barracks.
1957, December 6	**Elvis appears at another WDIA Goodwill Revue and is photographed with various famous Black musicians.**
1957, December 20	Induction notice sent from Memphis draft board.
1958, January 3	RCA suggests an Elvis tunes classical album, but the Colonel rejects it.
1958, January 7	'Don't' is released and it reaches number 1 on the *Billboard* Top 100 singles chart.
1958, January 15	Elvis starts initial work on *King Creole*.
1958, c. March 11	Elvis finishes his duties on *King Creole*.
1958, March 24	**Presley reports to the draft board.**
1958, April 7	'Wear My Ring Around Your Neck' released as a single. It reaches number 3 on *Billboard*'s Top 100 singles chart.
1958, June 10	'Hard Headed Woman' single released. It reaches number 4 on *Billboard*'s singles chart early in August.
1958, July 1	*King Creole Vol. 1* EP released. It tops the EP chart.
1958, July 2	***King Creole* opens in movie houses across the USA.**
1958, July 29	*King Creole Vol. 2* EP released, and also comes to top the EP chart.
1958, August 14	**Elvis's mother Gladys dies.**
1958, September 19	*King Creole* soundtrack album released. It makes number 2 on the *Billboard* Top Pop Album charts.
1958, September 22	**Elvis stages a press conference and boards a ship bound for Germany to continue his army duty.**
1958, October 21	'One Night' / 'I Got Stung' single released. The two sides peak at number 4 and 8 on *Billboard*'s singles chart in November and December.
1958, November 18	*Elvis Sails* EP released today. It peaks at number 2 in January on *Billboard*'s EP chart.
1958, December 13	Colonel Parker suggests idea for Hawaiian movie.
1959, March 3	Elvis visits Munich to date a girl he likes.
1959, March 10	'I Need Your Love Tonight' / '(Now and Then There's) A Fool Such As I' single released today. The two sides peak in the top 5 in this same month.
1959, June 13	Elvis takes an army break in Munich, then Paris.
1959, June 23	'A Big Hunk O' Love' released as a single today. It tops the US *Billboard* singles chart in October.

1959, September 13	Priscilla Beaulieu introduced to Elvis at his house party in Germany.
1959, December 6	Elvis starts karate lessons with German master Jürgen Seydel.
1960, January 6	Elvis travels to Paris on break from army.
1960, February 11	Promoted to full Sergeant by the army.
1960, March 1	Army press conference held in Germany.
1960, March 2	Elvis leaves Germany.
1960, March 5	**Release from army.**
1960, March 7	Post-army press conference held in Memphis.
1960, March 26	Elvis tapes *Frank Sinatra—Timex Show* in Miami.
1960, April 8	*Elvis Is Back!* LP is released. It reaches number 2 on the *Billboard* Top LPs chart.
1960, April 21	*G.I. Blues* preproduction begins in Los Angeles; Elvis reports for duty.
1960, April 25	'Stuck On You' tops the US *Billboard* singles chart.
1960, May 12	The *Frank Sinatra—Timex Show* airs on ABC.
1960, May 28	Elvis visits Las Vegas.
1960, June 17	Presley requests to be put on army standby, rather than active reserve.
1960, July 21	First degree blackbelt in karate received.
1960, August 1	Elvis starts work on *Flaming Star*.
1960, August 15	'It's Now Or Never' tops the US *Billboard* singles chart.
1960, September 9	Lease signed on new Beverly Hills residence on Perugia Way.
1960, October 1	*G.I. Blues* soundtrack album released. It tops the *Billboard* album charts.
1960, October 4	Filming finished on *Flaming Star*.
1960, November 2	New film deal for Elvis: $500,000 plus half the profits.
1960, November 9	Filming begins on *Wild in the Country*.
1960, November 10	*His Hand in Mine* gospel LP is released. It gets near the top ten of the *Billboard* Top Pop Album chart.
1960, November 23	***G.I. Blues* opens in movie theatres across America.**
1960, November 28	'Are You Lonesome Tonight' tops the US *Billboard* singles chart.
1960, December 4	Colonel Parker suggests *USS Arizona* benefit show.
1960, December 22	***Flaming Star* goes on exhibition in cinemas.**
1961, February 4	Junior Smith, Elvis's cousin, dies of alcohol poisoning.
1961, February 25	"Elvis Presley Day" declared. Elvis does an Ellis Auditorium show to raise funds for the Elvis Presley Youth Center in Tupelo.
1961, March 8	Elvis honoured in Nashville and meets Johnny Bragg of the Prisonaires.

1961, March 20	'Surrender' tops the US *Billboard* singles chart and Elvis starts work at Paramount on *Blue Hawaii*.
1961, March 25	***USS Arizona* memorial press conference and benefit show in Honolulu.**
1961, March 27	*Blue Hawaii* location filming work begins.
1961, May 2	Single featuring 'I Feel So Bad' is released. It reaches number 5 early in June.
1961, May 23	Filming ends on *Blue Hawaii*.
1961, June 17	*Something for Everybody* LP released today. It goes on to dominate the *Billboard* Top LPs chart.
1961, June 22	***Wild in the Country* opens in movie houses across the USA.**
1961, July 11	Filming begins for *Follow That Dream*.
1961, August 8	'(Marie's the Name) His Latest Flame' / 'Little Sister' single released today. Both eventually peak in the top 5.
1961, August 28	*Follow That Dream*'s principal photography ends.
1961, September 1	Elvis visits Las Vegas on vacation for most of this month.
1961, October 20	*Blue Hawaii* album released today. It dominates the album charts.
1961, October 23	*Kid Galahad* begins filming.
1961, November 22	***Blue Hawaii* opens across the country. Elvis moves his LA residence to Bellagio Road today.**
1961, November 23	'Can't Help Falling in Love / Rock-A-Hula Baby' single released today. The A-side later peaks at number 2 on *Billboard*'s singles chart.
1961, December 20	Filming finishes on *Kid Galahad*.
1962, January 3	Colonel arranges a new contract for Elvis on RCA, to last until 1966. It increases recorded output, income, and splits side deals down the middle between the manager and his client.
1962, January 10	IRS investigate Elvis's tax returns.
1962, March 26	Elvis arrives for work to start making *Girls! Girls! Girls!*
1962, April 11	*Follow That Dream* EP released today. It indicates a momentary return to form on the EP chart when it goes top 5.
1962, April 21	'Good Luck Charm' tops the US *Billboard* singles chart.
1962, May 23	***Follow That Dream* opens in movie theatres across America.**
1962, June 5	*Pot Luck with Elvis* album released and makes the top 5 of the *Billboard* Top LPs chart.
1962, June 12	*Girls! Girls! Girls!* publicity stills taken; filming has finished.
1962, June 19	Elvis heads for Las Vegas with Priscilla.

APPENDICES

1962, July 17	'She's Not You' single released today. It makes number 5 on *Billboard*'s singles chart in September.
1962, August 28	Elvis starts work on *It Happened at the World's Fair*.
1962, August 29	***Kid Galahad* opens nationally.**
1962, August 30	Colonel ups the RCA deal to include more bonus money and to run until 1969.
1962, October 2	'Return to Sender' single released today. It rises to number 2 on *Billboard*'s singles chart in November.
1962, October 9	Work finished on *It Happened at the World's Fair*. Elvis sees Johnnie Ray play Las Vegas.
1962, October 21	***Girls! Girls! Girls!* opens in movie houses across America.**
1962, November 9	*Girls! Girls! Girls!* soundtrack LP released. It goes on to make the top 5.
1963, January 28	*Fun in Acapulco* begins principal photography.
1963, March 2	Elvis meets with Priscilla's parents to arrange for her to live in Memphis.
1963, March 18	Elvis completes his duties on *Fun in Acapulco*.
1963, April 10	***It Happened at the World's Fair* opens in movie theatres across the USA. A soundtrack album is released at the same time. It makes the top 5.**
1963, c. June 18	'(You're the) Devil in Disguise' released this month. It peaks at number 3 on *Billboard*'s singles chart in August.
1963, July 9	Presley begins work on *Viva Las Vegas*.
1963, September 11	Elvis wraps up his contribution to *Viva Las Vegas*.
1963, October 1	'Bossa Nova Baby' from *Fun in Acapulco* released. It makes number 8 on *Billboard*'s singles chart in November.
1963, October 7	Elvis begins his work on *Kissin' Cousins*.
1963, November 1	*Fun in Acapulco* soundtrack LP is released. It goes top 5.
1963, November 14	Elvis finishes work on *Kissin' Cousins* with publicity shots.
1963, November 27	***Fun in Acapulco* screens at cinemas across the country.**
1964, February 9	The Beatles appear on *The Ed Sullivan Show*; Elvis and his manager send a telegram of support.
1964, February 26	Presley starts work on *Roustabout*, a Paramount drama about carnival life.
1964, April 2	*Kissin' Cousins* soundtrack LP released today. It peaks at number 6 on the charts.
1964, April 20	**Elvis learns that the profits from his movies help Hal Wallis fund more critically regarded films, like**

	the biopic *Becket*. End of principal photography for *Roustabout*.
1964, May 13	Elvis borrows a life-changing spiritual book, *The Impersonal Life*, from his hairdresser, Larry Geller.
1964, May 14	Elvis finishes his duties on *Roustabout*.
1964, June 17	*Viva Las Vegas* gets its nationwide opening.
1964, June 22	*Girl Happy* begins principal photography.
1964, August 12	Elvis finishes work on *Girl Happy*.
1964, September 21	Shelby County police make Elvis a Special Deputy Sheriff.
1964, October 6	Elvis starts work on *Tickle Me*.
1964, October 20	*Roustabout* soundtrack album released. It reaches number 1 on *Billboard*'s Top LP charts.
1964, November 11	*Roustabout* comes to movie houses across the USA.
1964, November 24	Elvis's duties end on *Tickle Me*.
1964, December 22	Colonel secures his benchmark figure of $1,000,000 per movie for Elvis.
1965, March 2	*Girl Happy* soundtrack LP released. It makes the top 10.
1965, March 5	Elvis thinks he sees the face of Joseph Stalin in clouds while travelling to Los Angeles.
1965, March 9	Elvis arrives to start work on *Harum Scarum*.
1965, April 6	'Crying in the Chapel' released today as a single. It ascends to number 3 on *Billboard*'s singles chart in June.
1965, April 7	*Girl Happy* debuts in theatres nationwide.
1965, April 18	Work finished on *Harum Scarum*.
1965, May 11	Elvis begins initial work on *Frankie and Johnny*.
1965, June 24	Final duties completed by Elvis on *Frankie and Johnny*.
1965, July 7	*Tickle Me* appears in cinemas across America.
1965, August 2	Elvis starts work on *Paradise Hawaiian Style*.
1965, August 10	*Elvis for Everyone!* album released and makes number 10 on the *Billboard* Top LPs chart.
1965, August 15	The Colonel and his client visit the memorial to the *USS Arizona* crew.
1965, September 11	Colonel Parker expresses doubts to press about whether he can control his client.
1965, October 1	Elvis finishes his duties on *Paradise Hawaiian Style*.
1965, November 3	*Harum Scarum* soundtrack LP released. It makes the top 10.
1965, November 24	*Harum Scarum* debuts in movie theatres across the USA.
1965, c. December 26	Elvis tries LSD at Graceland.
1966, February 3	Elvis arrives at his new LA home at Rocca Place in Bel Air.

1966, February 11	Presley begins work on MGM film *Spinout*.
1966, March 1	*Frankie and Johnny* soundtrack album released. It peaks at number 20.
1966, March 30	***Frankie and Johnny* debuts at theatres across the nation.**
1966, c. April 15	Elvis finishes his work on *Spinout* for MGM.
1966, June 10	*Paradise Hawaiian Style* soundtrack album is released. It peaks at number 15 on the *Billboard* Top LPs chart.
1966, July 6	***Paradise Hawaiian Style* debuts in US movie theatres.**
1966, July 11	Start of principal photography for *Double Trouble*.
1966, September 2	Elvis finishes his *Double Trouble* duties.
1966, September 27	The star begins work on *Easy Come, Easy Go*.
1966, October 31	*Spinout* soundtrack released. It reaches number 18 on the album chart.
1966, November 22	Elvis completes his stint on *Easy Come, Easy Go*.
1966, November 23	**Movie houses across the country show *Spinout*.**
1966, December 24	Elvis proposes to Priscilla.
1967, January 24	Colonel Parker renegotiates Elvis's RCA contract up to 1974.
1967, February 8	**Elvis makes first payment on a Mississippi ranch which he will rename the Circle G.**
1967, February 27	*How Great Thou Art* LP is released and makes the top 20 of the *Billboard* album chart.
1967, March 6	Presley belatedly starts work on *Clambake*.
1967, March 8	Colonel Parker writes to MGM requesting less cliched, more solid movie scripts for Elvis.
1967, March 27	***Easy Come, Easy Go* opens in theatres across the USA.**
1967, April 5	***Double Trouble* debuts at cinemas throughout the country.**
1967, April 27	Elvis finishes his *Clambake* duties.
1967, May 1	**Elvis and Priscilla get married at the Aladdin Hotel in Las Vegas.**
1967, c. May 7	Elvis buys a house on Hillcrest, part of Trousdale Estates in Beverly Hills.
1967, June 1	*Double Trouble* soundtrack album is released. It peaks just inside the top 50.
1967, June 19	Work gets underway for MGM's *Speedway*.
1967, August 7	End of Elvis's work on *Speedway*.
1967, September 29	"Elvis Presley Day" declared in Memphis.
1967, October 8	Presley shows up for work on *Stay Away, Joe*.
1967, October 10	*Clambake* soundtrack album released, but only just grazes the top 40.

1967, November 22	*Clambake* arrives in theatres across the country.
1967, November 28	Presley finishes work on *Stay Away, Joe*.
1968, January 12	NBC announce plans for an Elvis Christmas TV show.
1968, February 1	**Lisa Marie, Elvis's daughter, is born to Priscilla Presley in Memphis.**
1968, March 4	Elvis's duties begin on the making of *Live a Little, Love a Little*.
1968, March 8	***Stay Away, Joe* debuts in movie theatres across the country.**
1968, May 1	*Speedway* soundtrack album arrives ahead of the film, but goes on to sell poorly.
1968, May 7	Elvis finishes work on *Live a Little, Love a Little*.
1968, June 3	Preparatory rehearsal work begins on the NBC special.
1968, June 12	***Speedway* opens in cinemas across America.**
1968, June 27	Live with a studio audience, Elvis tapes the famous seated, jamming parts of his *Comeback Special*.
1968, June 29	The two famous 'stand up' segments of the NBC *Comeback Special* are taped today.
1968, July 8	Elvis starts work on *Charro!*
1968, August 28	*Charro!* duties finish for the singer.
1968, September 28	Dewey Phillips, the DJ who helped give Elvis his break, dies in Memphis.
1968, October 22	Elvis starts work on *The Trouble With Girls (And How to Get Into It)*.
1968, October 23	**Movie houses across the USA show *Live a Little, Love a Little*.**
1968, November 22	NBC Comeback Special 'live' album, *Elvis*, is released. It makes the top 10.
1968, December 3	**The *Comeback Special* airs on NBC.**
1968, December 18	Presley's duties on *The Trouble With Girls (And How to Get Into It)* are completed.
1969, January 13	**Elvis enters American Sound studio in Memphis.**
1969, February 17	Presley returns to American Sound.
1969, March 5	Elvis starts initial work in Hollywood on *Change of Habit*.
1969, March 13	***Charro!* opens in movie theatres across the USA.**
1969, April 14	'In The Ghetto' released as a single. It peaks at number 3 on *Billboard*'s singles chart in June.
1969, May 20	Circle G ranch sold, though eventually the buyer does not come up with all the money.
1969, June 17	*From Elvis in Memphis* album, which was recorded at American Sound, is released. It nears the top 10 *Billboard* Top LPs chart.

1969, July 31	Elvis returns to Las Vegas with a live show at the International Hotel.
1969, August 1	Press conference held to mark Elvis's return to live performance.
1969, August 31	First engagement of live shows in Las Vegas is successful and complete.
1969, September 3	*The Trouble With Girls (And How to Get Into It)* screens across the USA for the first time today.
1969, October 14	*From Memphis to Vegas / From Vegas to Memphis* part-live double album is released. It makes the number 12 slot.
1969, November 1	'Suspicious Minds' tops the US *Billboard* singles chart.
1969, November 10	*Change of Habit* screens in movie theatres across America.
1969, November 11	'Don't Cry Daddy' released as a single. It gradually peaks at number 6 on *Billboard*'s singles chart.
1969, December 12	Colonel arranges with RCA to re-release Elvis's albums on the budget, Camden label.
1970, January 26	Another month-long Las Vegas engagement begins.
1970, February 27	Elvis takes his live act beyond Las Vegas today. He holds a press conference and concert at the Houston Astrodome's *Live Stock and Rodeo*, playing for three nights in total.
1970, April 20	'The Wonder of You' is released as a single. It ascends to number 9 on *Billboard*'s singles chart in June.
1970, June 1	*On Stage* live album is released. It peaks at number 13.
1970, July 14	Filmed rehearsals start for the documentary, *That's The Way It Is*.
1970, August 10	The "Elvis Presley Summer Festival" of live engagements begins in Las Vegas.
1970, August 28	Elvis plays Las Vegas again despite receiving a death threat.
1970, September 7	The "Summer Festival" stint ends in Las Vegas and Elvis prepares to tour.
1970, October 17	At the Gospel Quartet Convention in the Ellis Auditorium, Elvis performs as part of a spontaneous quartet.
1970, November 11	*Elvis: That's The Way It Is* documentary opens in theatres across the USA. A live album is also released. It goes on to near the top 20 of the *Billboard* Top LPs chart.
1970, December 4	Elvis buys a bigger house on Monovale in Beverly Hills.
1970, December 21	Following an independent visit to the White House, Elvis Presley meets President Nixon.

1970, December 31	Elvis visits FBI headquarters in Washington, DC.
1971, January 2	*Elvis Country (I'm 10,000 Years Old)* album is released. It rises to number 12.
1971, January 16	**At the Ellis Auditorium in Memphis, Elvis accepts the honour of being one of the Junior Chamber of Commerce of America's Ten Outstanding Young Men of the Year.**
1971, January 26	New engagement starts at the International Hotel in Las Vegas.
1971, February 23	Las Vegas stint ends today.
1971, March 29	Presley seeks out the Memphis karate teacher, Kang Rhee.
1971, May 12	Still on his spiritual quest, Elvis visits Sri Daya Mata at the Self-Realization Center in California.
1971, June 1	In Tupelo, Elvis's very first home becomes a public exhibit.
1971, June 16	*Love Letters from Elvis* album released. It peaks at only 33, heralding an upcoming run of poor album sales.
1971, July 20	Elvis plays first of several regular stints at Lake Tahoe, Nevada.
1971, August 9	The second "Elvis Presley Summer Festival" begins in Las Vegas.
1971, September 6	Last show of "Summer Festival" gigs.
1971, October 6	Elvis stays at his recently purchased house on Monovale for the first time.
1971, October 20	*Elvis Sings the Wonderful World of Christmas* album is released.
1972, January 26	Opening show of a new engagement in Las Vegas.
1972, February 20	*Elvis Now* album is released. It fails to make the top 40.
1972, February 23	Priscilla tells Elvis that she is involved with karate champ Mike Stone.
1972, March 4	Elvis and Priscilla live apart, at different addresses in Beverly Hills.
1972, April 1	*He Touched Me* gospel album is released. It only reaches 79.
1972, May 9	**Madison Square Garden in New York plays host to an Elvis press conference and concert today. He plays four shows over three days, performing in the city for the first time since his 1950s TV appearances.**
1972, June 18	*Elvis: As Recorded at Madison Square Garden* live LP is released. It peaks at number 11.
1972, July 9	Tennessee beauty queen and future girlfriend Linda Thompson is introduced to Elvis.

1972, August 1	'Burning Love' released as a single on this day. It ascends the *Billboard* singles chart to peak at number 2 in October.
1972, August 4	New "Summer Festival" starts in Las Vegas.
1972, September 4	Press conference announces the *Aloha from Hawaii* concert satellite broadcast.
1972, November 1	***Elvis on Tour* documentary debuts in movie theatres across the country.**
1972, November 20	At an Elvis press conference in Honolulu, it is explained that *Aloha*'s takings will go to the Kui Lee Cancer Fund.
1973, January 13	Two nights at Honolulu International Center Arena in Hawaii are recorded for the *Aloha* satellite broadcast.
1973, January 26	Elvis begins a new stint live in Las Vegas.
1973, February 4	*Aloha from Hawaii via Satellite* live double album is released. It will go on to dominate the LP charts.
1973, February 18	Elvis attacked on stage by four men who he and his guards fight off.
1973, March 1	**Colonel negotiates a new seven-year RCA contract for Elvis and sells his whole pre-1973 back catalogue to label for $5.4 million.**
1973, April 4	***Aloha from Hawaii via Satellite* broadcast on TV to various nations.**
1973, May 19	After show cancellations, an LA attorney arranges for a private detective to find out who is over-supplying Elvis with prescription medication.
1973, July 16	*Elvis* (the 'Fool' album) is released, but fails to make the top 40.
1973, July 21	Elvis enters Stax studio in Memphis to start recording.
1973, August 6	New "Summer Festival" opens in Las Vegas.
1973, September 3	Festival of live shows reaches its conclusion with Elvis criticizing the hotel and afterwards trying to sack the Colonel backstage.
1973, October 1	*Raised on Rock* album released. It reaches number 50 on the charts.
1973, October 9	Elvis's divorce is finalized in court.
1973, December 10	Elvis goes to Stax studio again to record further material.
1974, January 2	*Elvis: A Legendary Performer Volume 1* compilation album is released and dominates the LP charts, indicating a thirst for classic material.
1974, January 26	Another Las Vegas engagement begins, only planned for two weeks this time as Elvis is not in peak health.
1974, February 9	Elvis closes his Las Vegas shows.
1974, March 1	Another tour starts in Tulsa.

1974, March 16	Elvis plays the first of three dates at the Mid-South Coliseum in Memphis, his first home town show since 1961.
1974, March 20	*Good Times* album released, but does poorly in sales.
1974, May 16	Another ten-day engagement begins at Lake Tahoe.
1974, July 4	Ed Parker and Elvis stage a karate demonstration in Memphis.
1974, July 7	*Elvis Recorded Live on Stage in Memphis* LP is released. It peaks at 33 in the charts.
1974, c. July 10	The Jungle Room is created in Graceland.
1974, August 20	Las Vegas "Summer Festival" begins with a reworked set list that is discarded by Elvis for subsequent dates.
1974, August 29	On stage, Elvis includes a karate demo in his set.
1974, September 2	Elvis unleashes a monologue on stage at his final "Summer Festival" night that will come to be known as "desert storm" amongst fans.
1974, September 16	In Memphis, Elvis stages another karate display for the press.
1974, c. October 1	Live spoken word comedy album *Having Fun with Elvis on Stage* is compiled from moments between songs and released this month. It sells poorly and fails to make the top 100.
1974, October 11	Elvis plays Tahoe for another four days.
1975, January 8	*Promised Land* LP is released. It peaks just inside the top 50.
1975, January 20	Elvis begins the process of buying his own jet aircraft.
1975, c. March 1	*Pure Gold* budget compilation album of earlier classics released this month. It made the top 5.
1975, March 18	Elvis's Las Vegas engagement begins today. It has been postponed due to his health.
1975, March 28	After attending Elvis's show, Barbara Streisand offers him a role in *A Star Is Born*.
1975, April 1	Las Vegas engagement closes.
1975, April 17	Elvis buys second-hand jet which he will rename as the Lisa Marie.
1975, May 5	Special benefit concert for Mississippi tornado victims staged in Jackson.
1975, May 7	The *Today* album is released. It peaks outside the top 50.
1975, September 2	Another aircraft, a Lockhead Jetstar, is purchased.
1975, November 25	Elvis borrows $350,000 in Memphis from the National Bank of Commerce.
1975, December 2	A two-week engagement begins in Las Vegas.
1975, December 15	Las Vegas engagement ends.

1976, January 6	*Elvis: A Legendary Performer Volume 2* compilation LP is released. It makes the top 10 on the LP charts.
1976, January 22	Colonel Parker creates a new contract in which live show income is split evenly between Elvis and himself.
1976, February 2	First RCA recording session to be held in the Jungle Room at Graceland.
1976, February 8	Jungle Room recording session ends today.
1976, March 22	*The Sun Sessions* classic compilation album is released. It reaches number 2 on the LP chart.
1976, May 1	*From Elvis Presley Boulevard, Memphis, Tennessee* album released today. It peaks at number 41.
1976, July 5	Elvis marks America's bicentennial with a show at the Mid-South Coliseum in Memphis.
1976, August 27	Larry Geller returns to Elvis's life and joins his tour in Texas.
1976, October 29	Another Jungle Room recording session is set up.
1976, November 23	An intoxicated Jerry Lee Lewis shows up at Graceland.
1976, December 2	Another Las Vegas stint is begun.
1976, December 12	Elvis's engagement finishes in Las Vegas and he is comforted by televangelist Rex Humbard after the show.
1977, January 26	Elvis proposes to girlfriend Ginger Alden.
1977, c. March 1	*Welcome to My World* compilation album released this month. It peaks at number 4.
1977, March 31	Last three dates of Louisiana area tour cancelled due to ill health.
1977, June 14	President Jimmy Carter calls Elvis in response to his own attempt at contact, aiming to help his friend George Klein's legal case.
1977, June 19	**Live show filmed in Omaha for *Elvis in Concert*, a CBS-TV special.**
1977, June 21	**Second concert filmed for the CBS-TV special, this one in Rapid City, South Dakota.**
1977, June 26	Elvis does a particularly good show, by recent standards, in Indianapolis.
1977, July 19	*Moody Blue* album is released. It peaks at number 3, but reaches number 1 on the Top Country Albums chart.
1977, August 4	*Elvis: What Happened?* is released: written by Elvis's ex-bodyguards, and heralded for several weeks by serializations in newspapers, this book radically exposes Elvis's human failings.
1977, August 16	Elvis found dead in Graceland.

Appendix 3:

Elvis's Sun Sessions and Singles Releases[1]

Date	Tracks
July 1954 (two visits)	Recording: 'Harbor Lights', 'I Love You Because', 'That's All Right', 'Blue Moon of Kentucky'
July 1954	**Single release:** 'That's All Right' / 'Blue Moon of Kentucky'
August 1954	Recording: *'Blue Moon'*[2]
September 1954	Recording: 'Tomorrow Night', 'I'll Never Let You Go (Little Darlin')', 'Satisfied', 'Just Because', 'Good Rockin' Tonight', 'I Don't Care if the Sun Don't Shine'
September 1954	**Single release:** 'Good Rockin' Tonight' / 'I Don't Care if the Sun Don't Shine'
November 1954	Recording: *'Milkcow Blues Boogie', 'You're a Heartbreaker'*
January 1955	**Single release:** 'Milkcow Blues Boogie' / 'You're a Heartbreaker'
February 1955	Recording: *'I Got a Woman', 'Tryin' to Get to You', 'Baby Let's Play House'*
March 1955	Recording: *'You're A Heartbreaker', 'I'm Left, You're Right, She's Gone', 'I'm Left,You're Right, She's Gone' (slow version), 'How Do You Think I Feel'*
July 1955	Recording: *'I Forgot to Remember to Forget', 'Mystery Train', 'Tryin' to Get to You'*
July 1955	**Single release:** 'Baby Let's Play House' / 'I'm Left, You're Right, She's Gone'
August 1955	**Single release:** 'Mystery Train' / 'I Forgot to Remember to Forget'
November 1955	Recording: *'When It Rains, It Really Pours'*

Appendix 4:

Elvis's Major Television Appearances[1]

Date	Scope	Channel	Show	Songs	Fee
28.1.56	National	CBS	Stage Show (aka The Dorsey Brothers Show, introduced by Bill Randle)	'Shake, Rattle & Roll / Flip, Flop & Fly', 'I Got a Woman'	$1250
4.2.56	National	CBS	Stage Show	'Baby Let's Play House', 'Tutti Frutti'	$1250
11.2.56	National	CBS	Stage Show	'Blue Suede Shoes', 'Heartbreak Hotel'	$1250
18.2.56	National	CBS	Stage Show	'Tutti Frutti', 'I Was The One'	$1250
17.3.56	National	CBS	Stage Show	'Blue Suede Shoes', 'Heartbreak Hotel'	$1500
24.3.56	National	CBS	Stage Show	'Money Honey', 'Heartbreak Hotel'	$1500
3.4.56	National	NBC	The Milton Berle Show	'Heartbreak Hotel', 'Blue Suede Shoes'	$3000
5.6.56	National	NBC	The Milton Berle Show	'I Want You, I Need You, I Love You', 'Hound Dog'	$5000
16.6.56	Local (Memphis)	WHBQ-TV	Wink Martindale's Dance Party	Interview	Unknown
1.7.56	National	NBC	The Steve Allen Show	'I Want You, I Need You, I Love You', 'Hound Dog' (plus comedy sketch with Andy Griffith)	$5000

1.7.56	Local (New York)	WRCA-TV	*Hy Gardner Calling*	Interview	Unknown
9.9.56	National	CBS	*Toast of the Town* (aka *The Ed Sullivan Show*)	'Don't Be Cruel', 'Love Me Tender', 'Ready Teddy', 'Hound Dog'	$15,000
28.10.56	National	CBS	*Toast of the Town*	'Don't Be Cruel', 'Love Me', 'Love Me Tender', 'Hound Dog'	$15,000
6.1.57	National	CBS	*Toast of the Town*	'Hound Dog', 'Love Me Tender', 'Heartbreak Hotel', 'Don't Be Cruel', 'Too Much', 'When My Blue Moon Turns to Gold Again' [all shot from the waist up] and 'Peace in the Valley'	$15,000
12.5.60	National	ABC	*The Frank Sinatra Timex Special: Welcome Home Elvis*	'Fame and Fortune', 'Stuck On You', 'Witchcraft'	$125,000
3.12.68	National	NBC	*Singer Presents Elvis* (aka *The Comeback Special* aka *The '68 Special*)	Over twenty songs including 'Trouble', 'Memories', 'One Night', 'Tiger Man' and 'If I Can Dream'	$1,250,000 (included in package deal with a feature film)
4.4.73[2]	International	NBC	*Aloha from Hawaii*	Over twenty songs including 'Burning Love', 'My Way' and 'I'll Remember You'	Elvis was not paid. He raised $75,000 for Kui Lee Cancer Fund
3.10.77	National	CBS	*Elvis in Concert*	Over ten songs including 'How Great Thou Art'	$750,000

Appendix 5:

Fictional Narrative Feature Films

Title	Studio	Director	Sub-genre
Love Me Tender (1956) b/w	20th Century Fox	Robert Webb	Civil war Western
Loving You (1957)	Paramount	Hal Kanter	Country biopic
Jailhouse Rock (1957) b/w	MGM	Richard Thorpe	Prison drama
King Creole (1958) b/w	Paramount	Michael Curtiz	Biopic drama
G.I. Blues (1960)	Paramount	Norman Taurog	Post-war romcom
Flaming Star (1960)	20th Century Fox	Don Siegel	Western
Wild in the Country (1961)	20th Century Fox	Philip Dunne	Youth drama
Blue Hawaii (1961)	Paramount	Norman Taurog	Vacation romcom
Follow That Dream (1962)	United Artists	Gordon Douglas	Light comedy
Kid Galahad (1962)	United Artists	Phil Karlson	Carefree drama
Girls! Girls! Girls! (1962)	Paramount	Norman Taurog	Carefree drama
It Happened at the World's Fair (1963)	MGM	Norman Taurog	Carefree drama
Fun in Acapulco (1963)	Paramount	Richard Thorpe	Romantic comedy
Kissin' Cousins (1964)	MGM	Gene Nelson	Comedy
Viva Las Vegas (1964)	MGM	George Sidney	Romantic comedy
Roustabout (1964)	Paramount	John Rich	Circus drama

Girl Happy (1965)	MGM	Boris Sagal	Beach party
Tickle Me (1965)	Allied Artists	Norman Taurog	Children's comedy
Harum Scarum (1965)	MGM	Gene Nelson	Children's comedy
Frankie and Johnny (1966)	United Artists	Frederick de Cordova	Musical
Paradise, Hawaiian Style (1966)	Paramount	D. Michael Moore	Beach party
Spinout (1966)	MGM	Norman Taurog	Racing-driver romance
Easy Come, Easy Go (1967)	Paramount	John Rich	Treasure-hunt caper
Double Trouble (1967)	MGM	Norman Taurog	Comedy caper
Clambake (1967)	Levy-Gardner-Laven	Arthur Nadal	Lifeswap class drama
Stay Away, Joe (1968)	MGM	Peter Tewksbury	Western comedy
Speedway (1968)	MGM	Norman Taurog	Racing-driver caper
Live a Little, Love a Little (1968)	MGM	Norman Taurog	Carefree romcom
Charro! (1969)	National General	Charles Marquis Warren	Western
The Trouble With Girls (1969)	MGM	Peter Tewksbury	Comedy mystery
Change of Habit (1969)	NBC/Universal	William Graham	Carefree drama

Appendix 6:

Key RCA Live and Studio Albums[1]

Name	Key genres	US release date	Example tracks	Key points
Elvis Presley	Rock'n'roll	March 1956	'Blue Suede Shoes', 'Tutti Frutti', 'Money Honey'	Included Sun material, but not 'Heartbreak Hotel'.
Elvis	Rock'n'roll	October 1956	'Love Me', 'Paralyzed', 'Ready Teddy', 'Old Shep'	Emulated the hybrid genres of the Sun sessions.
Elvis' Christmas Album	Mix of blues, ballads and carols	October 1957	'Santa Claus Is Back in Town', 'White Christmas', 'Blue Christmas', 'Silent Night', 'O Little Town of Bethlehem'	Irving Berlin hated Elvis's performance of 'White Christmas', which of course was a Bing Crosby movie song.
Elvis Is Back!	Mix of doo-woppy pop, blues and other genres	April 1960	'Fever', 'Such a Night', 'Reconsider Baby'	Elvis's first stereo album: a diverse return to form after the army.
His Hand in Mine	Gospel	November 1960	'Milky White Way', 'Working on the Building'	A first gospel album in wake of the *Peace in the Valley* EP.
Something for Everybody	Mix of swinging pop and ballad material	June 1961	'I Slipped, I Stumbled, I Fell', 'I'm Comin' Home'	Backing vocalist Millie Kirkham sang on tracks like 'There's Always Me'.
Pot Luck with Elvis	Up-tempo pop	June 1962	'Kiss Me Quick', 'Suspicion'	Dominated by Doc Pomus and Mort Shuman material.

Album	Genre	Date	Key tracks	Notes
How Great Thou Art	Gospel	March 1967	'How Great Thou Art', 'Run On', 'In the Garden'	An ethereal showcase of Elvis's sacred music.
From Elvis in Memphis	Blue-eyed soul, country	June 1969	'Long Black Limousine', 'Only the Strong Survive', 'In the Ghetto'	Material from the widely acclaimed American Sound sessions.
From Memphis to Vegas / From Vegas to Memphis	A mix of live rock'n'roll and more songs from American Sound Studio	November 1969	'Hound Dog', 'Suspicious Minds', 'Stranger in My Own Home Town'	Elvis's first double LP: the first disc represented Elvis's first live LP; the second, studio session material.
On Stage	Diverse collection of Vegas show covers	June 1970	'Polk Salad Annie', 'The Wonder of You', 'Yesterday', 'Release Me (And Let Me Love Again)'	In-concert piece from February 1971 with a fresh, contemporary, mature feel.
That's The Way It Is	Classic ballads and mellow country pop	December 1970	'I Just Can't Help Believin'', 'Patch It Up', 'I've Lost You', 'Just Pretend'	Las Vegas concert documentary and Nashville session material.
Elvis Country (I'm 10,000 Years Old)	Country	January 1971	'Funny How Time Slips Away', 'I Washed My Hands in Muddy Water'	Unusual genre concept album that explored Elvis's country roots.
Love Letters from Elvis	Pop and ballads	June 1971	'Heart of Rome', 'Love Letters', 'It Ain't No Big Thing (But It's Growing)', 'Got My Mojo Working'	Passable collection of left-over material from the *Elvis Country* sessions.

Album	Genre	Date	Tracks	Notes
Elvis Sings the Wonderful World of Christmas	Carols and swinging Christmas staples	October 1971	'Merry Christmas Baby', 'O Come, All Ye Faithful'	Elvis's second Christmas album.
Elvis Now	Range of genres including country and gospel	January 1972	'Hey Jude', 'Until It's Time for You to Go', 'Early Morning Rain'	Compilation of oddments from previous sessions.
He Touched Me	Contemporary gospel	April 1972	'He Touched Me', 'Lead Me, Guide Me', 'Amazing Grace'	Elvis's final studio gospel album, featuring a range of musicians including Joe Esposito on guitar.
Elvis: As Recorded at Madison Square Garden	Diverse rock'n'roll and country live material	June 1972	'You've Lost That Lovin' Feeling', 'The Impossible Dream', 'Can't Help Falling in Love'	Rush-released live album of Elvis triumphing in New York.
Aloha from Hawaii via Satellite	Wide range of live material	February 1973	'Burning Love', 'You Gave Me a Mountain', 'Steamroller Blues', 'I'll Remember You'	Double album accompanying the international broadcast.
Elvis (sometimes called *The Fool*)	Pop, rock ballads	July 1973	'Fool', 'I'll Take You Home Again Kathleen', 'It's Impossible'	Diverse album in the wake of *Aloha* that included Elvis on piano.
Good Times	Rock, country, ballads	March 1974	'Good Time Charlie's Got the Blues', 'My Boy'	Rueful result of Elvis's Stax sessions.
Elvis Recorded Live on Stage in Memphis	Rock'n'roll, gospel, live staples	July 1974	'Tryin' to Get to You', 'Lawdy Miss Clawdy', 'An American Trilogy'	Live staples sung to the home town crowd.

Having Fun with Elvis on Stage	Spoken word	October 1974	n/a	Odd collection of live concert interludes: makes a case for Elvis as a stand-up comic.
Promised Land	Rock'n'roll, rock, country	January 1975	'Promised Land', 'You Asked Me To', 'There's a Honkytonk Angel (Who'll Take Me Back In)', 'Mr. Songman'	More from the Stax sessions.
Today	Country, rock	May 1975	'T-R-O-U-B-L-E', 'And I Love You So', 'I Can Help', 'Green, Green Grass of Home'	Diverse material from Elvis's final recording studio sessions.
From Elvis Presley Boulevard, Memphis Tennessee	Adult contemporary ballads	May 1976	'Hurt', 'For the Heart', 'Blue Eyes Crying in the Rain'	Recorded in Graceland.
Moody Blue	Adult contemporary ballads	July 1977	'Moody Blue', 'Way Down', 'Unchained Melody'	Mix of Graceland session and live concert material.

Appendix 7:

Recording the *Comeback Special*[1]

Date	Place	Activity
June 3–16	Binder's Office, Sunset Boulevard	Informal rehearsals
June 20–24	Western Recorders, Hollywood	Audio for production segments pre-recorded in the studio
June 25	NBC, Burbank	Press conference and dressing-room rehearsal
June 27	NBC, Burbank	'Warm-up' rehearsal
June 27	NBC, Burbank	Live boxing ring 'sit down' jam sessions
June 28	NBC, Burbank	Playback/overdub session for gospel sequence, bordello scene and 'Guitar Man'
June 29	NBC, Burbank	Two 'stand up' boxing ring segments taped
June 30	NBC, Burbank	Further taping of 'Guitar Man' road medley and 'If I Can Dream' finale

Notes

Introduction

1. Jerry Hopkins, *Elvis: A Biography* (London: Open Gate Books, 1971), 64.
2. Slavoj Žižek, *Event: Philosophy in Transit* (London: Penguin Books, 2014), 2.
3. Žižek, *Event*, 3 (emphasis in original).
4. Nik Cohn, *Awopbopaloobop Alopbamboom* (St Albans: Granada, 1973), 23.
5. Pierre Bourdieu, *Distinction: A Social Critique of the Judgement of Taste* (Cambridge: Harvard University Press, 1984).
6. Bourdieu, *Distinction*.
7. See John Fiske, "The Cultural Economy of Fandom," in *The Adoring Audience: Fan Culture and Popular Media*, ed. Lisa Lewis (Abingdon: Routledge, 1992), 30–49; Simon Frith, *Performing Rites: On the Value of Popular Music* (Cambridge: Harvard University Press, 1996).
8. Amongst other things, Elvis had interests in Beethoven, opera and a film by Max Ophuls.
9. Theodor Adorno, *Introduction to the Sociology of Music* (New York: Seabury Press, 1976), 13.
10. Michael Bonner, "Quentin Tarantino Chooses His 10 Favourite Records," *Uncut*, August 19, 2019, https://www.uncut.co.uk/blog/quentin-tarantino-chooses-his-10-favourite-records-27610
11. Key contributions to academic debates on authenticity have included Simon Frith, "The Real Thing—Bruce Springsteen" (1988), reprinted in *The Rock History Reader*, ed. Theo Cateforis (New York: Routledge, 2012), 237–44; Jeremy Gilbert and Ewan Pearson, *Discographies: Dance, Music, Culture and the Politics of Sound* (New York: Routledge, 1999), and Alan Moore, "Authenticity as Authentication," *Popular Music* 21, no. 2 (2002): 209–23.
12. Cory Messenger, "Act Naturally: Elvis Presley, the Beatles and 'Rocksploitation,'" *Screening the Past* 12 (2014), http://www.screeningthepast.com/2014/12/act-naturally-elvis-presley-the-beatles-and-%e2%80%9crocksploitation%e2%80%9d/
13. Adam Bruno Ulam, *The Fall of the American University* (New York: Library Press, 1972), 79.
14. Greil Marcus, *Mystery Train: Images of America in Rock'n'Roll Music* (London: Omnibus Press, 1977).

15 Greil Marcus, *Dead Elvis: A Chronicle of Cultural Obsession* (Cambridge: Harvard University Press, 1999 [1991]).
16 Herbert Marcuse, "An Essay on Liberation," 1969, https://www.marxists.org/reference/archive/marcuse/works/1969/essay-liberation.htm
17 Marcuse, "An Essay on Liberation."
18 Herbert Marcuse, "Art as Revolutionary Weapon," YouTube video, 48:46, 1970. Reproduced October 16, 2016, https://www.youtube.com/watch?v=9livubNajl4
19 I am thinking, of course, of *Brown v. the Board of Education of Topeka*.
20 Karl Marx, "The Eighteenth Brumaire of Louis Bonaparte," 1852, https://www.marxists.org/archive/marx/works/1852/18th-brumaire/ch01.htm
21 Marx, "The Eighteenth Brumaire of Louis Bonaparte."
22 Cornel West, "Ware Lecture by Cornel West, General Assembly 2015," 2015, https://www.uua.org/multiculturalism/ga/ware-west
23 Gilbert Garcia, "Caught in a Trap," *Broward Palm Beach New Times*, January 21, 1999, https://www.browardpalmbeach.com/music/caught-in-a-trap-6331586
24 Peter Guralnick, *Careless Love: The Unmaking of Elvis Presley* (London: Abacus, 1999), xiv.
25 Marcus, *Dead Elvis*, xii.

Chapter 1 Roots

1 Glen Jeansonne, David Luhrssen and Dan Sokolovic, *Elvis Presley, Reluctant Rebel: His Life and Our Times* (Santa Barbara: Praeger, 2011), 46.
2 This was probably a flat fee. While it could be seen as exploiting the artist, Sam's strategy in effect risked his own capital for the rewards that came if a record was distributed.
3 Louis Cantor, *Wheelin' on Beale* (New York: Pharos Books, 1992), 112–13.
4 Ray Connolly, "Sam Phillips Plus Johnny Cash, Carl Perkins and Roy Orbison," *Radio Times*, September 1973, https://www.rayconnolly.co.uk/sam-phillips/
5 Connolly, "Sam Phillips Plus Johnny Cash, Carl Perkins and Roy Orbison."
6 Rufus Thomas then worked as disc jockey at WDIA and had later success with his daughter Carla in 1959 singing 'Cause I Love You' on Satellite Records (an early incarnation of Stax). His long running career as a novelty artist consolidated his place as a fixture on the Memphis music scene.
7 Some sources suggest that the Prisonaires may have met Elvis in the summer of 1953 in Sun Studio.
8 Connolly, "Sam Phillips Plus Johnny Cash, Carl Perkins and Roy Orbison."
9 Jerry Osborne, *Elvis: Word for Word* (New York: Gramercy Books, 2000), 37.
10 Ken Burke and Dan Griffin, *The Blue Moon Boys: The Story of Elvis Presley's Band* (Chicago: Chicago Review Press, 2006), 29.
11 He sang 'Old Shep' on October 3, 1945, at the Mississippi-Alabama State Fair. On November 6, 1948, he performed 'Leaf on a Tree' at Milam Junior High School. Elvis sang 'Cold, Cold Icy Fingers' and 'Old Shep' at the Christmas show at Humes. In April 1953, the Humes High students put on their final year 'Annual Minstrel' show and Elvis propped his foot up on a chair to cradle his guitar and sing Teresa Brewer's showy ballad 'Till I Waltz Again with You'. Despite the event's rather traditional title and programme, there is no evidence that Elvis or his classmates actually performed in blackface.
12 Ernst Jørgensen, *Elvis Presley: A Life in Music. The Complete Recording Sessions* (St Martin's Press: New York, 1998), 9.
13 Burke and Griffin, *The Blue Moon Boys*, 12.

14 *Sun Days with Elvis*, DVD, directed by Bernard Roughton (Sydney: Payless Entertainment, 2002).
15 Peter Guralnick and Ernst Jørgensen, *Elvis Day by Day: The Definitive Record of His Life and Music* (New York: Ballantine Books, 1999), 12.
16 Guralnick interviewed many local White musicians and concluded that "they simply didn't think of it." Peter Guralnick, *Last Train to Memphis: The Rise of Elvis Presley* (London: Abacus, 1994), 58.
17 Guralnick, *Last Train to Memphis*, 62.
18 John Potter, "Elvis Presley to Rap: Moments of Change since the Forties," in J. Potter, *Vocal Authority: Singing Style and Ideology* (Cambridge: Cambridge University Press, 1998), 139.
19 Jørgensen, *Elvis Presley: A Life in Music*, 10.
20 Jørgensen, *Elvis Presley: A Life in Music*, 10.
21 Connolly, "Sam Phillips Plus Johnny Cash, Carl Perkins and Roy Orbison."
22 Few facts about Elvis's life remain undisputed. See Julia Aparin, "He Never Got Above His Raising: An Ethnographic Study of a Working Class Response to Elvis Presley" (PhD diss., University of Pennsylvania, 1988), 44; Elaine Dundy, *Elvis and Gladys* (London: Pimlico, 1995), 65; Patrick Lacy, *Elvis Decoded: A Fan's Guide to Deciphering the Myths and Misinformation* (Bloomington: Author House, 2006). Music historian Lee Cotton (*Did Elvis Sing in Your Hometown?* [Sacramento: High Sierra Books, 1995], 233), for instance, found 70 concert shows from the 1950s were unverifiable.
23 Favius Friedman, *Meet Elvis Presley* (New York: Scholastic Book Services, 1973), 17.
24 Jim Black, *Elvis on the Road to Stardom 1955–1956* (London: WH Allen, 1988), 22.
25 Guralnick, *Last Train to Memphis*, 84.
26 Burke and Griffin, *The Blue Moon Boys*, 76.
27 Burke and Griffin, *The Blue Moon Boys*, 25.
28 Scotty said this in the documentary, *Classic Albums: Elvis Presley* (Marre, 2001).
29 Guralnick, *Last Train to Memphis*, 92.
30 This insight comes from a public interview that Peter Guralnick conducted with Sam Phillips, London South Bank Centre, July 7, 1999.
31 Jørgensen, *Elvis Presley: A Life in Music*, 11.
32 *Classic Albums: Elvis Presley*, DVD, directed by Jeremy Marre (New York: Eagle Vision, 2001).
33 The song was later released as a splice of takes 2 and 4 by RCA. Jørgensen, *Elvis Presley: A Life in Music*, 12.
34 Guralnick, *Last Train to Memphis*, 95.
35 Osborne, *Elvis: Word for Word*, 72.
36 *Classic Albums: Elvis Presley*, DVD.
37 There is an outside chance that they may also have recorded 'Tiger Man'. Jørgensen, *Elvis Presley: A Life in Music*, 13.
38 Connolly, "Sam Phillips Plus Johnny Cash, Carl Perkins and Roy Orbison."
39 David Neale, *Roots of Elvis* (New York: iUniverse, 2003), 27.
40 Connolly, "Sam Phillips Plus Johnny Cash, Carl Perkins and Roy Orbison."
41 Connolly, "Sam Phillips Plus Johnny Cash, Carl Perkins and Roy Orbison."
42 Eder notes that Elvis's version of 'That's All Right' may have been part inspired by two other Crudup recordings: 'If I Get Lucky' and 'Dirt Road Blues'. Mike Eder, *Elvis Music FAQ* (Milwaukee: Backbeat Books, 2013), 2.
43 Potter, "Elvis Presley to Rap," 139.
44 Burke and Griffin, *The Blue Moon Boys*, 14.
45 Osborne, *Elvis: Word for Word*, 6.
46 The constant tic-a-tic of Black's percussive style came to define a rockabilly. Burke and Griffin, *The Blue Moon Boys*, 36.
47 *Classic Albums: Elvis Presley*, DVD.

48 *Classic Albums: Elvis Presley*, DVD.
49 A good example here is to compare Carl Perkins's version of 'Blue Suede Shoes' with Elvis's rendition. Perkins is more measured and metered, less urgent and excessive.
50 I am thinking here of Alain Locke's essay anthropology, *The New Negro* (1925; repr., New York: Simon & Schuster, 1992).
51 Cantor, *Wheelin' on Beale*, 20.
52 Cantor, *Wheelin' on Beale*, 30, 13 and 21.
53 Cantor, *Wheelin' on Beale*, 48.
54 Cantor, *Wheelin' on Beale*, 164.
55 Cantor, *Wheelin' on Beale*, 164.
56 Cantor, *Wheelin' on Beale*, 167.
57 Cantor, *Wheelin' on Beale*, 165.
58 Connolly, "Sam Phillips Plus Johnny Cash, Carl Perkins and Roy Orbison."
59 Black, *Elvis on the Road to Stardom*, 25; Jørgensen, *Elvis Presley: A Life in Music*, 15.
60 Black, *Elvis on the Road to Stardom*, 26.
61 Taken from an interview with Richards shown in *Classic Albums: Elvis Presley*, DVD.
62 Burke and Griffin, *The Blue Moon Boys*, 20.
63 Jørgensen, *Elvis Presley: A Life in Music*, 13.
64 His words can be heard after the "alternative" early take of the song on *The Sun Sessions* CD released by RCA in 1990.
65 Ernst Jørgensen, *A Boy from Tupelo: The Complete 1953–55 Recordings* (New York: FTD Books, 2012), 52–53.
66 Connolly, "Sam Phillips Plus Johnny Cash, Carl Perkins and Roy Orbison."
67 Jørgensen, *A Boy from Tupelo*, 26 (emphasis in original).
68 Burke and Griffin, *The Blue Moon Boys*, 44.
69 *Classic Albums: Elvis Presley*, DVD.
70 Jørgensen, *A Boy from Tupelo*, 51.
71 Burke and Griffin, *The Blue Moon Boys*, 45.
72 Black, *Elvis on the Road to Stardom*, 26; Burke and Griffin, *The Blue Moon Boys*, 43.
73 Jørgensen, *A Boy from Tupelo*, 39.
74 James Ausborn—Elvis's childhood friend and brother of Mississippi Slim—discusses this on Mike Freeman's DVD documentary: *Elvis' Memphis*, DVD, directed by Gerry Malir (London: Artsmagic, 2000).
75 Brewster was a leading light in Memphis' Black culture who wrote songs for Clara Ward and Mahalia Jackson, and was eventually honoured by the Smithsonian. Cantor, *Wheelin' on Beale*, 61.
76 Osborne, *Elvis: Word for Word*, 1.
77 Bob Groom, "Tigerman: Elvis and the Blues," in *Aspects of Elvis*, eds. Adam Clayson and Spencer Leigh (London: Sidgwick and Jackson, 1994), 73–85.
78 Philip Ennis, *The Seventh Stream: The Emergence of Rock'n'Roll in American Popular Music* (Hanover: Wesleyan University Press, 1992), 236.
79 Elvis biographer Jerry Hopkins (*Elvis: A Biography*, 5), attributed this quote to a recollection from Marion Keisker about what Sam said. Gilbert Rodman (*Elvis After Elvis* [London: Routledge, 1996], 31–34) showed how different versions of the quote reflected different writers' perspectives on the Elvis myth. Albert Goldman's version, for example, implied racism and exploitation: "a White *boy* who could sing like a *nigger*" (*Elvis* [Middlesex: Penguin, 1982], 129; emphasis mine). When Greil Marcus called Keisker, she vehemently denied that Sam had ever used such a word. His actions—for example desegregating his studio at a time when even the café next door was segregated—tend to support her claim, though he did focus on White rockabillies after Elvis's music exploded. Ironically, however, Sam's wealth most likely came more from his investment in the Holiday Inn chain than from his music.

80　Though press stories quickly showed pictures of Elvis, the Sun singles did not have picture sleeves—some early fans may not initially have seen their hero. Osborne, *Elvis: Word for Word*, 72.
81　Eric Lott, *Love and Theft: Blackface Minstrelsy and the American Working Class* (Oxford: Oxford University Press, 1995), 55.
82　"The Spiritual Soul of Elvis," episode in *The Definitive Elvis* DVD box set, directed by Eduardo Eguia Dibildox (Los Angeles: Passport International Entertainment, 2002).
83　*Sam Phillips: The Man Who Invented Rock'n'Roll*, TV movie, directed by Morgan Neville (Los Angeles: Peter Jones Productions, 2000).
84　Cornel West, in *Examined Life*, DVD, directed by Astra Taylor (New York: Zeitgeist Films, 2010).
85　Nicholas Dawidoff, *In the Country of Country: A Journey to the Roots of American Music* (London: Faber and Faber, 2005), 144.
86　Gael Sweeney, "The King of White Trash Culture: Elvis Presley and the Aesthetics of Excess," in *White Trash: Race and Class in America*, eds. Matt Wray and Annalee Newitz (New York: Routledge, 1997), 253.
87　Vernon Chadwick, ed., *In Search of Elvis: Music, Art, Race, Religion* (Boulder: Westview Press, 1997), xv.
88　*Classic Albums: Elvis Presley*, DVD.
89　Linda Martin and Kerry Segrave, *Anti-rock: The Opposition to Rock'n'Roll* (New York: Da Capo, 1988), 41.
90　Peter Guralnick, "How Did Elvis Get Turned into a Racist?" *New York Times*, August 11, 2007, http://www.nytimes.com/2007/08/11/opinion/11guralnick.html?pagewanted=all&_r=0
91　Guralnick, "How Did Elvis Get Turned into a Racist?"
92　George Plasketes, *Images of Elvis Presley in American Popular Culture 1977–1997: The Mystery Train* (Binghampton, NY: Hayworth Press, 1997), 26.
93　Dave Marsh, *Elvis* (London: Omnibus Press, 1992 [1982]), 47.
94　Cantor, *Wheelin' on Beale*, 142.
95　Cantor, *Wheelin' on Beale*, 196. George Klein noted, however, that perhaps only about 1% of the audience at Elvis's live shows was Black, so the Goodwill Revue audience may simply have been pleased to see any big name performer.
96　Guralnick and Jørgensen, *Elvis Day by Day*, 116.
97　*Classic Albums: Elvis Presley*, DVD.
98　Behind the universality lies a much older and pervasive colonialist, Freudian assumption: that soul was *originally* Black because Black folk had access to authentic feelings that more civilized (and therefore repressed) White folk did not.
99　Klein said this on Mike Freeman's DVD documentary *Elvis' Memphis*, 2000.
100　Cantor, *Wheelin' on Beale*, 8–9.
101　Osborne, *Elvis: Word for Word*, 97.
102　Plasketes, *Images of Elvis Presley*, 53.
103　For instance, Elvis visited Nat D. Williams at WDIA—the Black radio station—with the aim of convincing him to play a wider range of records on his show. Cantor, *Wheelin' on Beale*, 192.
104　Jørgensen, *A Boy from Tupelo*, 138.
105　See Greil Marcus, et al., *Rockabilly: The Twang Heard 'Round the World* (Minneapolis: Voyageur Press, 2011); Stephen Tucker, "Rethinking Elvis and the Rockabilly Moment," in *In Search of Elvis: Music, Art, Race, Religion*, ed. Vernon Chadwick (Boulder: Westview Press, 1997), 19–28.
106　*Classic Albums: Elvis Presley*, DVD.
107　Potter, "Elvis Presley to Rap," 135.
108　Fabian Holt, *Genre in Popular Music* (Chicago: University of Chicago Press, 2007), 63–80.

109 Dawidoff, *In the Country of Country*, 144.
110 Guralnick said this on *Classic Albums: Elvis Presley*, DVD.
111 *Sam Phillips: The Man Who Invented Rock'n'Roll*, TV movie.
112 See Jørgensen, *A Boy from Tupelo*, 15; Burke and Griffin, *The Blue Moon Boys*, 34–35.
113 Jørgensen, *A Boy from Tupelo*, 23.
114 Jørgensen, *Elvis Presley: A Life in Music*, 19.
115 Jørgensen, *Elvis Presley: A Life in Music*, 15.
116 Burke and Griffin, *The Blue Moon Boys*, 36.
117 *Classic Albums: Elvis Presley*, DVD.
118 This scene, in which an upstart musician upstages more staid veteran performers, was re-staged in Elvis's semi-biographic feature film *Loving You*. Unfortunately, the event is lost to history. The only photos of Elvis at the Shell capture him backstage when he performed there the following year with Johnny Cash as the opening act.
119 Osborne, *Elvis: Word for Word*, 53.
120 Jørgensen, *A Boy from Tupelo*, 28.
121 Elvis said this at a show in Omaha, June 19, 1977.
122 Jørgensen, *Elvis Presley: A Life in Music*, 19.
123 RussellFamilyTV, "Elvis Presley I Forgot to Remember to Forget October 1, 1955. Unreleased LIVE Track Hayride," YouTube video, 3:33, 1955. Reproduced, July 16, 2012, http://www.youtube.com/watch?v=U3EofaQBFco
124 Jørgensen, *A Boy from Tupelo*, 150.
125 Osborne, *Elvis: Word for Word*, 5.
126 Jørgensen, *Elvis Presley: A Life in Music*, 17.
127 Jørgensen, *Elvis Presley: A Life in Music*, 15.
128 Jørgensen, *Elvis Presley: A Life in Music*, 16.
129 Jørgensen, *Elvis Presley: A Life in Music*, 17.
130 Burke and Griffin, *The Blue Moon Boys*, 35.
131 Jørgensen, *Elvis Presley: A Life in Music*, 16. Eder says some Sun tapes were lost before 1956. Eder, *Elvis Music FAQ*, 23.
132 Jørgensen, *Elvis Presley: A Life in Music*, 16.
133 Jørgensen, *Elvis Presley: A Life in Music*, 17.
134 Burke and Griffin, *The Blue Moon Boys*, 15.
135 Eder suggests that 'Milkcow Blues Boogie's false start may have limited its airplay. Eder, *Elvis Music FAQ*, 19.
136 Jørgensen, *Elvis Presley: A Life in Music*, 21.
137 Jørgensen, *Elvis Presley: A Life in Music*, 25.
138 Jørgensen, *Elvis Presley: A Life in Music*, 27.
139 Jørgensen, *A Boy from Tupelo*, 137.
140 Parker's widow Loanne discussed his time with Gene Austin here: http://www.rockabillyhall.com/ColTom.html
141 Alanna Nash, *The Colonel: The Extraordinary Story of Colonel Tom Parker and Elvis Presley* (New York: Simon & Schuster, 2003), 81.
142 Jørgensen, *Elvis Presley: A Life in Music*, 20.
143 Burke and Griffin, *The Blue Moon Boys*, 72.
144 *Classic Albums: Elvis Presley*, DVD.
145 Jørgensen, *Elvis Presley: A Life in Music*, 23.
146 Jørgensen, *Elvis Presley: A Life in Music*, 25.
147 Jørgensen, *Elvis Presley: A Life in Music*, 29.
148 Jørgensen, *Elvis Presley: A Life in Music*, 27.
149 Elvis *could* have graced more than one regional television spot around that time.
150 Sources differ about whether Neal or Parker arranged this booking. Burke and Griffin claim that Randle knew Elvis was signed to RCA by this point (*The Blue Moon Boys*, 73).

151 Burke and Griffin, *The Blue Moon Boys*, 73.
152 Burke and Griffin, *The Blue Moon Boys*, 75.
153 Jørgensen, *Elvis Presley: A Life in Music*, 28.
154 Jørgensen, *A Boy from Tupelo*, 137.
155 Osborne, *Elvis: Word for Word*, 58–59.
156 Burke and Griffin, *The Blue Moon Boys*, 76.
157 When Elvis was signed to RCA, Scotty and Bill were not contracted but paid union scale like session players. They were also disliked by Steve Sholes, who found their interruptions in recording sessions raised the cost of studio time (Guralnick and Jørgensen, *Elvis Day by Day*, 112). The two musicians had been promised a slot to record their own instrumental album late in 1957; when studio time failed to materialize, they resigned from Elvis's employ, but were retained for live performance work. Once Elvis was conscripted, Scotty joined Jack Clement and Slim Wallace at Fernwood Records and produced a hit called 'Tragedy' for Thomas Wayne, the brother of Johnny Cash's guitarist.
158 Burke and Griffin, *The Blue Moon Boys*, 19.
159 *Classic Albums: Elvis Presley*, DVD.
160 Parker was keen to strike a deal before any new Sun releases. RCA's interest might have waned with a poorly-selling single. A national hit might have raised Sam's asking price.
161 Parker's approved calculations on Peabody Hotel notepaper included a 25% cut for himself from two chunks: $1000 of income for Hill & Range publishers, and the RCA Victor bonus for Elvis. The singer only saw $4500 of the total.
162 Jørgensen, *Elvis Presley: A Life in Music*, 32.
163 Jørgensen, *Elvis Presley: A Life in Music*, 32.
164 This claim came from Chick Crumpacker—who was an RCA promotions manager in 1956—on the documentary, *Classic Albums: Elvis Presley*, DVD.
165 Osborne, *Elvis: Word for Word*, 13.
166 *Classic Albums: Elvis Presley*, DVD.
167 Potter, "Elvis Presley to Rap," 140.
168 Jørgensen, *Elvis Presley: A Life in Music*, 77.
169 Potter, "Elvis Presley to Rap," 140.
170 Potter, "Elvis Presley to Rap," 141.
171 Marcus, *Mystery Train*, 182.
172 George Cotkin, *Existential America* (Baltimore: Johns Hopkins University Press, 2003), 1.
173 Friedman, *Meet Elvis Presley*, 11 (emphasis in original).
174 Michael Bertrand, *Race, Rock, and Elvis* (Chicago: University of Illinois Press, 2005), 24.
175 Richard Peterson, "Why 1955? Explaining the Advent of Rock Music," *Popular Music* 9, no. 1 (1990): 97–116.
176 Lennon's comment was apparently made as early as November 1962, probably making him the first and most famous Elvis "big bang" theorist. Chris Hutchins and Peter Thompson, *Elvis Meets the Beatles: The Untold Story of their Entangled Lives* (London: Smith Gryphon, 1994), 52.
177 See Susan Doll, *Understanding Elvis: Southern Roots vs Star Image* (New York: Garland, 1998); Linda Ray Pratt, "Elvis, or the Ironies of a Southern Identity," in *The Elvis Reader: Texts and Sources on the King of Rock'n'Roll*, ed. Kevin Quain (New York: St Martin's Press, 1992), 93–103; John Shelton Reed, "Elvis as Southerner," in *In Search of Elvis: Music, Art, Race, Religion*, ed. Vernon Chadwick (Boulder: Westview Press, 1997), 75–92; Karen Cox, "The South and Mass Culture," *Journal of Southern History* 75, no. 3 (2009): 677–90.

178 This must have been particularly galling given that Elvis had a real-life twin brother called Jesse who died at birth.
179 David Jansson, "Internal Orientalism in America: WJ Cash's *Mind of the South* and the Spatial Construction of American National Identity," *Political Geography* 22, no. 3 (2003): 293–316.
180 A good example of this was Sam Phillips's awkward banter with the host on *The David Letterman Show* in 1986.
181 Black, *Elvis on the Road to Stardom*, 51. The clean-cut Boone and Elvis have often been contrasted and pitted against each other. Boone was from a more middle-class Northern background and studiously avoided the edge that Elvis brought to performance. However, the two were never enemies. After *Radio-TV Mirror* announced that Elvis and Pat Boone were antagonistic, Elvis said to an August 1956 interviewer, "Pat Boone and I are very good friends." Osborne, *Elvis: Word for Word*, 61.
182 *Classic Albums: Elvis Presley*, DVD.
183 Jørgensen, *Elvis Presley: A Life in Music*, 68.
184 Jørgensen, *Elvis Presley: A Life in Music*, 114.
185 Jørgensen, *Elvis Presley: A Life in Music*, 43.
186 *Classic Albums: Elvis Presley*, DVD.
187 *Classic Albums: Elvis Presley*, DVD.
188 Adam Victor, *The Elvis Encyclopedia* (New York: Overlook Duckworth, 2008), 136.
189 Jørgensen, *Elvis Presley: A Life in Music*, 48.
190 Jørgensen, *Elvis Presley: A Life in Music*, 51–55.
191 *Elvis: Love Me Tender, Geraldo* newscast, director unknown (New York: ABC, 1977).
192 Peter Carlin, *Paul McCartney: A Life* (New York: Touchstone, 2009), 22.
193 *CBS Special News Report*, newscast, director unknown (New York: CBS, 1977, August 18).
194 It is worth noting Leerom Medovoi's complex thesis that these changing attitudes to sex may also have been associated with the political need of America to win the Cold War. In other words, through Elvis and others, sex became a kind of freedom doctrine associated with the authentic expression of individual identity *and the promotion of a materialist consumer culture*. These individualist philosophies indirectly encouraged 'young' postcolonial countries to avoid aligning themselves with communism or religious collectivism, and thus stay open for capitalist trade with the USA. Leerom Medovoi, *Rebels: Youth and the Cold War Origins of Identity* (Durham: Duke University Press, 2005).
195 Milton Berle, "Milton Berle," *The Interviews—Television Academy Foundation*, 28:24, 1996. Reproduced, May 28, 2013, https://interviews.televisionacademy.com/interviews/milton-berle
196 Hopkins, *Elvis: A Biography*, 114.
197 Black, *Elvis on the Road to Stardom*, 129.
198 Parker is alleged to have made a leaflet called *Elvis Presley: Why Does He Drive the Girls Wild?* See Alfred Wertheimer, *Elvis '56: In the Beginning* (London: Pimlico, 1994), 96.
199 Cantor, *Wheelin' on Beale*, 167.
200 This comment was originally made in relation to an *Ed Sullivan Show* appearance in the 1950s by *The Catholic Sun*. Charles Karult repeated it on a *CBS Special News Report*, which aired August 18, 1977. Hopkins, *Elvis: A Biography*, 143.
201 Osborne, *Elvis: Word for Word*, 51.
202 Osborne, *Elvis: Word for Word*, 73.
203 Goldman, *Elvis* (1982), 519.
204 From *CBS Special News Report*, which aired August 18, 1977.

205 This claim came from Gordon Stoker of the Jordanaires in Mike Freeman's DVD *Beyond Elvis's Memphis*. Elvis had never undertaken dance training and on *Jailhouse Rock* the others were choreographed around him. *Beyond Elvis's Memphis*, DVD, directed by Gerry Malir (London: Artsmagic, 2008).
206 Osborne, *Elvis: Word for Word*, 79.
207 Guralnick, *Last Train to Memphis*, 293.
208 'I Want You, I Need You, I Love You' was made an A-side by RCA and constituted Elvis's first shot at success as a ballads artist.
209 Griffith, who had his own folksy charm, later played an Elvis-like "every man" character in Elia Kazan's 1957 movie *A Face in the Crowd*. The film explored the possibility that a populist country singer might transition to party politics.
210 Osborne, *Elvis: Word for Word*, 41.
211 Jørgensen, *Elvis Presley: A Life in Music*, 68.
212 Jake Austen, *TV-a-Go-Go: Rock on TV from* American Bandstand *to* American Idol (Chicago: Chicago Review Press, 2005), 16.
213 Jørgensen, *Elvis Presley: A Life in Music*, 74.
214 *Elvis' Memphis*, DVD.
215 Ronnie McDowell, Edie Hand and Joe Meador, *The Genuine Elvis* (Gretna: Pelican Publishing, 2010), 13.
216 Marjorie Garber makes connections between Valentino, Liberace and Elvis. Marjorie Garber, "The Transvestite Continuum: Liberace—Valentino—Elvis," in M. Garber, *Vested Interests: Cross Dressing and Cultural Anxiety* (New York: Routledge, 1992), 353–74.
217 David Shumway, "Authenticity: Modernity, Stardom and Rock'n'Roll," *Modernity/Modernism* 14, no. 3 (2007): 527–33.
218 Maxine Craig, *Sorry I Don't Dance: Why Men Refuse to Move* (New York: Oxford University Press, 2014), 85.
219 Persistent rumours disparagingly suggested "the Presley phallus as marionette": a lead bar, sausage or toilet roll tube. See Goldman, *Elvis* (1982), 199; Garber, "The Transvestite Continuum," 366; Bill Burk, *Early Elvis: The Sun Years* (Memphis: Propwash, 1997), 136.
220 From *Elvis: Summer of '56*, DVD, directed by Stuart Goldman (New York: Fisher Klingenstein Films, 2011).
221 Medovoi, *Rebels*, 195.
222 Potter, "Elvis Presley to Rap," 147.
223 Mark Duffett, "Understanding Elvis: Presley, Power and Performance" (PhD diss., University of Wales, Aberystwyth, 1998).
224 Duffett, "Understanding Elvis."
225 Osborne, *Elvis: Word for Word*, 56.
226 See Sean O'Neal, *Elvis Inc.: The Fall and Rise of the Presley Empire* (Rocklin, CA: Prima Publishing, 1996), 114 (picture inset); Dundy, *Elvis and Gladys*, 302.
227 This introduction can be heard before 'Heartbreak Hotel' on Elvis Presley (performer), *Elvis: A Portrait in Words and Music*, 1996, Start Entertainment/Musketeer MUCD95 17, compact discs.
228 Goldman, *Elvis* (1982), 240. Nearly a century earlier, onlookers reported a kind of human puppetry in blackface as singers seemed to have legs of wood, wire and springs. Lott, *Love and Theft*, 116.
229 Connolly, "Sam Phillips Plus Johnny Cash, Carl Perkins and Roy Orbison." The Million Dollar Quartet session was released much later.
230 Jørgensen, *Elvis Presley: A Life in Music*, 73.
231 Elvis can be heard on episode two of the DVD documentary: *Elvis by the Presleys*, DVD, directed by Rob Klug (New York: CBS, 2005).
232 Osborne, *Elvis: Word for Word*, 91.

233 From a public interview that Peter Guralnick conducted with Sam Phillips, London South Bank Centre, July 7, 1999.
234 *Beyond Elvis's Memphis*, DVD.
235 "The Spiritual Soul of Elvis," in *The Definitive Elvis*, DVD.
236 Burke and Griffin, *The Blue Moon Boys*, 60.
237 Osborne, *Elvis: Word for Word*, 71.
238 Osborne, *Elvis: Word for Word*, 71.
239 Jørgensen, *Elvis Presley: A Life in Music*, 93.
240 Susan Buck-Morss, *The Origin of Negative Dialectics: Theodor W. Adorno, Walter Benjamin and the Frankfurt Institute* (Hassocks: Harvester, 1977), 278.
241 Potter, "Elvis Presley to Rap," 142.
242 Osborne, *Elvis: Word for Word*, 70.
243 Jason Toynbee, *Making Popular Music: Musicians, Creativity and Institutions* (London: Arnold, 2000).
244 Although Elvis had a particular wide sphere of musical influences, initially he did not like jazz. Burke and Griffin, *The Blue Moon Boys*, 62.
245 "The Spiritual Soul of Elvis," in *The Definitive Elvis*, DVD.
246 Simon Frith, "Wise Men Say," in *Aspects of Elvis*, eds. Adam Clayson and Spencer Leigh (London: Sidgwick and Jackson, 1994), 282.
247 Charlie Hodge on "The Spiritual Soul of Elvis," in *The Definitive Elvis*, DVD.
248 Kathy Westmoreland, *Elvis and Kathy* (California: Glendale House, 1987), 229.
249 *He Touched Me: The Gospel Music of Elvis Presley*, DVD, directed by Michael Merriman (London: EMI, 2000).
250 This can be heard at the end of the CD, *A Hundred Years From Now: Essential Elvis 4* (RCA 07863 66866 4, 1996).
251 Elvis's Sun reconstruction of 'I Don't Care if the Sun Don't Shine' is a case in point. Dean Martin's showy Hollywood version came first, but Elvis turned the song around into a breezy, hillbilly ditty by adding a jaunty, folksy touch.
252 Osborne, *Elvis: Word for Word*, 77.
253 Elvis did write the lyrics to one song, 'You'll Be Gone', which was a reworking of Cole Porter's famous 'Begin the Beguine', but his suggestions were never used.
254 The latter charge was, of course, offered more vocally when he took a songwriting credit.
255 Jørgensen, *Elvis Presley: A Life in Music*, 178.
256 Jørgensen, *Elvis Presley: A Life in Music*, 305.
257 Stoker was interviewed in *Beyond Elvis's Memphis*, DVD.
258 *Classic Albums: Elvis Presley*, DVD.
259 *Classic Albums: Elvis Presley*, DVD.
260 Charles Keil, "Participatory Discrepancies and the Power of Music," *Cultural Anthropology* 2, no. 3 (1987): 275–83.
261 *Classic Albums: Elvis Presley*, DVD.
262 *Classic Albums: Elvis Presley*, DVD.
263 Jørgensen, *Elvis Presley: A Life in Music*, 92.
264 Jørgensen, *Elvis Presley: A Life in Music*, 54.
265 *Beyond Elvis's Memphis*, DVD.
266 Jørgensen, *Elvis Presley: A Life in Music*, 163.
267 *Beyond Elvis's Memphis*, DVD.
268 D.J. Fontana said this in the documentary, *Classic Albums: Elvis Presley*, DVD.
269 Jørgensen, *Elvis Presley: A Life in Music*, 23.
270 Osborne, *Elvis: Word for Word*, 10.
271 Jørgensen, *Elvis Presley: A Life in Music*, 110.
272 *Beyond Elvis's Memphis*, DVD.
273 Jørgensen, *Elvis Presley: A Life in Music*, 181.

274 "The Spiritual Soul of Elvis," in *The Definitive Elvis*, DVD.
275 *Sam Phillips: The Man Who Invented Rock'n'Roll*, TV movie.
276 When Elvis re-opened in Vegas, he was so taken with the bass singer he tried to find and employ him.
277 Eder, *Elvis Music FAQ*, 183.
278 Jake Hess explained that Elvis never made the move, because he would have put so many people around him out of work.
279 Jørgensen, *Elvis Presley: A Life in Music*, 7.
280 *He Touched Me*, DVD.
281 *He Touched Me*, DVD.
282 Osborne, *Elvis: Word for Word*, 30.
283 Osborne, *Elvis: Word for Word*, 13.
284 Osborne, *Elvis: Word for Word*, 70.
285 Osborne, *Elvis: Word for Word*, 53.
286 The Colonel also suggested that Elvis record the gospel staple 'Just a Closer Walk with Thee', which—before Red Foley's hit rendition in 1950—had a former life as a hymn performed at New Orleans funerals by jazz musicians. Elvis never cut the song in the studio, though a home recording eventually surfaced (Jørgensen, *Elvis Presley: A Life in Music*, 76).
287 Jørgensen, *Elvis Presley: A Life in Music*, 87.
288 Jørgensen, *Elvis Presley: A Life in Music*, 95.
289 Elvis was credited with arranging these numbers.
290 Jørgensen, *Elvis Presley: A Life in Music*, 141.
291 Marsh, *Elvis*, 158.
292 Jørgensen, *Elvis Presley: A Life in Music*, 237 and 244.
293 Other original members included Donnie Sumner and Tim Baty.
294 *He Touched Me*, DVD.
295 Mark Duffett, "Elvis' Gospel Music: Between the Secular and the Spiritual?" *Religions* 6, no. 1 (2015): 195.
296 Charles Reagan Wilson, "'Just a Little Talk with Jesus': Elvis Presley, Religious Music and Southern Spirituality," *Southern Cultures* 12, no. 4 (2006): 74–91.
297 Here is an interesting comparison: In classical music any labour that virtuoso singers put into their vocal technique is *made visible* through tutorials at institutions such as singing schools. By contrast, in rock or pop a singer's education comes through *invisible* means, such as copying records and performing live, and the lack of visibility shapes perceptions of it as intuitive and untutored. Such differences give the impression of instinctual talent that in turn helps to place the form lower down the cultural hierarchy. The gospel quartet tradition represents an intermediary sphere: vernacular and professional, based on some evident training and apprenticeship. It is notable here that the Blackwood Brothers gospel outfit had an off-shoot called the Songfellows. Elvis failed his audition to that group, while the Blackwoods passed *theirs* to a show that Elvis also failed to crack: *Arthur Godfrey's Talent Scouts*. To some degree, then, in his life story, Elvis's interest in gospel perhaps appears to represent an endearing compensation for a kind of *failed* professionalism.
298 *He Touched Me*, DVD.
299 Charles Wolfe, "Presley and the Gospel Tradition," in *The Elvis Reader: Texts and Sources on the King of Rock'n'Roll*, ed. Kevin Quain (New York: St Martin's Press, 1992), 13–28.
300 Lionel Crane, "Rock Age Idol: He's Riding the Crest of a Teenage Tidal Wave," *Daily Mirror*, April 30, 1956, 9.
301 Doll, *Understanding Elvis*, 76.
302 Marcus, *Mystery Train*, 137.

303 Holly George-Warren and Patricia Romanowski, *The Rolling Stone Encyclopedia of Rock'n'Roll* (New York: Rolling Stone Press, 2005), 774.
304 Dale Bailey, *American Nightmares: The Haunted House Formula in American Popular Fiction* (Wisconsin: Popular Press, 2009), 91.
305 Joel Williamson, *Elvis Presley: A Southern Life* (New York: Oxford University Press, 2015), 40.
306 Mark Duffett, *Understanding Fandom: An Introduction to the Study of Media Fan Culture* (New York: Bloomsbury, 2013), 44.
307 From *Beyond Elvis's Memphis*, CD.
308 Émile Durkheim, *The Elementary Forms of Religious Life* (Oxford: Oxford University Press, 2008 [1912]), 158.
309 Durkheim, *Elementary Forms of Religious Life*, 226.
310 Aparin, "He Never Got Above His Raising," 78.
311 Robert Gordon, *The King on the Road: Live on Tour 1954 to 1977* (London: Hamlyn, 1996), 35.
312 Duffett, *Understanding Fandom*, 333.
313 Mark Duffett, "Boosting Elvis: A Content Analysis of Editorial Stories from One Fan Club Magazine," *Participations* 9, no. 2 (2012): 317–36, http://www.participations.org/Volume%209/Issue%202/18%20Duffett.pdf
314 Durkheim, *Elementary Forms of Religious Life*, 116.

Chapter 2 Image

1 Jørgensen, *Elvis Presley: A Life in Music*, 112.
2 Osborne, *Elvis: Word for Word*, 54.
3 Jørgensen, *Elvis Presley: A Life in Music*, 171. For a discussion of Wallis, see Thomas Schatz, "Hal Wallis: Producer to the Stars, by Bernard F. Dick," *Film Quarterly* 59, no. 2 (2005): 67–68.
4 From the DVD documentary, *Elvis & June: A Love Story*, DVD, directed by Stuart Goldman (New York: BCI Eclipse, 2002).
5 Osborne, *Elvis: Word for Word*, 24.
6 Peter Nazareth, "Elvis as Anthology," in *In Search of Elvis: Music, Art, Race, Religion*, ed. Vernon Chadwick (Boulder: Westview Press, 1997), 37–74.
7 Victor, *The Elvis Encyclopedia*, 167.
8 Jørgensen, *Elvis Presley: A Life in Music*, 88.
9 Jørgensen, *Elvis Presley: A Life in Music*, 91–92.
10 Osborne, *Elvis: Word for Word*, 43.
11 Sigmund Freud, *The Essentials of Psychoanalysis* (London: Vintage Books, 2005 [1926]), 32.
12 Aparin, "He Never Got Above His Raising," 24.
13 Alan Fortas, *Elvis from Memphis to Hollywood* (Ann Arbor, MI: Popular Culture Ink, 1992), 92.
14 Osborne, *Elvis: Word for Word*, 11.
15 Osborne, *Elvis: Word for Word*, 14.
16 Osborne, *Elvis: Word for Word*, 67 (emphasis mine).
17 Douglas Brode, *Elvis Cinema and Popular Culture* (Jefferson: McFarland, 2006), 17.
18 Dundy, *Elvis and Gladys*, 13.
19 Elvis's closeness to his mother may have functioned in a similar way for him as Little Richard's homosexuality and campness did *for him*: it made the singer seem less of a dangerous outsider. For further discussion of this process, see Wiseman-Trowse, who recounts Stanley Booth's imagined dialogue between Elvis and Gladys in 1968. Nathan Wiseman-Trowse, "Oedipus Wrecks: Cave and the Presley Myth," in *Cultural*

Seeds: Essays on the Work of Nick Cave, eds. Karen Welberry and Tanya Dalziell (Farnham: Ashgate, 2009), 162.
20 Brode, *Elvis Cinema and Popular Culture*, 17.
21 Brode, *Elvis Cinema and Popular Culture*, 137.
22 Brode, *Elvis Cinema and Popular Culture*, 17. Also see Pat Broeske and Peter Brown, "Once Priscilla Gave Birth, Elvis Rejected Her," *Daily Mail*, July 11, 1997.
23 West's words are reproduced in Osborne, *Elvis: Word for Word*, 305.
24 Bertrand, *Race, Rock, and Elvis*, 81.
25 Osborne, *Elvis: Word for Word*, 43.
26 Jørgensen, *Elvis Presley: A Life in Music*, 106.
27 Medovoi, *Rebels*, 196.
28 Joel Whitburn, *A Century of Pop Music* (Wisconsin: Record Research Inc., 1999), 82.
29 Black, *Elvis on the Road to Stardom*, 19.
30 See Keightley's chapter on musical hybridization and high modernity. Keir Keightley, "Un Voyage via Barquinho: Global Circulation, Musical Hybridization and Adult Modernity, 1961–9," in *Migrating Music*, eds. Jason Toynbee and Byron Duek (Abingdon: Routledge, 2011), 112–26.
31 Brode, *Elvis Cinema and Popular Culture*, 107.
32 Dave Harker, *One for the Money* (London: Hutchinson, 1980), 61.
33 Sue Wise, "Sexing Elvis," in *On Record: Rock, Pop and the Written Word*, eds. Simon Frith and Andrew Goodwin (1984; repr., London: Routledge, 1990), 390–98.
34 Referencing patriotism, the *G.I. Blues* trailer was tagged, "It's the Red, White and G.I. Blues."
35 Brode, *Elvis Cinema and Popular Culture*, 250.
36 The frequent use of studio sets also added a dream-like quality to the films, a bit like in Alfred Hitchcock movies from the time.
37 Jørgensen, *Elvis Presley: A Life in Music*, 142.
38 Jørgensen, *Elvis Presley: A Life in Music*, 136.
39 Jørgensen, *Elvis Presley: A Life in Music*, 145–46.
40 Jørgensen, *Elvis Presley: A Life in Music*, 43.
41 Guralnick and Jørgensen, *Elvis Day by Day*, 116.
42 By the late 1950s the Hollywood studio system had entered a period of uncertainty. The Paramount Decision had put pay to vertical integration and guaranteed profits. Television emerged to compete for the family audience. The major studios soon learned to lever their distribution systems and skim box office takings from lucrative youth pictures. In this environment, studio operations sprang up to capitalize on the youth market with cheap but edgy independent fare. A new generation of filmmakers emerged. Promotional use of the director's name eventually became a key marketing strategy. While many 1960s star actors exploited their off-screen publicity, Elvis was promoted in a way that was closer to the old Hollywood style. He could be relied upon to carry a picture and remained a bankable asset. In industry terms, however, he was gradually integrated into Hollywood's newer practices, later working with lesser known directors, smaller budgets, and alternating his commitments between major studios and independent production companies such as National General Pictures, Levy-Gardner-Laven and Rhodes Pictures.
43 Mick Farren, *Elvis in His Own Words* (London: WH Allen, 1981), 7.
44 Jørgensen, *Elvis Presley: A Life in Music*, 98.
45 Jørgensen, *Elvis Presley: A Life in Music*, 113.
46 Raymond Weinstein, "Occupation G.I. Blues: Postwar Germany During and After Elvis Presley's Tour," *Journal of Popular Culture* 39, no. 1 (2006): 126–49.
47 Jørgensen, *Elvis Presley: A Life in Music*, 118.
48 Jørgensen, *Elvis Presley: A Life in Music*, 114–15.
49 Jørgensen, *Elvis Presley: A Life in Music*, 118–19.

50 Rare army home recordings can be found on the Memphis Recording Service CD, *Off Duty with Private Presley* (Memphis Recording Service, MRS30065859, 2010).
51 Jørgensen, *Elvis Presley: A Life in Music*, 112.
52 Hopkins, *Elvis: A Biography*, 227.
53 Phil Davidson, "Lamar Fike: Member of Elvis Presley's Famed Inner Circle, the Memphis Mafia," *The Independent*, February 26, 2011, http://www.independent.co.uk/news/obituaries/lamar-fike-member-of-elvis-presleys-famed-inner-circle-the-memphis-mafia-2226112.html
54 Jørgensen, *Elvis Presley: A Life in Music*, 156.
55 Jørgensen, *Elvis Presley: A Life in Music*, 115.
56 Jørgensen, *Elvis Presley: A Life in Music*, 119.
57 Jørgensen, *Elvis Presley: A Life in Music*, 120.
58 The song was loved by Parker's wife Marie. Jørgensen, *Elvis Presley: A Life in Music*, 127.
59 Jørgensen, *Elvis Presley: A Life in Music*, 126.
60 Jørgensen, *Elvis Presley: A Life in Music*, 127.
61 Jørgensen, *Elvis Presley: A Life in Music*, 120.
62 Jørgensen, *Elvis Presley: A Life in Music*, 128.
63 Jørgensen, *Elvis Presley: A Life in Music*, 135.
64 Richard Meltzer, *The Aesthetics of Rock* (1970; repr., New York: Da Capo, 1987), 40.
65 Meltzer, *Aesthetics of Rock*, 98.
66 Jørgensen, *Elvis Presley: A Life in Music*, 9.
67 Dawidoff, *In the Country of Country*, 183.
68 Freud, *Essentials of Psychoanalysis*, 410.
69 Peter Haining, ed., *The Elvis Presley Scrapbooks, 1955–1965* (London: Robert Hale, 1991), 70.
70 Jørgensen, *Elvis Presley: A Life in Music*, 183.
71 Dancing was quite racy in this whole movie, which led to protests by the Legion of Decency and the banning of the film in Gozo, near Malta.
72 This expressionist dance scene offers an example of how Elvis's inability to jive worked in his favour. As he shakes to the music, others around him move exuberantly, anchoring him in a subtly masculine role as the generative centre of spectacle.
73 Jørgensen, *Elvis Presley: A Life in Music*, 160.
74 Jørgensen, *Elvis Presley: A Life in Music*, 164.
75 Jørgensen, *Elvis Presley: A Life in Music*, 198.
76 Some sources said that the Colonel tried, after Hank Williams's death in 1953, to persuade studios to make a biopic. Others suggest that he withheld Elvis from acting in the venture.
77 Guralnick and Jørgensen, *Elvis Day by Day*, 163.
78 Scott Schindler and Andy Schwartz, *Icons of Rock* (Westport: Greenwood Press, 2007), 16.
79 Jørgensen, *Elvis Presley: A Life in Music*, 186.
80 Guralnick, *Careless Love*, 159.
81 Freud, *Essentials of Psychoanalysis*, 32.
82 Except Gladys Presley, and perhaps Marion Keisker, there are no *obvious* equivalent "good" or "bad" mothers, but many women—from songwriter Mae Boren Axton and screenwriter Sally Benson to RCA executive Joan Deary—did play significant roles in Elvis's career. The telling of his myth has, arguably, relegated these women.
83 See Fortas, *Elvis from Memphis to Hollywood*, 15; Marsh, *Elvis*, 1.
84 See Priscilla Presley, *Elvis and Me* (London: Century, 1985), 198; Goldman, *Elvis* (1982), 440.
85 Cindy Hazen and Mike Freeman, *Memphis Elvis-Style* (Winston-Salem: John F Blair, 1997), 9.

86 Guralnick, *Last Train to Memphis*, 213.
87 Westmoreland, *Elvis and Kathy*, 244.
88 Hugh Baker and Yuval Taylor, "Heartbreak Hotel: The Art and Artifice of Elvis Presley, Nashville January 10, 1956," in *Faking It: The Quest for Authenticity in Popular Music* (London: Faber and Faber, 2007), 33.
89 The Elvis fan community always had a conflicted relationship with Parker. While Presley was alive, the Colonel cultivated a special relationship with fan clubs and allowed the singer to personalize his communication to different territories. He also negotiated occasional access to shows and meet-and-greet sessions for club leaders. After Elvis died, Parker took part in events with fans in 1978, 1984 and 1987, helping to raise money for the Elvis Presley Memorial Foundation in Tupelo. Fans understood that he was a living link to a past that they had lost, but some also blamed him for Elvis's problems. Consequently, while fan club leaders cordially courted Parker, their rank and file members would occasionally ostracize each other for meeting him at Elvis events.
90 C. Haynes, "Elvis: In the Twilight of Memory," *Official Elvis Presley Fan Club of Great Britain Magazine* 7, 1997, 18.
91 Plasketes, *Images of Elvis Presley*, 10.
92 Dundy, *Elvis and Gladys*, 288.
93 Dee Presley et al., *Elvis, We Love You Tender* (London: New English Library, 1980), 78.
94 Guralnick, *Last Train to Memphis*, 358.
95 Bertrand, *Race, Rock, and Elvis*.
96 Susan Doll, *Elvis for Dummies* (Hoboken: John Wiley & Sons, 2009), 192.
97 See, for instance, Aparin, "He Never Got Above His Raising," 59; Wertheimer, *Elvis '56*, 96; and O'Neal, *Elvis Inc.*, 72.
98 Burke and Griffin, *The Blue Moon Boys*, 70.
99 A photo insert in one book shows Colonel Parker as a Mexican General and Santa Claus. Joe Esposito, *Good Rockin' Tonight* (New York: Simon & Schuster, 1994), 128. See also Fortas, *Elvis from Memphis to Hollywood*, 162.
100 Osborne, *Elvis: Word for Word*, 15.
101 Black, *Elvis on the Road to Stardom*, 66.
102 Jackson Baker, "Perfectly Normal," *Memphis Flyer* 442 (1997): 33.
103 Fortas, *Elvis from Memphis to Hollywood*, 168.
104 Goldman, *Elvis* (1982), 702.
105 See Goldman, *Elvis* (1982), 203; Gail Brewer-Giorgio, *The Elvis Files: Was His Death Faked?* (New York: Shapolsky, 1990), 84.
106 See Marge Crumbaker and Gabe Tucker, *Up and Down with Elvis Presley* (Sevenoaks: New English Library, 1981), 193; Esposito, *Good Rockin' Tonight*, 251; Scotty Moore, *That's All Right Elvis: The Untold Story of Elvis' First Guitarist and Manager* (New York: Schirmer Books, 1997), 227.
107 Chet Flippo, *Graceland: The Living Legacy of Elvis Presley* (London: Hamlyn, 1994), 17.
108 See Dundy, *Elvis and Gladys*, 237; Guralnick, *Last Train to Memphis*, 207.
109 See Presley, *Elvis and Me*, 209; Crumbaker and Tucker, *Up and Down with Elvis Presley*, 37.
110 See Esposito, *Good Rockin' Tonight*, 143; Jay Cocks, "Last Stop on the Mystery Train," *Time*, August 29, 1977, 24.
111 Chris Hutchins, "No, I Don't Take Half of What Elvis Earns," *The People*, January 26, 1997, 6–8.
112 Jørgensen, *Elvis Presley: A Life in Music*, 175.
113 Jørgensen, *Elvis Presley: A Life in Music*, 190.
114 "Elvis and the Colonel," an episode of the *Definitive Elvis* box set, directed by Eduardo Eguia Dibildox (Los Angeles: Passport International Entertainment, 2002).

115 Plasketes, *Images of Elvis Presley*, 76.
116 Thanks to Keir Keightley for alerting me to this particular Warhol, in his paper on Tin Pan Alley at the 2014 Edinburgh event, *Studying Music: An International Conference in Honour of Simon Frith*. The print was first bought by Salvador Dali and sold for $1.5 million in 2010.
117 Dundy, *Elvis and Gladys*, 282.
118 Jørgensen, *Elvis Presley: A Life in Music*, 171.
119 Jørgensen, *Elvis Presley: A Life in Music*, 173.
120 Jørgensen, *Elvis Presley: A Life in Music*, 198.
121 Jørgensen, *Elvis Presley: A Life in Music*, 231.
122 Jørgensen, *Elvis Presley: A Life in Music*, 133.
123 Jørgensen, *Elvis Presley: A Life in Music*, 134.
124 Jørgensen, *Elvis Presley: A Life in Music*, 103.
125 Jørgensen, *Elvis Presley: A Life in Music*, 137.
126 Jørgensen, *Elvis Presley: A Life in Music*, 149.
127 Jørgensen, *Elvis Presley: A Life in Music*, 164.
128 Jørgensen, *Elvis Presley: A Life in Music*, 156.
129 Jørgensen, *Elvis Presley: A Life in Music*, 85.
130 Jørgensen, *Elvis Presley: A Life in Music*, 128.
131 Jørgensen, *Elvis Presley: A Life in Music*, 129.
132 Jørgensen, *Elvis Presley: A Life in Music*, 76.
133 Jørgensen, *Elvis Presley: A Life in Music*, 77.
134 Jørgensen, *Elvis Presley: A Life in Music*, 158.
135 Jørgensen, *Elvis Presley: A Life in Music*, 81.
136 Jørgensen, *Elvis Presley: A Life in Music*, 165.
137 Jørgensen, *Elvis Presley: A Life in Music*, 191.
138 By this point Elvis sometimes sang strong songs in weak films.
139 Hopkins, *Elvis: A Biography*, 299.
140 Jørgensen, *Elvis Presley: A Life in Music*, 239.
141 See Jørgensen, *Elvis Presley: A Life in Music*, 160; Gillian Gaar, *Return of the King: Elvis Presley's Great Comeback* (London: Jawbone, 2010), 43.
142 Mark Duffett, "Walking in Memphis? Elvis Heritage between Fan Fantasy and Built Environment," in *Redefining Mainstream Popular Music*, eds. Sarah Baker, Andy Bennett and Jodie Taylor (New York: Routledge, 2013), 111.

Chapter 3   Comeback

1 Jane Wright, "The Adult Elvis [letter]," *Elvis Monthly* 4, no. 12 (1963): 29.
2 Jørgensen, *Elvis Presley: A Life in Music*, 217.
3 Gaar, *Return of the King*, 206. For a full discussion of the Nixon meeting, see Connie Kirchberg and Marc Hendrickx, *Elvis Presley, Richard Nixon and the American Dream* (Jefferson: McFarland, 1999); Egil Krogh, *Dear Mr President: The Day Elvis Met Nixon* (Minnesota: Pejam PR, 1993).
4 Marsh, *Elvis*, 161.
5 Marsh, *Elvis*, 158.
6 Jørgensen, *Elvis Presley: A Life in Music*, 206.
7 This was a song that Dylan wrote but others released. Marsh, *Elvis*, 162; Jørgensen, *Elvis Presley: A Life in Music*, 214.
8 Marsh, *Elvis*, 156.
9 I have only seen stills of this press conference and do not know whether any footage actually exists.
10 Guralnick and Jørgensen, *Elvis Day by Day*, 244.

11 Henry Jenkins, *Textual Poachers: Television Fans and Participatory Culture* (New York: Routledge, 1992), 11.
12 Marsh, *Elvis*, 162.
13 Binder himself explained it was a reel to reel Christmas promotion to radio that consisted of Christmas songs, pre-recorded interview answers, and spaces where the local disc jockey could insert himself or herself asking questions. See David Adams, "Interview with Steve Binder, Director of Elvis's '68 Comeback Special," *Elvis Australia*, 2005, http://www.elvis.com.au/presley/interview_steve_binder.shtml#sthash. gtgBx1Eu.dpbs. See also Jørgensen, *Elvis Presley: A Life in Music*, 245. Jerry Hopkins, however, suggested that the Colonel gave Binder an *Easter* special that had broadcast one of Elvis's religious albums and prompted a large number of fan letters. Hopkins, *Elvis: A Biography*, 336.
14 Singer had a package deal with NBC. Their sewing machines had no immediate connection with Elvis's music, except a female audience.
15 Guralnick, *Careless Love*, 293.
16 After Elvis's TV special, in 1970 Binder went on to produce one for Liza Minnelli and later directed specials for Mac Davis, Barry Manilow, Olivia Newton-John and Diana Ross.
17 Jørgensen, *Elvis Presley: A Life in Music*, 245.
18 The compère Steve Allen, of course, had awkwardly "tamed" Elvis in the summer of 1956 on his national television show. Steve Binder was later recruited for the ill-fated, Allen-financed series *Jazz Scene USA*. In May 1964, Binder also directed an episode of the revamped *Steve Allen Show*.
19 Guralnick, *Careless Love*, 294.
20 Guralnick, *Careless Love*, 303.
21 Just to confuse matters, there was also a 1968 LP called *Singer Presents Elvis Singing Flaming Star and Others*.
22 Adams, "Interview with Steve Binder."
23 Adams, "Interview with Steve Binder."
24 Guralnick, *Careless Love*, 295.
25 Adams, "Interview with Steve Binder."
26 Adams, "Interview with Steve Binder."
27 The *Special* showcased a number of sartorial personae and reflected different eras of Elvis's pre-existing celebrity image. Ian Inglis suggests that Elvis's varied dressing for the *Special* "had [comparatively] little sense of artifice or irony, and revealed instead a confusion *about* identity rather than a play *with* identity." However, dressing in denims, for instance, showed that Elvis was firmly *in character*, echoing his artificial Hollywood roles. Ian Inglis, "The Road Not Taken. Elvis Presley: *Comeback Special*, NBC TV Studios, Hollywood. December 3, 1968," in *Performance and Popular Music: History, Place and Time*, ed. Ian Inglis (Aldershot: Ashgate, 2006), 47.
28 LeGault, who was the same age as Elvis, had been a stunt double for him since *Girls! Girls! Girls!* in 1962, but was also a disc jockey and music performer in his own right.
29 Hopkins, *Elvis: A Biography*, 343.
30 Guralnick, *Careless Love*, 307.
31 Marsh, *Elvis*, 177.
32 Guralnick, *Careless Love*, 297.
33 Hopkins, *Elvis: A Biography*, 337.
34 Marsh, *Elvis*, 166.
35 Adams, "Interview with Steve Binder."
36 Binder's office was at 8833. Guralnick and Jørgensen, *Elvis Day by Day*, 241.
37 See Hopkins, *Elvis: A Biography*, 338; Guralnick, *Careless Love*, 298. According to one patron, the bar was frequented by other celebrities. See: http://www.hollywoodhangover.com/htm_files/classic_cat_on_the_strip.htm.

38 Marsh, *Elvis*, 169. Elvis was also not recognized by at least one tourist on a studio tour of the Johnny Carson stage at Burbank. Adams, "Interview with Steve Binder."
39 Adams, "Interview with Steve Binder."
40 Apparently the Colonel charged $250,000 for the walk-on. Guralnick, *Careless Love*, 296.
41 Independent production credits began with Leiber and Stoller's work for Jerry Wexler, so Parker started his career before the role became recognized.
42 Adams, "Interview with Steve Binder."
43 Adams, "Interview with Steve Binder." With its neon sign, Bob's Big Boy has itself become iconic of 1950s coffee shops.
44 See Guralnick, *Careless Love*, 311; Hopkins, *Elvis: A Biography*, 344.
45 Adams, "Interview with Steve Binder."
46 Guralnick and Jørgensen, *Elvis Day by Day*, 244.
47 Jerry Schilling, *Me and a Guy Called Elvis: My Lifelong Friendship with Elvis Presley* (New York: Gotham Books, 2006), 191.
48 Hopkins, *Elvis: A Biography*, 337.
49 Adams, "Interview with Steve Binder."
50 See the review of Steve Binder and Jo Tunzi's book '68 at 40—Retrospective here: http://www.elvisinfonet.com/bookreview_JAT68at40.html
51 Hopkins, *Elvis: A Biography*, 340. Jerry Hopkins claimed that there were audio tapes made of these four or five hour dressing-room jams. To my knowledge, however, while the boxing ring studio rehearsals have been released, these tapes have never surfaced.
52 Jørgensen, *Elvis Presley: A Life in Music*, 247.
53 Bill Black died during an operation to remove a brain tumour in 1965. Elvis avoided the funeral to avoid creating a media circus and he visited Black's family in private afterwards. Had Black survived, he may not have been interested in participating in the *Comeback* taping, given the way that he had been marginalized in Elvis's earlier career and the success of his own band, the Bill Black Combo.
54 Jørgensen, *Elvis Presley: A Life in Music*, 253.
55 Jørgensen, *Elvis Presley: A Life in Music*, 248.
56 Marsh, *Elvis*, 169.
57 Guralnick, *Careless Love*, 305.
58 Hopkins, *Elvis: A Biography*, 346.
59 At least one Alfred Wertheimer signature publicity shot of Elvis back in the 1950s features the singer posed with a peaked cap on a motorbike, but closer inspection reveals that he is wearing a Lansky shirt, not a leather jacket. Off-stage photos are a different matter—a few have surfaced of Elvis in leather because he was an avid motorcycle rider. There are some early shots of him on motorbikes wearing leather.
60 Bill Osgerby, *Biker: Truth and Myth* (Lewes: Ivy Press, 2005), 34.
61 While Elvis wore denim in his film roles, he eschewed it elsewhere because he associated it with manual labour.
62 Doll, *Elvis for Dummies*, 184.
63 Hopkins, *Elvis: A Biography*, 339.
64 Guralnick, *Careless Love*, 307.
65 Marcus, *Mystery Train*, 144.
66 Interviewer David Adams said to Binder, "He was like a caged tiger on stage." Binder replied, "Well I think he was." Adams, "Interview with Steve Binder."
67 Black, *Elvis on the Road to Stardom*, 129.
68 Guralnick, *Careless Love*, 308.
69 Gaar, *Return of the King*, 78.
70 Guralnick, *Careless Love*, 312. According to Jørgensen, Elvis asked Binder, "What if nobody likes me?" Jørgensen, *Elvis Presley: A Life in Music*, 255.

71 Hopkins, *Elvis: A Biography*, 344.
72 Marsh, *Elvis*, 176.
73 Marsh, *Elvis*, 177.
74 Guralnick, *Careless Love*, 314.
75 Victor, *The Elvis Encyclopedia*, 329.
76 'Always on My Mind', a ballad co-written by Mark James that Elvis recorded well after the *Comeback*, is a case in point. Brenda Lee sang the tune as a tragic country number sung in 1971. Elvis recorded it in March 1972, intending it to be used as a B-side on the single of Red West's 'Separate Ways'. When the single sold over a million in the USA, it was reversed for UK release so 'Separate Ways' was the B-side. 'Always on My Mind' then became a staple in Elvis's live set, with footage of its recording being included on the 1981 documentary feature, *This Is Elvis*. Since then, it has been featured on well over 15 different compilation albums including Sony's *Voices: The Official Album of the 2006 World Cup*. The song was successfully covered by Willie Nelson and reinvented by the Pet Shop Boys. Many people now see it as a central part of the Elvis canon; something that got there through popular demand rather than saturation marketing.
77 See Guralnick, *Careless Love*, 311; Hopkins, *Elvis: A Biography*, 344.
78 See, for instance, Hopkins, *Elvis: A Biography*, 345; Marsh, *Elvis*, 196.
79 Adams, "Interview with Steve Binder."
80 Mark Duffett, "Caught in a Trap? Beyond Pop Theory's 'Butch' Construction of Male Elvis Fans," *Popular Music* 20, no. 3 (2001): 395–408.
81 Guralnick, *Careless Love*, 297.
82 Guralnick, *Careless Love*, 298.
83 Marsh, *Elvis*, 176.
84 Marsh, *Elvis*, 176.
85 Guralnick, *Careless Love*, 305. According to Jørgensen, it was 'I'll Be Home for Christmas' (Jørgensen, *Elvis Presley: A Life in Music*, 248). Binder himself suggested, 'I Believe' (Adams, "Interview with Steve Binder").
86 Binder asked both Goldenberg and Brown to work on the song. He said, "But if we can put it in the lyrics of a song, he's never gonna know what we did. So I asked them to go home and write a song about the philosophy of what I was hearing from Elvis personally." In the event, Brown wrote the song, so Goldenberg dropped his own credit. Adams, "Interview with Steve Binder."
87 Martin Luther King, "I Have A Dream," *American Rhetoric: Top 100 Speeches*, 1963, http://www.americanrhetoric.com/speeches/mlkihaveadream.htm
88 What is particularly interesting here is that King had earlier described rock'n'roll as a "degrading and immoral" influence. Bertrand, *Race, Rock, and Elvis*, 101.
89 Jørgensen, *Elvis Presley: A Life in Music*, 251. See also Guralnick, *Careless Love*, 310; Marsh, *Elvis*, 181.
90 Guralnick, *Careless Love*, 316.
91 Guralnick and Jørgensen, *Elvis Day by Day*, 245.
92 After "threats" from the Colonel, Brown agreed to cut Hill & Range in on the publishing revenue. Marsh, *Elvis*, 181.
93 Jørgensen, *Elvis Presley: A Life in Music*, 248. In theory at least, this suggests that Elvis "believed" in *Change of Habit*. It was a rare moment in which one of his fictional features did *directly*—if superficially—represent contemporary social problems.
94 Hopkins, *Elvis: A Biography*, 345.
95 Hopkins, *Elvis: A Biography*, 345.
96 Doll, *Elvis for Dummies*, 184.
97 Jørgensen, *Elvis Presley: A Life in Music*, 262.
98 Pat Broeske and Peter Brown, *Down at the End of Lonely Street: The Life and Death of Elvis Presley* (London: Arrow Books, 1998), 338.

99   See Rodman, *Elvis After Elvis*, 174; Inglis, "The Road Not Taken," 51.
100 Guralnick, *Careless Love*, 317.
101 Inglis, "The Road Not Taken," 49.
102 Marsh, *Elvis*, 176.
103 Bill Malone, *Don't Get Above Your Raisin'* (Chicago: University of Illinois Press, 2002), 182.
104 Victor, *The Elvis Encyclopedia*, 67.
105 Victor, *The Elvis Encyclopedia*, 67.
106 Brode, *Elvis Cinema and Popular Culture*, 269.
107 Brode, *Elvis Cinema and Popular Culture*, 280.
108 Dusty's album, which contained 'Son of a Preacher Man', was not produced by Chips, but by a super-team from Atlantic consisting of Jerry Wexler, Arif Mardin and Tom Dowd.
109 Doll, *Elvis for Dummies*, 185.
110 Ironically, the engulfed publisher was called American Music.
111 American Sound's house musicians included guitarist Reggie Young, bassists Tommy Cogbill and Mike Leech, Gene Chrisman on drums, and Bobby Wood and Bobby Emmons on keyboards.
112 For material offered to Elvis see Jørgensen, *Elvis Presley: A Life in Music*, 269.
113 Jørgensen, *Elvis Presley: A Life in Music*, 271.
114 Jørgensen, *Elvis Presley: A Life in Music*, 273.
115 Victor, *The Elvis Encyclopedia*, 16.
116 Moman had also evoked the insecurities of Felton Jarvis, who felt his role was being usurped.
117 Doll, *Elvis for Dummies*, 185.
118 Guralnick and Jørgensen, *Elvis Day by Day*, 257.
119 Jørgensen, *Elvis Presley: A Life in Music*, 277.
120 In the 1970s, Elvis created a live sound that blended contributions from a range of sources, including a White female soprano, Black female gospel trio, White rock band, male gospel quartet, and full orchestra.
121 Jørgensen, *Elvis Presley: A Life in Music*, 272.
122 Guralnick and Jørgensen, *Elvis Day by Day*, 252.
123 The Sweet Inspirations had already backed Van Morrison, Dusty Springfield and Aretha Franklin. They also had successful releases of their own on Atlantic Records.
124 Guralnick and Jørgensen, *Elvis Day by Day*, 258.
125 Guralnick and Jørgensen, *Elvis Day by Day*, 262.
126 Others included Pat Boone, Petula Clark, Henry Mancini, George Hamilton, Angie Dickinson, Dick Clark, Ann-Margret, Fats Domino and Phil Ochs.
127 Doll, *Elvis for Dummies*, 191.
128 Doll, *Elvis for Dummies*, 192.
129 Doll, *Elvis for Dummies*, 192.
130 Doll, *Elvis for Dummies*, 193.
131 Guralnick and Jørgensen, *Elvis Day by Day*, 259.
132 Doll, *Elvis for Dummies*, 194.
133 Doll, *Elvis for Dummies*, 197.
134 The way that Elvis's costumes, comments and music vary between each show in the 1970s has become a significant focus for fans and bootleg collectors.
135 Neale, *Roots of Elvis*, 104.
136 Radano's discussion of racialization of "hot" rhythm is relevant here: Ronald Radano, "Hot Fantasies: American Modernism and the Idea of Black Rhythm," in *Music and the Racial Imagination*, eds. Ronald Radano and Philip V. Bohlman (London: University of Chicago Press, 2000), 459–82. Also see Jon Michael Spencer, "A Revolutionary Sexual Persona: Elvis Presley and the White Acquiescence of Black Rhythms," in *In

Search of Elvis: Music, Art, Race, Religion, ed. Vernon Chadwick (Boulder: Westview Press, 1997), 109–22.
137 See Ger Rijff's posting here: http://www.elvisechoesofthepast.com/rock-n-roll-king-vs-calypso-king/
138 *He Touched Me*, DVD. It is also notable that in Elvis dated Rita Moreno, and from 1973 onwards Jerry Schilling dated (and later married) Myrna Smith. See: http://www.elvisinfonet.com/myrna.html
139 Doll, *Elvis for Dummies*, 195.
140 Doll, *Elvis for Dummies*, 196.
141 *Elvis: His Best Friend Remembers*, DVD, directed by Terry Moloney (Los Angeles: Proletariat Filmworks, 2002).
142 *Elvis: True Stories*, DVD, directed by Peter J. Barton (Dartford: Delta Home Entertainment, 2004).
143 Marcus, *Mystery Train*, 138.
144 Marcus, *Mystery Train*, 137.
145 Medovoi, *Rebels*, 192.
146 Lisa Parks and Melissa McCartney, "Elvis Goes Global: *Aloha! Live Via Satellite* and Music/Tourism/Television," in *Medium Cool: Music Videos from Soundies to Cellphones*, eds. Roger Beebee and Jason Middleton (Durham: Duke University Press, 2007), 254.
147 Parks and McCartney, "Elvis Goes Global," 262.
148 Parks and McCartney, "Elvis Goes Global," 264.
149 See Marcus, *Mystery Train*, 140; Marsh, *Elvis*, 234; Presley et al., *We Love You Tender*, 166–68.
150 S. Hunter, "Discovering Elvis," *Elvis Monthly* 334 (1987): 21.
151 See Ed Parker, *Inside Elvis* (Orange, CA: Rampart House, 1978), 7; Jerry Hopkins, *Elvis: The Final Years* (London: WH Allen, 1980), 65; Aparin, "He Never Got Above His Raising," 71.
152 See Robert Matthew-Walker, *Elvis Presley: A Study in Music* (Tunbridge Wells: Midas Books, 1979), 93; Trevor Cajion, "Red West: This Is What Happened. Part One," *Elvis: The Man and His Music* 22 (1994).
153 David Brackett, "The Electro-Acoustic Mirror: Voices in American Pop," *Critical Quarterly* 37, no. 2 (1995): 12.

Chapter 4 Phenomenon

1 See Adams, "Interview with Steve Binder."
2 Jørgensen, *Elvis Presley: A Life in Music*, 151.
3 Guralnick, *Careless Love*, 635.
4 Victor Livingston, "Hefty and Hot, Elvis Still Carries Weight with Fans," *St. Petersburg Times*, April 28, 1975.
5 Lynn Spigel, "Communicating with the Dead: Elvis as Medium," *Camera Obscura* 8, no. 2 (1990): 177.
6 Bourdieu, *Distinction*, 191.
7 Bourdieu, *Distinction*, 374.
8 Douglas Martin, "Mary Jenkins Langston, 78, Cook for Presley," *New York Times*, June 5, 2000, https://www.nytimes.com/2000/06/05/us/mary-jenkins-langston-78-cook-for-presley.html.
9 Colin Escott, *Good Rockin' Tonight: Sun Records and the Birth of Rock 'n' Roll* (London: Virgin, 1992), 77.
10 Heather Robertson, "Tell Us That You Love Us, Elvis P.," *Maclean's* 88, no. 9 (1975): 84.

11 Mark Duffett, "Elvis Presley and Susan Boyle: Bodies of Controversy," *Journal of Popular Music Studies* 23, no. 2 (2011): 166–89.
12 The Phantom, "Elvis in Concert," *Elvis Monthly* 334 (1987): 15.
13 The Phantom, "Elvis in Concert," 17.
14 The Phantom, "Elvis in Concert," 20.
15 Guralnick, *Careless Love*, 638.
16 Theodor Adorno, "On the Fetish Character in Music and the Regression of Listening" (1938), in *Essays on Music*, ed. Richard Leppert (Berkeley: University of California Press, 2002), 295.
17 Frith, *Performing Rites*, 193.
18 Frith, *Performing Rites*, 193.
19 Frith, *Performing Rites*, 193.
20 Stephen Harper, "Madly Famous: Narratives of Mental Illness and Celebrity Culture," in *Framing Celebrity*, eds. Su Holmes and Sean Redmond (London: Routledge, 2006), 317.
21 Sonya Brown, "An Obscure Middle Ground: Size Acceptance Narratives and Photographs of 'Real Women'," *Feminist Media Studies* 5, no. 2 (2005): 249.
22 Katariina Kyrölä, "The Fat Gendered Body in/as a Closet," *Feminist Media Studies* 5, no. 1 (2005): 99.
23 This draws on the discussion in Christina Fisanick, "'One Thing I Know for Sure': Oprah Is Fat Phobic," *Feminist Media Studies* 5, no. 2 (2005): 94.
24 Crumbaker and Tucker, *Up and Down with Elvis Presley*, 165.
25 Guralnick, *Careless Love*, 643.
26 Spigel, "Communicating with the Dead," 195.
27 Mick Farren, *Speed-Speed-Speedfreak: A Fast History of Amphetamine* (Port Townsend: Feral House, 2010), 65.
28 Victor, *The Elvis Encyclopedia*, 119.
29 *Telerama*, "Bobby Gillespie (Primal Scream): Foot, Iggy Pop, Ecstasy," YouTube video, 9:22 (quote begins at 6:49), October 18, 2018, https://www.youtube.com/watch?v=FNWGHBhSSBo.
30 Victor, *The Elvis Encyclopedia*, 119.
31 See, for instance, Tony Parsons discussing Bowie's *Low* album. Dylan Jones, *David Bowie: An Oral History* (New York: Penguin Random House, 2018), 247.
32 Guralnick, *Careless Love*, 556.
33 On Disc 2 of the *Comeback Special Deluxe Edition*, NBC executive Bob Finkel compared Elvis to Howard Hughes. *Comeback Special Deluxe Edition*, DVD, directed by Steve Binder (New York: Sony BMG, 2004). Pat Broeske and Peter Brown's *Down at the End of Lonely Street*, 1998, also makes reference to Elvis as a doomed figure. A decade after Albert Goldman released *Elvis*, he returned with another book called *Elvis: The Last 24 Hours* (London: Pan Books, 1991), which claimed the star had committed suicide.
34 David Ritz, ed., *Elvis by the Presleys* (New York: Crown Archetype, 2005), 214–15.
35 Larry Geller, *If I Can Dream: Elvis's Own Story* (London: Century, 1989), 271.
36 Marcus, *Mystery Train*, 138–39.
37 R. Serge Denisoff and George Plasketes, *True Disbelievers: The Elvis Contagion* (New Brunswick: Transaction Publishers, 1995).
38 Irene Ilott, "Did Elvis Die of Boredom?," *British Journal of Occupational Therapy* 70, no. 10 (2007): 415. See also Stephan Rössner, "'Are You Lonesome Tonight?' Elvis Presley 1935–1977," *Obesity Reviews* 11, no. 9 (2010): 688–89.
39 In an intriguing interview with Gary James, Paul Lichter questioned the standard version of events for that day. See: http://www.classicbands.com/PaulLichterInterview.html.

40 Neal Gregory and Janice Gregory, *When Elvis Died: Media Overload and the Origins of the Elvis Cult* (New York: Pharos Books, 1992), 32.
41 Simon Frith, "Frankie Said, But What Did They Mean?" in *Consumption, Identity and Style: Marketing, Meanings and the Packaging of Pleasure*, ed. A. Tomlinson (London: Routledge, 1990), 178.
42 See Terri Anderson, "RCA to Re-release 16 Presley Chart Toppers," *Music Week*, April 30, 1977, 4; C. White and J. Hayward, "Consumers Rush for Elvis Product," *Music Week*, August 27, 1977: 4.
43 Gregory and Gregory, *When Elvis Died*, 189.
44 Tony Byworth, "Shelby Singleton and Sun: A Galaxy of a Back Catalogue," *Music Week*, December 17, 1977: 20.
45 L. Eliscu, "Elvis Souvenir Sales Hit Multi-Million Mark," *Music Week*, November 5, 1977: 10.
46 Matthew-Walker, *Elvis Presley: A Study in Music*, 83.
47 John Tobler and Richard Wootton, *Elvis: The Legend and the Music* (London: Optimum Books, 1983), 164.
48 Spigel, "Communicating with the Dead," 178.
49 Michael Bertrand, "How Much Does It Cost If It's Free? The Selling (Out) of Elvis Presley," in *Rock Brands: Selling Sound in a Media Saturated Culture*, ed. Elizabeth Barfoot-Christian (Lanham: Lexington Books, 2011), 291–324.
50 The other co-executors were accountant Joseph Hanks (who retired from his post in 1990) and the Memphis branch of the National Bank of Commerce.
51 From: "The King is Dead, But Long Lives The King in a Showbiz Bonanza," *People Weekly*, October 10, 1977.
52 Ted Harrison, *Elvis People: The Cult of the King* (London: Fount, 1992), 78.
53 O'Neal, *Elvis Inc.*, 217.
54 The celebrity chef Jamie Oliver is a case in point. Beyoncé and Jay-Z, however, were unsuccessful when they tried to trademark the name of their daughter, Blue Ivy. See Nicholas Hawkins, "Tangled Up in 'Blue Ivy': Beyoncé Battles Massachusetts Wedding Planner in Trademark Dispute," *IP Watchdog*, October 21, 2019, https://www.ipwatchdog.com/2019/10/21/tangled-blue-ivy-beyonce-battles-massachusetts-wedding-planner-trademark-dispute/id=114659/.
55 See David Wall, "Reconstructing the Soul of Elvis: The Social Development and Legal Maintenance of Elvis Presley," *International Journal of the Sociology of Law* 24, no. 2 (1996): 117–43; David Wall, "Policing Elvis: Legal Action and the Shaping of Post Mortem Celebrity Culture as Contested Space," *Entertainment Law* 2, no. 3 (2003): 35–69.
56 See Wright for a discussion of the *Velvet Elvis* case. Wright notes that parody is a grey legal area. Deborah Wright, "Don't Be Cruel: Scope of Parody Curtailed in Elvis Presley Enterprises, Inc. v. Capece," *Golden Gate University Law Review* 29, no. 3 (1999): 683–714.
57 Another example is the angry on-stage monologue from a show in Las Vegas from September 2, 1974, released on numerous bootlegs.
58 See, for example, Lee Goldman, "Elvis Is Alive, But He Shouldn't Be: The Right of Publicity Revisited," *Brigham Young University Law Review* 3 (1992): 597–628; O'Neal, *Elvis Inc*.
59 Doll, *Elvis for Dummies*, 188.
60 Duffett, *Understanding Fandom*.
61 See David Alderman, "The Politics of Saving the King's Court: Why We Should Take Elvis Fans Seriously," *Business Perspectives* 14, no. 3 (2002): 46–77; Duffett, *Understanding Fandom*.

62 John Fiske, "Elvis: A Body of Controversy," in idem, *Power Plays, Power Works* (London: Verso, 1993), 90–120.
63 Harry Sewlall, "'Image, Music, Text': Elvis Presley as a Postmodern, Semiotic Construct," *Journal of Literary Studies* 26, no. 2 (2010): 44–57.
64 See: http://www.rare-elvis.de/html/collectibles_2.html
65 Charles Thompson and James Cole, *The Death of Elvis: What Really Happened* (London: Robert Hale, 1991), 66.
66 Red West et al., *Elvis: What Happened?* (New York: Ballantine, 1977), 323.
67 Marty Lacker, *Elvis: Portrait of a Friend* (Memphis: Wimmer Brothers Books, 1979), 259.
68 West et al., *Elvis: What Happened?*, publisher's note.
69 Presley et al., *We Love You Tender*, 383.
70 Lacker, *Elvis: Portrait of a Friend*, 290.
71 Victor, *The Elvis Encyclopedia*, 141.
72 Graceland secretaries and members of the Memphis Mafia would sometimes reply to fans on Elvis's behalf and fake his signature.
73 See Westmoreland, *Elvis and Kathy*, 294; Parker, *Inside Elvis*, 160.
74 Other media products include various made-for-television biopics and series: *Elvis* (Carpenter, 1979), *Elvis and the Beauty Queen* (Trikonis, 1981), *Elvis and Me* (Peerce, 1988), *Elvis and the Colonel* (Graham, 1993), and *Elvis* (Sadwith, 2005).
75 Eggers may have suggested a different kind of biography. In the 1960s he formed Poppy Records, which released the country folk music of Townes Van Zandt. After changing the label's name to Tomato, Eggers released a remastered radio broadcast Elvis LP in 1984 called *Roots Revolution: Louisiana Hayride*.
76 Hopkins, *Elvis: The Final Years*, v.
77 William Grimes, "Albert Goldman, Biographer, Is Dead at 66," *New York Times*, March 30, 1994, http://www.nytimes.com/1994/03/30/obituaries/albert-goldman-biographer-is-dead-at-66.html?src=pm.
78 Guralnick, *Last Train to Memphis*, 362.
79 Goldman, *Elvis: The Last 24 Hours*, 187.
80 Goldman, *Elvis* (1982), 519.
81 R. Walters, "The Myth Lives On," *New York Times Book Review* 86, no. 33 (1981): 27. A decade later, Goldman procured a $225,000 advance on a relatively poor-selling, 1991 sequel *Elvis: The Last 24 Hours*, which set out to prove that the star committed suicide.
82 Marsh, *Elvis*, xi.
83 Frith, "Wise Men Say," 279.
84 Hamm's request is reproduced in Frith, "Wise Men Say," 279.
85 Geller, *If I Can Dream*, 136.
86 Brewer-Giorgio, *The Elvis Files*, 264.
87 Tony Myers, *Routledge Critical Thinkers: Slavoj Žižek* (New York: Routledge, 2003), 74.
88 Grimes, "Albert Goldman, Biographer, Is Dead at 66." First published in the [*Village*] *Voice Literary Supplement* in 1981.
89 James G. Ballard, "Fallen Idol: *Elvis* by Albert Goldman," in *A User's Guide to the Millennium*, ed. James G. Ballard (New York: Picador, 1996), 40.
90 Plasketes, *Images of Elvis Presley*.
91 All stereotypes contain a heavily distorted element of truth. While the media circus about Elvis "sightings" was designed to imply that fans could not tell their desires from reality, Denisoff and Plasketes (in their book *True Disbelievers*) reported on a small faction of true fans who supposedly *did* suspect that Elvis was alive and hiding from the public. Almost all Elvis fans, however, not only knew, understood and lamented

that their hero was gone; they also saw media representations implying otherwise as gross insults to their community.

92 Andy Kershaw, *No Off Switch: An Autobiography* (London: Virgin Books, 2012), 258.
93 Harrison, *Elvis People*, 102.
94 Harrison, *Elvis People*, 75.
95 The idea of Elvis fandom as religion dismissed fans as misguided believers. One problem at the time was that researchers lacked an appropriate vocabulary to talk about fandom and affect. Their wholesale borrowing of the religious metaphor was, at best, however, ill considered. At worst it aimed to deliberately damage the image of music fandom. Mark Duffett, "False Faith or False Comparison? A Critique of the Religious Interpretation of Elvis Fan Culture," *Popular Music and Society* 26, no. 4 (2003): 513–22.
96 For a sustained example, see Rupert Till, *Pop Cults: Religion and Popular Music* (London: Continuum Press, 2010). For a critique of the religiosity idea, see Duffett, "False Faith or False Comparison?"
97 Jenkins, *Textual Poachers*, 11.
98 Garber, "The Transvestite Continuum," 368.
99 Peter Stromberg, "Elvis Alive? The Ideology of American Consumerism," *Journal of Popular Culture* 24, no. 3 (1990): 17; Mark Duffett, "Transcending Audience Generalizations: Consumerism Reconsidered in the Case of Elvis Presley Fans," *Popular Music and Society* 24, no. 2 (2000): 75–91.
100 Stephen Hinerman, "I'll Be Here with You: Fans, Fantasy and the Figure of Elvis," in *The Adoring Audience: Fan Culture and Popular Media*, ed. Lisa Lewis (Abingdon: Routledge, 1992), 107.
101 There were other commercial ventures that added to this confusion by drawing on the notion that Elvis was a mystical romance hero. Gail Brewer-Giorgio's novel *Orion* (New York: Tudor, 1979), for instance, centred on a masked mystery singer who claimed to be Elvis. One impersonator, Jimmy Ellis, took the concept a step further and turned it into a stage act, but his popularity rapidly declined after he took off the mask. Lucy De Barbin's book *Are You Lonesome Tonight?* (London: Ebury Press, 1987) announced that its author had a love child with Elvis.
102 Mary Hancock-Hinds, *Infinite Elvis: An Annotated Bibliography* (Chicago: A Capella, 2001), 265.
103 Some examples of this alternative tradition include Matthew-Walker's critical musicology (*Elvis Presley: A Study in Music*), music research by Richard Middleton and other contributions in Jac Tharpe, ed., *Elvis: Images and Fancies* (London: Star Books, 1980), Aparin, "He Never Got Above His Raising", contributions by Simon Frith and others to Clayson and Leigh, *Aspects of Elvis*, and the excellent work of Michael Bertrand (*Race, Rock, and Elvis* and "How Much Does It Cost If It's Free?").
104 David Zurawik, "Bill Clinton's Sax on Arsenio Hall Still Resonates in Memorable Moments," *The Baltimore Sun*, December 27, 1992, http://articles.baltimoresun.com/1992-12-27/features/1992362178_1_clinton-arsenio-hall-hall-show
105 See: https://web.archive.org/web/20130316015528/https://www.elvispresleynews.com/BorisYeltsin.html
106 Duffett, *Understanding Elvis*, 228.
107 By "official" I mean RCA/BMG/Sony releases. I have not even counted those legally licensed to other operations. See: http://www.elvisoncd.com/frame.htm?http://www.elvisoncd.com/EIGENECD_a-z/ftd-label/ourmemoriesofelvis.htm
108 While BMG and then Sony's buy-outs of RCA have ameliorated this issue, it has not entirely disappeared. In the summer of 2013, EPE announced their intention to sue RCA's German branch to contest the token annual sum it paid after the Colonel's famous 1973 royalties waiver deal. See: http://www.prweb.com/releases/2011/8/prweb8755663.htm.

109 By licensing much of Elvis's older material in the 1970s to budget labels like Camden and Pickwick, RCA effectively offloaded promotional risk. The label then focused its marketing resources on other artists such as David Bowie.
110 Guralnick and Jørgensen, *Elvis Day by Day*, 255.
111 Adams, "Interview with Steve Binder."
112 Carl Arlington, "Joan Deary Didn't Find Any Skeletons in Elvis' Graceland Closets, Just a Record Bonanza," *People*, March, 12, 1984, https://people.com/archive/joan-deary-didnt-find-any-skeletons-in-elvis-graceland-closets-just-a-record-bonanza-vol-22-no-23/
113 Greg Geller's 1985 re-issues to commemorate the 50th anniversary of Elvis's birth tended to focus on familiar material.
114 Matt Hills, *Triumph of a Time Lord: Regenerating Doctor Who in the Twenty-first Century* (New York: IB Tauris, 2010), 54.
115 Semon and Jørgensen first met face to face in BMG's London office in 1985. They had already worked together at a distance on Elvis releases. One of their earliest successes was the album project, *Essential Elvis: The First Movies*, which was issued in the UK, then released in the USA because fans demanded it on import. The album mostly consisted of rare, unreleased alternative takes and helped people understand how Elvis's music was fashioned in the studio. Its success was unprecedented. See: http://www.elvisinfonet.com/interview_rogersemon.html
116 Taken from Jørgensen's interview with *Crawdaddy* magazine reproduced here: https://www.elvis.com.au/presley/video-interview-with-ernst-jorgensen.shtml.
117 See: https://www.elvis.com.au/presley/prince-from-another-planet-2-lp-vinyl-release.shtml.
118 Joan Deary oversaw two compilations in 1979 called *Our Memories of Elvis* which removed Felton Jarvis's overdubs and exposed the "pure" sound of Elvis's voice. Fan demand for an associated 2010 Victrola bootleg and the rediscovery of previously unreleased tracks prompted FTD to issue a 38-track *Pure Elvis Sound* compilation of its own in 2012. See: http://www.elvisinfonet.com/ftd_review_memories_of_elvis.html.
119 See: https://www.elvis.com.au/presley/cd/cd-the-complete-elvis-presley-masters-30-cd-box-set.shtml
120 Nash, *The Colonel*, 339.
121 See: https://web.archive.org/web/20140330174825/http://www.coremediagroup.com/pdf/Elvis%20Backstage%20Press%20Release%20-%20EPE%20&%20CEASARS.pdf
122 Greil Marcus, "Elvis Again," *The Threepenny Review*, winter 2003, http://www.threepennyreview.com/samples/marcus_w03.html
123 To my knowledge, Lisa Marie was the first person to create an endorsed posthumous duet with her father: 1997's 'Don't Cry Daddy'. Ten years later, with the help of rotoscoping techniques and a tribute artist, Celine Dion duetted 'If I Can Dream' with Elvis's image on ABC's *American Idol*. Late in 2013 Susan Boyle was also paired with Elvis on a charity duet recording of 'O Come, All Ye Faithful' that unsuccessfully aimed for the Christmas number one slot.
124 Mark Fisher, "The Metaphysics of Crackle: Afrofuturism and Hauntology," *Dancecult* 5, no. 2 (2013): 43.
125 Fisher, "The Metaphysics of Crackle," 49.
126 Fans who hear bootlegs of shows that they attended often have crystal-clear recall.
127 Michel Foucault, "What is an Author?," in *Language, Counter-Memory, Practice: Selected Essays and Interviews*, ed. Donald Bouchard (New York: Cornell University Press, 1977), 114.
128 From Mike Freeman's DVD, *Beyond Elvis's Memphis*.
129 Marsh, *Elvis*, 162.
130 Brode, *Elvis Cinema and Popular Culture*, 284.

131 Wanda Powell Heagy, *East Tupelo and Elvis: That's The Way It Was* (Saltillo: Tillo, 2010), 242.
132 Ken Sharp, *Elvis Presley: Writing for the King* (New York: FTD Books, 2006), 291.

Appendix 2

1 For a concert log of Elvis's tour dates, see Gordon, *The King on the Road*, 202–7.

Appendix 3

1 This list does not include the two visits that Elvis made to capture amateur vanity recordings, the rehearsal he may have made to sing 'Without You' in June 1954, or the famous Million Dollar Quartet session that Elvis participated in later, when he visited Sun after signing to RCA.
2 This session is disputed, as 'Blue Moon' could have been recorded earlier. Jørgensen, *A Boy from Tupelo*, 36.

Appendix 4

1 Some of Elvis's local or unsubstantiated appearances have not been included here. Neither have press conferences or news footage segments.
2 The date is for the USA airing. *Aloha from Hawaii* was initially broadcast live elsewhere, January 14, 1973.

Appendix 6

1 These are only the studio and live LPs released while Elvis was alive. The list does not include full compilations or movie soundtracks. Also, because of the choice of material, sometimes the line between studio albums and compilations was breached.

Appendix 7

1 Summarized from Guralnick and Jørgensen, *Elvis Day by Day*, 241–45. Also see: http://www.keithflynn.com/recording-sessions/60_index_03.html

Bibliography

Adams, David. "Interview with Steve Binder, Director of Elvis's '68 Comeback Special." *Elvis Australia* (2005). http://www.elvis.com.au/presley/interview_steve_binder.shtml#sthash.gtgBx1Eu.dpbs

Adorno, Theodor. *Introduction to the Sociology of Music*. New York: Seabury Press, 1976.

—. "On the Fetish Character in Music and the Regression of Listening" (1938). Reprinted in *Essays on Music*, edited by Richard Leppert, 288–317. Berkeley: University of California Press, 2002.

Alderman, David. "The Politics of Saving the King's Court: Why We Should Take Elvis Fans Seriously." *Business Perspectives* 14, no. 3 (2002): 46–77.

Anderson, Terri. "RCA to Re-release 16 Presley Chart Toppers." *Music Week*, April 30, 1977.

Aparin, Julia. "He Never Got Above His Raising: An Ethnographic Study of a Working Class Response to Elvis Presley." PhD diss., University of Pennsylvania, 1988.

Arlington, Carl. "Joan Deary Didn't Find Any Skeletons in Elvis' Graceland Closets, Just a Record Bonanza." *People*, March 12, 1984. https://people.com/archive/joan-deary-didnt-find-any-skeletons-in-elvis-graceland-closets-just-a-record-bonanza-vol-22-no-23/

Austen, Jake. *TV-a-Go-Go: Rock on TV from* American Bandstand *to* American Idol. Chicago: Chicago Review Press, 2005.

Bailey, Dale. *American Nightmares: The Haunted House Formula in American Popular Fiction*. Wisconsin: Popular Press, 2009.

Baker, David. "Elvis Goes to Hollywood: Authenticity, Resistance, Commodification and the Mainstream." In *Redefining Mainstream Popular Music*, edited by Sarah Baker, Andy Bennett and Jodie Taylor, 89–101. New York: Routledge, 2013.

Baker, Hugh, and Yuval Taylor. "Heartbreak Hotel: The Art and Artifice of Elvis Presley, Nashville January 10, 1956." In H. Barker and Y. Taylor, *Faking It: The Quest for Authenticity in Popular Music*. London: Faber and Faber, 2007.

Baker, Jackson. "Perfectly Normal." *Memphis Flyer* 442 (1997): 33.

Ballard, James G. "Fallen Idol: *Elvis* by Albert Goldman." In *A User's Guide to the Millennium*, edited by James G. Ballard, 39–40. New York: Picador, 1996.

Berle, Milton. "Milton Berle." *The Interviews—Television Academy Foundation*, 28:24, 1996. Reproduced, May 28, 2013. https://interviews.televisionacademy.com/interviews/milton-berle

Bertrand, Michael. *Race, Rock, and Elvis*. Chicago: University of Illinois Press, 2005.

—. "How Much Does It Cost If It's Free? The Selling (Out) of Elvis Presley." In *Rock Brands: Selling Sound in a Media Saturated Culture*, edited by Elizabeth Barfoot-Christian, 291–324. Lanham: Lexington Books, 2011.

Black, Jim. *Elvis on the Road to Stardom 1955–1956*. London: WH Allen, 1988.
Bonner, Michael. "Quentin Tarantino Chooses His 10 Favourite Records." *Uncut*, August 19, 2019. https://www.uncut.co.uk/blog/quentin-tarantino-chooses-his-10-favourite-records-27610
Bourdieu, Pierre. *Distinction: A Social Critique of the Judgement of Taste*. Cambridge: Harvard University Press, 1984.
Brackett, David. "The Electro-Acoustic Mirror: Voices in American Pop." *Critical Quarterly* 37, no. 2 (1995): 11–27.
Brewer-Giorgio, Gail. *Orion*. New York: Tudor, 1979.
—. *The Elvis Files: Was His Death Faked?* New York: Shapolsky, 1990.
Brode, Douglas. *Elvis Cinema and Popular Culture*. Jefferson: McFarland, 2006.
Broeske, Pat, and Peter Brown. "He Binged on Junk Food." *Daily Mail*, July 9, 1997a.
—. "Once Priscilla Gave Birth, Elvis Rejected Her." *Daily Mail*, July 11, 1997b.
—. *Down at the End of Lonely Street: The Life and Death of Elvis Presley*. London: Arrow Books, 1998.
Brown, Sonya. "An Obscure Middle Ground: Size Acceptance Narratives and Photographs of 'Real Women.'" *Feminist Media Studies* 5, no. 2 (2005): 237–60.
Buchanan, Catherine. "A Comparative Analysis of Name and Likeness Rights in the United States and England." *Golden Gate University Law Review* 18, no. 301 (1988): 301–70.
Buck-Morss, Susan. 1977. *The Origin of Negative Dialectics: Theodor W. Adorno, Walter Benjamin and the Frankfurt Institute*. Hassocks: Harvester, 1977.
Burk, Bill. *Early Elvis: The Sun Years*. Memphis: Propwash, 1997.
Burke, Ken, and Dan Griffin. *The Blue Moon Boys: The Story of Elvis Presley's Band*. Chicago: Chicago Review Press, 2006.
Buskin, Richard. *Elvis: Memories and Memorabilia*. London: Salamander, 1995.
Byworth, Tony. "Shelby Singleton and Sun: A Galaxy of a Back Catalogue." *Music Week*, December 17, 1977.
Cajiao, Trevor. "Red West: This Is What Happened. Part One." *Elvis: The Man and His Music* 22 (1994).
Cantor, Louis. *Wheelin' on Beale*. New York: Pharos Books, 1992.
—. *Dewey and Elvis: The Life and Times of a Rock'n'Roll Deejay*. Chicago: University of Illinois Press, 2005.
Carlin, Peter. *Paul McCartney: A Life*. New York: Touchstone, 2009.
Chadwick, Vernon, ed. *In Search of Elvis: Music, Art, Race, Religion*. Boulder: Westview Press, 1997.
Christgau, Robert. "Now It Can Be Told." 1994. http://www.robertchristgau.com/xg/misc/rbgoldm2-94.php
Clayson, Adam. "Snowmen: The Manager and his Client." In *Aspects of Elvis: Tryin' to Get to You*, edited by Adam Clayson and Spencer Leigh, 50–55. London: Sidgwick and Jackson, 1994.
Cocks, Jay. "Last Stop on the Mystery Train." *Time*, August 29, 1977.
Cohn, Nik. *Awopbopaloobop Alopbamboom*. St Albans: Granada, 1973.
Connelly, Charlie. *In Search of Elvis*. London: Abacus, 2007.
Connolly, Ray. "Sam Phillips Plus Johnny Cash, Carl Perkins and Roy Orbison." *Radio Times*, September 1973. https://www.rayconnolly.co.uk/sam-phillips/
Cortez, Diego. *Private Elvis*. Stuttgart: FEY, 1978.
Cotkin, George. *Existential America*. Baltimore: Johns Hopkins University Press, 2003.
Cotton, Lee. *Did Elvis Sing in Your Hometown?* Sacramento: High Sierra Books, 1995.
Cowan, Sharon. "The Elvis We Deserve: The Social Regulation of Sex/Gender and Sexuality through Cultural Representations of 'The King.'" *Law, Culture and the Humanities* 6, no. 2 (2010): 221–44.

Cox, Karen. "The South and Mass Culture." *Journal of Southern History* 75, no. 3 (2009): 677–90.
Craig, Maxine. *Sorry I Don't Dance: Why Men Refuse to Move*. New York: Oxford University Press, 2014.
Crane, Lionel. "Rock Age Idol: He's Riding the Crest of a Teenage Tidal Wave." *Daily Mirror*, April 30, 1956.
Crumbaker, Marge, and Gabe Tucker. *Up and Down with Elvis Presley*. Sevenoaks: New English Library, 1981.
Davidson, Phil. "Lamar Fike: Member of Elvis Presley's Famed Inner Circle, the Memphis Mafia." *The Independent*, February 26, 2011.
http://www.independent.co.uk/news/obituaries/lamar-fike-member-of-elvis-presleys-famed-inner-circle-the-memphis-mafia-2226112.html
Dawidoff, Nicholas. *In the Country of Country: A Journey to the Roots of American Music*. London: Faber and Faber, 2005.
De Barbin, Lucy. *Are You Lonesome Tonight? The Untold Story of Elvis Presley's One True Love and the Child He Never Knew*. London: Ebury Press, 1987.
Denisoff, R. Serge, and George Plasketes. *True Disbelievers: The Elvis Contagion*. New Brunswick: Transaction Publishers, 1995.
Doll, Susan. *Understanding Elvis: Southern Roots vs Star Image*. New York: Garland, 1998.
—. *Elvis for Dummies*. Hoboken: John Wiley & Sons, 2009.
Doss, Erika. *Elvis Culture: Fans, Faith and Image*. Kansas: University of Kansas Press, 1999.
Duffett, Mark. "Understanding Elvis: Presley, Power and Performance." PhD diss., University of Wales, Aberystwyth, 1998.
—. "Transcending Audience Generalizations: Consumerism Reconsidered in the Case of Elvis Presley Fans." *Popular Music and Society* 24, no. 2 (2000): 75–91.
—. "Caught in a Trap? Beyond Pop Theory's 'Butch' Construction of Male Elvis Fans." *Popular Music* 20, no. 3 (2001): 395–408.
—. "False Faith or False Comparison? A Critique of the Religious Interpretation of Elvis Fan Culture." *Popular Music and Society* 26, no. 4 (2003): 513–22.
—. "Elvis Presley and Susan Boyle: Bodies of Controversy." *Journal of Popular Music Studies* 23, no. 2 (2011): 166–89.
—. "Walking in Memphis? Elvis Heritage between Fan Fantasy and Built Environment." In *Redefining Mainstream Popular Music*, edited by Sarah Baker, Andy Bennett and Jodie Taylor, 102–13. New York: Routledge, 2013.
—. "Boosting Elvis: A Content Analysis of Editorial Stories from One Fan Club Magazine." *Participations* 9, no. 2 (2012): 317–36.
http://www.participations.org/Volume%209/Issue%202/18%20Duffett.pdf
—. *Understanding Fandom: An Introduction to the Study of Media Fan Culture*. New York: Bloomsbury, 2013.
—. "Elvis' Gospel Music: Between the Secular and the Spiritual?" *Religions* 6, no. 1 (2015): 182–203.
—. *Counting Down Elvis: His 100 Finest Songs*. Lanham: Rowman & Littlefield, 2018.
Dumas, Chris. *Un-American Psycho: Brian De Palma and the Political Invisible*. Bristol: Intellect Books, 2012.
Dundy, Elaine. *Elvis and Gladys*. London: Pimlico, 1995.
Durkheim, Émile. *The Elementary Forms of Religious Life*. Oxford: Oxford University Press, 2008 [1912].
Eder, Mike. *Elvis Music FAQ*. Milwaukee: Backbeat Books, 2013.
Eliscu, L. "Elvis Souvenir Sales Hit Multi-Million Mark." *Music Week*, November 5, 1977.
Ennis, Philip. *The Seventh Stream: The Emergence of Rock'n'Roll in American Popular Music*. Hanover: Wesleyan University Press, 1992.

Escott, Colin. *Good Rockin' Tonight: Sun Records and the Birth of Rock 'n' Roll*. London: Virgin, 1992.
Esposito, Joe. *Good Rockin' Tonight*. New York: Simon & Schuster, 1994.
Farren, Mick. *Elvis in His Own Words*. London: WH Allen, 1981.
—. *Speed-Speed-Speedfreak: A Fast History of Amphetamine*. Port Townsend: Feral House, 2010.
Fisanick, Christina. "'One Thing I Know for Sure': Oprah Is Fat Phobic." *Feminist Media Studies* 5, no. 2 (2005): 93–95.
Fisher, Mark. "The Metaphysics of Crackle: Afrofuturism and Hauntology." *Dancecult* 5, no. 2 (2013): 42–55.
Fiske, John. "The Cultural Economy of Fandom." In *The Adoring Audience: Fan Culture and Popular Media*, edited by Lisa Lewis, 30–49. Abingdon: Routledge, 1992.
—. "Elvis: A Body of Controversy." In Fiske, *Power Plays, Power Works*, 90–120. London: Verso, 1993.
Flippo, Chet. *Graceland: The Living Legacy of Elvis Presley*. London: Hamlyn, 1994.
Fortas, Alan. *Elvis from Memphis to Hollywood*. Ann Arbor, MI: Popular Culture Ink, 1992.
Foucault, Michel. "What Is an Author?" In *Language, Counter-Memory, Practice: Selected Essays and Interviews*, edited by Donald Bouchard, 113–38. New York: Cornell University Press, 1977.
Freud, Sigmund. *The Essentials of Psychoanalysis*. London: Vintage Books, 2005 [1926].
Friedman, Favius. *Meet Elvis Presley*. New York: Scholastic Book Services, 1973.
Frith, Simon. "Frankie Said, But What Did They Mean?" In *Consumption, Identity and Style: Marketing, Meanings and the Packaging of Pleasure*, edited by A. Tomlinson, 172–85. London: Routledge, 1990.
—. "Wise Men Say." In *Aspects of Elvis*, edited by Adam Clayson and Spencer Leigh, 275–87. London: Sidgwick and Jackson, 1994.
—. *Performing Rites: On the Value of Popular Music*. Cambridge: Harvard University Press, 1996.
—. "The Real Thing—Bruce Springsteen." (1988). Reprinted in *The Rock History Reader*, edited by Theo Cateforis, 237–44. New York: Routledge, 2012.
Gaar, Gillian. *Return of the King: Elvis Presley's Great Comeback*. London: Jawbone, 2010.
Garber, Marjorie. "The Transvestite Continuum: Liberace—Valentino—Elvis." In *Vested Interests: Cross Dressing and Cultural Anxiety*, 353–74. New York: Routledge, 1992.
Garcia, Gilbert. "Caught in a Trap." *Broward Palm Beach New Times*, January 21, 1999. https://www.browardpalmbeach.com/music/caught-in-a-trap-6331586
Geller, Larry. *If I Can Dream: Elvis's Own Story*. London: Century, 1989.
George-Warren, Holly, and Patricia Romanowski. *The Rolling Stone Encyclopedia of Rock'n'Roll*. New York: Rolling Stone Press, 2005.
Gilbert, Jeremy, and Ewan Pearson. *Discographies: Dance, Music, Culture and the Politics of Sound*. New York: Routledge, 1999.
Goldman, Albert. *Elvis*. Middlesex: Penguin, 1982.
—. *Elvis: The Last 24 Hours*. London: Pan Books, 1991.
Goldman, Lee. "Elvis Is Alive, But He Shouldn't Be: The Right of Publicity Revisited." *Brigham Young University Law Review* 3 (1992): 597–628.
Gordon, Robert. *The King on the Road: Live on Tour 1954 to 1977*. London: Hamlyn, 1996.
Gregory, Neal, and Janice Gregory. *When Elvis Died: Media Overload and the Origins of the Elvis Cult*. New York: Pharos Books, 1992.
—. "When Elvis Died: Enshrining a Legend." In *In Search of Elvis: Music, Art, Race, Religion*, edited by Vernon Chadwick, 225–42. Boulder: Westview Press, 1997.
Grimes, William. "Albert Goldman, Biographer, Is Dead at 66." *New York Times*, March 30, 1994. http://www.nytimes.com/1994/03/30/obituaries/albert-goldman-biographer-is-dead-at-66.html?src=pm

Groom, Bob. "Tigerman: Elvis and the Blues." In *Aspects of Elvis*, edited by Adam Clayson and Spencer Leigh, 73–85. London: Sidgwick and Jackson, 1994.

Guralnick, Peter. *Last Train to Memphis: The Rise of Elvis Presley*. London: Abacus, 1994.

—. *Careless Love: The Unmaking of Elvis Presley*. London: Abacus, 1999.

—. "How Did Elvis Get Turned into a Racist?" *New York Times*, August 11, 2007. http://www.nytimes.com/2007/08/11/opinion/11guralnick.html?pagewanted=all&_r=0

Guralnick, Peter, and Ernst Jørgensen. *Elvis Day by Day: The Definitive Record of His Life and Music*. New York: Ballantine Books, 1999.

Haining, Peter, ed. *Elvis in Private*. New York: St Martin's Press, 1987.

—. ed. *The Elvis Presley Scrapbooks, 1955–1965*. London: Robert Hale, 1991.

Hammontree, Patsy. *Elvis Presley: A Bio-Bibliography*. London: Aldwych Press, 1985.

Hancock-Hinds, Mary. *Infinite Elvis: An Annotated Bibliography*. Chicago: A Capella, 2001.

Harker, Dave. *One for the Money*. London: Hutchinson, 1980.

Harper, Stephen. "Madly Famous: Narratives of Mental Illness and Celebrity Culture." In *Framing Celebrity*, edited by Su Holmes and Sean Redmond, 311–28. London: Routledge, 2006.

Harrison, Ted. *Elvis People: The Cult of the King*. London: Fount, 1992.

Hawkins, Nicholas. "Tangled Up in 'Blue Ivy': Beyoncé Battles Massachusetts Wedding Planner in Trademark Dispute." *IP Watchdog*, October 21, 2019. https://www.ipwatchdog.com/2019/10/21/tangled-blue-ivy-beyonce-battles-massachusetts-wedding-planner-trademark-dispute/id=114659/

Haynes, C. "Elvis: In the Twilight of Memory." *Official Elvis Presley Fan Club of Great Britain Magazine* 7 (1997).

Hazen, Cindy, and Mike Freeman. *Memphis Elvis-Style*. Winston-Salem: John F Blair, 1997.

Heagy, Wanda Powell. *East Tupelo and Elvis: That's The Way It Was*. Saltillo: Tillo, 2010.

Hills, Matt. *Triumph of a Time Lord: Regenerating Doctor Who in the Twenty-first Century*. New York: IB Tauris, 2010.

Hinerman, Stephen. "I'll Be Here with You: Fans, Fantasy and the Figure of Elvis." In *The Adoring Audience: Fan Culture and Popular Media*, edited by Lisa Lewis, 107–34. Abingdon: Routledge, 1992.

Holt, Fabian. *Genre in Popular Music*. Chicago: University of Chicago Press, 2007.

Holzer, Hans. *Elvis Presley Speaks: The Astonishing Evidence of Spiritual Contact with Elvis from Beyond the Grave*. Los Angeles: New English Library, 1981.

Hopkins, Jerry. *Elvis: A Biography*. London: Open Gate Books, 1971.

—. *Elvis: The Final Years*. London: WH Allen, 1980.

Hunter, S. "Discovering Elvis." *Elvis Monthly* 334 (1987): 21.

Hutchins, Chris, and Peter Thompson. *Elvis Meets the Beatles: The Untold Story of their Entangled Lives*. London: Smith Gryphon, 1994.

Hutchins, Chris. "No, I Don't Take Half of What Elvis Earns." *The People*, January 26, 1997.

Ilott, Irene. "Did Elvis Die of Boredom?" *British Journal of Occupational Therapy* 70, no. 10 (2007): 415.

Inglis, Ian. "The Road Not Taken. Elvis Presley: *Comeback Special*, NBC TV Studios, Hollywood. December 3, 1968." In *Performance and Popular Music: History, Place and Time*, edited by Ian Inglis, 41–51. Aldershot: Ashgate, 2006.

Jansson, David. "Internal Orientalism in America: WJ Cash's *Mind of the South* and the Spatial Construction of American National Identity." *Political Geography* 22, no. 3 (2003): 293–316.

Jarman-Ivens, Freya. "'Don't Cry, Daddy': The Degeneration of Elvis Presley's Musical Masculinity." In *Oh Boy! Masculinities and Popular Music*, edited by Frey Jarman-Ivens, 161–82. London: Routledge, 2007.

Jeansonne, Glen, David Luhrssen and Dan Sokolovic. *Elvis Presley, Reluctant Rebel: His Life and Our Times*. Santa Barbara: Praeger, 2011.

Jenkins, Henry. *Textual Poachers: Television Fans and Participatory Culture.* New York: Routledge, 1992.
Jones, Dylan. *David Bowie: An Oral History.* New York: Penguin Random House, 2018.
Jørgensen, Ernst. "From Demark to RCA: On the Road with Elvis, Scotty, and Bill." In *In Search of Elvis: Music, Art, Race, Religion,* edited by Vernon Chadwick, 29–36. Boulder: Westview Press, 1997.
—. *Elvis Presley: A Life in Music. The Complete Recording Sessions.* New York: St Martin's Press, 1998.
—. *A Boy from Tupelo: The Complete 1953–55 Recordings.* New York: FTD Books, 2012.
Keightley, Keir. "Un Voyage via Barquinho: Global Circulation, Musical Hybridization and Adult Modernity, 1961–9." In *Migrating Music,* edited by Jason Toynbee and Byron Duek, 112–26. Abingdon: Routledge, 2011.
Keil, Charles. "Participatory Discrepancies and the Power of Music." *Cultural Anthropology* 2, no. 3 (1987): 275–83.
Kershaw, Andy. *No Off Switch: An Autobiography.* London: Virgin Books, 2012.
King, Barry. "Articulating Stardom." *Screen* 26, no. 5 (1985): 27–51.
King, Martin Luther. "I Have A Dream." *American Rhetoric: Top 100 Speeches,* 1963. http://www.americanrhetoric.com/speeches/mlkihaveadream.htm
Kirchberg, Connie, and Marc Hendrickx. *Elvis Presley, Richard Nixon and the American Dream.* Jefferson: McFarland, 1999.
Klein, George. *Elvis: My Best Man.* London: Virgin Books, 2011.
Koslowski, Rich. *The King.* Marietta, GA: Top Shelf Productions, 2005.
Krogh, Egil. *Dear Mr President: The Day Elvis Met Nixon.* Minnesota: Pejam PR, 1993.
Kyrölä, Katariina. "The Fat Gendered Body in/as a Closet." *Feminist Media Studies* 5, no. 1 (2005): 99–102.
Lacker, Marty. *Elvis: Portrait of a Friend.* Memphis: Wimmer Brothers Books, 1979.
Lacy, Patrick. *Elvis Decoded: A Fan's Guide to Deciphering the Myths and Misinformation.* Bloomington: Author House, 2006.
Levy, Alan. *Operation Elvis.* London: Consul Books, 1962.
Lichter, Paul. *Elvis in Hollywood.* New York: Simon & Schuster, 1975.
—. *The Boy Who Dared to Rock: The Definitive Elvis.* New York: Doubleday, 1978.
Livingston, Victor. "Hefty and Hot, Elvis Still Carries Weight with Fans." *St. Petersburg Times,* April 28, 1975.
Locke, Alain. *The New Negro* (1925). Reprint, New York: Simon & Schuster, 1992.
Lott, Eric. *Love and Theft: Blackface Minstrelsy and the American Working Class.* Oxford: Oxford University Press, 1995.
Malone, Bill. *Don't Get Above Your Raisin'.* Chicago: University of Illinois Press, 2002.
Marcus, Greil. *Mystery Train: Images of America in Rock'n'Roll Music.* London: Omnibus Press, 1977.
—. *Dead Elvis: A Chronicle of Cultural Obsession.* Cambridge: Harvard University Press, 1999 [1991].
—. 'Elvis Again.' *The Threepenny Review,* winter (2003). http://www.threepennyreview.com/samples/marcus_w03.html
Marcus, Greil, et al. *Rockabilly: The Twang Heard 'Round the World.* Minneapolis: Voyageur Press, 2011.
Marcuse, Herbert. *Eros and Civilization.* New York: Vintage, 1955.
—. "An Essay on Liberation." 1969. https://www.marxists.org/reference/archive/marcuse/works/1969/essay-liberation.htm
—. "Art as Revolutionary Weapon." YouTube video, 48:46, 1970. Reproduced, October 16, 2016. https://www.youtube.com/watch?v=9livubNajl4
Marsh, Dave. *Elvis.* London: Omnibus Press, 1992 [1982].

Martin, Douglas. "Mary Jenkins Langston, 78, Cook for Presley." *New York Times*, June 5, 2000. http://www.nytimes.com/2000/06/05/us/mary-jenkins-langston-78-cook-for-presley.html

Martin, Linda, and Kerry Segrave. *Anti-rock: The Opposition to Rock'n'Roll*. New York: Da Capo, 1988.

Marx, Karl. "The Eighteenth Brumaire of Louis Bonaparte." 1852. https://www.marxists.org/archive/marx/works/1852/18th-brumaire/ch01.htm

Matthew-Walker, Robert. *Elvis Presley: A Study in Music*. Tunbridge Wells: Midas Books, 1979.

McDowell, Ronnie, Edie Hand and Joe Meador. *The Genuine Elvis*. Gretna: Pelican Publishing, 2010.

Medovoi, Leerom. *Rebels: Youth and the Cold War Origins of Identity*. Durham: Duke University Press, 2005.

Meltzer, Richard. *The Aesthetics of Rock* (1970). Reprint, New York: Da Capo, 1987.

Messenger, Cory. "Act Naturally: Elvis Presley, the Beatles and 'Rocksploitation.'" *Screening the Past* 12 (2014). http://www.screeningthepast.com/2014/12/act-naturally-elvis-presley-the-beatles-and-%e2%80%9crocksploitation%e2%80%9d/

Middleton, Richard. "All Shook Up?" In *The Elvis Reader: Texts and Sources on the King of Rock'n'Roll*, edited by Kevin Quain, 3–12. New York: St Martin's Press, 1992.

Moody, Raymond. *Elvis After Life: Unusual Psychic Experiences Surrounding the Death of a Superstar*. Atlanta: Peachtree Publishers, 1987.

Moore, Alan. "Authenticity as Authentication." *Popular Music* 21, no. 2 (2002): 209–23.

Moore, Scotty. *That's All Right Elvis: The Untold Story of Elvis' First Guitarist and Manager*. New York: Schirmer Books, 1997.

Moscheo, Joe. *The Gospel Side of Elvis*. New York: Centre Street, 2007.

Myers, Tony. *Routledge Critical Thinkers: Slavoj Žižek*. New York: Routledge, 2003.

Nash, Alanna. *The Colonel: The Extraordinary Story of Colonel Tom Parker and Elvis Presley*. New York: Simon & Schuster, 2003.

Nazareth, Peter. "Elvis as Anthology." In *In Search of Elvis: Music, Art, Race, Religion*, edited by Vernon Chadwick, 37–74. Boulder: Westview Press, 1997.

Neale, David. *Roots of Elvis*. New York: iUniverse, 2003.

O'Neal, Sean. *Elvis Inc.: The Fall and Rise of the Presley Empire*. Rocklin, CA: Prima Publishing, 1996.

Osborne, Jerry. *Elvis: Word for Word*. New York: Gramercy Books, 2000.

Osgerby, Bill. *Biker: Truth and Myth*. Lewes: Ivy Press, 2005.

Parker, Ed. *Inside Elvis*. Orange, CA: Rampart House, 1978.

Parks, Lisa, and Melissa McCartney. "Elvis Goes Global: *Aloha! Live via Satellite* and Music/Tourism/Television." In *Medium Cool: Music Videos from Soundies to Cellphones*, edited by Roger Beebee and Jason Middleton, 252–68. Durham: Duke University Press, 2007.

Peterson, Richard. "Why 1955? Explaining the Advent of Rock Music." *Popular Music* 9, no. 1 (1990): 97–116.

Plasketes, George. *Images of Elvis Presley in American Popular Culture 1977–1997: The Mystery Train*. Binghampton, NY: Hayworth Press, 1997.

Potter, John. "Elvis Presley to Rap: Moments of Change since the Forties." In *Vocal Authority: Singing Style and Ideology*, 133–57. Cambridge: Cambridge University Press, 1998.

Pratt, Ray. *Rhythm and Resistance: Explorations in the Political Use of Popular Music*. New York: Praeger, 1990.

Presley, Dee, et al. *Elvis, We Love You Tender*. London: New English Library, 1980.

Presley, Priscilla. *Elvis and Me*. London: Century, 1985.

Presley, Vester. *A Presley Speaks*. Memphis: Wimmer Books, 1988.

Quain, Kevin, ed. *The Elvis Reader: Texts and Sources on the King of Rock'n'Roll*. New York: St Martin's Press, 1992.

Radano, Ronald. "Hot Fantasies: American Modernism and the Idea of Black Rhythm." In *Music and the Racial Imagination*, edited by Ronald Radano and Philip V. Bohlman, 459–82. London: University of Chicago Press, 2000.
Reece, Gregory. *Elvis Religion: The Cult of the King*. London: IB Tauris, 2006.
Ritz, David, ed. *Elvis by the Presleys*. New York: Crown Archetype, 2005.
Robertson, Heather. "Tell Us That You Love Us, Elvis P." *Maclean's* 88, no. 9 (1975): 84.
Rodman, Gilbert. *Elvis After Elvis*. London: Routledge, 1996.
Rössner, Stephan. "'Are You Lonesome Tonight?' Elvis Presley 1935–1977." *Obesity Reviews* 11, no. 9 (2010): 688–89.
RussellFamilyTV. "Elvis Presley I Forgot to Remember to Forget October 1, 1955. Unreleased LIVE Track Hayride." YouTube video, 3:33, 1955. Reproduced, July 16, 2012. http://www.youtube.com/watch?v=U3EofaQBFco
Schatz, Thomas. "Hal Wallis: Producer to the Stars, by Bernard F. Dick." *Film Quarterly* 59, no. 2 (2005): 67–68.
Schilling, Jerry. *Me and a Guy Called Elvis: My Lifelong Friendship with Elvis Presley*. New York: Gotham Books, 2006.
Schindler, Scott, and Andy Schwartz. *Icons of Rock*. Westport: Greenwood Press, 2007.
Sewlall, Harry. "'Image, Music, Text': Elvis Presley as a Postmodern, Semiotic Construct." *Journal of Literary Studies* 26, no. 2 (2010): 44–57.
Sharp, Ken. *Elvis Presley: Writing for the King*. New York: FTD Books, 2006.
Shelton Reed, John. "Elvis as Southerner." In *In Search of Elvis: Music, Art, Race, Religion*, edited by Vernon Chadwick, 75–92. Boulder: Westview Press, 1997.
Shumway, David. "Authenticity: Modernity, Stardom and Rock'n'Roll." *Modernity/Modernism* 14, no. 3 (2007): 527–33.
Spencer, Jon Michael. "A Revolutionary Sexual Persona: Elvis Presley and the White Acquiescence of Black Rhythms." In *In Search of Elvis: Music, Art, Race, Religion*, edited by Vernon Chadwick, 109–22. Boulder: Westview Press, 1997.
Spigel, Lynn. "Communicating with the Dead: Elvis as Medium." *Camera Obscura* 8, no. 2 (1990): 176–205.
Stromberg, Peter. "Elvis Alive? The Ideology of American Consumerism." *Journal of Popular Culture* 24, no. 3 (1990): 11–19.
Sweeney, Gael. "The King of White Trash Culture: Elvis Presley and the Aesthetics of Excess." In *White Trash: Race and Class in America*, edited by Matt Wray and Annalee Newitz, 249–66. New York: Routledge, 1997.
Telerama. "Bobby Gillespie (Primal Scream): Foot, Iggy Pop, Ecstasy." YouTube video, 9:22, October 18, 2018. https://www.youtube.com/watch?v=FNWGHBhSSBo
Tharpe, Jac, ed. *Elvis: Images and Fancies*. London: Star Books, 1980.
The Phantom. "Elvis in Concert." *Elvis Monthly* 334 (1987).
Thompson, Charles, and James Cole. *The Death of Elvis: What Really Happened*. London: Robert Hale, 1991.
Till, Rupert. *Pop Cults: Religion and Popular Music*. London: Continuum Press, 2010.
Tobler, John, and Richard Wootton. *Elvis: The Legend and the Music*. London: Optimum Books, 1983.
Toynbee, Jason. *Making Popular Music: Musicians, Creativity and Institutions*. London: Arnold, 2000.
Tucker, Stephen. "Rethinking Elvis and the Rockabilly Moment." In *In Search of Elvis: Music, Art, Race, Religion*, edited by Vernon Chadwick, 19–28. Boulder: Westview Press, 1997.
Ulam, Adam Bruno. *The Fall of the American University*. New York: Library Press, 1972.
Victor, Adam. *The Elvis Encyclopedia*. New York: Overlook Duckworth, 2008.
Wall, David. "Reconstructing the Soul of Elvis: The Social Development and Legal Maintenance of Elvis Presley." *International Journal of the Sociology of Law* 24, no. 2 (1996): 117–43.

—. "Policing Elvis: Legal Action and the Shaping of Post Mortem Celebrity Culture as Contested Space." *Entertainment Law* 2, no. 3 (2003): 35–69.
Walters, R. "The Myth Lives On." *New York Times Book Review* 86, no. 33 (1981): 27.
Warhol, Andy. *The Andy Warhol Diaries*. New York: Warner Books, 1989.
Weinstein, Raymond. "Occupation G.I. Blues: Postwar Germany During and After Elvis Presley's Tour." *Journal of Popular Culture* 39, no. 1 (2006): 126–49.
Wertheimer, Alfred. *Elvis '56: In the Beginning*. London: Pimlico, 1994.
West, Cornel. "Ware Lecture by Cornel West, General Assembly 2015." 2015. https://www.uua.org/multiculturalism/ga/ware-west
West, Red, Sonny West, Dave Hebler and Steve Dunleavy. *Elvis: What Happened?* New York: Ballantine, 1977.
Westmoreland, Kathy. *Elvis and Kathy*. California: Glendale House, 1987.
Whitburn, Joel. *A Century of Pop Music*. Wisconsin: Record Research Inc., 1999.
Whitcomb, Ian. *After the Ball: Pop Music from Rag to Rock*. Baltimore: Penguin, 1972.
White, C., and J. Hayward. "Consumers Rush for Elvis Product." *Music Week*, August 27, 1977.
Williamson, Joel. *Elvis Presley: A Southern Life*. New York: Oxford University Press, 2015.
Wilson, Charles Reagan, "'Just a Little Talk with Jesus': Elvis Presley, Religious Music and Southern Spirituality." *Southern Cultures* 12, no. 4 (2006): 74–91.
Wise, Sue. "Sexing Elvis." 1984. Reproduced in *On Record: Rock, Pop and the Written Word*, edited by Simon Frith and Andrew Goodwin, 390–98. London: Routledge, 1990.
Wiseman-Trowse, Nathan. "Oedipus Wrecks: Cave and the Presley Myth." In *Cultural Seeds: Essays on the Work of Nick Cave*, edited by Karen Welberry and Tanya Dalziell, 153–67. Farnham: Ashgate, 2009.
Wolfe, Charles. "Presley and the Gospel Tradition." In *The Elvis Reader: Texts and Sources on the King of Rock'n'Roll*, edited by Kevin Quain, 13–28. New York: St Martin's Press, 1992.
Wright, Deborah. "Don't Be Cruel: Scope of Parody Curtailed in Elvis Presley Enterprises, Inc. v. Capece." *Golden Gate University Law Review* 29, no. 3 (1999): 683–714.
Wright, Jane. "The Adult Elvis [letter]." *Elvis Monthly* 4, no. 12 (1963): 29.
Yancy, Becky. *My Life with Elvis*. New York: Warner Books, 1977.
Žižek, Slavoj. *Event: Philosophy in Transit*. London: Penguin Books, 2014.
Zurawik, David. 1992. "Bill Clinton's Sax on Arsenio Hall Still Resonates in Memorable Moments." *The Baltimore Sun*, December 27, 1992. http://articles.baltimoresun.com/1992-12-27/features/1992362178_1_clinton-arsenio-hall-hall-show.

Index

20th Century Fox 96, 190
2001: A Space Odyssey 133
50,000,000 Fans Can't Be Wrong 68

'A Big Hunk O' Love' 87, 132, 175
A Boy From Tupelo 163
'A Cane and a High Starch Collar' 75
'A Little Less Conversation' 164
A Star Is Born 185
A Stone for Danny Fisher 80
A Walk on the Wild Side 103
Abbey Road 130
ABC 88, 108, 123, 129, 176, 189, 222
Abel, Robert 119
Aberbach, Jean 75, 103
   see also Hill & Range
ABG *see* Authentic Brands Group 163
Academy Awards 86, 105
Adams, Gerald Drayson 97
The Addams Family 81
Adidge, Pierre 119
Adorno, Theodor 4, 56, 101, 139
aesthetics 5–6, 10, 73, 97, 101, 156
African Americans 10, 23, 28–9, 32–3, 120–1
   slavery 27–8
      Emancipation Proclamation 27
   see also Black music; civil rights
'After Loving You' 126
'Ain't No Grave Can Keep My Body Down' 121
Aladdin Hotel 170, 182

Alden, Ginger 186
Ali, Muhammad 163
'All My Trials' 131
'All Shook Up' 43, 89, 103, 174
All You Need is Love (documentary series) 2
All-Night Gospel singing sessions 62, 64, 170, 172, 174
Allen, Steve *see The Steve Allen Show*
Allied Artists 191
Aloha from Hawaii via Satellite 13, 106, 130–4, 164, 167, 169, 184–5, 189, 194, 223
   double album 184
Alpert, Herb 131
'Also Sprach Zarathustra' 127
'Always on My Mind' 215
'Amazing Grace' 194
Ambassador Hotel 120
America 1, 3, 6–9, 29, 66, 81, 95, 107, 113, 128, 132, 138, 159, 166–7
   bicentennial 186
   foreign policy 159
American dream 7, 44, 58, 73, 75, 101, 133
American Graffiti 123
American Idol 163, 222
American International Pictures 82
American Sound studio 13, 99, 106, 123–8, 130, 149, 169, 181, 193, 216
'An American Trilogy' 131–3, 195
An Essay on Liberation 9
'And I Love You So' 195

Andress, Ursula 84–5
Andrus, Sherman 55, 57, 65
Anka, Paul 83, 131
Ann-Margret 93–4, 216
Anthology album series 160
'Any Day Now' 126
'Any Way You Want Me' 47
Apollo Management Group 163
Are You Lonesome Tonight? (book) 221
'Are You Lonesome Tonight?' 88, 176
Arnold, Eddy 39, 41, 63, 86
The Arsenio Hall Show 158–9
art 7–10, 101, 166
Arthur Godfrey's Talent Scouts 40, 171, 207
'As Long As I Have You' 81
ASCAP 147
Asher, William 82
Astaire, Fred 58
Atkins, Chet 29, 34, 61, 64, 107
Atlantic Records 41, 124, 216
Ausborn, James 200
Austin, Gene 39
Authentic Brands Group 163
authenticity 7–8, 13, 19, 30, 57–9, 65, 117–18, 122, 141, 165, 197, 201, 204, 215
Avalon, Frankie 83
Avon Books 153
Awopbopaloobop Alopbamboom 1
Axton, Mae Boren 42, 210

baby boomers 14, 73, 158–9
'Baby Let's Play House' 34, 60–1, 171, 188
'Baby, What You Want Me to Do' 115
Bacharach, Burt 126
Baker, LaVern 23, 39
Bakhtin, Mikhail 145
Ballard, J.G. 153
'Barcarolle' 102
barn storming 19
'Battle Hymn of the Republic' 131
Baty, Tim 207
Baum, Bernie 97, 102
BBC 90, 137
B.B. King 31, 167
Beach Boys, the 83, 88
Beach Party 82

Beale Street 81, 121, 150
'Bear Cat' 16
Bearde, Chris 110, 114
Beatles 7–8, 51, 56, 58, 102, 107–8, 115, 125, 127, 129–30, 134, 166, 178
see also individual Beatles by name
Becket 179
Beethoven, Ludwig van 110, 197
'Begin the Beguine' 206
Beinstock, Freddy 103
Belafonte, Harry 121, 129
Belew, Bill 115, 118, 122
Bennett, Roy 75–6
Bennett, Tony 42
Benson Records 64
Benson, Sally 93, 210
Berkey, John 157
Berle, Milton see *The Milton Berle Show*
Berlin, Irving 58, 63, 166, 192
Berlingieri, Annibale 101
Berry, Chuck 3, 123
Bertrand, Michael 44, 147, 221
Beyoncé 219
Bieber, Justin 143
Big Bill Broonzy 128
'Big Boss Man' 108
Big Chief 36
Big Joe Turner 39
Big Mama Thornton 16, 47
Billboard 26–7, 31, 39, 54, 90, 103, 172–82, 184
Binder, Steve 58, 109–15, 120–2, 125, 130, 136, 160, 196, 213–15, 218
biography 11, 72, 97, 120, 150–4, 223
Black music 5–6, 9, 21, 24, 27–9, 31–2, 94
Black, Bill 19–22, 25, 27, 36–8, 41, 45, 55, 89, 170–2, 203, 214
  Bill Black Combo, the 214
Black, Johnny 20
Blackface 27–8, 131, 198, 205
Blackwell, Otis 46–7, 54, 102
Blackwood Brothers 62, 172, 207
Bland, Bobby "Blue" 31
Blitz Bingo 163
'Blowin' in the Wind' 108
The Blue Bird 112
'Blue Christmas' 63, 122, 192
'Blue Eyes Crying in the Rain' 195

Blue Hawaii 82–3, 96, 134, 177, 190
   album 104, 177
Blue Ivy 219
Blue Moon Boys, the 26, 35, 37–8, 168, 171–2
'Blue Moon' 38, 187, 223
'Blue Moon of Kentucky' 25–6, 168, 170–1, 187
'Blue Suede Shoes' 42, 45–7, 127, 131, 188, 192, 200
bluegrass 25
blues 14–16, 21–4, 26–7, 29, 32–5, 43, 47, 52, 56, 58, 73, 90, 125, 128, 130, 166–7, 192
blues rock revival 108
Blye, Allan 110, 114
BMG 161, 221–2
BMI 14, 147
bobby soxers 17
Bogert, Dick 161
Bon Air club 20, 35–6, 171
Bond, Eddie 170
Boone, Pat 40, 46, 88, 172, 204, 216
bootlegs 72, 146, 160–3, 216, 219, 222, 225
bossa nova 75
'Bossa Nova Baby' 59, 178
Bourdieu, Pierre 3, 56, 137
Bowie, David 123, 143, 166, 218, 222
Boyle, Susan 222
Bragg, Johnny 176
Brando, Marlon 74, 115
Breedlove, Jimmy 102
Brewer-Giorgio, Gail 221
Brewer, Teresa 198
Brewster, W. Herbert 27, 200
'Bridge Over Troubled Water' 130, 134
Brill Building 103
British Invasion 108, 121
Broeske, Pat 218
Brown v. the Board of Education of Topeka 198
Brown, Earl 122, 215
Brown, James 32, 110
Brown, Peter 218
Brown, Ruth 23
Bruce, Lenny 152
Buffalo Studio 163
'The Bullfighter Was a Lady' 85

Bureau of Narcotics and Dangerous Drugs 107
The Burger and the King 137
Burgess Jr, John 42
Burnette, Dorsey 19
'Burning Love' 130, 184, 189, 194
Burton, James 126
Bush, George W. 159
Bush, Laura 159
Bye Bye Birdie 51
Byron, Lord 51

'C'mon Everybody' 94
Cadillac 61, 171
Camden label 182, 222
Campbell's Elvis 101
'Can't Help Falling in Love' 127, 132, 177, 194
Cantor, Louis 24, 31
Capece, Barry 149
Cárdenas, Elsa 84
Careless Love 97
Carter Sisters, the 40
Carter, Jimmy 124, 186
Cash, Johnny 40, 53–4, 96, 142, 173, 202–3
Catholic Sun, The 204
'Cause I Love You' 198
CBS 37, 40, 48–50, 123, 136, 139, 149, 168–9, 172–3, 186, 188–9
'CC Rider' 128
Change of Habit 53, 84, 94–6, 121, 169, 181–2, 191, 215
Charles, Ray 39, 94, 108
Charlie's Records 17
Charms, the 39
Charro! 94, 121, 181, 191
Chess Records 3, 16
Chisca Hotel 23, 25, 149, 174
Chong, Tommy 151
Chrisman, Gene 216
Christian music 64–5, 124
Christmas 63, 86, 109, 114, 122, 149, 181, 197–8, 213, 222
Christmas Duets 164
chronotopic imagination 146, 160
CinemaScope 82
Circle G ranch 149, 180–1

Cirque du Soleil 164
civil rights 6, 10, 32, 57, 72–3, 92, 95, 107, 120–1
    Black History Month 167
    Black Panthers 107
CKX Inc. 163
Clambake 180–1, 191
    album 180
Clark, Dick 216
Clark, Petula 109, 121, 216
Clash, the 47
Classic Cat club 113
classical music 9, 55, 110, 166, 175, 207
Clement, Jack 203
'The Climb' 94
Clinton, Bill 158–9
Clovers, the 39
Coasters, the 23, 102
Cogbill, Tommy 216
Cohn, Nik 1
Cold War 15, 159, 204
'Cold, Cold, Icy Fingers' 198
Cole, Nat King *see* Nat King Cole
Colonel Parker 39–42, 44–5, 50–51, 58, 61, 63, 68, 70, 84–8, 95, 97–100, 102–3, 110, 113–14, 122, 126–7, 136, 141, 144, 147–8, 152, 160, 163, 171–80, 182, 184, 186, 207, 210–11, 213–15, 221
    dancing chickens 99
colonialism 27, 201, 204
Coltrane, John 8
Columbia label 16, 41, 162
Columbia Pictures 82
Columbia University 152
Comeback Special 1, 12–13, 58, 95, 99, 106, 108–26, 128–9, 132, 151, 160, 164, 167, 169, 181, 189, 196, 213–15, 218
    "boxing ring" stage 111, 114–15, 117, 119, 196, 214
    bordello sequence 112, 196
    Deluxe Edition (DVD set) 218
    live audience 113–14
commodification 5, 12, 18, 66, 96, 141–2, 154
Como, Perry 42, 45, 109
consumerism 15, 71, 101, 138, 154, 157, 159, 204
Conversations on Elvis event 135

Core Media Group 163
counterculture 10, 72, 92, 107, 118
country music 35, 37, 40, 57, 89, 193–5, 205, 215
    country folk 35–6, 220
Country Song Roundup 138
Cramer, Floyd 40
"crass commercialism" argument 4–6, 150, 154–6
Creedence Clearwater Revival 128–9
Crosby, Bing 38–9, 43, 192
Crown Electric 35, 171
Crudup, Arthur 21–2, 38, 46, 57, 199
Crump, Edward "Boss" 23, 51
Crumpacker, Chick 40, 47, 203
'Cry' 17
'Crying in the Chapel' 179
Cuban Missile Crisis 96
cultural capital 3, 146, 156
    see also taste
Curtiz, Michael 56, 80, 190

Dali, Salvador 212
'Danny Boy' 87
Danova, Cesare 93
David, Mack 38
Davis Sisters 40
Davis, Mac 119, 125, 213
Davis, Miles 8
Davis, Oscar 39
Day, Doris 82, 85
De Barbin, Lucy 221
de Cordova, Frederick 94, 191
De Quincey, Thomas 152
Dead Elvis 150
The Dean Martin Show 110
Dean, James 73, 76–7
Dean, Jimmy 40, 64
Deary, Joan 160–1, 210, 222
Dee, Sandra 82
DeMetrius, Claude 103
Denisoff, R. Serge 145, 220
Diamond, Neil 124, 128, 130
Dice Clay, Andrew 3–6, 8, 12
Dickinson, Angie 216
Dion, Celine 222
'Dirt Road Blues' 199
disco 152

Diskin, Tom 40
'Dixie' 131
'Dixieland Rock' 80
Doll, Susan 45, 99, 116, 125, 127, 129
Domasin, Larry 85
'Dominic' 102, 104
Domino, Fats 23, 108, 216
'Don't' 175
'Don't Be Cruel' 43, 46–7, 50, 173, 189
'Don't Cry Daddy' 183, 222
doo-wop 16, 18, 54, 192
Doris Day 123
Dorsey Brothers *see Stage Show*
Dorsey, Thomas 50
Doss, Erika 158
Double Trouble 180, 191
  album 180
Douglas, Gordon 190
Dowd, Tom 216
Down at the End of Lonely Street 218
"Dr. Nick" *see* Nichopoulos, George
Dr. No 84
Drifters, the 23, 39, 87
Duchamp, Marcel 101
Dundy, Elaine 77, 98
Dunleavy, Steve 151
Dunne, Philip 96, 190
Durkheim, Émile 67–9
  see also totemism
Dylan, Bob 8, 57, 108, 121, 166, 212

Eagles Hall 40
Eagle's Nest 37, 171
'Early Morning Rain' 194
East of Eden 77
East Trigg Baptist Church 27
Easter 63, 213
Easy Come, Easy Go 180, 191
easy listening 131, 166
Economist, The 101
Edgren, Stig 164
The Ed Sullivan Show 31, 50–1, 53–4, 62, 80, 86, 115, 168, 173, 178, 189, 204
effervescence 67
Eggers, Kevin 152, 220
Eight Elvises 101
'El Toro' 85

The Elementary Forms of Religious Life 67
Ellis Auditorium 31, 62, 64, 170, 172, 174, 176, 182–3
Ellis, Jimmy 221
Elvis
  and acting 72
  as adolescent on screen 73
  agency 8, 61, 97–100, 107, 110, 167
  altercations 173–4, 184
  army service 6, 71, 86–7, 169, 175–6, 210
  attacked on stage 184
  audience, children 53, 75, 85, 95, 97, 104–5, 191
  as auteur 59
  badge collecting 107, 179
  ballads 39, 63, 85, 87, 89, 192–3, 205
  Black culture 27–9, 31–4
  "butch god" image 83, 119
  career as rollercoaster 2, 8, 72, 143–5
  "castrated" metaphorically 89, 90–2, 118
  celebrity image 11, 66, 72, 86, 94, 141, 148, 152
  and class 3, 7, 31, 71, 81, 95, 97, 133, 137–8
  clothing 37, 51–2, 106, 111, 115, 118, 122, 131–2, 213–14
  colour-blindness 17, 30–1, 120, 129, 167, 217
  contracts
    film 96, 100, 176, 179
    live music 127, 129, 186
    Louisiana Hayride 38, 41, 98, 172
    management 171–2, 186
    merchandising 147, 173
    record 41, 172–3, 177, 180, 203
  and contradictions 53, 152
  as "country cousin" 73–5, 124
  creativity 8, 19–20, 22, 54–5
  creolized racial identity 33, 52, 81, 113
  death 141, 145, 160, 169, 186
  death threat 182
  democratic ideals 7, 9, 31, 70–1
  "desert storm" monologue 185, 219
  diet 137–8
  divorce 134, 140, 184

INDEX **237**

and entertainment 2, 50, 65, 72–3, 75, 80, 90–1, 96, 104, 116, 130, 142–3, 150–1, 158, 163
entrapped by fame 44, 145
estate 79, 144, 147–50, 160
as event 1, 165–6
as family entertainer 50, 53, 70–1, 73, 80, 90–2, 95, 104, 109, 116
as fan 55
father figures, "good", in career 64, 112, 130, 161
film canonization 105
funeral 100
gift 7, 55, 67, 97, 146, 151, 154, 166
grace 11
and gospel music 29, 61–5, 111, 153, 216
heritage in Memphis 149–50
and Hollywood 15, 39, 58, 70, 83–4, 86, 91–2, 100, 117, 140, 168–9, 209, 213
as hologram 164
as humanitarian 69
as icon 3–4, 8, 37, 58–9, 66, 70, 72, 75, 86, 91, 95, 101, 105–7, 111–13, 123, 132–4, 142, 144, 148, 150, 153–4, 160, 163–7
and individualism 8, 70, 150, 167, 204
inner pain 140, 143
jet planes 73, 137, 185
as juvenile delinquent on screen 73, 75–6, 80, 115–17
"loss of nerve" in relation to race 8
marital separation 183
marketing 42, 57, 83, 86, 89, 91, 163–4, 173, 209
marriage day 169, 180
masculinity 51–2, 83, 94, 116–18, 131–2, 141
merchandising 41, 144–5, 147–8, 173
messianic role 6, 95, 155
music
    race mixing 21, 25, 33, 48, 52, 166, 216
    rarities 160–3
    remastering 161, 164, 220
    remixing 164
    signature catalogue 45, 119, 164

stereo 192
studio technology 88
musical skills 58, 60–1
informality and amateurism 12, 54–6, 59, 114, 207
musical taste 22, 35, 56, 166
and narcissism 36, 56, 113, 155
and Native Americans 74–5, 167
and nervousness 36–7
nicknames 1, 4–5, 51, 83, 90–1, 166
Oedipus complex 12, 76–7, 79–81, 91–2, 97–8, 113, 118, 132, 134, 208
personal finances 185
    posthumous 147
    tax returns 177
personal politics 107
and popular music studies 3
and populism 70–1, 146
and prescription drugs 142–5, 151–2, 154, 184
press conferences 100, 108, 127, 130, 169, 173–7, 182–4, 196, 212, 223
prompting racial assimilation 30–3, 74
as rebel 9, 44, 78, 87
religious faith 61, 63, 75, 186
residences
    Alabama Avenue 20, 24
    Audubon Drive 78
    Bellagio Road 177
    Hillcrest, Trousdale Estates 180
    Lauderdale Courts 19–20, 170
    Monovale 182–3
    Perugia Way 176
    Rocca Place 179
    see also Graceland
self-redemption 12
as sex symbol 4, 53, 61, 83, 91, 116, 120, 141, 205
sexual persona 36, 51–3, 116–18
as song interpreter 8, 56–9
as songster-like 90
as Southerner 45–6, 50, 73, 116, 122, 132, 137
stagecraft 36, 48–9, 77, 80, 85, 117–18, 132
stamps 157
tabloid press coverage 143
"teddy bear" image 83, 119

UK tour proposals 174
"U.S. male" reading 83–84, 86, 92
vocal style 4, 22–3, 39, 43, 58, 139–40, 143, 153, 165–6, 207
weight gain 136–7, 139–40
Elvis (Albert Goldman biography) 152, 218
Elvis (album) 174, 192
Elvis (*Comeback Special* album) 181
Elvis (the 'Fool' album) 184, 194
Elvis After Elvis 150
Elvis After Life 157
Elvis Answers Back 50, 55–6, 58, 63, 78
Elvis Aron Presley album set 160
Elvis is Back! 89, 177, 197
Elvis' Christmas Album 174, 192
Elvis cinema, themes and genres 73, 190–1
Elvis in Concert 139, 146, 149, 169, 186, 189
Elvis: The Concert 164
Elvis Country (I'm 10,000 Years Old) 183, 193
Elvis Culture: Fans, Faith and Image 158
Elvis for Everyone! 179
Elvis: The Final Years 152
Elvis's Greatest Shit 72
Elvis in Hollywood 151
Elvis impersonators *see* Elvis tribute artists
Elvis: The Last 24 Hours 218, 220
Elvis: A Legendary Performer Volume 1 184
Elvis: A Legendary Performer Volume 2 186
Elvis Monthly 106
Elvis Now 183, 194
Elvis People: The Cult of the King 155
Elvis by the Presleys (book) 144
Elvis by the Presleys (DVD) 205
Elvis Presley album 47, 172, 192
Elvis Presley Boulevard 148, 160
Elvis Presley Charitable Foundation 149
"Elvis Presley Day" 124, 176, 180
Elvis Presley Enterprises 68, 147–50, 159–60, 164, 219, 221
Elvis Presley Memorial Foundation 211

Elvis Presley's Memphis restaurant and bar 149
Elvis Presley Music 103, 125
Elvis Presley Speaks (book) 157–8
Elvis Presley Speaks (magazine) 150
"Elvis Presley Summer Festival" 182–5
Elvis Presley Youth Center 176
Elvis: Prince from Another Planet 162
Elvis: As Recorded at Madison Square Garden 130, 183, 194
Elvis Recorded Live on Stage in Memphis 185, 195
Elvis Sails EP 87, 175
Elvis Sings Christmas Songs EP 174
Elvis Sings the Wonderful World of Christmas 183, 194
Elvis Special annuals 151
Elvis: That's The Way It Is 130, 169, 182, 193
Elvis on Tour 119, 130, 169, 184
Elvis tribute artists 141, 148–9, 154–5, 166, 221–2
Elvis: True Stories 132
Elvis Vol. 1 EP 173
Elvis Week 155, 159
Elvis: What Happened? 145, 151, 169, 186
Emhardt, Robert 95
Emmons, Bobby 216
EPE *see* Elvis Presley Enterprises
Ertegun, Ahmet 41
Esposito, Joe 87, 100, 132, 152–3, 194
Essential Elvis: The First Movies 222
Everly Brothers, the 166
existential issues 12, 14, 43–4, 75, 80, 113, 116–18, 134–5, 144–6
exploitation film 82, 96, 103, 166
'The Eyes of Texas' 94

Factors Etc 147–8
Factors Incorporated 147
'Fame and Fortune' 189
family, nuclear 90
fans 3–4, 7, 13, 36, 53, 55–6, 65, 67–9, 74, 95, 97–9, 104–5, 109, 114, 119, 137–8, 140, 144–9, 152–65, 211, 216, 220–2
boosting 69, 117, 146–7
closet fans 3

INDEX **239**

fan fiction 79
female 52, 73, 82, 92, 104, 117, 119, 156, 162
    interpreted as religious 155–6, 221
    as living culture 146, 155
Farren, Mick 86, 142
FBI 183
feminism 83, 140
    see also women's liberation
Ferguson, Bert 23
Fernwood Records 89, 203
Ferra, Christine 61
'Fever' 88, 131, 134, 192
field recording 15, 21
Fike, Lamar 87–8, 152
Finkel, Bob 109–10, 114, 121, 218
First Assemblies of God church 61–2
'The First Time Ever I Saw Your Face' 129
Fisher, Eddie 42
Fiske, John 150
Flack, Roberta 129
Flaming Star 74–5, 101, 176, 190, 213
'Flip, Flop & Fly' 188
Foley, Red 207
folk 6, 27, 29, 35–6, 57–8, 65, 75, 102, 131, 157, 167, 220
    folk blues 27, 29, 33, 121
    see also country music, country folk
Follow That Dream 74, 84, 177, 190
    EP 177
Follow That Dream label 162, 222
Fontana, D.J. 34, 40, 45, 48, 60, 89, 115, 206
Fonz, the 166
'Fool' 184, 194
'Fool, Fool, Fool' 39
Forrest Gump 6
Fortas, Alan 77, 87, 115
Foucault, Michel 165
Four Seasons, the 83
Fox *see* 20th Century Fox
Frankie and Johnny 94–6, 179–80, 191
    album 180
Franklin, Aretha 216
The Frank Sinatra Timex Show: Welcome Home Elvis 88, 176, 189
Freddie Bell and the Bellboys 47

Freud, Sigmund 9, 12, 76–7, 79, 91, 97, 117, 156–7, 201
    see also Elvis, Oedipus complex
Friedman, Favius 19, 44, 151
From Elvis in Memphis 125, 181, 193
From Elvis Presley Boulevard, Memphis, Tennessee 135, 186, 195
From Memphis to Vegas / From Vegas to Memphis 127, 182, 193
FTD *see* Follow That Dream label
Fun in Acapulco 59, 84–85, 93–4, 178, 190
    album 178
'Funny How Time Slips Away' 193

Garber, Marjorie 51, 157
Gardner, Hy 50, 79, 189
Geissler, Harry 148
Geller, Larry 144–5, 153, 169, 179, 186
General Electric 161
generations
    generational change 9, 107
    see also baby boomers
'Gentle on My Mind' 125
Georgia Tech 110
Geraldo 153
Giant, Bill 97, 102
G.I. Blues 71, 74, 86, 88–9, 91–3, 102–3, 110, 176, 190
Gidget 82
Gillespie, Bobby 142
Girl Happy 82, 84, 179, 191
    album 179
'The Girl of My Best Friend' 86
'Girl Next Door Went A-Walking' 89
Girls! Girls! Girls! 84, 102, 105, 177–8, 190, 213
    album 178
Gladys Music 103, 125
Gleason, Jackie 45
Golden Celebration album set 161
'Golden Coins' 104
Golden Laurel Award 105
'Golden Years' 123
Goldenberg, Billy 110, 116–18, 215
Goldman, Albert 152–4, 157–8, 200, 218, 220
'Good Luck Charm' 59, 177

'Good Rockin' Tonight' 38–9, 90, 171, 187
'Good Time Charlie's Got the Blues' 134, 194
Good Times 185, 194
Good, Jack 91
gospel music 61–5, 89, 110, 153, 192–6, 207
   spirituals 61–2
   see also individual recordings
Gospel Quartet Convention 182
'Got a Lot o' Livin' to Do' 78, 103
'Got My Mojo Working' 193
'Gotta Let You Go' 16
Graceland 136, 145–9, 155, 163, 169, 174, 179, 181, 186, 195, 220
   Jungle Room 159, 185–6
Graceland Crossing shopping mall 148
Graham, William 191
Grammy Awards 65, 111
Grand Ole Opry 17, 19, 25, 37, 61, 171
Grant, Cary 127
Grant's department store 23
'Green, Green Grass of Home' 195
Griffith, Andy 50, 205
'Guitar Man' 108, 111–12, 118, 196
Guralnick, Peter 11–12, 17–18, 22, 31, 34–5, 41, 50, 60, 97, 105, 110–12, 115–16, 118–20, 122, 125–7, 141, 152, 199, 206

Haley, Bill 39–40, 56, 123, 172
Hamilton, George 96, 216
Hamilton, Roy 63, 102, 125
Hamm, Charles 153
Hancock-Hinds, Mary 158
Hanks, Joseph 219
Happy Days 123
'Harbor Lights' 21, 187
'Hard Headed Woman' 81, 175
Harker, Dave 83
Harmonizing Four, the 62
Harrison, George 130
Harrison, Ted 155
Harry & Lena 129
Hart, Lorenz 38
'Harum Holiday' 104
Harum Scarum 73, 104, 179, 191

Having Fun with Elvis on Stage 156, 185, 195
HBO 160
He Touched Me 183, 194
'He Touched Me' 62, 64
'Heart of Rome' 193
Heartbreak Hotel, the 150
'Heartbreak Hotel' 22, 31, 42–3, 45–6, 61, 114, 116, 158, 172, 188–9, 192, 205
'Hearts of Stone' 39
Hebler, Dave 151
hedonism 13, 75, 82, 84, 128
Heffner, Hugh 49
Hess, Jake 63–4, 207
'Hey Jude' 125, 127, 194
'Hey Little Girl' 104
Hi-Hat club 170
'Hi-Heel Sneakers' 108
High Noon Round Up 35
Hill & Range 41, 75, 86, 88, 102–3, 125, 203, 215
Hilton Hawaii Village Waikiki Beach 164
Hinerman, Stephen 157
His Hand in Mine 63, 176, 192
Hitchcock, Alfred 77, 209
Ho, Don 131
Hodge, Charlie 57, 87, 115, 119, 126, 132, 152
Holzer, Hans 157
Honolulu International Center 164, 184
Honolulu Stadium 175
Hootenanny Hoot 96
Hopkins, Jerry 116, 151–2, 213
"hot" rhythm 216
'Hound Dog' 16, 46–7, 50, 57, 87, 117, 127, 131, 168, 173, 188–9, 193
Houston Astrodome 129, 169, 182
How Great Thou Art 62, 64, 126, 180, 193
'How Great Thou Art' 64, 189
Howe, Bones 110, 113–14
Howlin' Wolf 23
Hullabaloo 110
Humbard, Rex 186
Humes High School *see* L.C. Humes High School
Hurricane Katrina 149
'Hurt' 98, 134, 195

INDEX   **241**

hurt/comfort 79
Hutchins, Chris 100
Hy Gardner Calling 189
   see also Gardner, Hy

'I Believe' 63
'I Don't Care if the Sun Don't Shine' 38–9, 61, 171, 187, 206
'I Don't Hurt Anymore' 20
'I Feel So Bad' 177
'I Forgot to Remember to Forget' 37, 42, 171, 187
'I Got a Woman' 39, 187–8
'I Got Stung' 175
'I Just Can't Help Believin'' 193
'I Love You Because' 20, 187
'I Slipped, I Stumbled, I Fell' 192
'I Want to Be Free' 76
'I Want You, I Need You, I Love You' 50, 173, 188, 205
'I Was The One' 61, 188
'I Washed My Hands in Muddy Water' 193
'I'll Be Home for Christmas' 215
'I'll Never Let You Go (Little Darlin')' 27, 187
'I'll Never Stand in Your Way' 18, 170
'I'll Remember You' 131, 189, 194
'I'll Take You Home Again Kathleen' 194
'I'm Comin' Home' 192
'I'm Gonna Walk Dem Golden Stairs' 63
'I'm Left, You're Right, She's Gone' 171, 187
'I'm So Lonesome I Could Cry' 131
'I've Got Confidence' 64
'I've Lost You' 193
'If I Can Dream' 57, 72, 122–3, 167, 189, 196, 222
'If I Didn't Care' 20
'If I Get Lucky' 199
'If You Talk in Your Sleep' 88
"imagined memories" 160
Imperials, the 55, 57, 62, 64, 126
The Impersonal Life 169, 179
impersonators see Elvis tribute artists
'The Impossible Dream' 194
'In the Garden' 196
'In the Ghetto' 72, 95, 125–6, 149, 181, 193

Ink Spots, the 18, 20, 90
International Hotel 126–7, 169, 182
'It Ain't No Big Thing (But It's Growing)' 193
It Happened at the World's Fair 53, 178, 190
   album 178
'It Hurts Me' 112, 114
It Takes a Thief 123
'It Wouldn't Be The Same Without You' 18, 170
'It's Impossible' 194
'It's Now or Never' 86, 89, 176
'It's Over' 131
Ivory Joe Hunter 23

Jackie Brenston and his Delta Cats 16
Jackson, Mahalia 200
Jackson, Michael 166
Jagger, Mick 167
Jailhouse Rock 53, 60, 75–6, 91, 97–8, 101, 112, 116–17, 174–5, 190, 205
   EP 175
'Jailhouse Rock' 76
Jamboree Attractions 39
James Bond 84
James, Joni 18
James, Mark 125, 215
Jarvis, Felton 61, 105, 108, 124, 216, 222
Jay-Z 219
Jaycees see Junior Chamber of Commerce
jazz 56, 61, 75, 80–1, 206–7
Jazz Scene USA 213
Jenkins, Henry 109, 156
Jessup, Susan 74
Jet magazine 174
'Johnny B. Goode' 3
Johnson, Robert 8
Jolson, Al 58, 88
Jones, Carolyn 81
Jordanaires, the 34, 42, 50, 59–65, 68, 81, 89, 94, 135, 205
Jørgensen, Ernst 17, 38–9, 46–7, 56, 89, 109, 115, 122, 125–6, 161–3, 214–15
'Joshua Fit the Battle' 63
Juanico, June 52, 72, 98
Jubilee Four, the 94
Junior Chamber of Commerce 169, 183

'Just Because' 38, 187
'Just a Closer Walk with Thee' 207
Just For You EP 174
'Just Pretend' 193
'Just Walkin' in the Rain' 16
JXL 164

Kanter, Hal 53, 190
karate 29, 112, 127, 154, 176, 183, 185
Karlson, Phil 60, 190
Karult, Charles 48, 204
Katz Drugs store 37, 171
Katzman, Sam 96, 104
Kaye, Florence 97, 102
Kazan, Elia 77, 205
Keightley, Keir 209
Keisker, Marion 1, 18–19, 36, 39, 170, 200, 210
Kennedy, Bobby 120
Kennedy, Kern 55
'Kentucky Rain' 125
Kerkorian, Kirk 126
Kern, Don 31
Kershaw, Andy 155–6
Kid Galahad 60, 94, 177–8, 190
King Creole 56, 74, 80–1, 85, 91, 113, 116, 175, 190
   album 175
   Vol 1. EP 175
   Vol 2. EP 175
'King Creole' 81
The King of Rock'n'Roll: The Complete '50s Masters 162
'King of the Whole Wide World' 60
King, B.B. *see* B.B. King
King, Martin Luther 32–3, 120, 122, 167
Kinsey, Alfred 15
Kirkham, Millie 192
'Kiss Me Quick' 103, 192
Kissin' Cousins 73–4, 96–7, 178, 190
   album 178
Klein, George 21, 25, 31–2, 37, 51, 87, 124, 166, 186, 201
KMAC 72
Knight, Gladys 108
Koizumi, Junichiro 159
Kollis, Ed 125
Korean conflict 15, 19, 86

Kraftwerk 8
Kubrick, Stanley 133
Kui Lee Cancer Fund 131, 184, 193
KWEM 20
KWKH 37

Lacker, Marty 87–8, 124
Ladies Home Journal 151
Laine, Frankie 130
Lake Tahoe 183, 185
Lamar-Airways shopping center 37
Langston, Mary Jenkins 137
Lansky, Bernard 26
Lansky's clothing store 45, 150, 214
Last Train to Memphis 11
Lastfogel, Abe 86, 126
Laughton, Charles 50
'Lawdy Miss Clawdy' 95, 119, 195
Lawhead, Gordon 23
L.C. Humes High School 25, 51, 87, 135, 170, 198
'Lead Me, Guide Me' 194
Leadbelly 21, 58, 128
'Leaf on a Tree' 198
Lee, Brenda 215
Lee, Kui 131
Lee, Peggy 88
Leech, Mike 126, 216
LeGault, Lance 96, 111, 116, 213
Leiber, Jerry 16, 47, 54–6, 58, 63, 75–6, 81, 86, 93–4, 102–3, 214
Lennon, John 44, 90–1, 203
   "before Elvis, there was nothing" quote 44
   "Elvis died when he went in the army" quote 90
Leo, Malcolm 119
'Let It Be Me' 128
'(Let Me Be) Your Teddy Bear' 174
'Let's Go to That Land' 62
Levy-Gardner-Laven 191, 209
Lewis, Jerry 61, 86
Lewis, Jerry Lee 53–4, 123, 142, 186
Lewis, Smiley 117
liberal humanism 28–9
Lichter, Paul 151, 218
Life magazine 31, 152
Lightnin' Hopkins 23

Lincoln, Abraham 27, 167
lip-synching 40, 104, 111, 122
Little Richard 23, 45–6, 208
'Little Sister' 103, 177
'The Little White Cloud That Cried' 17
Live a Little, Love a Little 110, 181, 191
Locke, Alain 200
Locke, Dixie 59
Loew's theatre 70
Logan, Horace 37
Lomax, John 15
'Lonesome Cowboy' 57
'Long Black Limousine' 124, 193
'Long Tall Sally' 54
'The Lord's Prayer' 57
Lorraine Motel 120
The Lost Album / For the Asking 104
Louis, Joe Hill 15
Louisiana Hayride 34, 37–8, 40–1, 98, 162, 168, 171–2
Louvin Brothers 29
Love Letters from Elvis 183, 193
'Love Letters' 107, 193
'Love Me' 54, 131, 173, 189, 192
Love Me Tender 54, 70, 73, 168, 173, 190
'Love Me Tender' 82, 88–90, 153, 159, 173, 189
Loving You 53, 74–7, 80–1, 103, 134, 173–4, 190, 202
   album 174
   EP 174
Low 218
LSD 179
Lucas, George 123
Lukas, Paul 93
Lynrd Skynyrd 128

MacColl, Ewan 129
Maclean's 138
Madison Square Garden 100, 130, 162, 169, 183, 194
Maeterlinck, Maurice 112
mainstream 2, 15, 26–7, 71, 89, 105, 109, 120–1, 127, 166–7
Malone, Bill 123
Mancini, Henry 216
Manilow, Barry 213

Marcus, Greil 8, 43, 66, 105, 144, 153, 163, 165, 200
Marcuse, Herbert 9–10
Mardin, Arif 216
'Marguerita' 85
'(Marie's the Name) His Latest Flame' 103, 177
marketplace, the 3–5, 16, 19, 23, 30, 51, 57, 66, 71, 73, 83–4, 99, 104, 134, 161–2, 164, 167
MARL Metal Products 170
Marley, Bob 8
Marsh, Dave 97, 108
Martin, Dean 38–9, 42, 86, 110, 206
Martindale, Wink 17
Marxism 8–10, 83, 139
mass culture criticism 4
   see also commodification; consumerism; "crass commercialism" argument; Adorno, Theodor
Matthau, Walter 81
McCartney, Paul 48
McGraw-Hill 152–3
'Mean Woman Blues' 103
Meet Elvis Presley 151
melting pot 7, 29, 71, 73, 75, 81, 113, 125, 129
Meltzer, Richard 89
Melville, Herman 112
'Memories' 111, 119, 189
Memphis Commercial Appeal 32, 125, 150
Memphis Mafia 87–8, 110, 151, 159, 220
Memphis Press-Scimitar 17, 32, 53, 78
Memphis Recording Service 15, 78, 168, 170
Memphis Recording Service 210
'Merry Christmas Baby' 194
'Mexico' 85
Meyer, Alan 148
MGM 75–6, 82, 96, 100, 104, 130, 174, 180, 190–1
Mid-South Coliseum 164, 185–6
Midnight Globe 97
Milam Junior High School 198
'Milkcow Blues Boogie' 27, 39, 128, 171, 187, 202

'Milky White Way' 57, 63, 192
Miller, Mitch 41
Million Dollar Quartet 54, 166, 173, 205, 223
The Milton Berle Show 45–6, 48, 50, 172–3, 188
Minnelli, Liza 213
Mirabelle 83
"Mississippi Burning" trial 120
Mississippi Slim 200
Mississippi-Alabama Fair and Dairy Show 53, 170, 173, 198
Mister Will You Marry Me 93
modernity 7, 11, 45, 57, 72, 113, 128, 133, 138, 142, 166
Moman, Chips 61, 124–5, 216
'Money Honey' 39, 188, 192
Monroe, Bill 25, 171
Monroe, Marilyn 49, 93
Monroe, Matt 64
Monroe, Vaughn 42
Moody Blue 135–6, 186, 195
'Moody Blue' 195
Moody, Raymond 157
moon landing 132–3
'Moonlight Sonata' 110
Moore, D. Michael 191
Moore, Scotty 19–22, 24, 27–8, 35–9, 41, 45, 56, 81, 89, 111, 115, 170–2, 174, 199, 203
Moreno, Rita 31, 217
Morris, Bobby 127
Morrison, Jim 151, 166
Morrison, Van 216
Moscheo, Joe 62
Mother Maybelle and the Carter Sisters 40
'Mr. Songman' 195
MTV 134, 147, 150, 158
MTV Unplugged 123
Muddy Waters 23
Muhoberac, Larry 110, 126
Murdoch, Rupert 151
music industry 8, 101–2
musical eras 8
musicals 70, 191
'Muss I Denn' 102

'My Baby Left Me' 46
'My Boy' 194
'My Happiness' 18, 90, 168, 170
'My Way' 131, 189
Mystery Train (book) 144, 153
'Mystery Train' 39, 42, 60, 171, 187

Nadal, Arthur 191
NASA 132
Nashville sound 34
Nat King Cole 24
National Bank of Commerce 219
National Entertainment Collectibles Association 163
National Film Registry 97
National General Pictures 196, 209
National Star, The 151
Nazareth, Peter 74
NBC 1, 12, 45, 58, 106, 108–10, 112, 114–15, 123, 125–6, 160, 169, 173, 181, 188–9, 196, 213, 218
Neal S. Blaisdell Centre 164
Neal, Bob 35, 37–8, 40–1, 45, 147, 171–2
Nelson, Gene 97, 105, 190–1
New Dimensions 64
New Frontier Hotel 47, 126, 172
New Orleans 40, 80, 207
'New Orleans' 80
New York 16, 38, 46–7, 83, 102, 130, 162, 168–9, 172–3, 183, 189, 194
New York Times 123, 137, 152
Newbury, Mickey 131
Newton-John, Olivia 213
Nichopoulos, George 144, 152
Nielsen, Sherrill (Shaun) 64
Nixon, Richard 107, 130, 132, 169, 182, 212
'No Room to Rhumba in a Sports Car' 85
Nogar, Thorne 54
North Alabama Citizen's Council 31
nostalgia 3, 11, 13, 115, 125, 165
   "keeping his memory alive" 146–50, 154
   for rock'n'roll 123, 138
'(Now and Then There's) A Fool Such As I' 87, 175
NYPD 123

INDEX **245**

'O Come, All Ye Faithful' 194, 222
'O Little Town of Bethlehem' 63, 192
'O Sole Mio' 64, 89
Obama, Barack 167
Ochs, Michael 28
Ochs, Phil 107, 216
Odetta 121
Odetta at Carnegie Hall 121
Oedipus Rex 76
Off Duty with Private Presley 210
Okeh label 16
'Old Shep' 54, 192, 198
Oliver, Jamie 219
On Stage 127–8, 130, 182, 193
'One Night' 12, 87, 115–17, 175, 189
'Only the Strong Survive' 193
Orbison, Roy 59, 173
orientalism 45, 97
Orion 221
Our Memories of Elvis 222
Overton Park Shell 35–6, 171, 173, 202
The Ozzie and Harriet Show 126

Packard, Vance 48
Page, Patti 102
Paget, Debra 173
Palmer, Tony 2
Pan American 26
Paradise Hawaiian Style 179–80, 191
    album 180
'Paralyzed' 54, 192
Paramount 38, 70, 74, 84, 88, 96, 103, 108,
    172, 177–8, 190–1, 209
Parker, Ed 185
Parker, Junior 31, 39
Parker, Thomas Andrew *see* Colonel
    Parker
Parks, Rosa 185
"participatory discrepancies" 60
Pasternak, Joe 82
'Patch It Up' 193
pathography 11
Payne, Leon 20
Peabody Hotel 32, 203
Peace in the Valley EP 63, 174, 192
Peacock Records 16
Penguin publisher 153
Pentecostal church 61

People magazine 160
People, The 100
Pepper, John 23
Perkins, Carl 46, 53–4, 173, 200
permissive society 73
Perryman, Tom 26, 40
Pet Shop Boys, the 215
Peterson, Richard 14
Petula 121
Phillips label 15
Phillips, Dewey 15, 23–6, 35, 170, 181
Phillips, Sam 15, 17–22, 25, 30, 35, 37, 41,
    57, 61, 112, 126–7, 130, 142, 170, 200
    "Negro sound and Negro feel" quote
    27, 200
Physician's Desk Reference 75, 144
Pickwick label 222
The Pied Piper of Cleveland 40
pill, contraceptive 82
Plasketes, George 31, 33, 101, 145, 150,
    220
Playboy 4–5, 93
Poindexter, Doug 20, 38
'Polk Salad Annie' 128, 193
Pomus, Doc 102–3, 192
Pond, Steve 93
pop (music genre) 2, 16, 18, 21, 24, 30, 38,
    42, 56, 58, 65, 82–3, 89–90, 103, 106,
    124–5, 130, 134, 150, 157, 166, 172–6,
    192–4, 207
Poplar Tunes 17, 149
Poppy Records 220
popular culture 5, 9, 25, 27, 66, 77, 124,
    150, 152, 158, 167
Porter, Cole 206
Pot Luck with Elvis 177, 192
'Power of My Love' 125
Precision Tool 170
Presley Place 149
Presley, Elvis *see* Elvis
Presley, Gladys 13, 17–19, 44, 51, 64–5,
    77–80, 87, 89–91, 100, 118, 140, 142,
    169–70, 175, 208, 210
Presley, Jesse Garon 44–5, 79, 85, 204
Presley, Lisa Marie 147, 149, 163, 181, 222
Presley, Minnie Mae 147
Presley, Priscilla 79, 90, 136, 147, 152, 163,
    169, 176–8, 180–1, 183

Presley, Vernon 13, 42, 79, 98, 100, 147, 152, 170
Presley, Vester 17
primitivism 27–9, 117, 133
Prince from Another Planet see Elvis: Prince from Another Planet
Prisonaires, the 16–7, 57, 98, 176, 198
Promised Land 185, 195
'Promised Land' 195
'Proud Mary' 128
Prowse, Juliet 92
Psycho 77
The Public Ear 106
Pulp Fiction 7
Pure Elvis Sound 222
Pure Gold 185
Pussy Riot 8

Quatro, Suzi 123
'Que Sera, Sera' 87
The Question of Lay Analysis 77, 97

R&B 16–17, 23–7, 31, 34–5, 50, 58, 76, 90, 94, 122, 125, 172
Rabbit's Foot Minstrels 16
racism 6, 10–11, 95, 200
radio 14, 23–4, 109, 147
    formatting 26
    and race 17, 23–25
Radio Recorders studio 54, 56, 63, 76, 110
Radio-TV Mirror 204
Rainey, Ma 128
Raised on Rock 184
Randle, Bill 40, 45–6, 172, 188, 203
Ray, Johnnie 16–17, 45, 52, 178
RCA
    label 22, 38–44, 52, 54, 76, 81, 86–7, 96, 100, 102–3, 107, 129–30, 136, 146–7, 150, 156, 160–2, 168, 172–3, 175–8, 180, 184, 186, 192, 203, 221–2
    release strategy 47, 68, 89, 103, 147, 160, 175, 205
    Studio B 57, 63, 88, 124
'Ready Teddy' 189, 192
'Reconsider Baby' 192
Record World 115
Red, Hot and Blue 23–4

Red Skelton 123
Reed, Jerry 108, 112, 124
Reeves, Jim 131
'Release Me (And Let Me Love Again)' 128
The Reporter 152
'Return to Sender' 178
Rhee, Kang 183
Rhodes Pictures 209
Rich, John 190–1
Richard, Cliff 166
Richards, Keith 25, 32
Right This Way 100
Robbins, Marty 130
Robertson, Heather 138
rock (music genre) 1–2, 10, 47, 49, 57–8, 108, 110, 123–5, 128, 130, 133–4, 142–3, 151–2, 165, 194–5, 207, 216
rock'n'roll 5–6, 14, 16, 18, 26, 31, 42, 49–50, 57, 66, 72–3, 76–7, 82, 87, 89–90, 103, 106–8, 110, 115–17, 123, 127–8, 134, 137–8, 142, 153, 166–7, 192–5
rockabilly 1, 34, 46, 52–3, 57, 138, 166, 199
'Rock-A-Hula Baby' 177
'Rocket 88' 16
Rodman, Gilbert 150, 200
Rogers, Jaime 111
Rogers, Richard 38
Rolling Stone magazine 66, 151
Rolling Stones, the 25, 32, 51, 110, 166
Romero, Alex 76
Roots Revolution: Louisiana Hayride 220
Ross, Diana 213
rotoscoping 222
Roustabout 93, 180, 195
    album 93, 179
Royal Philharmonic Orchestra 164
'Rubberneckin'' 95
'Run On' 193
'Runaway' 128

sacredness 67–8, 156
sacred music *see* gospel music
Sainte-Marie, Buffy 134, 167–8
samba 83
Sands of the Desert 104
Sands Hotel 47

Sands, Tommy 39, 63, 171
Sanitation Strike of February 1968 32
'Santa Claus Is Back in Town' 63, 119, 122, 192
Saperstein, Hank 147, 173
Sarnoff, Tom 109
Satellite Records 198
'Satisfied' 38, 187
'Saved' 115, 128
Scared Stiff 39, 61
Scheff, Jerry 126
Schilling, Jerry 87–8, 114, 217
Schroeder, Aaron 47, 75, 103, 132
Scott, Lizabeth 74, 80
SDS 107
Sedaka, Neil 52
'See See Rider' 127–8, 130, 132
Self-Realization Center 183
Semon, Roger 161
'Separate Ways' 88, 134, 215
The Seven Year Itch 93
Sex Pistols, the 166
Sexual Behaviour in the Human Female 15
sexual liberation 6, 9, 15, 49, 76, 84, 90–1, 116, 118, 166
Seydel, Jürgen 176
'Shake, Rattle and Roll' 39, 46, 188
Shannon, Del 83, 128
Shaughnessy, Mickey 76
Shaw, Sid 148
'She's Not You' 178
Sholes, Steve 40, 42, 47, 103, 160, 203
Shuman, Mort 102–3, 192
Shumway, David 51–2
Sidney, George 51, 190
Siegel, Don 74, 190
'Silent Night' 192
Sinatra, Frank 17, 42, 64, 71, 74, 88, 119, 131, 166, 176, 189
  see also *The Frank Sinatra Timex Show: Welcome Home Elvis*
Singer Presents Elvis see Comeback Special
Singer Presents Elvis Singing Flaming Star and Others album 213
Singer Sewing Machine Company 109–10, 213

Singleton, Shelby 146
Skippy 86
slapback 22
Sleepy-Eyed John 37
Smith, Billy 51
Smith, Johnny 17
Smith, Junior 176
Smith, Louise 51
Smith, Myrna 129, 217
Smithsonian Institute 157, 200
Snow, Hank 20, 36, 39–41, 63, 172
Snow, Jimmie Rodgers 40
'So Close, Yet So Far (From Paradise)' 104
'So Glad You're Mine' 46
'Softly, As I Leave You' 64
Solt, Andrew 119
Something For Everybody 71, 103, 177, 192
'Something' 130
'Sometimes I Feel Like a Motherless Child' 121
'Son of a Preacher Man' 216
Songfellows, the 62, 64, 207
songwriting 58–9
Sonny Burgess and the Pacers 55
Sonny and Cher 131
Sony Music 161–3, 215, 221
soul 9, 28, 32, 58, 60, 65, 101, 166, 201
  blue-eyed 125, 193
'Sound Advice' 104
South, Joe 129
South, national predicament 123–4
  stereotype 4, 96–7
Southsploitation 96
Special News Report 49, 202–5
Spector, Phil 166
Speedway 110, 180, 191
  album 181
Speer Family, the 64
Spinout 180, 191
  album 180
spirituals see gospel music
Spreen, Glen 126
Springfield, Dusty 124, 216
Squires, Dorothy 131
Sri Daya Mata 183
Stafford, Jo 20
Stage Show 44, 50, 168, 172, 188
Stalin, Joseph 179

248 ELVIS

Stamps, the 64
Stardust, Alvin 123
Starlite Wranglers 19–20, 35, 38, 171
Statesman, the 36, 64
Stax label 120, 198
Stax studio 124, 184, 194–5, 198
'Stay Away' 102
Stay Away, Joe 102, 105, 180–1, 191
'Stay Away, Joe' 102
'Steadfast, Loyal and True' 81
'Steamroller Blues' 130, 194
The Steve Allen Show 50, 109, 168, 173, 188, 213
Stewart, Rod 151
Stoker, Gordon 55, 59–61, 205
Stoller, Mike 16, 47, 54–5, 58, 63, 75–6, 81, 86, 93–4, 102–3, 214
Stone, Mike 183
Strange, Billy 110, 119
'Stranger in My Own Home Town' 125, 193
Streisand, Barbara 127, 185
Stromberg, Peter 157
'Stuck On You' 88, 176, 189
Stutzman, Mark 157
'Such a Night' 87, 192
Sullivan, Ed see *The Ed Sullivan Show*
'Summer Kisses, Winter Tears' 75
Sumner, Donnie 207
Sumner, J.D. 62, 64
Sun Records 1, 14, 16–18, 20, 25, 35, 38–9, 41–3, 46–7, 54, 57, 61, 90, 130, 146, 168, 171, 187, 201, 203
and race 15–16
release strategy 46, 201
The Sun Sessions 5, 186, 200
Sun studio 15, 18–20, 40, 42, 53–4, 60, 73, 135, 142, 149, 168, 173, 223
equipment 15, 17
and race 28
Taylor's restaurant 17
Sun, The 151
Sunshine Boys, the 62
'Surrender' 177
'Suspicion' 192
'Suspicious Minds' 125–7, 131, 182, 193
Suzore No. 2 movie theatre 24
'Sweet Caroline' 128, 130

'Sweet Home Chicago' 167
Sweet Inspirations, the 126, 129, 216
see also Smith, Myrna
'Swing Down Sweet Chariot' 63

'Take My Hand, Precious Lord' 63
The T.A.M.I. Show 110, 121
Tarantino, Quentin 5–8, 12
taste 3, 56, 59, 78, 98–9, 108, 119, 138, 140, 144, 154–6, 166
see also cultural capital
Taurog, Norman 53, 71, 86, 92, 96, 105, 110, 190–5
Taylor, James 130
Taylor, Vince 115
television 44, 49, 106, 108, 111, 123, 126, 133–4, 188–9, 202, 209
see also specific TV shows and appearances
Temple, Shirley 101
Tepper, Sid 75
Tewksbury, Peter 105, 110, 191
Tharpe, Sister Rosetta 62
'That's All Right' 20–22, 24–26, 35, 61, 149, 168, 170–1, 187, 199
That's The Way It Is see Elvis: That's The Way It Is
'That's When Your Heartaches Begin' 18, 135, 168, 170
'(There'll Be) Peace in the Valley (For Me)' 51, 189
see also *Peace in the Valley* EP
'There's Always Me' 192
This Is Elvis 119
Thomas, Carla 198
Thomas, Rufus 16, 26, 31, 198
Thompson, Claude 111, 122
Thompson, Linda 136, 143, 183
Thorpe, Richard 75, 190
Through My Eyes 152
Tickle Me 105, 179–80, 191
'Tiger Man' 119, 189, 199
'Till I Waltz Again with You' 170, 198
Tily, H. Coleman 42
'The Times They Are a-Changing' 121
Timex 88, 176, 189
Tin Pan Alley 8, 38, 58, 102, 166, 212
Tipler family 35

Tippy and the Clovers 59
Toast of the Town see The Ed Sullivan Show
Today 185, 195
'Today, Tomorrow and Forever' 94
Tomato label 223
'Tomorrow is a Long Time' 108
'Tomorrow Night' 38, 187
'Tonight Is So Right for Love' 102
'Too Much' 54, 173, 189
totemism 12, 65–9, 95, 113, 117, 132, 134, 146, 153, 155
tourism, global in 1950s and 1960s 83
Town & Country Jubilee 40
'Tragedy' 203
transdiscursivity 165–6
'Treat Me Nice' 76
'T-R-O-U-B-L-E' 195
'Trouble' 59, 80, 111, 189
The Trouble With Girls 110, 181–2, 191
True Disbelievers 220
'True Love Travels on a Gravel Road' 126
'Tryin' to Get to You' 187, 195
Tubb, Ernest 63, 102, 171
Tucker, Tommy 108
Tupelo 17, 27, 53, 61, 74, 132, 160, 168, 170, 173–4, 176, 178, 183, 211
  Shake Rag ghetto 27
  Tupelo Hardware Store 170
Turner, Ike 16
Tutt, Ronnie 126
'Tutti Frutti' 45–7, 188, 192
TV Guide 123
'Tweedle Dee' 39
Tyler, Judy 76

'Unchained Melody' 136, 195
United Artists 190
United Paint Company 98
Universal 191
Universally Elvis Fan Club of Memphis 69
'Until It's Time for You to Go' 134, 194
'U.S. Male' 108
USS Arizona 169, 176–7, 179
USS Hancock 45, 172

Valentine 83
Valentino, Rudolph 104, 205

van Kuijk, Andreas Cornelis 99
  see also Colonel Parker
Vanguard label 121
Variety 75, 85, 137
Vaudeville 45, 81
Velvet Elvis club 149
vernacular music genres 14–15, 23, 26–7, 45, 55, 57–8, 61, 65, 75, 121, 123, 126, 142, 157, 166, 207
  racial segregation of 30, 42
  see also individual music genres
Victor label *see* RCA
Victrola label 222
Vietnam conflict 107
Village Voice 153
Vincent, Gene 115
'Vino, Dinero y Amour' 84–5
Vinton, Bobby 83
Viva Elvis 164
Viva Las Vegas 93, 96, 105, 111, 178–9, 190
Viva Las Vegas / Roustabout album 93
Voice (group) 64
Voices: The Official Album of the 2006 World Cup 215

Waits, Tom 47
Wakely, Jimmy 18
'Walk a Mile in My Shoes' 72, 129
Walker, Ray 60, 62, 65, 68
Wall, David 148
Wallace, Slim 203
Wallis, Hal 70, 84, 103, 140, 172, 178, 208
Ward, Clara 200
Warhol, Andy 101, 212
Warren, Charles Marquis 94, 191
Watergate 132
Waters, Muddy *see* Muddy Waters
'Way Down' 135, 195
Wayne, Sid 105
Wayne, Thomas 89, 203
WDIA 17, 23–4, 31, 168, 173, 175, 198, 201
  Goodwill Revue 31, 168, 173, 175, 201
'We Call On Him' 64
'Wear My Ring Around Your Neck' 175
'Wearin' That Loved-On Look' 125
Webb, Robert 70, 190
Weinshanker, Joel 163

Weisman, Ben 102–3, 105
Weiss, Allan 84
Welcome to My World 135, 186
'Welcome to My World' 131
Wells, Alan 113
Wertheimer, Alfred 214
West Coast music 64
West, Cornel 10–11
West, Mae 36
West, Red 79, 87–8, 134, 151, 215
West, Sonny 151
Western Recorders studio 196
Wexler, Jerry 124, 214, 216
'What Now My Love' 131
'What'd I Say' 94, 127
WHBQ 23–5, 27, 35, 37, 170
WHBQ-TV 188
Wheeler, Onie 40
'When It Rains, It Really Pours' 187
'When My Blue Moon Turns to Gold Again' 189
Where the Boys Are 82
Whitburn, Joel 83
'White Christmas' 63, 192
White House 107, 167, 182
White supremacy 10–11, 31, 158
White, Barry 141, 166
White, Tony Joe 128
Whitman, Slim 35–6
Wilburn Brothers 40
Wild in the Country 74, 96, 176–7, 190
The Wild One 115
Wilkinson, John 126
William Morris Agency 41, 45, 86, 126
Williams, Andy 109, 131
Williams, Hank 20, 96, 131, 142–3, 210
Williams, Nat D. 23, 201
Williams, Robert 150
Williams, Tennessee 80
Wilson, Charles Reagan 65
Winehouse, Amy 143
Wink Martindale's Dance Party 17, 188
Wise, Fred 102

Wise, Sue 83
'Witchcraft' 88, 189
'Without You' 19, 171, 223
The Wizard of Oz 114
WMAL-TV 40
WMPS 35
women's liberation 10, 73, 81, 84
'The Wonder of You' 128, 182, 193
Wood, Bobby 216
'Wooden Heart' 86, 102
'Working on the Building' 192
World War II 15
Wortham, Red 19
WRCA-TV 189
WREC 15
Wyche, Sid 132

'The Yellow Rose of Texas' 94
Yeltsin, Boris 159
'Yesterday' 127–8, 193
'You Asked Me To' 57, 195
'You Belong to Me' 20
'You Don't Know Me' 108
'You Gave Me a Mountain' 130, 134, 194
'You'll Be Gone' 206
'You'll Never Walk Alone' 64
'You're a Heartbreaker' 39, 171, 187
'You're the Boss' 93
'(You're the) Devil in Disguise' 102, 178
'(You're So Square) Baby I Don't Care' 55, 76
Young Lovers 150
Young, Faron 40
Young, Reggie 216
Your Cheatin' Heart 96
youth 1, 5–6, 13, 15–16, 27, 29, 34, 39, 45–6, 48, 51, 57, 66, 70–3, 75–6, 78–9, 82–3, 90–1, 107–8, 113, 121, 124, 137–8, 141, 166, 174, 176, 190, 209

Zemeckis, Robert 6
Žižek, Slavoj 1, 153
Zurawick, David 158

www.ingramcontent.com/pod-product-compliance
Lightning Source LLC
Chambersburg PA
CBHW062012220426
43662CB00010B/1303